The Complete
Book of Astrology

ST. MARTIN'S GRIFFIN ≈ NEW YORK

Ada Aubin and June Rifkin

The Complete
Book of Astrology

THE COMPLETE BOOK OF ASTROLOGY. Copyright © 1998 by Ada Aubin and June
Rifkin. All rights reserved. Printed in the United States of America. No part of
this book may be used or reproduced in any manner whatsoever without written
permission except in the case of brief quotations embodied in critical articles or
reviews. For information, address St. Martin's Press, 175 Fifth Avenue, New
York, N.Y. 10010.

Design by Kate H. Kim

Library of Congress Cataloging-in-Publication Data

Aubin, Ada.
    The complete book of astrology / by Ada Aubin and June Rifkin. —
1st ed.
        p.   cm.
    Includes bibliographical references and index.
    ISBN 0-312-18070-5
    1. Astrology.   I. Rifkin, June.   II. Title.
BF1708.1.A89   1998
133.5—dc21   97-46412
                                                       CIP

First St. Martin's Griffin Edition: July 1998

10 9 8 7 6 5 4 3 2 1

This book is dedicated to the past masters.

Thank you,
Ada

★

Contents

ix ☾ Contents

Acknowledgments

Working on this book was a fascinating experience. My many conversations with Ada were, as they have been for over a decade, enlightening and thought provoking. In addition to Ada, I'd like to thank the following people who supported me during this project: my dear friend Lorraine Bates, who introduced me to Ada; my friend and agent Peter Rubie, who suggested my participation in the book; my husband, Dick, and son, Colin, for their patience and understanding and for having to endure many deliveries of pizza and Chinese food; and everyone else who didn't change the subject, walk away, or look askance when told I was writing a book on astrology.

—June Rifkin

★
An Astrologer's Creed

I sincerely believe . . .

That astrology is a true and divine science and art and, as such, its abuse or misuse would be sacrilegious.

That I must continually strive to be worthy of further enlightenment by the Source of All Knowledge and that I may truly serve Him and my fellow man.

That I will not attempt to guide or advise anyone where my knowledge of astrology shows me it is not for me to do so, as when my own horoscope indicates serious afflictions to another's chart.

That I shall have a sympathetic understanding of the weaknesses of humanity. Never ridiculing, condemning, or becoming accessory before the fact of wrongdoing, I shall endeavor to lift up, encourage, and help as follows:

Where there is ignorance, I will endeavor to enlighten.
Where there is fear, I will encourage confidence and faith.
Where there is hate, I will counsel love.
Where there is error, I will encourage truth.
Where there are unstable emotions and hysteria, I will
*   attempt to calm and encourage deliberation.*
Where there is sin, I will encourage virtue.
Where there is greed, I will encourage selflessness.

That if I am not to be a hypocrite, I must live this science to the best of my ability as well as preach it. "For it is by their works that ye shall know them."

That I shall teach that which I have found to be true, to all desiring to learn, who are worthy of being taught.

That knowledge in itself is useless unless applied. That if misapplied, it can be destructive; it must be properly applied.

That properly applied knowledge is wisdom and that wisdom can free one from so-called "fate."

—Anonymous

★

Chapter One

What Is Astrology?

Approaching the Millennium

The year 2000 is upon us. It brings with it the close of a decade and century and the start of a new millennium. Much has been written about and speculated upon this milestone . . . from the prophecies of Nostradamus to the Book of Revelation to the superstitious fringe groups living in pockets of the United States. The pessimists and naysayers foresee destruction and doom; the optimistic and enlightened, a chance for peace and renewal. Depending on the perspective, it can represent the end . . . or the beginning.

In its simplest terms, the millennium is nothing more than a thousand-year span of time. In astrological terms, approximately every 2,000-to-2,500-year period represents an "age." Each age is ruled by a sign of the Zodiac and has brought focus to a particular development of mankind. This can be demonstrated by archaeological discovery and recorded history. The earliest relevant age would be during the existence of the caveman about ten thousand years ago in the Age of Leo. The beginning of Egyptian rule, Judaic law, and Oriental philosophy (the Tao) had their foundations set during the Age of Taurus (4000–2000 B.C. approximately). The Age of Aries (2000 B.C. to A.D. 1) brought aggression and advancement. Aries, a fire sign, ruled the age when ancient Greece was in its glory, Moses led the Jews out of Egypt, and Rome was building its vast empire. It was also an age of artistic and philosophical expression and discovery. The birth of Christ signified the beginning of the Age of Pisces (A.D. 1–2000), the sign of fishes, a symbol equated with Christianity. The Pisces Age has given rise to religion, vision, and spirituality, and as the twelfth (and last) sign of the Zodiac, it brings a fusion and culmination of all that has come before it.

Although the Fifth Dimension sang about it in the 1960s, only now are we actually experiencing the "dawning of the Age of Aquarius." Technically, the Aquarian Age doesn't begin until sometime after the year 2000, but its anticipation thirty years ago made for a hit record, the Broadway musical *Hair*, and the emerging hippie culture of peace and love. It was also the time when astrology was introduced to the masses.

Baby boomers may recall, with either nostalgia or embarrassment, parading around in bell-bottoms and Nehru jackets asking "What's your sign?" of everyone they met. Most were probably unaware of what it meant to be a Pisces or Sagittarius—touting your sign was simply a way to be sociable and "groovy." If anything was known of astrology, it was most likely the superficial personality traits of the Sun Signs and those with whom you were compatible. It was a time when horoscopes were read with tentative interest in the daily newspaper, trying to make the one-line prediction fit your life at that moment. (It brings to mind a routine by comedian Robert Klein about the vagueness of the daily horoscope: "*A good day to ask for a raise.* Hmm . . . you know, if I *had* a job, I *would* ask for a raise!")

Then, sometime after the disco era in the late seventies/early eighties, as society traded in its polyester shirts and platform shoes for wool suits and briefcases, the world became more pragmatic and business-oriented. At the same time, the astrology craze waned and its leaders and aficionados silently retreated. The subject would pop up occasionally, however, usually in supermarket tabloids and daytime TV talk shows hawking "Predictions for the Year," which primarily focused on the fates of celebrities and politicians and, in retrospect, poorly at that.

But now, as the Aquarian Age dawns, astrology is making a comeback. What was formerly classified as "occult" has now become "New Age," giving the mystical and spiritual a newfound air of intelligence and legitimacy. In fact, the nineties have become the decade of the New Age.

Since the middle of the century, the world has undergone great and rapid advancement in communication, information, and technology. It is both exciting and frightening. As a result, people are searching for stability and answers . . . for themselves, their loved ones, society, and the world in general. Be it through meditation, music, holistic living, or renewed interest in the family religion, the path to enlightenment and a quest for purpose is becoming clearer, and perhaps a little gridlocked, as the century comes to a close. The nineties are teaching us the responsibilities we must undertake, for ourselves and those around us, to reach the new century in a receptive, aware state. Aquarius is a sign that allows us to tap knowledge and to discipline ourselves. It is a mental sign seeking balance, and without balance there can be no growth—body, mind, and soul must function in unison.

Astrology can offer knowledge. It can map for us those ways or roads that are most relevant and productive. The birth chart reveals the many facets of the individual, opening up the possibilities of one's life for self-discovery, career, relationships, and other personal goals. It can make sense of the senseless or chaotic and provide structure, purpose, and, most valuably, promise.

It has been said that when the student is ready, the teacher appears. For anyone with a candid interest or curiosity who wishes to explore and study the wondrous complexities of this ancient craft, this book exists to feed the mind, explore the past, present, and future of astrology, and offer insight and information on this complex and fascinating subject. It's time to shed old and distorted impressions—astrologers do *not* parade around in beads and caftans and have crystal balls—and to take a renewed look at this complex body of knowledge that has existed, been examined, and used since early man beheld the sky and stars above him.

Through study of astrology, the millennium can prove to be a hopeful and exciting time. It begins, simply, with an open and inquisitive mind.

What Is Astrology?

Astrology is both an art form and a science—the "science of possibilities." It deals with the effects that the planets (including the Sun and the Moon) have on the human being. The interaction between planets and a person born at a given time has been set into a system that explains, with accuracy, his potentials. A birth chart, or horoscope, is a personal road map that provides clear-cut and effective explanations for the challenges a personality undertakes.

Astrology has withstood the test of time and, as a result, has embodied and undertaken the delineation of human nature. The configuration of symbols and signs in a birth chart can help to time and understand events in your life. It provides insight into relationships, family, career, and, most importantly, the potentials and limitations of an individual.

Astrology deals with both mental and physical maturation. It holds the key to the correction of attitudes that affect your life. The objective in studying and understanding astrology is to provide and produce self-awareness. It is extremely difficult to attain full self-awareness, but the rewards bring harmony and balance into our lives. Awareness of ourselves ultimately enhances our objectivity about life and how we relate to and interact with others. Astrology is an excellent diagnostic tool that can assist us in achieving the desired objectivity.

The History of Astrology

The history of astrology is as old as the history of man. The need to relate to the cosmos was common to all ancient civilizations. Some bits and pieces of artifacts that predate recorded history were used in rituals for the worship of the heavenly bodies. Early man needed to place himself within the context of the vast universe. He was a tireless observer who was aware of his vulnerability.

The high priest or priestess was the selected person who would devote his or her life to the study and/or practice of this knowledge. It was serious business as the entire culture depended on such a person, as in the case of the Native American medicine man.

The genesis of astrology is unknown, but all cultures claim it. The I Ching of the Chinese has astrology based on Moon cycles. The Kabbalah represents the work of the Jewish mystics. Egypt has left monuments to its astrological practices, as have the Islamic world and the cultures of ancient Greece and Rome. Even Europe collected, and held in high position, astrological knowledge, clear to the Middle Ages.

Astrology as a mystical science represents the development of the human psyche. This body of knowledge grows and changes as the human being undergoes his evolution. The notion that astrology is a religion has led many to fear and misunderstand this excellent diagnostic tool. Astrology has coexisted with the dogmatic faiths for centuries without difficulty. The Torah does not deny the Kabbalah, but confirms it. The I Ching doesn't contradict the Tao, but enhances it.

The political/religious developments throughout Europe during and after the Middle Ages put astrology underground. The great astrologer and clairvoyant Michel de Nostradamus wrote his prophecies in metaphoric quatrains, using a language that combined Latin and old French, as a subterfuge to avoid being accused of heresy by the church. This is when the infamous side of astrology was born. This powerful tool became used as a weapon. This knowledge gave the advantage to those who used it for personal gain. During World War II, Adolf Hitler used astrologers in hopes of outsmarting the Allies; little did he know the Allies were using astrologers to outflank him. This selfish motive backfired, since "service to others" is a prepossession that an astrologer should not violate.

The introduction of psychiatry into modern culture relegated astrology to being a "poor relation." Psychiatrists have undertaken the study of human nature and, in so doing, have coined a language that has expanded the definitions of planets and circumstances found in a chart. One cannot help but see the approaching union between these two sciences.

Carl Jung, the renowned Swiss psychologist and student of Sigmund Freud, took astrology seriously. He philosophically separated from Freud as he studied the subject and pursued psychology on a separate and independent level. He believed in "synchronicity," which is the concept that certain events on Earth, both global and personal, coincide in time with similar planetary relations in astronomy. Jung coined the terms *collective unconscious* and *archetypes*, which also describe the purpose and significance of astrology. Michel Gauquelin, a French psychologist, studied and wrote of how the positions of the planets in a birth chart reflected the personality and profession of an individual.

The contributions to astrology are endless. This ancient body of knowledge is vast and, when properly used, can provide an insight into the personality like no other tool. As we enter the Aquarian Age, the quest will be to discover our authentic personalities, not just live with the ones constructed for us. It is a time for enlightenment so that we may avoid the mistakes of the past.

Predestination Versus Free Will

The discussion of predestination versus free will has a long history. The school of thought that states that we are wholly responsible for our actions cannot explain the many occurrences that are out of context in our lives. The construction and study of an astrological chart directs and points out the objectives and goals of our lives. It is quite easy to foresee or experience a transit—a planet that triggers another planet restricts us to that phase or lesson. The response can occur at three levels, depending on one's spiritual development: at the physical level, with all its obvious manifestations; at the emotional level, subjecting ourselves to psychic traumas; or at the theoretical level, where one can, through love and patience, transcend the growing pains experienced.

When this knowledge is placed within the framework of a chart, the planets and the signs in their given houses can be seen as an inevitable lesson. The empty houses represent free will. How free? The opportunity to use empty houses is important, particularly when part of a tee square. In that configuration, there will be leakage, wasted energy, or perhaps an opportunity to untangle the difficulties of such a hard aspect.

Astrology accepts the concept that we choose our parents, our economic level, our race, and in our collective unconscious, the knowledge of past lives. This "package" of choices is for the purpose of advancing our souls. Sometimes we must also go back in order to undo past mistakes. By doing so, we progress to the next level of development.

This opportunity for advancement can be disrupted by a personality that changes in midstream. For example, the alcoholic or drug abuser drops out and stops his chart, just as surely as a suicide does. But these merely act as delays. The individual will come back and repeat that life until he has overcome the action. Each time he will face the value of life and living in various modes.

Although a case can be made for predestination, the recognition of man's will figures strongly into the equation. A great sadness is suffered when the will is broken. The difficulty that such a person experiences sometimes leads to heights of accomplishment; yet in another person, it becomes his undoing. In the end, each person must balance his life. He must strike when it is in his power to do so and allow the universe to take over when it is out of his hands.

As stated time and time again within astrological circles, "The stars incline, they do not compel."

★

Chapter Two

Elements of Astrology

The Zodiac

The Zodiac is a belt of fixed stars that circle the Earth. The correlation between these stars, the seasons, and human behavior has evolved into the study of astrology.

The Zodiac is made up of twelve constellations, or signs, each holding thirty degrees. Each of these signs spans about a four-week period within a calendar year. The latitude and longitude of the birth chart will alter the number of degrees in a house or, for that matter, the sign that appears in a given house. This backdrop of stars for the travel of the Sun Sign describes its archetype. As in astronomy, the positions of clustered stars define the various constellations seen in the sky, and these have been given names based upon the patterns they make. Each of the twelve signs of the Zodiac reflects its corresponding ancient constellation.

The symbols or "glyphs" that have been assigned to the constellations have varied points of origin. Egypt, ancient Greece, China, and India have influenced the system that is now used as a shorthand. The study of ancient cultures will enrich the knowledge of the Zodiac, as these constellations and symbols were not born out of a simplistic "look at the sky," but out of a need in each culture for man to understand his place in the scheme of creation. As each planet moves through the Zodiac, it travels from sign to sign, where it takes on a different trait in each placement.

Signs of the Zodiac

The twelve signs of the Zodiac are

Aries	Ram	♈	Rules First House
Taurus	Bull	♉	Rules Second House
Gemini	Twins	♊	Rules Third House
Cancer	Crab	♋	Rules Fourth House
Leo	Lion	♌	Rules Fifth House
Virgo	Virgin	♍	Rules Sixth House
Libra	Scales	♎	Rules Seventh House
Scorpio	Scorpion	♏	Rules Eighth House
Sagittarius	Centaur/Archer	♐	Rules Ninth House
Capricorn	Goat	♑	Rules Tenth House
Aquarius	Water Bearer	♒	Rules Eleventh House
Pisces	Fish	♓	Rules Twelfth House

The signs and their individual characteristics will be covered in detail when we explore the Sun Signs in Chapter 4.

The Planets

The field of astrology is influenced by ten planets, which include the Sun and the Moon (which are not really planets but, respectively, a star and a satellite of Earth). These planets, and their relationship to Earth and their individual transits, are studied to determine the personalities and potentials of every individual. The planets are basically raw energy. We are affected by such energy in the way we either choose or choose not to respond to it.

Sun	☉	Jupiter	♃
Moon	☽	Saturn	♄
Mercury	☿	Uranus	♅
Venus	♀	Neptune	♆
Mars	♂	Pluto	♇

Since the Sun, Moon, Mercury, Venus, and Mars move quickly and are in close proximity to each other, they are considered "personal planets." These planets take within two years to complete their orbits and therefore have a more personal and noticeable impact on our lives.

Jupiter and Saturn are "viewpoint planets." Their orbits span a greater length of time and impact the transition of decades upon our lives.

Uranus, Neptune, and Pluto are outer, or "transpersonal," planets. This group of planets has a more generational rather than personal influence.

The placement of planets in a birth chart and their changing positions thereafter are what give depth to a horoscope, taking it further beyond the analysis of the Sun Sign.

RETROGRADE PLANETS

A retrograde action is a planet slowing down. In contrast to the velocity of Earth, it appears to be going backward. No planet ever goes backward or leaves its orbit. It is always moving forward. The apparent backward motion of a retrograde is simply the loss of velocity. The Sun and Moon never go into retrograde motion.

Retrograde planets represent work that must be achieved in this lifetime because it was not accomplished or reconciled in a past life.

The Houses

As the Earth completes one full rotation in a twenty-four-hour day, the whole Zodiac passes over it. As the signs divide the Zodiac into twelve four-week segments of the year, the houses divide it into twelve two-hour periods of the day. The first house, which begins approximately at dawn, rests on the ascendant or eastern horizon. Each house represents a different facet of life as well as personal and public conditions.

First House—The first house cusp represents the first cardinal point. It is the entrance of the ego and deals with the self. When there are planets in this house, it indicates that you must reconcile your ego. If there are no planets there, it indicates that there is no ego problem.

The first house is also the house of your ascendant or rising sign, as well as your ego. It represents your appearance, your best foot forward, and what you project to others. It represents your personality and your outlook. Personal actions, personal instincts—those things that belong to the self are in this first house.

Second House—The second house is personal concepts and ideas. It is also the house of resources. It is the fashion in which you display values and personal obligations, such as earning, spending, and how you establish your financial standing.

Third House—The third house is communications. This is also the house of memories. It is the house associated with learning—either the ability to learn or the misfortune of learning (or mental) difficulties.

This is the house of siblings. It is also the house associated with short-term transportation and local travel.

Fourth House—The fourth house is associated with the soul's inheritance, family, and the home. It represents nurturing, roots, and, most importantly, our mothers. Your inheritance from your mother enters in the fourth house.

This is also the house of beginning and ending, and the entrance of the soul. People with prominent planets in the fourth house deal with real estate and property.

Fifth House—The fifth house is the house of talent and procreation, whether it be children, self-esteem, or creative forces and endeavors.

The fifth house is also the house of romance, fun, drama, physical outlets, and self-expression.

Sixth House—The sixth house is environment. It is also the house of health because there is an internal environment as well as an external environment, and those two, one against the other, affect, establish, or risk your health, as the case might be.

This house not only represents the environment of the home but the work environment as well—how you would be employed.

The sixth house represents your own ambitions as well as service to others.

Seventh House—The seventh house is the descendant point, the opposite point of the rising or ascendant point. The seventh house is where sociability is displayed, where partners are taken on, and where you balance your ego with the egos of others.

This is the house where open enemies and competitors will arise. It is also the house of partnerships, relationships, marriages, legal partnerships, and cooperation.

Eighth House—The eighth house is the other house of partnerships because it opposes the second house: my ideas versus your ideas. You bring to any relationship not just your ego, but concepts and ideas. You have a background, a history, a standard. You have a whole procedure that has been part of your life, and when you take on a partner, you have to reconcile your standards with your partner's standards.

This house has always been associated with sexuality and psychic sexual energy.

It is also both the house of inheritances and the house of great losses. Many people with planets in that eighth house tend to lose their inheritances.

Ninth House—The ninth house is the elevation of the mind. It is considered the house of higher education—not only formal education, religion, or philosophy, but the ability for abstract knowledge. Through the ninth house, you acquire understanding that forms your attitude.

The ninth house is the house of teaching, education, and publishing. It is also the house of in-laws and long journeys.

Tenth House—The tenth house is the house of duties, responsibilities, personal status—it represents what has been done with what you acquired in the fourth house. In the tenth house, you will be judged. You will have a whole lifetime to take your inheritance and translate it into what the world will judge as success or failure.

The tenth house is the house of father. It is the house of prestige and career, reputation and law.

Eleventh House—The eleventh house is sorting. It sorts out who your friends and associates are, what you have done with your creativity—in essence, what you have accomplished. It is the house of goals and objectives.

The eleventh house represents the groups, associations, and people that you deal with as well as the responsibility to or association with the children of others, whether it be as a teacher or stepparent. The eleventh house also relates to your social responsibility.

Twelfth House—The twelfth house is the ultimate house and has always been feared because it is both the house of confinement and the house of the greatest depth of creativity, knowledge, and resources. It is the house of the soul's transformation. If you flow with that twelfth house, it can be a great source for tapping a reservoir of information, knowledge, and past-life contact.

The objective of the twelfth house is to confine your ego because your ego must transmute. It must mature, develop, and rise beyond narcissistic pleasures and desires in order to acquire what it wants. The conflict between what you need and what you want can be totally destructive to the soul. This is the house of karma or the end of it.

The twelfth house also rules hospitals and institutions.

HOUSE POSITIONS

Angular Houses—If planets in a chart come off an angle—that means in the first, fourth, seventh, or tenth house position—those planets are powerful and active and are going to work overtly.

If you have many angular planets in your chart, it means that you have been assigned a task that distinguishes you from your own generation. You are going to either be far more advanced or be in charge of current or subsequent generations.

Succedent Houses—If many planets in your chart are situated in the second, fifth, eighth, and eleventh house positions, they will impact your emotions and desires.

Cadent Houses—If many planets in your chart are situated in the third, sixth, ninth, and twelfth house positions, they will have a more subliminal influence, most noticeably in mental energy.

The Natural Zodiac

The "natural" Zodiac begins with Aries, which coincides with the vernal equinox or first day of spring. Aries appears on and rules the first cusp (ascendant) and house of the natural Zodiac, which, when placed on a "wheel," appears on the eastern horizon.

The Natural Zodiac

Hemispheres

The lower or southern hemisphere, which goes from Aries to Cancer to Libra, has a significance in a chart. The signs of this hemisphere tend to be primitive. These houses are involved with introspection, so when planets are placed in this hemisphere, it means that, sooner or later, you will go through introspection.

From Aries to the north position of Capricorn to Libra is the upper or northern hemisphere. The signs of this hemisphere tend to be complex. The houses here are more outward and extroverted. When planets are placed in this hemisphere, you will interact with others.

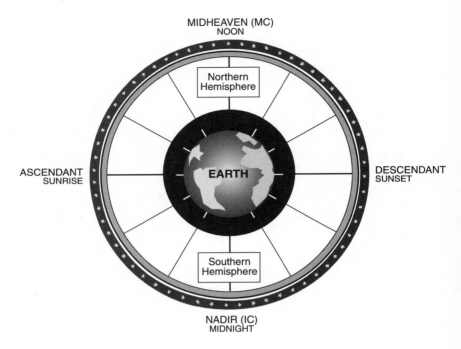

Ascendant, Midheaven, Descendant, and Nadir

The significant points in the cycle of each day are when the Sun rises, culminates, sets, and anticulminates.

The ascendant appears on the cusp of the first house, occurring at sunrise. This position reflects your personality and who you are to the outside world.

The midheaven, or medium coeli (MC), is reached at around noon and occupies the highest point of a chart. Embodied in that position is a reflection of what you have become and how you are perceived and judged by the world.

The descendant point occurs when the Sun has reached the sunset position.

At midnight, the Sun reaches the nadir position, or imum coeli (IC), which is the lowest point, directly opposite the midheaven.

Crosses (Quadruplicities or Modes)

When the circle of the natural Zodiac is squared, it creates four segments, each segment having a particular value and area of development:

1st segment   = the development of the ego
2nd segment = the development of intuition and awareness
                  of the self
3rd segment = reflection and objectivity
4th segment = karma

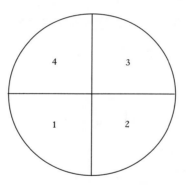

The division of the circle into four segments produces crosses that are significant to our emotional and spiritual development. Crosses, also referred to as quadruplicities or modes, are four signs in opposition. An opposition is an opportunity for objectivity. It allows you to see someone else's side of the picture in balance with your own perspective. In astrology, there are three kinds of crosses.

CARDINAL CROSS

The points from Aries to Libra and Capricorn to Cancer create a cardinal point or cardinal cross. This is the first of the three crosses or quadruplicities. *Cardinal*, in Latin, means "hinges of the door." These four points are extremely important in the development of the psyche because cardinal represents the beginning, the opening of the door to a new path. These four points work toward initiating something, whether it be the evolution of a personality or a soul.

Cardinal signs tend to be initiators by nature. They are champions of causes that can benefit their fellow man.

Cardinal Cross

Fixed Cross

Mutable Cross

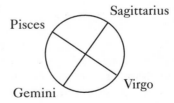

FIXED CROSS

The fixed cross is commonly called the "cross of the soul." The four signs of the fixed cross are Taurus, Leo, Scorpio, and Aquarius. These signs have a tendency to be inflexible, particularly in their opinions.

The fixed signs carry an innate fear of rejection and a morbid dread of change. They find it difficult to alter emotions and also hold grudges. To evolve spiritually and maintain their physical well-being, they must find methods of release and heal old wounds.

MUTABLE CROSS

The third cross is the mutable cross or "the common cross." It represents whether your paths—your chosen paths—have any value or if you have outgrown them.

The four signs of the mutable cross are Gemini, Virgo, Sagittarius, and Pisces. The mutable signs are usually flexible and adaptable by nature. But they are also volatile, changeable, and inconsistent and need to handle things in a healthy way in order to avoid detrimental effects on the central nervous system.

In esoteric astrology, where the concept of past lives is addressed, the mutable cross is usually indicative of lifetimes spent in churches or as men (or women) of the cloth. As a result, mutable signs often carry a sense of inhibition and introspection.

The Elements (Triplicities)

The elements, also referred to as triplicities, represent a method of operation for the Sun Sign. There are four elements—fire, earth, air, and water—with three Sun Signs in each element.

Fire—The three fire signs are Aries, Leo, and Sagittarius. Fire represents the will. The will is the spirit within an individual. It is enthusiastic, directed energy. Fire is always looking for a challenge and taking spirited action for the benefit of the self.

Earth—The three earth signs are Taurus, Virgo, and Capricorn. Earth represents structure and that which is solid and tangible. It represents the senses. Earth signs deal with the material world comfortably. They have an innately suspicious attitude toward the unseen, so they rely on their senses—touch, taste, smell, sight, and hearing—for confirmation.

Air—The three air signs are Gemini, Libra, and Aquarius. Air represents concepts, ideas, and abstract expression. These concepts are expressed through many forms—painting, sculpture, writing, and the like. Air signs are idea people. They are involved with their ideas but not with their emotions.

Water—The three water signs are Cancer, Scorpio, and Pisces. Water has been noted as a difficult but potentially wonderful element. Water, unlike any of the other elements, lacks consistency. It will take the form and shape of the vessel that holds it. Water represents intuition and the ability to feel. The water signs tend to understand and deal with other people's feelings.

BALANCE OF ELEMENTS

If you take the ten planets in your chart and make note of the signs in which they are placed, you can then determine the balance of the four elements. Having one or no planets in any element indicates a lack; having four or more planets in any element indicates an abundance.

It is interesting to note that when a person is lacking an element in his chart, he will invariably be attracted to someone who possesses that which he lacks.

Lack of Fire/Too Much Fire—The lack of fire indicates a broken will. This person is vulnerable because lacking fire indicates that he doesn't have a joie de vivre, the challenge or the enthusiasm that makes life wonderful. His quest in life is to devise a method by which he can display his will.

Having too much fire creates a tenacious individual. His willfulness and inflexibility cast an overbearing attitude over every challenge he encounters. This quality is difficult on relationships because this individual's will to do as he sees fit can stampede over somebody else's life.

Lack of Earth/Too Much Earth—A lack of earth signs creates an insecurity. This person does not feel grounded and lacks the consistency needed to produce mastery. He usually loses faith in what he is doing and doesn't turn the corner to see success on the other side. This is the individual who can quit just before he wins.

Too much earth produces a self-reliance and security that borders on laziness. This individual is constructive and confident in his work and other practical activities so that he provides himself with the security he needs. However, this can be an unimaginative individual who although consistent, successful, and a potentially good earner will not be the type who will venture into any type of speculation or risk.

Lack of Air/Too Much Air—If air is lacking in a chart, it produces a need for learning and a search for concepts. This individual is considered a borderline genius—his quest for knowledge ultimately produces a bright, intelligent person.

Too much air in a chart creates a woolly headed individual who spins ideas and concepts, but doesn't get anything up off the drawing board. There is too much thought and not enough action to complete or conquer anything.

Lack of Water/Too Much Water—An individual who lacks water in his chart is unable to feel for or understand the feelings of others. He therefore creates emotional scenes to produce sensations, making him callous and unapproachable.

Too much water, on the other hand, cripples a person because he becomes soaked—literally inundated by his emotions. This individual is not just overwhelmed by his own emotions, but is stimulated by the emotions of others, leaving himself vulnerable and his emotional energy and resources sapped.

Balanced Elements—The individual with a relatively balanced chart (any combination of 3/2/3/2) is going to revert to his own needs in a crisis. He will find his own equilibrium and then take action.

COMBINATIONS OF ELEMENTS

Many charts display a predominance of two elements. The combination of these elements will impact the motivations and actions of an individual.

Fire/Air—All fire and air signs are masculine, so the high concepts of air and the will of fire make for a masculine, forward-moving individual who can promote his concepts and ideas. This individual might have strong verbal ability, as in the case of a lawyer, or might have an optimistic, almost humorous attitude about life.

Water/Earth—This is an easy combination. When water and earth are emphasized, there is an ability to harness the power of emotions. Earth confines, which gives structure and form to water and hence, emotions. The result is a creativity that allows water/earth to be expressive and artistic.

Air/Water—The air/water combination is challenging because these two elements are in direct opposition to each other. Earth is passive and feminine; air is masculine and intellectually aggressive. The energies that each projects are so distinctly different that when these elements combine, they begin to create odd combinations. At the most positive level, an air/water combination can develop a type of feeling/intuition that can lead to some degree of comfort. When the intuition of water combines with the concepts of air, it begins to create ideas that are worthwhile and satisfying to both of those elements. Once the physical and psychological difficulties created by these incongruous elements are overcome, this combination can produce an imaginative and genuinely creative individual with specialized skills who can deal with people effectively and be involved in the healing arts.

Earth/Air—The combination of earth and air creates a contradictory push/pull. Earth is grounded and tangible while air is lofty, rising above everyday circumstances. When these elements combine, they create an individual who has one foot in each camp and is not quite sure who and what he is and how he is supposed to operate. When a harmony is achieved between earth and air, it develops the ability to sort out those concepts and notions that are of value. Since air produces a lot of ideas, earth will take these ideas and give them structure and balance.

An earth/air person tends to distrust impulses and emotionalism—he thinks in a broad but concise way. This is an individual who can distribute wealth, commodities, and materials and who will work hard to take care of everyone he loves.

Fire/Water—The combination of fire/water is extremely combustible. When water is heated by fire, it bubbles and boils. This is a person who becomes impulsive, who takes his feelings and puts action behind them, whether right or wrong. Logic is overshadowed by emotion.

The individual with this combination is extremely sensitive and worried about what others think. He has a need to sell himself and explain to the world who he is and what he is about. He suffers emotional swings because there is a conflict between water's need for security—needing to hang on and bond—and fire's ego, which simply wants to go forth.

With discipline, this conflict can be conquered and this individual can accomplish a great deal because he is able to express emotion without losing perimeters. At his worst, however, this person is a little firecracker, exploding all over the place because of deep, internal frustration. It is difficult to control these mood swings, and they can lead to troubled relationships.

Earth/Fire—The combination of earth and fire results in what noted astrologer Zipporah Dobyns referred to as the steamroller. This individual has enormous drive and a need to take action. He will either spring into action over an idea or, if he discovers that it has no practical value, completely eliminate it. The creative energy of fire mixed with the plotting and planning of earth is a successful combination. This person can take a small business and turn it into a large, successful business. He possesses enormous faith and patience in all undertakings, believing that everything planned and acted upon will eventually be realized.

On the other hand, if the energy created by the earth/fire combination is not disciplined, the negative side of the steamroller is the individual who will challenge and trample on the ideas of others. He must learn to accept that there are different ways of doing things and that different doesn't necessarily mean better or worse, right or wrong. His productivity is admirable but his sensitivity needs to be improved.

Groups

The signs of the Zodiac can also be classified in groups—emotional, intellectual, and theoretical. Each group consists of four signs, one of each element—fire, earth, air, and water.

The Emotional Group—There are four signs in the emotional group— Aries, Taurus, Gemini, and Cancer—which are also the first four signs of the Zodiac. Signs of the emotional group are unable to control their emotions before speaking or acting. Even when they strive to handle things at an intellectual level, their emotions come through. If the signs of this group begin suppressing their emotions, psychosomatic illnesses will develop.

The emotional group must learn to displace emotions; to think and then react. This is the "I" group. Its objective is to learn to identify the self.

The Intellectual Group—The intellectual group consists of Leo, Virgo, Libra, and Scorpio, which are the four middle signs of the Zodiac. This group takes its thinking, responses, and emotions and filters everything through intellect. The signs in this group tell you how they think, not how they feel, because they don't have contact with their feelings. They disassociate themselves from their emotions in order to intellectualize.

This group has to be taught to stop thinking and to act. Otherwise, they'll sit and pontificate on the ramifications of everything without ever responding or moving.

The intellectual group is the "we" group. They are concerned with others, they have partnerships—somebody else's ego is involved in this intellectualizing. They can take things from their head, filter them through the gut, and succeed for the benefit of themselves and others.

The Theoretical Group—The theoretical group includes the signs of Sagittarius, Capricorn, Aquarius, and Pisces, the last four signs of the Zodiac. This is the most complicated group of the three—their illnesses are worse and their actions can be extreme. When they are positive, they can be superb and reach enormous heights; when they are negative, they can go completely down the tubes.

Theoretical signs take their emotions and instead of intellectualizing, they transcend them. They live in the world of ought to be, could be, and should be—these signs can "should" you to death. The inherent difficulty for the theoretical group is dealing with "what is." When you talk to theoretical signs about an issue, just when you thought you had explained how things are, they'll go off on a tangent of what could, should, ought to be, and may be and forget about what "is." They need to learn the law of cause and effect. They must learn to practice what they preach to others.

This group is considered the "universal" group. Their egos are satisfied and developed by the responses of large groups—institutions, corporations, etc.

Gender

The signs of the Zodiac are either masculine or feminine. The gender of a sign is also referred to as positive or negative, active or passive, and extroverted or introverted. The various terminologies associated with the gender quality can be confusing. Positive/negative does not mean good/bad. Furthermore, a woman in a masculine sign does not lack femininity any more than a man in a feminine sign lacks masculinity. For example, Libra, which is a masculine sign, is ruled by Venus, which is a planet of refinement, beauty, and femininity; Scorpio, a feminine sign, is aggressive and powerful, traits which are considered masculine.

There is always a striving for balance between opposing traits. However, men and women in opposite gender signs often face certain challenges that are determined and influenced by the rest of the natal chart. These influences will be addressed and illustrated in greater detail in the Sun Signs chapter.

The qualities of masculine and feminine also apply to the influence of one's parents. The six masculine signs of Aries, Gemini, Leo, Libra, Sagittarius, and Aquarius are considered "father dominated." If you are born under one of these Sun Signs, you entered into this life to deal with and work out issues with your father. Those issues are not necessarily good or bad. It only means that within maturation you must come to terms with dad.

The same is true of the six feminine signs—Taurus, Cancer, Virgo, Scorpio, Capricorn, and Pisces. If you are born under one of these Sun Signs, you will deal with and work out issues relating to your mother.

The Sun, which represents the father, is the chosen destiny you are here to work out and fulfill. The Moon, which represents the mother, personifies your physical and emotional inheritance that leads to your medical history or karma. This is of particular influence if your Moon is placed in the fourth house.

Moon Nodes and Polarities

Within a natal chart, besides planets and signs, are nodes. These are imaginary lines that represent the path of the Moon when it is circling the Earth. The Moon crosses at two points in its course—the first is called the North Node (☊), or Dragon's Head, and the second is called the South Node (☋), or Dragon's Tail. These points, which oppose each other, are karmic and important. The North Node represents movement and fulfillment, while the South Node represents complacency and old habits. Both the North and the South Nodes are always in retrograde action and must be reconciled or else they will create frustration. Since the human being cannot always reach a middle ground, he tends to go toward either one node or the other. A balance must be struck between the pull of the North and South Nodes to establish well-centeredness.

Aries/Libra Polarity—In Aries/Libra what you have is self-will versus personal freedom. It is also the reconciliation between your ego and the ego of others. The fiery/Mars quality of Aries versus the passive/Venus quality of Libra pulls back and forth. When you have a South Node in Aries versus a North Node in Libra, you already know the consequences of aggression. The reconciliation is not being passive but knowing when to use aggression and when to exhibit passivity. If you have a South Node in Libra versus a North Node in Aries, you will understand the consequences of indifference. Many times, passivity is interpreted as indifference.

When this polarity is in balance, and aggression and passivity are successfully integrated, Aries/Libra can become an excellent therapist or counselor because he innately understands the conflict of one's internal forces.

Taurus/Scorpio Polarity—The Taurus/Scorpio polarity represents self-indulgence and material possessions versus the value and respect of others. In Taurus, there is a tendency to give it all away versus Scorpio, which is always holding back. Scorpio is secretive and doesn't feel that he should inform you—if you don't know, educate yourself. If this polarity is integrated, it can help others to recognize their self-worth. People with this polarity can be at the top of their abilities particularly in careers related to finance or research.

Gemini/Sagittarius Polarity—The polarity of Gemini/Sagittarius is the self versus others. Gemini gathers information while Sagittarius processes information. When balanced, it integrates words with concepts, creating knowledge. These are referred to as the teaching nodes. When integrated, this makes for a great communicator.

Cancer/Capricorn Polarity—The polarity of Cancer/Capricorn is home versus economic life. It can be quite a pull, but an important one because it creates a tension between security and responsibility.

The Cancer/Capricorn polarity usually represents past-life starvation. That starvation through Capricorn can be a business failure or inability to succeed; through Cancer, it can be actual deprivation and starvation. Anxiety is inherent in this polarity as well as a need to integrate. A home business is a good option when this polarity is prominent.

Leo/Aquarius Polarity—The polarity of Leo/Aquarius is self-awareness versus the humanistic concern for others. This polarity is pushing and pulling between getting out of the self and unto others or retreating entirely within the self. When integrated, this polarity allows an individual to mingle, exchange ideas, and not lose the self, which can result in personal growth and achievement.

Virgo/Pisces Polarity—In the polarity of Virgo/Pisces, Virgo analyzes the parts while Pisces sees the whole picture. One must know what the components are in order to master the inner peace that can come from knowing. There is a patient-versus-doctor quality to this polarity—both signs are healers, both are communicators, both have sensitivity and knowledge. When integrated, this is an excellent polarity for doctors or any profession that involves the care or healing of others.

Zodiacal Sign Attributes

Sign	Ruler	Element	Cross	Group	Gender	Polarity
Aries	Mars	Fire	Cardinal	Emotional	Masculine	Libra
Taurus	Venus	Earth	Fixed	Emotional	Feminine	Scorpio
Gemini	Mercury	Air	Mutable	Emotional	Masculine	Sagittarius
Cancer	Moon	Water	Cardinal	Emotional	Feminine	Capricorn
Leo	Sun	Fire	Fixed	Intellectual	Masculine	Aquarius
Virgo	Mercury	Earth	Mutable	Intellectual	Feminine	Pisces
Libra	Venus	Air	Cardinal	Intellectual	Masculine	Aries
Scorpio	Pluto/Mars	Water	Fixed	Intellectual	Feminine	Taurus
Sagittarius	Jupiter	Fire	Mutable	Theoretical	Masculine	Gemini
Capricorn	Saturn	Earth	Cardinal	Theoretical	Feminine	Cancer
Aquarius	Uranus/Saturn	Air	Fixed	Theoretical	Masculine	Leo
Pisces	Neptune/Jupiter	Water	Mutable	Theoretical	Feminine	Virgo

★

Chapter Three

The Astrological Chart

What Is a Horoscope?

A natal horoscope, or birth chart, is a diagram in the form of a "wheel" that depicts the placement in the sky of signs, planets, and houses at the time of your birth. All of these factors, taken together, reflect your unique personality, potential, and possible path of endeavor. A horoscope can be determined for any occurrence—a marriage, a business, even the birth of a nation.

Horoscopes that appear in newspapers and magazines take into account factors influencing the Sun Signs. It is a broad perspective that assumes that everyone born under the same sign will act, respond, and experience events in a similar way. This is not really the case. Though much can be determined by a thorough examination of your Sun Sign, how many times have you met someone who shared your sign but with whom you had little in common? Although you have the same Sun Sign, you will most likely have different rising signs and Moon, Mercury, or Venus placements. People born under the same Sun Sign do share some basic characteristics, but *all* the planets in context make each and every one of us a pure individual in his or her own right.

Creating a Birth Chart

In today's high-tech world, the simplest and most accurate way to construct a birth chart is by computer. What took hours for the novice to calculate by hand is now available within minutes using a computer program. In fact, nowadays, most astrologers use computers themselves.

Putting together a chart by hand is not only time-consuming, but the task cannot be undertaken without the availability or purchase of several other books and resources that provide the information necessary for accurate chart construction. These reference books include an ephemeris, a book that lists the positions of all the planets, from a noon or midnight perspective, for any given month, day, and year; *Time Changes in the U.S.* by Doris Doane, which gives an accurate listing of standard and daylight saving time changes; *Longitudes and Latitudes for the U.S.A.* by Eugene Dernay, which determines the longitude and latitude of a city of birth; and a "table of houses," which gives the cusps of the houses for the degrees of latitude. Once these references have been secured, birth times must be converted to Greenwich mean time and then to sidereal time, degree compensations made, and hour corrections undertaken either from noon or midnight . . . it is a complicated process.

So, for the purposes of this book and to provide a rough idea as to where your planets were located at the time of your birth, a "Planet Finder" has been included at the back of this book so that you can quickly look up this information with ease and convenience. However, please note that these Planet Finder charts are approximations and do not guarantee total accuracy. For a more accurate and detailed horoscope that will also include planetary degrees, houses, and natal aspects, it is recommended that you subsequently have a chart created by a professional astrologer or astrological service, via a computer program, or by obtaining one over the Internet. Suggested resources are located in the appendix of this book.

The Key to an Accurate Birth Chart

To create an accurate birth chart, regardless of how the chart is developed or obtained, first and foremost you will need to know your date, time, and place of birth. If you don't know your time of birth, check your original birth certificate. If you don't have your original birth certificate, contact the Bureau of Records (or Vital Statistics) in your city and obtain a copy. Some bureaus refer to these certificates as "vault" copies because most birth certificates requested are computer-generated and do not contain this information. To provide it, a certified photocopy must be made of the original certificate, which is kept in a vault.

You might also contact the hospital in which you were born. Some hospitals will accommodate your request; others will not.

If neither of these methods works, ask your parents, grandparents, or other close relatives or family friends. Even if you don't discover an exact birth time, you should come away with a good estimate. If all else fails, use 6:00 A.M. as your time of birth. Even without knowing your time of birth, you will be able to get a fairly accurate indication of which signs your planets were placed in, even if you will not be able to determine house placements or your ascendant.

Reading a Birth Chart

If you have a birth chart constructed by a professional or computer, it will look somewhat like the following:

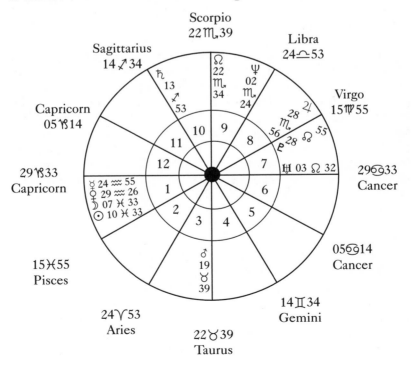

At first glance, you'll see a wheel filled with unfamiliar symbols and numbers. Making sense of this is easier than you think.

In addition to wheels, many computer programs also print out tables that allow you to see this information more clearly. Placing the information in a table makes it easier to understand and interpret, as shown with information taken from this example.

Planet	Glyph	Sign	Degrees	House
Moon	☽	Pisces	07♓33	1
Sun	☉	Pisces	10♓33	1
Mercury	☿	Aquarius	24♒55	1
Venus	♀	Aquarius	29♒26	1
Mars	♂	Taurus	19♉39	3
Jupiter	♃	Virgo	28♍56	8
Saturn	♄	Sagittarius	13♐53	10
Uranus	♅	Leo	28♌55	7
Neptune	♆	Scorpio	02♏24	9
Pluto	♇	Leo	28♌55	7
North Node	☊	Scorpio	22♏34	10
Ascendant	**ASC**	Capricorn	29♑26	1

It helps to familiarize yourself with the various glyphs used as a shorthand for the signs and planets. In this example, the configuration 07♓33 means 7 degrees, 33 minutes of Pisces.

Once you have all your planets in their signs and houses placed in a chart or table, you can easily look up the information in the following chapters to read the interpretations given.

Many computer-generated charts provide an aspect grid. This is a chart that displays the aspects or notable angles that various planets make to one another in a birth chart.

Aspects

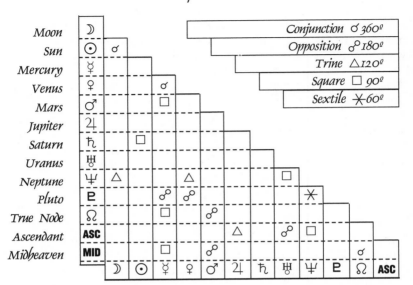

Explanation and interpretation of aspects are covered in Chapter 7.

How to Use This Book

The quickest and easiest way to get a first glimpse at your horoscope is to turn to the Planet Finder at the back of the book and look up the information that corresponds with your day, month, and year of birth. The information provided in the Planet Finder is fairly accurate provided you were born in North America. There are sample worksheets in the appendix that allow you to log this information as you go. As soon as you've completed the worksheets, you can begin reading the explanations of your Sun Sign, all your planets in their signs, your ascendant, distribution of elements, and so on. Since degrees of planets cannot be determined through this method, you might not be able to determine exact house placements at this time.

Interpretation

The three major factors to look at in interpretation are planets, signs, and houses. Planets represent energies or "what," signs represent "how" the planets operate, and houses represent the environment or "where."

Whether you are interpreting your own chart or that of a family member or friend, start with a broad perspective. Add up the number of planets you have in masculine and feminine signs to see if you are more active or passive. How many cardinal, fixed, and mutable planets do you have? Divide your planets into elements and see which ones dominate. Are you lacking fire? Air? Earth? Water? Do your planets tend to be emotional, intellectual, or theoretical in nature? These are some of the first attributes worth examining to give an overview of your unique traits.

Exploring all the characteristics and potentials in your chart is interesting, informative, and fun. As you begin your study of astrology and chart interpretation, you might find that certain traits show up several times, while others contradict each other. Keep in mind that sometimes you might read something about yourself that is dead-on while, other times, you might not readily relate to such a trait. The entire process has to be taken as a whole. Every person has a blend and balance of positive and negative traits, qualities that are dynamic, and qualities that are understated or subliminal. There are bright sides and dark sides; things that come easily and things that present challenges. As you pursue the path to self-awareness, you will become more open-minded about what you discover. Sometimes the things we learn that make us uncomfortable are the very things that eventually help us to grow. An affliction or hard aspect in a chart is a chance for understanding, overcoming obstacles, and, ultimately, greater personal development.

Chapter Four

The Sun Signs

Introduction to the Sun Signs

The twelve signs of the Zodiac comprise the zodiacal belt, which is the backdrop by which we identify the transit of Earth. We are geocentric, which means that our astrological orientation stems from our perspective of the planets from our view on Earth. As the Earth transits through its elliptical course, during any given month a particular sign will be a backdrop. These "Sun" Signs are consistent—the same Sun Sign appears at the same time each year. It takes the Earth twelve months to complete its rotation as it passes through each of the twelve Sun Signs.

Early in the development of man, he recognized the warmth, light, and energy he received from the Sun. The Sun Sign, like the Sun itself, is the most vital, energetic, and powerful part of a natal chart. It determines your position in life—your outlook, success, progress, and, most importantly, the manner in which you come to know yourself.

In psychological terms, the Sun Sign represents the unconscious part of your psyche that moves you toward the fulfillment of your instinctive needs. The Sun Sign contains your entire survival kit—how you relate, project, and respond to the world at large.

There are no good or bad Sun Signs; each has a unique set of qualities, both positive and negative. The Sun Sign is your chosen destiny. It is your personal spirit and will, and you are born to use it. It is something you cannot avoid but, instead, must understand and work through.

The Sun, in combination with your Moon and ascendant, defines the qualities of your personality in this chosen lifetime, but only the Sun carries your destiny—the other planets are actors in supporting roles.

Each Sun Sign is also divided into three thirty-degree sections called decanates. A decanate is a flavoring. It adds a personality edge to a particular Sun Sign. The first decanate spans zero to ten degrees; the second decanate is ten to twenty degrees; and the third decanate is twenty to thirty degrees. Your decanate will be flavored by one of three planets in the same element of your birth sign, depending on the degrees of your Sun at the time of your birth.

Depending on the year of your birth, the dates when the Sun enters each sign may differ by one day, so a well-calculated and constructed natal chart is necessary to ensure exact Sun Sign dates for any year.

The Sun Sign dates listed below reflect those noted at the time of publication.

THE SUN SIGNS

♈ ARIES (MARCH 21–APRIL 19)

Symbol—*The Ram*
Ruling Planet—*Mars*
Element—*Fire*
Cross—*Cardinal*
Group—*Emotional*
Gender—*Masculine*
House Ruled—*First*
Famous Arians—*Warren Beatty, Elton John, Vincent van Gogh, Thomas Jefferson, Tennessee Williams, Gloria Steinem, Harry Houdini, Marlon Brando*

BASIC PERSONALITY

Aries, the first sign of the Zodiac, represents the beginning. He is generous, moral, and has physical courage, which, given to him by his ruling planet of Mars, endows him with physical strength and stamina. Aries can be extremely intellectual and innovative, direct and forceful.

Aries is an initiator. He likes to get going, he likes to do—but that never guarantees that he will finish. He needs lots of praise and encouragement to keep going. Without this, he becomes anxiety-ridden and prone to failure.

Inside of Aries lurks an insecurity, a sense of inadequacy that often leads to extravagance, jealousy, or arrogance. The end result is disappointment and disillusionment. When Aries is troubled in this way, his physical courage, forcefulness, and directness become compulsive, even impulsive, as he gives little thought to his actions.

The urge to move is utmost to Aries, but he needs to learn to stand still, to stop and consider if there is, indeed, a reason to move. Since Aries is naturally fast, quick, and alert, he finds it hard to control his impulsiveness—as soon as a thought is in his brain, it's out of his mouth. He'll jump into the water and then realize he can't swim. He means well, but when things backfire, he gets anxious. If he holds back or tries to reconcile his impulses, he starts to feel guilty and then winds up in a bad funk.

Aries has an innate fear of rejection, which he often uses as a defense mechanism—he rejects for fear that he might be rejected. If he does not overcome this problem or receive positive stroking with the genuine care and love he requires, he will feel incomplete.

Aries desires success, and if he is not successful, it is usually of his own doing. He lacks a sense of proportion. He becomes overly optimistic, extravagant, or makes well-intended but grandiose claims that he cannot always back up. Should his expectations not be met, emotional problems ensue.

Aries is youthful, and since, astrologically, he is a beginner, he is often naive, lacks insight, and is unable to correctly assess human nature. He needs to develop self-awareness, which is something that takes maturity, education, and reinforcement. His instability—this itch that makes him go from one thing to the next—can, with the development of self-awareness, make him more consistent, allowing him to bring ideas and projects to completion and, ultimately, achieve.

Overall, Aries is basically strong, formidable, and successful. If he overcomes the fear of rejection and becomes secure in his actions and accomplishments, he will meet his ultimate objectives and destiny head-on.

TALENTS AND ABILITIES

Aries constantly expresses himself, so journalism is a good field of endeavor. As a journalist, he can actualize self-expression through travel, excitement, and "on the go" experiences. TV, radio, and theater can also safely provide Aries with outlets for the flights of fantasy to which he is heir. These are all good career fields that allow for change and little boredom.

Since Mars rules this sign and, mythologically, Mars is the ancient god of war, it makes Aries very much at home in any career in the military. Unless he has a strong disciplinarian influence, Aries is not likely to be self-disciplined. The military provides discipline, structure, and danger. It is a career field that will allow Aries to go where his courage is needed and where he can express his inner "knight in shining armor" qualities.

HEALTH AND PHYSICAL TRAITS

Aries rules the head, spinal cord, sensory nerves, face, and the lower jaw. Frequently, Aries has scars on his face.

Aries is also prone to nervous tension and anxiety. When Aries is ridden with guilt, in extreme cases it can produce impotency in the male and frigidity in the female.

FAMILY RELATIONSHIPS

Aries is a masculine/father-dominated sign, which means he has issues to work out with his father. The relationship between the Aries child and his father is basically one of fear. Whether good or bad, the father is more than likely going to be aggressive and manifest the very quality that Aries has to curb. Bearing the rest of the chart, he will have either an isolated/uncommunicative or aggressive/authoritative dad. He will imitate father's behavior while copying mother's emotional structure. If there is parental tension in the household, Aries starts feeling guilty and assumes that he's responsible for the rift. At that point, he tries his best to reconcile mom and dad. His needs turn egocentric and create selfishness.

The Aries child is an aggressive daredevil who will take his parents to task. He's always moving and doesn't hold still. It is best to give this child free rein but with guidance. Guidance is a means to get this child to think—he acts before he thinks and expects to find results after the action. It is nearly impossible to get him to understand the concept of consequences. The Aries child often winds up with scars and bruises because he is a born risk-taker. He must not be contained, but instead, learn to contain himself. Enrolling the Aries child in a martial arts class or some other structured activity or sport will help channel his energy.

PARTNERSHIPS

When relating to others, Aries is usually aggressive, talkative, and pushy—whether he's selling himself or just projecting his fears. He can't control himself—he is "on" all the time and can be an extremely tiring partner. He is sexually oriented, forceful, and spontaneous. Partnerships are difficult with Aries because he is innately afraid of rejection. Aries translates anything that puts off his desires, anything that isn't conducted when or how he wants it, as rejection. If this happens too often, jealousy is aroused. He can ram the walls or get sexually hysterical. He is insecure and slow to mature. Feelings must be explained to him. As a partner, it is recommended that you be gentle, soothing, and able to accept this immature sign. As Aries matures, he acquires sophistication, and therefore his rougher qualities begin to subside. He'll be a far better partner later in life—particularly after he passes midlife. At that point, his intelligence and accomplishments can show through.

DECANATES

First Decanate: Aries/Aries—(0 to 10 degrees or approximately March 21–30)

This decanate is doubly ruled by Mars so that Aries's Martian quality is very evident in this placement. The inability to think before expressing himself creates difficulty for this decanate. Aries/Aries is talkative; he moves around but is not conscious of the impact his indiscreet talk or actions have on someone else. He has little insight into other people. Since he acts without thinking, he's prone to repeat his mistakes over and over, always wondering why he elicits strange and negative reactions from others.

Secon∂ Decanate: Aries/Leo—(10 to 20 degrees or approximately March 31–April 9)

In this decanate, the influence of Leo and the Sun are going to tone down the native characteristics of Aries. He is going to be less self-centered and more "we" oriented. His ambitions are directed and he has a flair for drama and passion, which Leo amply provides. Aries/Leo is intense and emotional and needs lightening up. He has a low tolerance for pain and always thinks his pain is worse than everyone else's.

Thir∂ Decanate: Aries/Sagittarius—(20 to 30 degrees or approximately April 10–19)

Jupiter's influence on Sagittarius is going to give this decanate of Aries a whole different attitude. He is going to be far more outgoing and philosophical. He might be more physical and have well-disciplined energy, which can be favorably applied to sports and outdoor activities, as well as philosophical interests. This is the most restless of the decanates because that Jupiter quality that expands him will also keep him moving and focused.

♉ TAURUS (APRIL 20–MAY 20)

Symbol—*The Bull*
Ruling Planet—*Venus*
Element—*Earth*
Cross—*Fixed*
Group—*Emotional*
Gender—*Feminine*
House Ruled—*Second*
Famous Taureans—*Barbra Streisand, Adolf Hitler, Sigmund Freud, William Shakespeare, Candice Bergen, Bing Crosby, Queen Elizabeth II, Jerry Seinfeld*

BASIC PERSONALITY

Taurus, the second sign of the Zodiac, is conservative, a meticulous planner, and an extremely artistic individual. Taurus is honest and childlike. He is consistent, dependable, basically selfless, and generous. He has enormous willpower, is self-disciplined, and tenacious.

Taurus has power of the body. Because his physical structure is muscular and strong, Taurus can simply give of himself and then quickly regenerate. He possesses healing abilities that can provide great comfort to others.

A very sexual sign, Taurus is tuned in to the sensual needs of himself and his partners. His five senses—hearing, smell, taste, touch, and sight—are keen and well developed. Only an old or sick Taurus loses the use of his senses.

Taurus tends to derive security from the material, so he begins to amass. He uses possessions to compensate for whatever he feels is lacking in himself and in his life and to help lower anxieties about his insecurities.

Personality contradictions set in when there are negative afflictions for Taurus. This so-called conservative, meticulous planner can suddenly become a rigid, stubborn, selfish, and self-restricting individual. He might give you blind devotion, but you can be sure he expects it in return. If it is not obtained, he becomes hostile, resentful, suspicious, oversensitive, and hot-tempered.

Loyalty is utmost to Taurus; he is loyal and will test others' devotion. He loses his loyalty only as a result of having his ego attacked or being lied to—and if you lie to a Taurus, he will more than likely never trust you again.

Taurus automatically holds back and represses emotions and aggressions beyond the call of duty. Taurus wants to let go and move forward but is afraid that his actions might be considered unacceptable. Since Taurus is ruled by the refined and feminine planet of Venus, it makes him self-conscious and embarrassed by anything that is "gross." These suppressions often wind up producing overindulgences and excesses of all kinds—food, drink, sex . . . you name it.

There also exists in Taurus a morbid dread of change. Since he is a fixed sign, he finds it difficult to alter his emotions. He might change concepts or ideas, but his emotions stay bottled up. This makes him a master at holding grudges. Taurus takes it and takes it until he cannot take it anymore, and then, watch out—like a charging bull, he will simply explode and take you right over the hill with him. At that point, Taurus can throw tantrums like a baby whose outbursts can be triggered by the slightest thing, and he will care little about them.

To cope or to overcome old wounds, Taurus must find a more productive method of release. He must learn to hold his emotions, temper, and innate stubbornness in balance. Most importantly, he must learn how to forgive.

Taurus bases his security on knowing. Education and the enlargement of thought is vital to Taurus since he rules the second house, which represents the possession of concepts and the ability (or inability) to act on them.

Taurus reaches maturity somewhere at midlife, usually over the age of forty. About that time, he makes for a knowledgeable and stable person—one who will most likely have a long life and a youthful personality. If Taurus learns to understand and control his temper, he can work well under pressure, be creative and talented, capable and extraordinarily productive.

TALENTS AND ABILITIES

Since Venus rules the throat, Taurus usually possesses a beautiful speaking or singing voice—Barbra Streisand and Bing Crosby were both born under the sign of Taurus.

The influence of Venus produces an artistic ability and appreciation that makes Taurus a successful artist or writer.

Taurus is also a good money handler. He understands stocks and commodities and can make an excellent financier or accountant.

Since Taurus both amasses and preserves, he can be successful in restoration, renovation, and antiques.

Love of beautiful things allows Taurus to thrive as a clothing designer, makeup artist, perfumer, or jeweler.

HEALTH AND PHYSICAL TRAITS

Taurus rules the thyroid gland and the throat. Because Venus rules Taurus, it also rules the bloodstream and the sugar level in the pancreas.

Taurus needs a lot of exercise. He won't do it voluntarily and really has to be prodded into getting physical. Aerobics can be beneficial by helping Taurus sweat, expand the lungs, and clear the bloodstream. Blood has to clear itself of carbon, which Taurus retains and which slows him down, makes him tired, and turns him into a couch potato. Take heed, Taurus: It's time to get moving!

FAMILY RELATIONSHIPS

Taurus is a feminine/mother-dominated sign, so he's very much a reflection of his mother. Until he matures, he winds up emulating mother. Since his mother is usually strict and demanding, one of the things Taurus has to learn is not to become overbearing and impose his concepts and ideas on others, whether it be on family, friends, or associates. As a result of having a strong mother, many Taurus males fear that women have much too much power. This can create power struggles or simply become threatening to relationships.

As a parent, Taurus shines at handling babies—that natural healing and soothing quality is wonderful and nurturing to infants and children. The clashes usually start when a child is much older and begins having ideas of his or her own. That's the time Taurus must learn to let go.

The Taurus mother has a personal need to keep her children the cleanest and the smartest. She is loving and means well, but her sense of refinement is projected onto her children, wanting them to be the best. If she bears a child with a less cooperative Sun Sign, it will result in a clash and the Taurus mother will get hurt. She doesn't understand that the most important thing she can do is take her energy back and stop projecting herself onto her children. She must learn to look for her own identity and desires, go out and do her own thing, and get off her children's backs so that they can be true to themselves.

A Taurus dad is a nice, indulgent guy. He's placid and usually goes along with mom—he's a "good guy" and nurturing. Both Taurus parents are generous, love their children, and will indulge them.

PARTNERSHIPS

Overall, Taurus males and females make good partners. One of the difficulties a Taurus female has is that she projects her energy onto her husband. She is motherly and loving, sometimes to the point of smothering. She tends to be jealous and possessive.

The Taurus male wants adulation and recognition, particularly from his family. He is a good provider and needs his family to show appreciation for his efforts.

DECANATES

First Decanate: Taurus/Taurus—(0 to 10 degrees or approximately April 20–30)

In this decanate, Taurus can be stubborn and bullish; he will push rather than move gently. He is sexually oriented but predominantly sensual. Earth/Venus requires indulgence and pleasure, and Taurus will frequently indulge in food to sublimate what is lacking in other areas of his life. He resists emotional and psychological pain beyond the call of duty and can withstand anything. He can also be benevolent.

Second Decanate: Taurus/Virgo—(10 to 20 degrees or approximately May 1–10)

This Virgo/Mercury influence makes for a more intellectual Taurus. He is prone to think rather than act or respond. Taurus, in this decanate, doesn't want the contamination of others' input—he has to get the answers by himself. If afflicted, he might be unadaptable or unsociable.

Third Decanate: Taurus/Capricorn—(20 to 30 degrees or approximately May 11–20)

This decanate is influenced by Capricorn/Saturn, and Saturn is restrictive. Taurus is going to be more materialistic in this decanate. If afflicted, there can be a fear of deprivation, so Taurus must develop a trust in his abilities to make money or else he will wind up becoming stingy, pessimistic, conventional, and unwilling to take a chance. This decanate needs to develop faith and take seriously the concept that hard work and mastery can result in rewards.

♊ GEMINI (MAY 21–JUNE 20)

Symbol—*The Twins*
Ruling Planet—*Mercury*
Element—*Air*
Cross—*Mutable*
Group—*Emotional*
Gender—*Masculine*
House Ruled—*Third*
Famous Geminis—*John F. Kennedy, Marilyn Monroe, Bob Hope, Bob Dylan, Joe Namath, Clint Eastwood, Alanis Morissette*

BASIC PERSONALITY

Gemini, ruled by Mercury, is heady and intelligent, possessing lightning quickness of the mind. He is witty and articulate with a natural sense of comic timing. He is also an experience seeker, versatile, and adaptable.

Like all air signs, Gemini is a sign of extremes. He is also a double sign—the sign of the twins. This duality gives him both manual and mental dexterity, but also makes him inconsistent, superficial, irritable, and even irritating. He can become obsessive, compulsive, and excessively analytical about anything and everything.

Gemini is naturally nosy. He desires to know about others but, ironically, reveals little of himself. If afflicted, he can become emotionally dependent, which, in turn, spurs hostility—this is a person who can bite the hand that feeds him.

If negatively afflicted, Gemini's natural glibness and wit become distorted, making him a liar and a cheat. He has a cunning command of words and will verbally cut down his foes. At his worst, he can be cold-blooded and cynical with an "I don't care" attitude. This is one of the cruelest aspects of this personality—he can reach a point where he truly doesn't give a damn.

Gemini often feels inadequate, and that can make him hostile and adversarial. He'll argue and fight using a contradictory tactic—when you become emotional, he becomes intellectual; when you're cool, calm, and intellectual, he becomes overemotional. Whenever Gemini gets too overwhelmed or feels that he's not going to win, he will simply disappear. It takes a long time before Gemini learns to control the inconsistency in his nature. That's why he is often referred to as "a butterfly."

There is a constant striving for balance between mind and emotion within Gemini. He works to keep his logic and emotions on an even keel even if, ultimately, he winds up creating chaos around him.

To keep healthy and productive, Gemini must eventually accept the duality of his nature, which can be accomplished through education. When his intellect is enhanced and self-knowledge gained, Gemini becomes a sophisticated, adaptable, and easygoing individual—a delight, who is mentally stimulating and can think on his feet. When he becomes unrepressed, he will operate well under pressure, be free of anxiety, and be able to control his innate propensity toward overanalyzing himself and others.

TALENTS AND ABILITIES

As a master of words, Gemini thrives as a writer or an actor, particularly in the theater. In acting, that butterfly quality is an advantage—

Gemini can go from one role to another and get out of himself through his command of words. His innate sense of the ridiculous makes Gemini a good comedian, too.

Gemini possesses dexterity of hands, arms, legs, and feet and can be a good dancer. He is also successful in any form of sales.

HEALTH AND PHYSICAL TRAITS

Gemini rules the lungs, all fiber tissue, and the shoulders down to the hands.

Gemini tends to be lean unless afflicted. Because he's mutable, he has to take care of his central nervous system and periodically rest. He has a predisposition to nervousness and allergies and has to watch his diet. His emotional swings from logical to emotional may make him prone to manic-depression and, in highly afflicted cases, schizophrenia.

Gemini has to be careful, particularly if there is a Sagittarius aspect in his chart, of airborne and food-related allergies, which, if left untreated, can produce asthma. Gemini rules lungs, so expansion of the lungs through swimming, dancing, or similar pursuits is vital to him. He has to take care of his lungs or else run the risk of winding up with respiratory problems like emphysema.

FAMILY RELATIONSHIPS

Gemini is usually reared in a household where his mother and father are basically talkers. They don't touch each other and Gemini isn't privy to displays of physical affection. Everything that goes on in his household is so verbal in nature that Gemini learns that if he wants attention he is simply going to have to contradict everyone—it's the only way he will succeed at getting noticed. If he is not conscious of this action, he's going to spend the rest of his life contradicting situations and people simply for the sake of being heard. This will only result in his own unhappy and unhealthy isolation.

The Gemini child is attractive, talkative, and friendly. He is also restless, active, and nosy. It's hard to get his attention and even harder to keep it. He needs to learn to calm down. He needs sleep and good nutrition. He doesn't like restriction, so he will disassociate or create chaos to get attention or get his own way. The Gemini child needs mental challenges and discipline to keep going—he needs to learn mastery. You can't punish a Gemini child, but you can discipline him by arousing his interest and curiosity, helping him to finish and to keep consistent.

The Gemini parent is confusing and inconsistent, lacking the ability to provide personal attention. Though the Gemini parent cares about his child and the child's education, he often winds up getting more involved with the political issues of the school than the educational needs of his child.

PARTNERSHIPS

Partnerships are difficult for Gemini because he requires constant stimulation. He is easily bored, dislikes familiarity, and is always looking for change, particularly in his youth. He can be superficial in his personal relationships and business partnerships since he doesn't always hold up his end of the bargain.

In marriage, the partner of Gemini needs to adapt to the loneliness created by Gemini's need to roam. Geminis are not dependable and are usually not great earners until later in life. If you're in love with a Gemini, you will have to put up with a lot and identify your role in the relationship. The best approach is to take Gemini with a grain of salt and not be possessive—he's really not dangerous and will always come back home.

DECANATES

First Decanate: Gemini/Gemini—(0 to 10 degrees or approximately May 21–30)

Gemini's Mercury rulership is going to be strong here and emphasize that unstable, butterfly quality—talkative, babbling, but not necessarily cohesive. He is also going to play that mental game where when you're intellectual, he's emotional, and vice versa.

The first decanate of Gemini is indiscreet. He'll open his mouth and say things that are childlike but often hurtful.

Second Decanate: Gemini/Libra—(10 to 20 degrees or approximately May 31–June 10)

Gemini in this decanate, flavored by Libra/Venus, is artistic and has a creative flair. This Venus/Mercury combination creates a gentle, likable, and nonconfrontational Gemini. If afflicted, however, Gemini/

Libra can be mentally and physically lazy, and this can lead to a restlessness that leads nowhere. He will lack discipline, start but never finish, and ultimately prevent his artistic expression from blossoming.

Third Decanate: Gemini/Aquarius—(20 to 30 degrees or approximately June 11–20)

This decanate has the influence of Aquarius/Uranus, which combined with Gemini is excellent. It makes this Gemini quick-minded and prophetic. He can think beyond the present and instinctively know where the next business trend is heading and go straight for it. Gemini, in this decanate, has enormous ability for success in business, especially in science, medicine, big corporations, and group settings.

♋ CANCER (JUNE 21–JULY 22)

Symbol—*The Crab*
Ruling Planet—*Moon*
Element—*Water*
Cross—*Cardinal*
Group—*Emotional*
Gender—*Feminine*
House Ruled—*Fourth*
Famous Cancerians—*Princess Diana, Julius Caesar, Tom Hanks, Robin Williams, Ernest Hemingway, Louis Armstrong, Rembrandt, Henry VIII, Meryl Streep, O.J. Simpson, Bill Cosby, Sylvester Stallone*

BASIC PERSONALITY

Those born under the sign of Cancer are referred to as Moon children because they are vulnerable to the changing phases of the Moon, the ruling planet of Cancer.

Cancer is sensitive, shy, and retiring by nature. He has the ability to understand and feel for others in a psychic manner. Cancer is imaginative, dependable, conservative, and extremely loving. He has a great need to be loved, which can, in turn, lead to many disappointments of the heart.

Cancer is a family and home-oriented individual, and this extends to the workplace, town, country, or even the universal family. At any club, office, or community gathering, you'll find that it's usually Cancer who supplies the food—he makes sure there is coffee and cake and whatever else is necessary to secure the comfort of the group.

Cancer is inherently moody, which is traced to the waxing and waning of the Moon. If you're having trouble with a Cancer, wait two days . . . the Moon phases will alter and so will he.

When Cancer is negatively afflicted, he becomes touchy. Instead of being sensitive, he's prickly; instead of being shy, he's hostile. This ability to ensure that everyone has a cup of coffee and a piece of cake can transform into stinginess. He becomes spiteful and hardened and "tight as a crab's ass."

Part of Cancer's internal conflict is that he feels and senses, but doesn't necessarily interpret correctly—he misconstrues and personalizes things. If Cancer doesn't learn to catch himself doing this and discipline himself, he will become increasingly angry, hostile, and, eventually, paranoid.

By nature, Cancer is a collector and a hoarder. Unlike Taurus, whose propensity for collecting comes from a Venus-ruled desire for beauty and security, Cancer hoards out of self-stroking, self-caring, and possessiveness. Because Cancer usually has a difficult emotional life, which is common to all water signs, the deprivation of emotion and occasional bouts of self-pity make him possessive and hungry to hold on to everything. And it is truly a "hunger." No matter how successful, Cancer always harbors a need to be stroked and loved. Even when he receives it, he doesn't always recognize or believe it. Within Cancer is a void that exists from the moment he is born because Cancer/Capricorn is the "polarity of starvation." This means that in a past-life experience he more than likely starved. As a result, Cancer takes this unconscious physical starvation and brings it into this life as emotional starvation.

The strength or weakness of a Cancer Sun Sign, either physical or psychological, lies in the placement of the Moon within a chart.

It is interesting to note that the United States became a nation under Cancer—July 4, 1776—and the United States has become the caretaker of the world. The heart of this country, like Cancer itself, is selfless and shares its abundance.

TALENTS AND ABILITIES

Because of his emotional personality, Cancer makes a wonderful actor. In the world of business, he can be an excellent financier. His keen intuition and consuming need for security make the world of finance a wonderful and comfortable place for Cancer. There are many wealthy Cancerians. Once Cancer feels secure and achieves, he also becomes philanthropic.

The attic or closet of any Cancer, a collector by nature, will likely be filled with many interesting and valuable things—antiques, baseball cards, comic books, coins, memorabilia—that can be turned into a serious hobby or side business for profit.

With his inherent fear of starvation, you can also find Cancer involved with food as a restaurateur, chef, or caterer.

HEALTH AND PHYSICAL TRAITS

Cancer rules the breasts, stomach, spleen, and all elastic tissue. For Cancer, one of the difficulties of his life is going to be illness. The Cancer child usually starts out with a great many psychosomatic illnesses—his innate and acute emotional sensitivity and inconsistency leaves him physically vulnerable and "lacking."

Cancer is prone to digestive problems. Since he is afraid of starvation, he sometimes lacks digestive enzymes and can't digest food completely or make proper use of food internally. This can be resolved by dietary changes and improved eating habits. Overeating or eating disorders are quite typical of this sign. Cancer frequently nurtures himself through food.

Calcium shortages during maturation can create pregnancy problems. Cancer women are often unable to conceive or are prone to miscarriages. It is helpful for Cancer women to supplement their diets early in life with calcium, and to get lots of exercise—they have a tendency to be couch potatoes.

FAMILY RELATIONSHIPS

Cancer is a mother-dominated sign, so he spends his life copying mother. Depending on the placement of the Moon within the chart, this could be a love/hate relationship.

Cancer has trouble keeping his relationships with his parents in balance. His emotional inconsistency keeps him bouncing back and forth between the two, so that he can wind up playing a risky game of dividing mom and dad to conquer each separately and, ultimately, wind up achieving nothing.

The Cancer child is sensitive and picks up the emotional vibes in his household. Since he is also easily hurt, he often withdraws, feeling deprived and sorry for himself. He is basically shy but will always find a way to get what he needs. The Cancer child knows how to press the buttons of concern in others and is quick to complain.

As a parent, Cancer is possessive. The Cancer mother worries about her baby before it is born. Since she usually battles health problems and has difficulty overcoming her own history of illness, she often carries forth this concern and projects it on her children.

PARTNERSHIPS

Cancer is romantic. The Cancer male does not go looking for sex. Falling in love is the highest priority, for both men and women.

The Cancer male is in a relationship for the long haul. He enjoys romance and intimacy until his last breath. In the female, Cancer deems sex important for childbearing only and often turns away from her husband sexually early in the marriage. She is quite content being a housewife. For her, cleaning a window is more satisfying than a romp in bed. She becomes involved with the mechanics of family life and designates roles to each family member—dad is the provider, she is the caretaker, and so on. The Cancer female frequently gets into trouble because she exaggerates her emotional/physical weaknesses. Instead of being tired, she's sick; instead of saying something doesn't appeal to her, she gets a headache. She has a cop-out for everything.

If afflicted, Cancer can go from being romantic to being so domineering, tyrannical, and self-centered that it leaves little room for anyone else's ideas or feelings.

DECANATES

First Decanate: Cancer/Cancer—(0 to 10 degrees or approximately June 21–July 1)

The Moon influence results in an instability that can lead to unnecessary sensitivity and self-pity. Spite often grips this decanate. Cancer really has to learn how to control her emotional responses.

Water holds within it a primordial longing that is hard to define. It is a desire to return to the womb—Cancer wants comfort and has a longing to be protected and nurtured by a parent or spouse.

Secon∂ Decanate: Cancer/Scorpio—(10 to 20 degrees or approximately July 2–12)

The Scorpio/Pluto influence leads to some strong and powerful qualities. This Cancer can be psychic and make an excellent medium because he will have the ability to receive information from another source other than his ego. This is usually a wonderful and sensitive Cancer. If afflicted, however, he can be stubborn, domineering, jealous, and vindictive.

Thir∂ Decanate: Cancer/Pisces—(20 to 30 degrees or approximately July 13–22)

With the flavor of Pisces, Cancer will be sympathetic and have the ability to absorb and empathize. This is the most psychic of all of the Cancer decanates because the perceptions about people and things will be sharp. Badly aspected, this can switch to a form of martyrdom—someone who serves beyond the call of duty and can lose himself in an idealistic world-savior concept. He can become completely self-sacrificing toward a person, cause, or ideal, especially if it entails influencing the masses.

♌ LEO (JULY 23–AUGUST 22)

Symbol—*The Lion*
Ruling Planet—*Sun*
Element—*Fire*
Cross—*Fixed*
Group—*Intellectual*
Gender—*Masculine*
House Ruled—*Fifth*
Famous Leos—*Jacqueline Kennedy Onassis, Mae West, Carl Jung, Alfred Hitchcock, Napoleon, Dustin Hoffman, Robert Redford, Andy Warhol, Madonna, George Bernard Shaw, Fidel Castro, Whitney Houston*

BASIC PERSONALITY

Leo epitomizes the classic sense of masculinity. He represents energy and vital forces at the highest level. He is generous, loyal, dramatic, and outgoing—this is a sunny disposition in the truest sense of the word. The Sun rules Leo, and like the Sun, he positively shines.

Leo is masterful and dynamic, self-aware, and self-assured. Like an actor walking onto a stage and knowing every line and every spot where he has to stand, he commands that stage as if he owns it. He radiates strength and fortitude and possesses a high threshold for pain and adversity—there is little he cannot withstand.

Leo has enormous drive and a desire to succeed—he has the gift of leadership. He is a born leader who can motivate any group to success. He possesses a natural flair for inspiring others to think and act.

Fire signs, in general, are particularly intelligent; all they need is honing, polishing, and education. If Leo can go from acquiring information to applying it, he will invariably find success and, most importantly, develop wisdom.

Leo unintentionally draws envy from others. Even the most uneducated or unpolished Leo has a regal quality and a commanding gait to his walk. In the Leo male, the fashion in which he carries his body makes others feel attracted to yet threatened by him. In the female, it's a charisma, a self-assured quality about her that others tend to envy. These majestic, confident qualities are so unconscious to Leo that he needs to learn to curb them because they sometimes wind up becoming a disguise for doubt. Even with all of his self-confidence, Leo has a seed of doubt about himself. If that doubt takes hold and becomes more prominent than his positive qualities, his ego will start requiring constant reassurance.

If afflicted, Leo's majestic personality becomes proud, and pride often becomes blinding and dangerous. Leo is not a good judge of people and can easily be taken in. The greatest traumas are suffered by Leo, whether a Leo Sun, Moon, or ascendant. Leo is the "sign of victimization." He is overly sensitive to other people's needs. He has an overwhelming desire to please, which leads to the denial of his own needs so that someone else can benefit. This is what is meant by victimization. Leo is proud of his intelligence and needs to prove how smart he is. Assets can become liabilities when misused or abused.

Since Leo isn't a good judge of people, he is susceptible to flattery, which becomes his greatest undoing—it makes him arrogant, overbearing, and blustery.

Leo has an overwhelming desire to please, and this desire often leads to a denial of his own needs and energies. It can make him too easygoing and lazy like a fat cat on a windowsill. When you prod or demand something from Leo, he responds like a firecracker—he explodes with a quick, bad temper. Leo knows deep in his heart he has to move, but since he's always trying to please everybody, he winds up holding himself back or denying the self entirely. This creates depression because his seed of self-doubt becomes self-defeating.

When Leo is in touch with himself and recognizes his self-worth, his pride will no longer be a source of self-victimization and he is strong and secure—a shining light to himself and to those around him.

TALENTS AND ABILITIES

There is nothing finer than a Leo actor. He can thoroughly transform himself into any character or situation.

Radio or television announcing is perfect for the Leo male—the resonance in his voice is unmistakable. Even as a baby he sounds like a little foghorn. (Leo females, however, have voices that aren't as melodic and are almost squeaky.)

The Leo female has unquestionable intelligence and needs mental stimulation. With her keen retention of facts she makes a good accountant, people manager, or office manager. She needs to succeed. She loves big challenges and multifaceted responsibilities.

HEALTH AND PHYSICAL TRAITS

Leo rules the heart, which is the central pump of the body, mind, and soul universe.

Leo is strong and usually muscular. Both the male and female have a body structure that makes them powerful—a power that emanates from the level of the aura.

Leo has good posture, a smooth gait, and, like a lion, he is ready to pounce at every turn. The hair of Leo is unmistakable—abundant, thick, and beautiful.

FAMILY RELATIONSHIPS

As a father-dominated sign, the Leo male has issues to resolve with his father. He is afraid of being rejected by him, so he elevates his father to a level of which he might not always be deserving. Leo also develops a sense of competitiveness with his father in order to feel and identify with his own masculinity. The Leo female identifies with her father, too—she needs his strength and attention.

Interestingly, Leo himself makes a wonderful father. He is that rare bird who will often stay in a deteriorating marriage for the sake of his children. His intense relationship with his own father makes him protective and fearful of losing his children.

The Leo female makes a good mother, too. She is strong and supportive to her family. However, she should be careful not to be authoritative—she thinks she knows better and can be argumentative and demanding. She sets standards that are predicated on her opinions and ego with little insight into the talents and limitations of her children. The Leo mother sees her children as a reflection of herself. Her intentions are good but often too subjective.

The Leo child is stubborn and fixed. He is going to emulate his father. The Leo child is trusting, enthusiastic, and open—it's hard to deflate him. But if he feels put down, he gets very hurt. There is a dichotomy here—he's stubborn, but if he needs correction, his ego and self-esteem suffer. As masterful as he can be, he still needs lots of affection.

PARTNERSHIPS

Leo needs a mate. Regardless of whom he picks as a partner, the Leo male has great staying power and this will extend to the family—he's the big daddy. His partnerships are huge and his commitment strong.

The Leo female, on the other hand, is just the opposite. If a partner doesn't meet her standards, she will start to bully, expect change, and project her need to control right onto her partner.

If you're involved with a Leo, recognize that this is a demanding individual. You need to approach Leo with tenderness if you don't want him to roar. In handling a Leo, it helps to explain, in a gentle way, what your needs are—never demand.

DECANATES

First Decanate: Leo/Leo—(0 to 10 degrees or approximately July 23–August 2)

This vital Sun quality is ambitious, straightforward, and dignified. Leo is also a good friend who is loyal beyond the call of duty. This decanate also enjoys the good life—good times, good fellows, and good old fun.

If afflicted, this becomes a roaring lion—one who will not forgive and who will seek to avenge. He has a tendency to translate reprimands as indignations and is extremely self-conscious. This creates the inability to move to a more positive attitude. Lessons are harder for this Leo because of his self-righteousness. Leo is also embarrassed by his limitations. He hides this well, but all it does is compound the problem for him.

Second Decanate: Leo/Sagittarius—(10 to 20 degrees or approximately August 3–12)

This Leo, with the flavor of Sagittarius and Jupiter, is philosophical and cautious. He knows that there is more to life than material surroundings and immediate gratification. He is sociable, friendly, open, and aboveboard.

Should there be an affliction, this Jupiter flavoring is going to begin to overexpand, and this Leo is going to become bombastic and make promises he can't keep.

Third Decanate: Leo/Aries—(20 to 30 degrees or approximately August 13–22)

Mars energizes everything it touches. Therefore, when the Sun combines with the energy of Aries/Mars, this becomes a particularly strong Leo. This Leo can override his stubbornness. He can become courageous, independent, energized, and majestic in the truest sense of the word.

If afflicted, it can create someone who is afraid, who has that seed of doubt, and has to deal with rejection or the fear of rejection.

♍ VIRGO (AUGUST 23–SEPTEMBER 22)

Symbol—*The Virgin*
Ruling Planet—*Mercury*
Element—*Earth*
Cross—*Mutable*
Group—*Intellectual*
Gender—*Feminine*
House Ruled—*Sixth*
Famous Virgos—*Ingrid Bergman, Sean Connery, Queen Elizabeth I, D. H. Lawrence, Sophia Loren, Michael Jackson, Leonard Bernstein, H. G. Wells, Stephen King*

BASIC PERSONALITY

Virgo is methodical, talented, and hardworking. He is discriminating, tasteful, and reserved. Because he is ruled by Mercury, Virgo has the ability to examine things both abstractly and concretely. Highly intelligent and creative, he uses his analytical ability to see both sides of the coin. He is orderly and structured. And because he is mutable, he easily adapts to any environment.

On the negative side, Virgo can be carping, rigid, and critical. That wonderful Mercurial quality will turn sarcastic, making him the master of the put-down, condemning others to justify his own imperfections.

Because he is an earth sign, Virgo is a methodical planner who refuses input from other people. He can become snobbish and narrow-minded, discarding whomever he does not consider intellectual enough for his standards. This occurs because Virgo worries about intellectual contamination. He gravitates only to those he considers his "equals." With maturity, Virgo will hopefully realize that there is a difference between analysis and criticism. But until then, he takes everything as criticism.

Virgo has an underlying fear of success. He is aware that success can also bring notoriety, and he is more comfortable behind the scenes and working alone. Virgo is not motivated by fame and the limelight, but by his basic need to achieve and accomplish something of importance and value—something he can take pride in.

TALENTS AND ABILITIES

Virgo is talented, intelligent, and successful at whatever career or long-term goals he desires. He takes on enormous responsibility and is as hardworking as the day is long.

Virgo rules the sixth house, the house of health, which makes him successful in the medical field, whether as a doctor, nurse, or administrator.

Virgo is a superb communicator and excels in education, teaching, and writing.

HEALTH AND PHYSICAL TRAITS

Virgo rules the intestinal track. His food cannot be adulterated or else his body quickly responds with stomach and/or intestinal ailments. Virgo is also prone to food-related allergies.

Although Virgo possesses a self-healing ability, ironically, he also has a tendency toward hypochondria. He is obsessed with germs and won't drink out of someone else's glass or use a public toilet without first covering the seat. If afflicted, his concern with cleanliness might make him obsessive-compulsive about dirt and give him a severe fear of contamination. This makes Virgo feel vulnerable to all illnesses—both physical and mental. Michael Jackson, who is a Virgo, is a classic, albeit extreme, personification of this compulsion since he is often seen in public wearing gloves and/or a surgical mask.

FAMILY RELATIONSHIPS

Virgo comes from a household where condemnation, especially by the father, is predominant. His father will demand and condemn and so Virgo starts condemning others to justify his own imperfections. He is convinced that nothing and no one is perfect, including himself.

Mother is influential to the basic personality of Virgo, so much so that attitudes about partners and the world are derived from mother. Unfortunately, mother has a critical and/or condescending attitude about dad. Virgo needs to distance himself from this parental difficulty. If not, he'll develop trouble in love affairs and marriage because he will wind up feeling superior to and/or competitive with his mates. It is important for Virgo to work out his issues with his father—his outlooks on life and love depend on it.

The Virgo mother is meticulous—a little bit demanding, especially as her children get older. She has an enormous caring that equates to the setting of good standards. Though she appears to be loving and caring, she tends to demonstrate it in an intellectual, rather than physical or emotional, manner.

The Virgo father is a quietly roaming nonentity in a household. He really doesn't bother with children until they are much older and he can converse with them on an equal footing. At that point, he becomes more involved and responsive. More often than not, he's a shadow who will only be heard from when he is displeased.

Both parents must be careful not to invalidate the accomplishments of their children. If a child brings home a test score of 95, the Virgo parent tends to ask why it wasn't 100—to compare it to something greater or someone else's achievements.

PARTNERSHIPS

This is the only Sun Sign that can successfully marry its own sign. Two Virgos can have a long and happy marriage. They know how to self-analyze and adjust.

Although Virgo has many inhibitions, he still possesses a passionate quality. Once those inhibitions are shed, his passion knows no boundaries.

Because Virgo is dominated by mother and has issues to work out with father, relationship problems often exist. The Virgo male, in particular, is always seeking perfection in his mate. This is a difficult quandary for Virgo. He needs simply to accept and feel love and not analyze it or look for certainty. Love is something that cannot be analyzed—it must be felt in order to blossom and succeed.

DECANATES

First Decanate: Virgo/Virgo—(0 to 10 degrees or approximately August 23–September 1)

With a double Mercury rulership, this decanate of Virgo is quiet and shy with a tremendous need for solitude. He needs to learn to overcome loneliness and self-imposed isolation by accepting others rather than fearing them or shutting them out.

Second Decanate: Virgo/Capricorn—(10 to 20 degrees or approximately September 2–11)

Capricorn and Saturn tend to make for serious thinking. Virgo in this decanate can be an excellent teacher or healer.

This Virgo takes nothing for granted. He is basically inhibited and serious and never assumes or presumes—he tests and earns it. Virgo knows he has to work for everything but also knows, at the end of the line, he will reap the benefits. He is not looking for fame, notoriety, or adulation, but for security and a clean reputation.

If afflicted, there is an increase in moodiness, isolation, rigidity, and one-sidedness in this native.

Third Decanate: Virgo/Taurus—(20 to 30 degrees or approximately September 12–22)

Because Virgo is flavored by Taurus and Venus, he tends to be more fun-loving, friendly, and less compulsive in this decanate. He might enjoy the routine of everyday work, but will find a creative outlet. This decanate of Virgo also tends to have a flair for acting.

♎ LIBRA (SEPTEMBER 23–OCTOBER 23)

Symbol—*The Scales*
Ruling Planet—*Venus*
Element—*Air*
Cross—*Cardinal*
Group—*Intellectual*
Gender—*Masculine*
House Ruled—*Seventh*
Famous Librans—*John Lennon, Oscar Wilde, Barbara Walters, Brigitte Bardot, F. Scott Fitzgerald, Mahatma Gandhi, George Gershwin, Julie Andrews, Truman Capote, Mickey Mantle, Dwight D. Eisenhower*

BASIC PERSONALITY

Libra is a happy, generous, and realistic individual. Although a masculine sign, the rulership of Venus gives Libra an edge of refinement and femininity. Therefore, it is referred to as "she."

Libra is charming, amiable, gracious, and affectionate. As the sign of the scales, she is looking to keep a balance. She has a rare and important gift—she is a natural mediator who can objectively see both sides of the coin, making her the world's best judge. This ability of impartial thinking also makes Libra a great strategist. Libra sits back, examines every possibility and probability, devises her plan, and then takes action. She has the foresight to see what the other person is going to do or what the next move is.

Libra is a materialist. There is little spirituality in Libra; in fact, she's quite superficial in that area. If her ego is weak, she can also be self-indulgent like the caricature of the bonbon-eating lady on a satin sofa. Venus rulership influences her to amass material purely for the sake of reassurance and security. She can overindulge in food and/or sex as well.

Libra's ego is extremely vulnerable. When her equilibrium is balanced, she's fine; when it's not, she is easily hurt, worrisome, and anxious. Libra rules the seventh house, which is the house of partnerships, so she often looks for approval from her partners and, if she doesn't get it, becomes depressed. She doesn't like to be alone and needs a partner to feel whole. If Libra is afflicted, she will latch on to one partner after another . . . it doesn't matter who it is, as long as someone is there. Libra needs to develop self-reliance to strengthen her ego.

Libra wants peace at any price. She will compromise and suppress her feelings or hostilities for the sake of creating harmony. Libra gives up or gives in because she fears confrontation. This is not healthy, because swallowing anger and repressing emotions can have negative repercussions on Libra's health and well-being.

This tendency toward suppression also makes Libra forgetful. She may sometimes give the impression of being scatterbrained, but Libra is actually an intelligent human being who is simply avoiding. When Libra drops out, she retreats into counterproductive fantasy and illusion.

When Libra is positive, she has wonderful mental balance and mental health. Air signs are mental people—concepts and ideas people. When well-balanced, Libra is capable and accomplishes a great deal. When her innate sense of detachment and impartiality is favorably maximized, Libra can objectively view her own ideas and feelings and intelligently decide whether they are worth pursuing.

TALENTS AND ABILITIES

Libra possesses courage. There are many famous Libra generals and strategists—Eisenhower, for example. Libra has the fortitude and strategic aptitude to achieve success on the front lines. The ability to detach and impersonalize, influenced by the refinement of Venus, also makes Libra an excellent diplomat.

Libra's impartiality and balance make her a superb judge or mediator in the field of law. Most judges have a prominent Libra house, position, or a number of Libra planets in their charts.

Libra also excels in any field that requires a sense of symmetry or a keen eye for color—interior decorating or photography, for example. Libra can pass a picture hanging on a wall, notice that it's out of kilter by an eighth of an inch, and straighten it out automatically.

HEALTH AND PHYSICAL TRAITS

Libra rules the kidneys and the blood. She has a sweet tooth and has to be mindful of her pancreas and diet. As an air sign, Libra tends to be dry and should regularly consume liquids. Drinking a lot of clear water is beneficial to her health.

Libra can develop kidney stones or other kidney difficulties. The liver is also at risk if she is not careful about her health.

Because of Libra's need for mental balance, if negatively afflicted, she can suffer from mental illness, sometimes as severe as schizophrenia or catatonia. When Libra is mentally ill, she can withdraw completely from reality.

FAMILY RELATIONSHIPS

Libra is often born into strange circumstances and is frequently the product of unwed parents or a single mother. If she is born to a married couple, most likely the father is rarely there. He's either a workaholic or on the road.

The Libra mother views her children as reflections of herself. She enjoys primping and fussing over them and is generous, loving, and proud of her children.

The Libra father, on the other hand, is inferior. He competes for attention with his children—he will actually upstage his children to get noticed. He also lacks assertiveness. When it comes to discipline, he prefers for someone else to take the reins.

The Libra child is not consciously aware of tension in the household—she senses it in the gut. There is usually dissension between her parents, and that makes her quiet and withdrawn. She wants her parents to treat each other with respect and kindness. If there are overt marital tensions in the household, the Libra child will transcend the family and disassociate.

The Libra child is usually afraid to be alone—doesn't like to sleep alone, won't go to the bathroom by herself. She feels insecure and incomplete. This is a difficult placement for an only child.

In general, Libra is a quiet and darling child who is cooperative and eager to please. She is bright, perceptive, and wants to fit in. She avoids making waves or getting in the middle of controversy. The Libra child will not display anger or disappointment and might even smile when crying. However, as she matures, she will start to recognize and feel anger and hurt. Sooner or later Libra must learn to stand up and be counted.

PARTNERSHIPS

Libra is an affectionate sign; she is loving and demonstrative, but tends to fall in love with love. The Libra female is refined and loving, but if she finds that her wonderful "knight in shining armor" is rusted, she can fall out of love in an instant. She gets bored with her partner, and unless he can really hold her to the relationship, she is going to wander and have many partners or affairs.

The Libra male has many of the same qualities as the female. He, too, gets easily bored. He can lose himself in his career or other stimulating pursuit. He is easygoing, sociable, and prone to extramarital affairs. The Libra man prefers women who are self-sufficient, professional, and interested in work and achievements outside the home. He does not want to be bogged down with mundane details of life and is stimulated by an exciting and productive partner.

Libra rules the seventh house, which is the house of marriage and partnership, but that does not guarantee consistency. Laziness is a big problem for Libra. She can get bored with a partner and wind up in and out of marriages. Libra wants excitement and is always looking for "more."

DECANATES

First Decanate: Libra/Libra—(0 to 10 degrees or approximately September 23–October 2)

The double Venus quality makes for a good disposition. Venus produces an enormous power of attraction; she's refined and cultured and going to enchant people. Yet, it's a quality that works strictly for the "self."

Libra is artistic in this decanate and can work well with others. She can make a wonderful social worker.

Second Decanate: Libra/Aquarius—(10 to 20 degrees or approximately October 3–13)

This is an unconventional Libra; a Libra who is strong-minded and willing to stick her neck out. Uranus is daring; a power wielder. The male in this decanate has a natural agility and the leadership qualities to run a successful organization. The female sometimes becomes a bit too masculine in this situation and doesn't always feel comfortable or happy. She might develop an aggressive edge that conflicts with both her innate character and the refined influence of Venus.

Third Decanate: Libra/Gemini—(20 to 30 degrees or approximately October 14–23)

The influence of Gemini/Mercury gives this Libra an inquisitiveness and curiosity that lends itself to investigative careers or journalism. This Libra is out there getting the scoop and is always on the go. She has an abundance of energy and knows how to pace herself and achieve an end result without exhausting herself. When these talents are combined with physical attractiveness (which is prevalent in this decanate), Libra can also find success as a television reporter or anchorperson.

♏ SCORPIO (OCTOBER 24–NOVEMBER 21)

Symbol—*The Scorpion*
Ruling Planet—*Pluto/Mars*
Element—*Water*
Cross—*Fixed*
Group—*Intellectual*
Gender—*Feminine*
House Ruled—*Eighth*
Famous Scorpions—*Prince Charles, Richard Burton, Roseanne, Marie Curie, Martin Luther, Jonas Salk, Pablo Picasso, Billy Graham, Charles Manson, Theodore Roosevelt, Bill Gates, Ted Turner*

BASIC PERSONALITY

Scorpio rules one of the houses of the soul. He rules the genitals, too, and because of that, there have been more weird stories about Scorpio than you can shake a stick at.

Scorpio is a dual-planet sign. His ancient rulership was Mars, but in 1930, the planet Pluto was discovered, and its erratic qualities were applied to Scorpio. As a result, there is a Scorpio that answers to a Mars vibration and a Scorpio that answers to a Pluto vibration. That accounts for his passions and extremes.

When it comes to Scorpio, it's black or white. When it comes to

Scorpio, it's love or hate. He doesn't want you to like him, he wants you to love him. And if you can't love him, he would rather you hate him. There is no in-between.

Scorpio is purposeful. He is directed and dominant. He's a feminine, water sign with strong, covert energy. Scorpio emanates a potent aura that is the height of magnetism. He is emotional but also possesses an intellectual and persuasive power that is best illustrated, at its most negative level, by Charles Manson—that is how powerful this Scorpio can be. It is a power that can create fear. On the other hand, in a more positive light, there is Billy Graham, a man who has moved thousands of people with his faith.

Scorpio is extremely ambitious, fearless, and self-sufficient. At the negative level, though, he's a bully. Love, hate, anger, fear—these emotions run through him in full force making him hostile, cynical, and self-righteous. Have you ever seen a Scorpio brooding? He's menacing. And vengeful. *Vendetta* is a word created for Scorpio. He holds hostilities and grudges, and even if it takes twenty years, he will seek his revenge.

Scorpio has a death anxiety. He rules the eighth house, and this is where Pluto comes in—the planet of death/rebirth. Scorpio frequently has to contend with death. Whether it be the untimely death of a parent, a sibling, a mate, a friend . . . invariably, death will impact and influence his life.

Under the best circumstances, Scorpio can be protective of others, but if afflicted, possessiveness takes over. He becomes jealous and subsequently competitive—he wants to beat everybody and be the best. He's arrogant, brilliant, and dangerous. He becomes prideful and starts to identify himself through material possessions and through relationships with others. It creates an insecurity that can lead to stinginess and condemnation. The "I am the master, you are the slave," concept lies in the heart of Scorpio. He manifests this in partnerships, predominantly romantic relationships or marriage. Scorpio is possessive and controlling of others because he is afraid of rejection. An afflicted Scorpio hides his insecurities well.

The unconscious force that drives Scorpio is his free-flowing energy. It heightens his sexual drive. This is a person without inhibitions. His ego has one motive and that is to be responsible to the self. His sexuality is pure energy, and when afflicted, he becomes erotically obsessed. Scorpio lacks a censoring device, so he doesn't care about how others are impacted by his energy and sexuality—he has no guilt and is highly self-indulgent.

At a positive level, he can sublimate this powerful, sexual energy to produce healing. Scorpio has enormous healing abilities. He not only regenerates himself but others as well. This healing can be accomplished through religion, therapeutic guidance, or medicine.

TALENTS AND ABILITIES

Scorpio is the world's best imitator—if he sees you doing it once, he will do you one better. He has an incredible ability to learn and has great mental retention—he can instantly recall information and events.

Scorpio's powerful healing abilities make him an excellent doctor, surgeon, or diagnostician. He also makes a shrewd detective—Scorpio will look at you and see right through to the truth.

Scorpio is not as involved with ideas as with the power of ideas. He has executive qualities and enormous magnetism, which might even make him a good politician.

HEALTH AND PHYSICAL TRAITS

Scorpio usually has no inhibitions, but should there be, he will manifest them through physical difficulty. If there is a suppression of energy and a deviation in his normal bodily flows, he can develop heart problems.

Scorpio is a sign of excess. He has difficulty with self-control and will often overindulge in food or sex. Since Scorpio rules the genitals, males might experience prostate problems. Good health is dependent on exercise, something Scorpio dislikes.

FAMILY RELATIONSHIPS

Scorpio comes into the world with rejection. His father probably didn't want him, and his mother might not have wanted the pregnancy (particularly true of a Scorpio Moon placement). If this is the case, Scorpio innately knows it and is driven to compensate for that rejection. When he is born, he comes out swinging. This is something that Scorpio must learn to curb and overcome.

The Scorpio mother is poor. She is possessive and demanding of her children and finds it difficult to let them grow up. She is not particularly generous either. With a Scorpio mother, you've got to get your own and earn it yourself.

Fathers do a little bit better. Strangely enough, the Scorpio father is a more patient and determined dad than other Sun Signs. He has a good understanding of children, particularly his own. If afflicted, however, he will look at his children as a reflection of himself and have enormous but often unrealistic expectations of them.

The Scorpio child has many needs and will be boisterous about them. He is demanding and competitive, especially with siblings. If he can't get his needs met by his own family, the Scorpio child will find someone else's family to bond with.

This child is a natural brooder who can't sit still. He's a tough child who will not be placated. It is helpful for him to move and keep busy. An intelligent and perceptive child, Scorpio needs mental and physical stimulation. The Scorpio boy often takes his mother for granted, expecting her to take care of all his needs. As an adult, he winds up expecting his wife to do the same.

PARTNERSHIPS

Scorpio is prideful and often identifies himself through others. This is dangerous because, in many cases, Scorpio chooses a spouse not out of love, but because he or she has the right qualities to reflect or represent him.

Even the best Scorpio is not a romantic. Partners are chosen purely for ego positions. For Scorpio, there is no equality in a relationship—he has to be in charge, has to be the king (or queen). This is the way in which he asserts and identifies himself.

When Scorpio takes on a partner and family, he absorbs them and they become part of him. He is extremely possessive; what is his is truly his, and he cannot let go. Even when divorced, Scorpio is still not mentally divorced—he won't give up anything and that makes it hard for him to establish new relationships.

The Scorpio female also has a strong ego and has the notion that if she sexually satisfies a man, he will never go elsewhere. The Scorpio female doesn't fall in love. Although down-to-earth, she is demanding and thinks sex is a power that is endless. Once married, she is as possessive as the male.

The inability to strike an ego balance with a partner is the reason why Scorpio's relationships go askew. The best advice to Scorpio for a solid relationship is to learn to respect and consider your partner.

DECANATES

First Decanate: Scorpio/Scorpio—(0 to 10 degrees or approximately October 24–November 2)

Scorpio/Scorpio is an outwardly calm but secretive individual.

Scorpio in this decanate has a lack of polish. He is competitive and uses his will instead of strategy to get ahead. He can get pushy and has little concern for the consequences of his actions.

Second Decanate: Scorpio/Pisces—(10 to 20 degrees or approximately November 3–12)

This Scorpio, with the influence of Pisces/Neptune, needs to be elevated; he needs philosophical concepts and ethics. He must learn to take all his magnificent qualities and serve the world. By serving, through professional achievement or humanistic endeavors, Scorpio will avoid stinging others and, inevitably, himself.

Third Decanate: Scorpio/Cancer—(20 to 30 degrees or approximately November 13–21)

Scorpio has now taken on the Moon quality of Cancer, and this is Scorpio at his softest. He makes a fine psychologist or psychiatrist because the Moon/Pluto combination creates a great ability to empathize and sympathize and bestow a psychic kindness on others.

♐ SAGITTARIUS (NOVEMBER 22–DECEMBER 21)

Symbol—*The Archer*
Ruling Planet—*Jupiter*
Element—*Fire*
Cross—*Mutable*
Group—*Theoretical*
Gender—*Masculine*
House Ruled—*Ninth*
Famous Sagittarians—*Woody Allen, Winston Churchill, Mark Twain, Walt Disney, Noël Coward, Beethoven, Joe DiMaggio, Tina Turner, Steven Spielberg, Frank Sinatra*

BASIC PERSONALITY

Sagittarius has been given, by his ruling planet of Jupiter, an extraordinary gift of intuition. It's a gut feeling, a "knowing without knowing," because it is not intellectually or educationally based. It is an intuition that has been equated with luck.

Sagittarius is honest. He's versatile and optimistic, independent and friendly. In fact, Sagittarius considers even the most casual acquaintance his friend.

It is considered the "sign of the millionaire" because Sagittarius is usually born with a high IQ and is achievement driven.

Sagittarius also has a healthy, unconscious mechanism that keeps his psyche well-adjusted. At a positive level, this person is devoid of fear and neuroses. Sagittarius thrives on freedom and independence. A freewheeling individual, he has no inhibitions. He does not suppress or repress emotions like other Sun Signs.

If he is afflicted, however, he loses his competitive edge and drive. He will begin to suffer from doubt and then find it hard to trust his own instincts. He can start feeling claustrophobic, which can lead to wanderlust. In that state of mind, he thinks only of himself and begins eliminating his responsibilities. Sagittarius must learn that in order to achieve autonomy, he must meet his responsibilities first.

The ninth house, ruled by Sagittarius, is the house of theories, concepts, and philosophy. Quite often, Sagittarius thinks his perception is the only one. He has to deal with the fact that his truth is not the ultimate truth.

Sagittarius is a theoretical sign with the ability for abstract thinking. He can understand and decipher that which is not tangible. A creative individual, he can go beyond the limitations of touching, feeling, and seeing. He conceives things before they have been manifested. The inherent difficulty for Sagittarius is that because he's the one who has keen perception, he must take his ideas and instincts and bring them forth in a way that others can perceive and understand.

When Sagittarius is afflicted, he becomes rebellious and irresponsible. He gets careless about what he says, becoming extremely inaccurate and superficial, with little regard to his words or actions. He doesn't know how to hold his tongue, becomes impulsive and outspoken without stopping to deliberate. Even in a positive mode, he feels compelled to express himself candidly. You don't have to ask Sagittarius to tell you the truth—he will, whether you want to hear it or not. Sagittarius is unaware of the effects this has on others. Never argue or get into a heated discussion with a Sagittarius—he gets personal and attacks you at your weakest point. He will undermine you so that he can win the argument whether he is right or wrong.

If Sagittarius is chided for his outspokenness, if you can't see his sense of humor or handle him with a sense of humor, he lapses into resignation, and that is comparable to defeat. His drive diminishes and he becomes emotionally and mentally sloppy, careless, indifferent— all of the qualities of someone whose fire and spirit have been dampened.

The restrictions, limitations, and discipline of Sagittarius need to be handled carefully and philosophically. He sees everything as a challenge. Although he is theoretical, he doesn't always follow or conform to his own philosophies.

TALENTS AND ABILITIES

Since the ninth house is the area where religion and philosophy enter, Sagittarius can make a fine man of the cloth—minister, priest, nun, rabbi. His innate sense of abstract vision allows him to excel as an engineer, architect, or general contractor.

His natural sense of the absurd makes him a good comedian, and his personable manner makes him comfortable in sales. He thrives in any career that allows him freedom of movement.

A natural gambler, Sagittarius is always game to tackle something new. He is able and capable and carries a professional attitude toward his work.

HEALTH AND PHYSICAL TRAITS

Sagittarius rules the hips, sciatic nerve, and the liver. Since he is a mutable sign, he has a tendency for allergies, usually related to grains such as wheat or barley. Diet is important. Sagittarius doesn't take much interest in food; he eats to live but needs to be careful about what he eats or drinks. With a sensitive liver, it is recommended that Sagittarius abstain from alcohol, particularly grain-based liquors.

Sagittarius is mentally and physically self-regulating. He has the ability to heal his body through his mind. If he is afflicted, he loses that ability and he can no longer control the body or his psyche.

Naturally athletic and competitive, exercise is of great benefit to

Sagittarius but should not be overdone. He needs to be careful about running because it could be damaging or stressful to the hips. Swimming is an excellent alternative.

FAMILY RELATIONSHIPS

The Sagittarius mother is fairly good, but she doesn't like to have her lifestyle cramped. If she is not too obsessed with the need for personal independence, she can guide her children well and provide them with insight. She can make an excellent mother who will encourage and empower her children to great heights. She provides for her children but takes care of her needs, too. If she feels claustrophobic or that her freedom is being hampered, she can begin to neglect everything and everyone around her including herself.

The Sagittarian father is an out-and-out poor parent. "Home life" is not a priority to him because it restricts his freedom and independence.

Sagittarius is a father-dominated sign, and the Sagittarian child will be in a bad state because he might have a father who will not accept him or who will compete with him. This is particularly difficult for a little boy—he will be told that he doesn't measure up and his father will challenge him rather than empower him.

The Sagittarius female tends to compete with her sister(s) for father's (or even brother's) attention. She is looking for approval from dad, who, unfortunately, will probably never give it unless she has a good mother to help encourage dad's support.

The Sagittarius child is bright, tall, lean, and very quick. This is an active and social kid, gregarious, happy by nature, talkative, and animated. The Sagittarius child is intelligent and has a high IQ, regardless of the intellect or success of his parents. When he succeeds, however, he often becomes depressed—he has outdone his father and might incur his wrath. He might even develop a fear of success due to his concern about how it will impact his relationship with his father.

PARTNERSHIPS

When the Sagittarian male gets married, he becomes a married bachelor. He thinks his wife is the one who is married, not he. He makes decisions predicated on his needs and expects his wife to tag along. He is not romantic and is quite spontaneous about sex—when he wants it, he wants it now and his interest must be maintained. The

Sagittarius male doesn't trust women; his involvement with dad took precedence over his relationship with and the value of his mother, which winds up impairing his relationships with women. Sagittarius doesn't understand women and is basically chauvinistic. He has a partner in theory, and his relationships will remain stable as long as his partner meets all his "shoulds"; if she doesn't, he'll roam. He's a good provider, but that's it. He expects his mate to be available, consistent, and tolerant of his needs and wants, but he's not particularly trustworthy. He doesn't have what it takes to be a good partner.

The Sagittarius female, who grows up seeking her father's approval, will transfer that dynamic to other men. She is competitive with other women for the attentions of men and will subsequently select a partner she can also compete with. She is not the dependent type.

DECANATES

First Decanate: Sagittarius/Sagittarius—(0 to 10 degrees or approximately November 22–December 1)

This Sagittarius is talkative, restless, and interesting and makes a superb salesman. He is sociable, entertaining, and pleasant to be around. If afflicted, he becomes careless and sloppy—a liar, a gossip, and just plain manipulative.

Second Decanate: Sagittarius/Aries—(10 to 20 degrees or approximately December 2–11)

This decanate is adventurous and a risk-taker. He's the one who boarded the ship and sailed to the New World. Whatever he undertakes is important and necessary—he has a faith in himself that makes him able to be courageous, take chances, and, ultimately, achieve.

If afflicted, the adventurous nature of this Sagittarius will simply lead to foolhardiness.

Third Decanate: Sagittarius/Leo—(20 to 30 degrees or approximately December 12–21)

This is a powerful placement that almost guarantees success. Sagittarius is, in general, a successful sign, and if he isn't, it is through either his own undoing or an affliction that has not been overcome. The power of Leo combined with the intuitive power of Jupiter provides Sagittarius with an innate honing device that lets him know where to go, what to do, when to do it, and how to do it, regardless of others' support or belief in him. This is a successful position for fame and/or fortune.

♑ CAPRICORN (DECEMBER 22–JANUARY 19)

Symbol—*The Goat*
Ruling Planet—*Saturn*
Element—*Earth*
Cross—*Cardinal*
Group—*Theoretical*
Gender—*Feminine*
House Ruled—*Tenth*
Famous Capricorns—*Elvis Presley, Richard Nixon, Martin Luther King, Jr., Benjamin Franklin, Joan of Arc, Isaac Newton, Humphrey Bogart, Muhammad Ali, Cary Grant, Louis Pasteur, Jim Carrey*

BASIC PERSONALITY

Capricorn is determined, single-minded, and possesses directed energy. He doesn't fantasize, he visualizes. Capricorn will envision a goal, impress it in his mind, hold it dear to his heart, then carry through until that goal or desire is realized.

Because of Saturn's rulership, Capricorn is serious and seldom considered magnetic. Impressive, yes; but not magnetic. He is somewhat self-centered with an overdeveloped ego that gives him a high sense of responsibility. He can be extremely austere, relentless without observing, ruthless, and opportunistic. Capricorn can exercise a self-denial that allows him to win under any circumstance.

Capricorn has an inferiority complex that he compensates for by striving to maintain a strong public image. When he is in conflict, he can become egocentric, lapsing into a selfishness of distorted proportions whereby he becomes convinced of his own omnipotence.

Since Capricorn is in the polarity of starvation, his innate fear of starvation makes him hoard. He is not generous by nature and needs to learn how to share.

Several unconscious motives direct Capricorn. The first is a retentiveness that makes him downright stingy. The second is an anxiety about loss or failure. Even when Capricorn is aggressive, he is always defensive. If afflicted, he becomes rigid, and this inability to bend is accentuated by the repression of all impulses, making him unable to move forward. This is a troubling conflict for Capricorn given his usual innate and phenomenal strength and tenacity.

Capricorn is serious and very aware of his reputation. He is a planner and an enabler and will make many sacrifices to attain his goals. Single-minded, he systematically moves forward. The key word for Capricorn is *respect*. He believes that payback comes through hard work and is a stickler for playing by the rules.

TALENTS AND ABILITIES

Capricorn is an excellent organizer. His strong leadership skills and goal-oriented attitude can make him an effective chief executive of a major company.

Capricorn has a wonderful aptitude for math, which allows him to shine in banking, finance, real estate, building, or general contracting. His abilities are best placed under his own command since he knows where and how money is to be made.

HEALTH AND PHYSICAL TRAITS

Capricorn rules the skeletal structure, bones, and spinal column. Capricorn tends to be tall, but his knees and spine are vulnerable, and he generally has problems with his posture.

Capricorn often has a loss of body calcium and needs to supplement calcium in his diet. This is necessary to maintain the integrity of his bones and teeth, which can suffer if his diet is not rich in calcium.

FAMILY RELATIONSHIPS

This is probably one of the most mother-dominated signs of all. If you look at a Capricorn, you usually see his mother, both physically and in character.

The Capricorn mother must watch that she doesn't become all work and no play. She can be harsh with her children but also protective. The Capricorn father is basically domineering and always worried about what "people will say."

The Capricorn child is like an old person—serious and responsible. Ironically, as he matures, he retains his youth. Capricorn truly looks and gets better as he gets older.

The Capricorn child is resourceful. He's the hardworking paperboy who'll earn money to buy his own bicycle. Since he is mother-dominated, Capricorn will even go out and buy mom what she needs. Capricorn wants to get rid of dad; he doesn't know why mom needs him and wants to take dad's place. He is protective of his mother and deems his father useless. He frequently winds up parenting himself or becoming his own father.

PARTNERSHIPS

Capricorn has deep passions for human relationships. If he softens his retentiveness and inhibitions, he has boundless energy.

The Capricorn male is protective. He is not particularly romantic and not a playboy. He needs a wife and family. He is prone to marrying for social status, therefore his wife must come from a polished, well-educated, respectable family—he doesn't want scandals emerging from the past.

The Capricorn female is not fixated on the physical attractiveness of her mate—she is more interested in someone with a good career, a future, money, and respectability than in lust or romance. She wants a man who can afford her and who is a good provider.

Capricorn can be loving, although not demonstrative. He or she can be "in love" and inwardly passionate but is usually not good at showing it. It takes a rare partner to bring those qualities to the surface.

DECANATES

First Decanate: Capricorn/Capricorn—(0 to 10 degrees or approximately December 22–31)

The key word is *ambition*. Capricorn in this decanate is a meticulous planner who always has an objective—he can't live without one. True to his symbol, he's that mountain goat climbing straight up the hill, and if he slips a little bit, he will climb right back up again. If afflicted, he will think in terms of his own needs and desires, which will drive him to the point of climbing that mountain so fast he'll darn well fall right off it. Saturn has a way of making sure that everything gained is earned. If Capricorn manipulates, bypasses the ground rules, or is unethical, he'll fall from the highest place. That is guaranteed.

Second Decanate: Capricorn/Taurus—(10 to 20 degrees or approximately January 1–10)

The combination of Saturn/Venus can be softening to austere Capricorn. It allows him some self-love, which he's not prone to naturally. Venus is going to give him a quality that attracts. Females in this decanate are particularly pretty. They have a balance and structure to their appearance that is not usually present with Saturn.

If afflicted, Capricorn is going to be egocentric, self-centered, self-serving . . . he will be his own worst enemy and his own undoer.

Third Decanate: Capricorn/Virgo—(20 to 30 degrees or approximately January 11–19)

This combination makes Capricorn discriminating and intellectual, with a quickness of mind that borders on brilliance. In this decanate, Capricorn makes an excellent accountant, teacher, or journalist—the type you send out to get the news, which he does efficiently.

If afflicted, this Capricorn will be critical and demanding, and while he will be a good, hard worker, he will also expect everybody else to meet his standards. This is an individual who works more effectively alone.

♒ AQUARIUS (JANUARY 20–FEBRUARY 18)

Symbol—*The Water Bearer*
Ruling Planet—*Uranus/Saturn*
Element—*Air*
Cross—*Fixed*
Group—*Theoretical*
Gender—*Masculine*
House Ruled—*Eleventh*
Famous Aquarians—*Oprah Winfrey, Charles Darwin, Galileo, Clark Gable, Franklin D. Roosevelt, Abraham Lincoln, Thomas Edison, George Burns, Charles Dickens, Norman Rockwell, Ronald Reagan, John Travolta, Michael Jordan, Paul Newman*

BASIC PERSONALITY

Aquarius is often called the humanistic sign. Personable, he gets along with almost anyone. He is imaginative, generous, and often inspiring.

Aquarius is practical and always looking to improve the self. Before

Uranus ruled Aquarius, it was Saturn ruled, and Saturn makes certain that one becomes self-aware.

Aquarius has insights ahead of his time. He has the ability to tap into "race knowledge," the experience and knowledge of generations, which is stored in his collective unconscious. For Aquarius, knowledge is not for his self-preservation but the preservation of all man. His foresight enables him to go into the future. Since he must reconcile the past to get into the future, it creates a conflict—past versus future—back and forth inside his head. As a result, he needs to strike a mental balance and acquire boundaries so that he can avoid confusion or the type of abstract thinking that makes him unable to maintain his feet on the ground.

As a theoretical sign, Aquarius can ascend to a complex mental level and become woolly headed, obstinate, and antisocial. He can unintentionally isolate himself through preoccupation with his thoughts or endeavors. Occasionally, Aquarius becomes morbidly focused on unconventionality. He will create conflict and go against society, the environment, current morality, and so on, simply to challenge or shatter the status quo.

Aquarius is impressionable and easily swayed by others. The selection of his environment and peers is extremely important and influential to his healthy and productive development.

In a strong and positive position, Aquarius can be the most rational of individuals. Since he has the ability of foresight and prophecy, the insight he develops into other human beings can, ultimately, make him tactful and considerate.

TALENTS AND ABILITIES

Aquarius shines in service industries. His wonderful socialization skills allow him to succeed in any field that brings him in contact with other people, whether it be social work, humanitarian pursuits, public relations, or politics. Many American presidents have been born under the sign of Aquarius.

Aquarius excels at anything that involves mental stimulation or thinking as well as in any career in an electronics-related field. He makes an excellent engineer, scientist, inventor, electrician, or X-ray technician.

HEALTH AND PHYSICAL TRAITS

Aquarius rules the ankles, the cardiovascular system, and circulation. He is, by nature, not a physical being—you've got to get him up off his butt and moving because his natural tendency is to be contemplative and physically inert. It is beneficial for Aquarius to keep his diet light and get regular exercise.

Since he tends to overwork his mind, if he does not strike a balance between body and mind, Aquarius must watch out for mental breakdowns. The heady, mental qualities of Aquarius, when afflicted, can produce a loss of boundaries and a risk of mental withdrawal.

FAMILY RELATIONSHIPS

The Aquarian mother is generally unimpressive. She is occasionally good, but that depends on her willingness to accept routines that Aquarius doesn't like. She tends to be a mediocre homemaker—housekeeping is not her forte. Unless other planets influence the chart, she is basically sloppy. The reason she isn't meticulous or domestically adept is because her mind is usually elsewhere.

The Aquarius father is poor, too. Parenting from an Aquarius father is, at best, permissive. Like the mother, the father also doesn't care for routine and repetition. He will indulge his child in any way as long as he is not bothered. Although Aquarius parents truly love their children, they are not particularly meticulous about child-rearing in general.

The Aquarius child is independent but loves socializing with others. This is a little contradictory—he wants to be alone but doesn't want to be alone. You have to be careful with the Aquarian child because he will begin to identify with his friends and do exactly what they are doing. It is important for him to establish his own identity, as opposed to going along with the crowd.

The Aquarius child also needs to be mentally engaged. He doesn't always pay attention to what is going on or being said and will often only listen to part of a request. He lacks patience and easily becomes bored and oblivious. He needs to work at remembering things and beefing up his recall. Even a traumatic experience will be forgotten by an Aquarius child.

Maturity and sophistication can elevate this child, but he must be kept in school. Although he hates routines, he must be encouraged to stick it out, particularly where education is concerned. It will all pay off to his benefit in the end.

PARTNERSHIPS

Aquarius is often tall, lean, attractive, and not short of partners. He is romantic and enjoys anything that strokes his emotions. Aquarius loves to wine and dine, and to be courted. Once he finds someone to commit to, he is loyal. In fact, he might even tend to be dependent in his relationships. He rarely feels confined because his mind can easily go off onto another plane when necessary.

In a partnership, the downside of Aquarius is that he is not always focused and has his share of little quirks—he is forgetful and not overly domesticated. The Aquarius female is usually professional and intellectual rather than domestic. Sometimes she has problems recognizing her femininity and seeks constant validation from the men in her life.

DECANATES

First Decanate: Aquarius/Aquarius—(0 to 10 degrees or approximately January 20–29)

This Aquarius possesses a strong personality and truly marches to the beat of a different drummer. He is going to have difficulties because he doesn't want to adapt and can be positively pigheaded. While it is not imperative for him to adapt, he definitely needs to stop working up a resistance just for the sake of resisting.

Aquarius in this decanate is an innovator. He can foretell the future. However, if he imposes his insights or lacks the patience and finesse that is required to share his foresight and wait for the acceptance of his ideas by others, he will become overbearing—the type whom nobody wants to believe or deal with. He is not going to be understood, which will be lonely and difficult for him.

Second Decanate: Aquarius/Gemini—(10 to 20 degrees or approximately January 30–February 8)

The flighty, Mercurial quality of Gemini influencing this decanate creates a mind that roams all over the place. This is a friendly Aquarius who is sociable and active. The Aquarius/Gemini combination makes him nosy and curious as well as humanistic and congenial, so it produces a real social butterfly. This Aquarius can be sent all over the world and easily adapt to any place or culture.

Third Decanate: Aquarius/Libra—(20 to 30 degrees or approximately February 9–18)

Talk about flair! This is the artist who will be doing something at the consciousness-raising level, the one who can predict fashion or artistic trends, or who might choose a color that becomes popular next year.

If afflicted, this decanate of Aquarius also has the ability to detach emotionally and completely. He will leave you cold, be disinterested, and have absolutely no desire to empathize. He needs to be willing to make contact, to be vulnerable and unafraid of his feelings, so that instead of detaching, he can make emotional connections with others.

⊃⊂ PISCES (FEBRUARY 19–MARCH 20)

Symbol—*The Fish*
Ruling Planet—*Neptune/Jupiter*
Element—*Water*
Cross—*Mutable*
Group—*Theoretical*
Gender—*Feminine*
House Ruled—*Twelfth*
Famous Pisceans—*Elizabeth Taylor, Albert Einstein, Michelangelo, Frédéric Chopin, Victor Hugo, Rudolf Nureyev, John Steinbeck, George Washington, Cindy Crawford*

BASIC PERSONALITY

Pisces occupies the twelfth house and is ruled by Neptune. He also has a dual rulership since Jupiter ruled this sign in ancient times. Jupiter provides intuition while Neptune provides depth, making Pisces the deepest of all constellations.

Pisces is multifaceted and multitalented. It is the ultimate sign with qualities that encompass all signs of the Zodiac. Pisces is intuitive, imaginative, and possesses an insight into human nature that bestows him with compassion and an "others before me" attitude. He is empathetic and people oriented. As a theoretical sign, Pisces displays, feeds, and expresses his ego through other people. His innate sense of intuition provides him with an awareness of both his abilities and limitations. It enables Pisces to correct his fears so that he doesn't become vague and float out into never-never land.

A dual personality, Pisces is symbolized by two fish swimming in opposite directions. This opposing nature creates a split psyche. This means he can be a medium—Pisces can remove his ego so that he can read someone else's ego. He retains his identity while empathizing with others. At a positive level, this is wonderful because it gives Pisces psychic ability. He is able to think in the abstract and go beyond the boundaries and limitations of all the other Sun Signs. On the negative side, Neptune makes Pisces unpredictable and difficult to understand. His irrational fears can make him phobic. However, his chameleon quality allows him to withstand anything—he has the key to survival. On the other hand, it often handicaps Pisces because, unless he has been educated by self-awareness and knows how to control and appreciate his intuitive and psychic abilities, he doubts them. To counter this, Pisces must learn to use and depend on his gut.

Pisces picks up the vibrations of others. As a result, he often projects not just his own problems but the problems of those around him. This can be mentally and emotionally draining, so periodic isolation is healthy and important for Pisces—he needs to eliminate all stimulation and recuperate. When consumed by severe fear or anger, he can move away from people and isolate permanently. Meditation can be helpful to Pisces when all else has failed.

Although Pisces needs solitude, he fears being alone and sometimes develops a need to please for fear of being rejected. When negatively afflicted, or when frightened and uncertain, Pisces suffers terribly from the "what ifs." This makes it difficult for him to deal with "what is." He can become a loner or dependent and insecure. It's dangerous when Pisces starts depending on others for motivation or validation—he gets limited and nasty and, consequently, vindictive.

When afflicted, Pisces is lazy, vague, and lacks concentration. He can become overly emotional to the point of hysteria—in Pisces hysteria abounds when he is in doubt, afraid, or uncertain. He will become bad tempered and self-indulgent without boundaries. Pisces will hang on to imaginary hurts and misinterpret things. He will go to any length to satisfy his ego, becoming deceitful if need be. The self-indulgence of Pisces can reach epic proportions. When this occurs, he must get his central nervous system back into a relaxed state or else it will have negative effects upon his health.

Pisces is quick to jump to conclusions, so he must learn to hold judgment until his intuition proves the right or wrong of a situation. This way, he can relate to others without blaming or taking things personally. When this intuition is used as a self-disciplining device, Pisces is powerful and can accomplish a great deal.

With a good education, self-awareness, and fortitude, Pisces can be creative, artistic, and productive. The responsibility of Pisces is to do the right kind of juggling act where he can have a free flow back and forth between the abstract and the concrete. This will enable him to tap into others and make use of his own instincts and ideas.

TALENTS AND ABILITIES

Pisces is a multitalented sign. He can makes strides in the world of medicine, especially as a diagnostician or psychologist. Because he has visualization and an innate understanding and absorption of others, Pisces makes a great actor who can take on any role—be anything, do anything.

Pisces has a good sense of humor and could be a good comedian.

As talented as Pisces is, he also has a lazy streak. He wants others to do it for him. He thinks he is subtle. Suggestions abound, even when he is not willing to do the work. Pisces must learn that "doing it himself" is the only way to master. He must learn to strike a balance between laziness and industriousness and to focus his talents and master something.

HEALTH AND PHYSICAL TRAITS

Pisces rules the feet and all the filtration glands.

Physically, Pisces is not strong. Most of his health problems are central nervous system related. Since Pisces has to learn to overcome dependency, fear, and rejection, his internal struggles are exhausting. Regeneration is instrumental to the health and well-being of Pisces. He must take periodic breaks to relax and reenergize.

FAMILY RELATIONSHIPS

As a mother-dominated sign, Pisces tends to pick up on and imitate mother—good, bad, or indifferent. Mother is instrumental to Pisces, while father is a fantasy. It takes a long time for a Pisces to understand his father, if he is there at all. It is hard for a Pisces to know his father and vice versa. He has a crossed perception of dad that is oddly shaped by his mother's definition, father's actions (or inactions), and the truth. But it takes awhile to get the truth. Neptune doesn't allow for clarity, which makes it hard for Pisces to know who father is and where he fits in. This usually does not occur until later in life. If there is a relationship with dad, Pisces will bend over backward to please him.

The Pisces mother, like the other theoretical signs, is poor. Pisces tends to lack the consistency that is necessary to rear a child with the great security that every child needs. She can become a martyr, making her children feel guilty—that if she cares for her children, they owe her. The Pisces mother can be industrious and dutiful, particularly if her own mother was that way. But if her mother was lazy and disorganized, Pisces will manifest those traits.

The Pisces father is lazy. He can live vicariously through his offspring, which causes the child to fight for his identity because father is either projecting or rejecting his parental responsibility altogether.

The Pisces child has a difficult emotional life. The underlying problem is that he is conscious of the family and is sensitive—he picks up everybody's vibrations. He transcends his age in terms of this understanding but is helpless to do anything about it. When this becomes overwhelming or overstimulating, it causes him to withdraw. He escapes into fantasy or television. It is helpful for the Pisces child to keep busy and active so that he doesn't isolate and brood. The imagination of the Pisces child can be turned into something creative and positive for his development and growth.

PARTNERSHIPS

If Pisces emulates mother or can't let go of mother's impact, he will bring those characteristics to his partnerships. Pisces will have opinions about partners, particularly about men, based on mother's perceptions. For the Pisces man, if he finds he can't treat, act, or have his partner behave like his mother, there will be relationship difficulties. Pisces needs to be intelligent and flexible enough to recognize that his mate is his (or her) own person.

The Pisces female often has to succumb to her husband's demands, and when she doesn't want to do this, she will do what is requested in appearance only, then turn around and undermine her spouse. She can become sneaky.

Since he has an emotional personality, Pisces will often marry and wrap himself around a partner. Pisces is superficially dependent—he uses dependency as a control issue. He must stop trying to get his partner to do what he thinks his partner should do. When Pisces develops positively, he will realize that his security is not predicated on controlling circumstances or other people. He needs to be careful of control, even though it is not done overtly.

Although romantic, Pisces is not overly passionate and sometimes feels sex is a duty. He assumes that romance is all that is necessary in a relationship. An inherent loneliness in Pisces can be overcome by taking a "leap of faith," turning to spirituality, rather than a mate, for his security and strength. If Pisces finds and develops strength, he will discover that he actually has more to offer than his mate.

DECANATES

First Decanate: Pisces/Pisces—(0 to 10 degrees or approximately February 19–28)

Neptune can be frightening, so Pisces in the first decanate has a great deal to resolve. He must control the depth of his water quality and accept the fact that no one else is going to feel this depth of emotions, and while it may appear to be a lonely trip, the end result is enlightening. Pisces will eventually reach a point where he is not alone. This will happen when he can touch his soul or reach a spirituality of sorts. When this occurs, Pisces will recognize and be able to deal with his own emotional depth, unite with the universe, and cease to feel lonely. The enlightenment is a source of power that allows Pisces to be secure about himself.

If afflicted, Pisces will brood and feel sorry for himself or be overcome with either irrational fear of the unknown (which can relate to past lives), or the "what ifs." Although obsessing over the "what ifs" prevents him from fully enjoying the present, Pisces does this to overcome karma—the twelfth house, which Pisces rules.

Second Decanate: Pisces/Cancer—(10 to 20 degrees or approximately March 1–10)

This is perhaps the most difficult of the three decanates because that Cancer/Moon instability coupled with Neptune's fear can make for a moody, unhappy, self-pitying individual. Pisces has to learn to harden, to muster, and to have a faith—it will help to make movement with his life and goals. Without these tools, Pisces will become immobilized, afraid to take the next step because he is convinced the worst is going to happen. Pisces is capable of reaching the ultimate heights or the lowest of depths, depending on where his Moon takes him and what other afflictions or strengths may be revealed in the natal chart.

This decanate needs to get out of himself and do something for someone else—if too self-absorbed, it tires his system and takes its toll on his health.

Third Decanate: Pisces/Scorpio—(20 to 30 degrees or approximately March 11–20)

Since Scorpio is always strong, this decanate of Pisces also has the good fortune of being strong. The glitch here is that Scorpio brings an intensity that makes Pisces either very good or very bad—if Pisces is very good, he is phenomenal; but if he's very bad, he will be selfish, destructive, and narcissistic. He will use his strength as a self-serving tool that will most certainly prove to be his undoing.

On the other hand, if positive, Pisces can share his strength with others and serve. As he serves others, he becomes more dynamic and attractive.

Sun Through the Houses

Once you become familiar with your Sun Sign, you're going to find that it isn't always in its natural house; that is, the Sun Sign of Aries doesn't always land in the Aries-ruled first house, the Sun Sign of Taurus doesn't always land in the Taurus-ruled second house, and so on. It is purely dependent on your hour of birth and the rising sign (ascendant). Your rising sign is always in the first house, and it determines the placement of all your planets in their respective houses.

SUN IN THE FIRST HOUSE

When the Sun is occupying the first house, it becomes "head-on." This means it must experience, it must do. It takes on youthful, courageous, and enthusiastic qualities. In the first house, the Sun will be driven and will often jump without thinking.

If afflicted, this active, energetic quality turns into arrogance, which is nothing more than a cover for fear. The ego becomes stifled—sneaky on some occasions, bombastic on others. There is a tendency to overcompensate, to justify and explain itself, feeling as if it is not quite sure it has a right to be, due to an innate fear of rejection.

SUN IN THE SECOND HOUSE

The Sun desires anything material in nature. There is a need to develop the financial power necessary to obtain all the luxury, beauty, and possessions that this Venus-ruled house demands.

If afflicted, financial and material resources may be squandered. Although there is a natural grace in earning money, it will usually slip right through the fingers, sometimes through gambling. An affliction can either create laziness or the tendency to take things for granted.

SUN IN THE THIRD HOUSE

The Sun in this house has a need to express the self and be understood. It prompts a desire to be educated in ways that enhance both self-awareness and self-expression. A talent for communicating is apparent in this house, whether it be in writing, teaching, public speaking, or painting.

SUN IN THE FOURTH HOUSE

The Sun in this placement is going to be a nurturer. It is self-protecting and self-sustaining and needs to come in contact with the self. The Sun in this placement also has an innate need to amass and cling to possessions, feeling unstable and uncertain about its lot.

When afflicted, Sun in the fourth house is someone who really doesn't want to leave home. This is the thirty-five-year-old bachelor (or bachelorette) whom mom is still looking after because he craves the comfort and protection of home or is afraid to leave. This is also the type of person who, in a divorce case, would rather kill than lose possession of the house.

SUN IN THE FIFTH HOUSE

This is a powerful placement because the Sun is in domicile position in this house. No matter how weak the rest of a chart may be, with the Sun placed in the fifth house, the individual takes on a creative quality, performs without fear, and has a desire to express and accomplish.

A person with this placement seldom strays from a spouse or family. It is not his or her forte—he is honest and generally cannot handle more than one partner. Men with the Sun in this placement make devoted, affectionate, and committed fathers, even to the point of competing with their wives.

Should it be afflicted, unfortunately this is going to bring about a great deal of difficulty in these same areas. The individual might become unstable and wander. A father might either neglect his children or become so afraid of losing them that he becomes too possessive.

SUN IN THE SIXTH HOUSE

This is a plain old workaholic who just wants to improve and do. He tends to be a loner. If afflicted, he really doesn't know how to interact with the world at large. He will find himself exhausted by other people, which will consequently impact his central nervous system. He will frequently have to isolate himself so that he is able to regenerate.

In health matters this Sun is not a strong one and has a low vitality that will somehow have to be compensated for.

SUN IN THE SEVENTH HOUSE

When someone has a Sun placed here, he is considered a "much married" person who is always thinking in terms of "we." This person often surrenders his power to his partner. He doesn't realize he's giving his power away—he thinks that the partner is taking it and not being considerate. He doesn't feel he can operate without a partner and feels incomplete and, eventually, frustrated.

The individual with the Sun in this house needs to understand this dynamic and try to function on his own so that he comes to discover himself as a whole person.

SUN IN THE EIGHTH HOUSE

When a person has a Sun in this placement, his life might be tainted by death, whether it be a heart attack that he survives, a near-death experience, or the deaths of people who are important to him. When these losses occur, he has to pick up and regenerate and, eventually, let go. This letting go can be like a death in itself, but from that comes the ability to survive and experience "rebirth."

As a result, this placement is often influential to those whose careers are associated with death—hospice work, undertakers, funeral directors, and the like.

SUN IN THE NINTH HOUSE

The Sun placed here brings forth a natural ability to tap past-life knowledge and religion associated with philosophy, higher learning, and the expansion of the mind. This individual is usually much wiser than his education would denote.

If afflicted or under hardship, this philosophical, abstract quality turns into defiance, creating an individual who might suffer from wanderlust—he wants to be here, there, and everywhere but winds up nowhere.

A person with this placement has a great desire for adventure, travel, and knowledge.

SUN IN THE TENTH HOUSE

This placement indicates someone who is going to be before the public, someone who will have his fifteen minutes of fame at the very least. This is the house of power, and it produces an individual who works hard for prestige, achievement, and notoriety.

When afflicted, it creates an authoritative and dictatorial individual who is certain that his direction is the only way to go. He could wind up being on the lunatic fringe or in a cult or outside of regular government—definitely a person looking to be noticed.

SUN IN THE ELEVENTH HOUSE

This Sun has a lot of hopes and wishes all his own. This is the house of friendship, but a person with this placement needs to be cognizant not to spread himself so thin that he loses the ability to identify with anyone or anything in particular. Although the Sun in this house is always friendly, group-oriented, and a humanitarian with the world at large, he is also always on a continuous quest for his own identity.

If afflicted, the Sun in this house is going to get into the habit of rebelling just for the hell of it. He'll break down every order and be unconventional for the sake of being unconventional. He can be eccentric and odd.

SUN IN THE TWELFTH HOUSE

This Sun is mysterious. The twelfth house is the reservoir of wonderful past-life abilities, talents, and techniques. Yet, when the Sun is placed here, the misfortune is that the individual has a sensation of confinement. And often, he is confined. It can be a complete confinement such as a wheelchair or a jail term, or confinement through one's inner fears and limitations.

In this house, the Sun also experiences transmutation. The individual begins to slow down and listen. It might require a transit of Saturn or Jupiter over the Sun to reveal that this confinement or limitation doesn't really exist; it is usually self-imposed. The individual can go from feeling confined to listening to his subconscious. This allows him to flower. Talents emerge, perhaps some he never knew existed. This is the house where limitations can be transcended, and with transcendence comes liberation.

★

Chapter Five

Ascendants—Your Rising Sign

Rising Signs: An Overview

The ascendant, or rising sign, indicates how you see yourself. The position of your rising sign in relationship to your Sun and your Moon defines your unique personality. The rising sign is the third leg of this astrological trilogy—Sun, Moon, and ascendant—which represents your id, your conscience, and your superego.

The rising sign is your future. It acts as a protective layer, shielding your Sun and Moon Signs, so that they can develop. You are always your Sun Sign and Moon Sign, but the ascendant sign represents the socialization process. When integrated with the Sun and Moon, one is whole. Your rising sign is the part of your personality that is not going to leave you wide open, available to anybody's potshots or concepts and ideas. The rising sign is your best foot forward, the fashion in which you operate. It is who you let the world think you are.

As the Earth rotates every twenty-four hours, it brings a new rising sign on the horizon approximately every two hours. Whatever sign was on the horizon at your exact time of birth becomes your rising sign. It also determines where your first house is placed (and in what sign). Your rising sign is always in the first house of your birth chart on the eastern horizon.

ARIES RISING

The emotional sign of Aries represents ego. The simplest equation for a strong ego is knowing what you want and feeling you deserve it. In the case of Aries rising, when that is achieved, he comes to peace. When it is not, he winds up getting pushy, overbearing, and prone to temper tantrums. No matter how elevated the Sun Sign, an Aries rising needs to develop moderation, otherwise the friends and/or partners of an Aries rising are just going to walk away, leaving him to wonder, "What did I do?"

Aries rising is a materialist. He is not religiously or philosophically bent. The aggressive and impulsive Martian quality of Aries gives him physical and sexual energy. If Aries rising learns to sublimate this energy, there is no limit to what he can do. This is raw and crude energy that has to be channeled in a positive and productive manner, which can be accomplished through dancing, martial arts, sports, or crafts. This energy of Mars, without any kind of discipline or direction, will lead to difficulty and conflict with other people.

Youngsters with Aries rising can find themselves in accidents. These are children who have no foresight or fear of consequences. They need to be guided. Once guided and disciplined, that energy can be redirected into a more positive and structured quality to avoid the symbolic ramming of the horns against the wall.

Many successful people with this rising sign have careers and achievements associated with any number of things you find in the Aries Sun Sign, such as acting or the military. Aries rising is quick and intelligent.

TAURUS RISING

Taurus is ruled by Venus, and Venus filters out that which is gross to produce refinement. This will make Taurus rising appear placid and an easygoing pushover.

Taurus rising is emotional. He is also slow and deliberate. Once he puts his hooves in, he is going to follow through and do, no matter what. But he has to do it at his own pace—with any kind of prodding, pushing, or disturbance of his equilibrium, he is going to flare up like a bull.

Taurus rising has a natural affinity to all things that are lovely and refined. He likes good food, good wine, and good living conditions. He wants a comfortable, pleasurable, and enjoyable lifestyle and environment. He'll work for it, too. He possesses an energy and a love for labor that is endless.

Family and community oriented, Taurus rising will make sure that his children go to the best schools and live in the best home in the best community. He is very conscious of who the neighbors are and how he lives within his own home. He wants a lovely environment and will put a lot of energy into making his home beautiful. If he loses his equilibrium, he is going to get depressed if anything around him is dirty or does not live up to his high standards.

Sometimes Taurus rising has to prove himself over and over. It is a tedious, heartbreaking, and energy-consuming position that will eventually lead poor old Taurus rising to feeling as though his efforts are of little use. When this happens, he begins to get negative, lazy, and unkempt until inertia takes over, causing him to negate his positive qualities and strengths. As in the Taurus Sun Sign, Taurus rising doesn't want to unfold his temper. He is afraid that his temper will disturb his equilibrium and refined, Venus quality. To avoid conflict, he holds in and stockpiles his anger. But one day, when there is no more to be taken, the dam breaks and the bull charges.

This rising sign needs a great deal of physical affection—his five senses are keen, particularly touch. Taurus rising needs a lot of stroking and cuddling. As a baby, he's the one who'll want to sleep with his parents; as an adult, he can't walk in or out the door without kissing everybody.

GEMINI RISING

Gemini has a dual nature, and on the rising sign, that Mercurial quality is going to show up immediately. Gemini rising is fickle. He is doing a balancing act and can't afford to deal with everything as though it were going to be a career, so he touches and gathers here, picks a brain over there, and so on . . . he accumulates enough information to keep on going without staying in one place for too long.

Although Gemini rising is optimistic and quick of mind, he has to make sure that his thoughts and feelings are in unison so that he can become a better communicator. He must learn to be consistent so that he doesn't have difficulties with a partner. If he says one thing now and the opposite three hours later, his partner will perceive him as a liar and problems will ensue.

In a positive light, Gemini rising has mental agility, allowing him to excel in any form of writing, music, or even politics. Many individuals with this ascendant have achieved fame and success. If negative, Gemini rising can be nothing more than a gossip. He can play games, the most common of which is that, when you are intellectual with him, he is emotional, and vice versa. Worst of all, once he makes you lose your equilibrium or temper, he'll get very cold-blooded.

Gemini rising is quick and intellectual, with a great deal of retained knowledge and a good head for trivia. The downside is that he can also lack the depth to sustain any train of thought or action—he goes from one idea to the next. Gemini rising needs to master something or else he'll become a jack-of-all-trades and master of none.

Gemini rising works well in combination with a fixed Sun Sign, such as Taurus, Leo, Scorpio, or Aquarius. This is a wonderful opportunity if used correctly because it allows a fixed sign to see both sides of the coin.

CANCER RISING

Cancer rising is emotional and sentimental, sensitive, nurturing, and protective—the type who draws others to him.

Since the rising sign protects the rest of the chart and the Moon is the ruler of Cancer rising, it creates the appearance of vulnerability. As long as Cancer rising feels his vulnerability is not at risk, he is forthcoming. But should he feel any kind of threat, he is going to batten down the hatches, tighten up like a crab, and submerge. That vulnerability will turn to moodiness.

Cancer rising is always ready to get going. He likes to get things organized, to ensure the comfort of the home and the comfort of the self. He makes collection an art form. If afflicted, Cancer rising will hold on to material possessions above all else. He has a morbid fear of losing, so he is always collecting or initiating. As noted in the Sun Sign, Cancer is the polarity of starvation, so this innate fear of loss is manifested by hoarding and hanging on to everything because he is afraid of the inability to replace. Look in the basement of any Cancer rising and there will be a lifetime of memorabilia and artifacts.

The sensitivity of Cancer rising can lead to self-pity. There is nobody like a Cancer to feel sorry for himself—he thinks that he is being taken. As a result, he develops defense mechanisms—he gets prickly, overly annoyed, and touchy and can become extremely bitter and resentful.

Most difficulties of Cancer rising come from a need for emotional fortification. The misfortune of this is that when Cancer rising begins to feel sorry for himself, even if the reasons are legitimate, he begins to stroke his ego in a dangerous way, sometimes by escaping through the use of drugs or alcohol.

In a positive light, Cancer rising can be very effective. His intense emotions make him an excellent actor or successful in the arts. He can also provide a great deal of aid and comfort to others, tending to the sick and nurturing those who are less fortunate. In fact, giving his emotions away to benefit others is not only healthy for Cancer rising but can lead to a worthwhile vocation and a great deal of success.

LEO RISING

When Leo is rising, it personifies the image of a lion strutting with power and in stride. The Sun rules Leo rising and gives it a vitality and a dynamic personality. He radiates a sunny disposition, a magnetism, especially in the male (the female is also magnetic, but through no fault of her own, she has a tendency to draw envy). Powerful individuals will be drawn to the magnetic personality of Leo rising. As such, it almost guarantees that Leo rising is going to be an executive or in a position that puts him among people where leadership and executive abilities are important. Leo rising has an ability to make money.

By nature, Leo rising is easygoing. He loves color, has a certain flair, and excellent taste. He enjoys pomp and circumstance, ceremonies and uniforms. He relishes dressing up and being singled out from the rest. While he might dress in a black suit, he'll wear an outrageous tie just to be different—he aims to get attention. However, if this royal, magnificent animal is in any way afflicted, what you get is a downright broken ego, which leads to a sloppiness and a lack of self-esteem and self-respect. Once that happens, Leo becomes disrespectful. Drama is part of the Leo Sun, Moon, and rising sign. He can be effective and quite talented or, in the negative sense, take everything that happens and turn it into a melodramatic situation.

If afflicted, Leo rising can have a bad temper, display bossiness, and be susceptible to flattery. An old saying goes, "Flattery is like perfume—you sniff it, but you never swallow it." Leo rising must take heed because he can be manipulated and victimized by this vulnerability. But if he is fully aware of his abilities and strength, he can't be pushed or led by adulation.

Leo rising will never forget a favor. He has a long memory, so anyone who is kind, helpful, or trustworthy will wind up in the longestterm friendship imaginable. The misfortune of a betrayed Leo rising is that an injury to his ego will never be forgotten. Even if he has to deal with you, work with you, or be your companion, he will never trust you again.

VIRGO RISING

When we deal with Virgo rising, we are dealing with a loner. Virgo rising tires of people since they distract his focus and drain his energy. He loves labor and likes being alone. He doesn't want anyone hovering over him watching what he does. He's intelligent because he's ruled by Mercury and is also a veritable workhorse. Virgo rising is not bored by details. He easily and contentedly nitpicks, going through all the little mundane pieces that support major things. He is like an accountant who locates that missing penny with great satisfaction.

Virgo rising has an interesting and inquisitive mind. He learns things and stores away all this treasured information knowing that, sooner or later, when he has to find an answer or come up with some ingenious solution, he can tap into this valuable resource in the back of his head. As in the Virgo Sun Sign, he has an enormous ability for self-analysis, which can help him deal with his shortcomings.

If afflicted, Virgo rising will clean the stove until it shines but forget the sink and the rest of the kitchen. He gets too bogged down with perfecting the details so that other things wind up going to pot. Virgo rising is so busy breaking apart and taking care of segments that he quite often misses the big picture. He can be nitpicky, critical, condemning, or otherwise get himself into trouble.

What Virgo rising needs most is approval. Unfortunately, his background is usually one in which he draws criticism, so that, somewhere along the line, he will have to distinguish between being analyzed and being criticized, which, of course, are two very different things. Virgo rising doesn't handle criticism well, but he's awfully good at dishing it out. He is looking for perfection, but perfection, like beauty, is in the eye of the beholder. He needs to be more open and accepting of other people's flaws.

LIBRA RISING

Libra is ruled by the feminine planet of Venus, which endows Libra rising with a natural grace and beauty. The beauty that comes from Libra/Venus is a balanced beauty of both face and body.

Libra rising is concerned not only with graciousness and diplomacy but with stability. She needs to stabilize and be in complete command of her mental faculties. To maintain equilibrium, Libra rising needs to remove herself from anything that is nerve-racking—stress, tension, pressure—because she really doesn't handle it well.

To be in perfect balance is Libra rising's life quest. Out of that comes a strength and ability to detach and be nonjudgmental. Just like the Libra Sun Sign, Libra rising can look at a situation and be an excellent judge because she can see both sides of the coin, offer pure objectivity, and come to a fair and equitable conclusion. That's a rare gift that is not bestowed on other signs.

If afflicted, Libra rising won't give a damn. Her detachment is incredible because, although she will appear to be caring, underneath there won't be even a drop of concern. In matters of diplomacy, when it is necessary to speak and act in a cordial manner without a single emotion attached to it, this can be a formidable quality. But in personal relationships, it is nothing but trouble because a friend or mate will be looking to get a reaction and Libra rising will remain frustratingly cool, balanced, and unresponsive.

Venus rules everything that is artistic, beautifying, or that satisfies the senses. People with Libra rising are usually successful in any field related to that which is artistic—fashion design, art, acting, interior decorating, and the like.

Women and men with Libra rising have an overall physical attractiveness due to the symmetry of their bodies and facial features. It is the type of beauty that is everlasting. For example, Elizabeth Taylor has a Libra rising, and no matter what affects her—whether she gains weight or suffers through various illnesses—her beauty continues to surface and survive; it's beauty that cannot be destroyed.

SCORPIO RISING

When Scorpio is rising, it creates a personality so strong that you either love it or you hate it—there is no in-between. Scorpio rising, like the Scorpio Sun Sign, is an extremist. He can possess enormous magnetism or create repulsion. He can be absolutely darling or the most hateful individual—when he's good, he's very good, but when he's bad, he's awful.

Scorpio rising readily sorts out who is worthy in his life and whom he will annihilate. His energies flow without guilt, and he doesn't care whether you like him or not. If you like him, all the better, but if you don't, it's of little consequence to him. This attitude makes him stone-faced and austere in appearance. His eyes are piercing, but they're also meant to intimidate—they either send out a message to keep you away or they'll look right through you. They're eyes that can mesmerize you.

Scorpio risings are magnetic. They exude a psychic, sexual energy that flows freely and is attractive. If a Scorpio rising doesn't realize that he has this power, he will likely misuse it.

Scorpio is ruled by Pluto, which deals with the underworld. When afflicted, it can lead Scorpio rising into a controversial lifestyle and mischievous dealings that might eventually have him wind up where he least expects it—in jail or even dead—if he's not careful.

Positively, Scorpio rising's powerful energy can lead and influence large groups of people. If he dedicates himself to the service or welfare of others, he will become a truly formidable individual.

SAGITTARIUS RISING

Sagittarius rising has an uncanny ability to bend the will of the universe to serve him. This willful, broad-minded, and intuitive personality can attract and acquire financial security without thinking about it twice. On the other hand, if negatively aspected, he will develop a dangerous and narcissistic attitude that begins to take things for granted, believing he can have anything he wants.

Freewheeling, curious, elegant, and friendly, Sagittarius rising is charming, pleasant, talkative, and generous. Yet he's also extraordinarily fickle. When he gets bored and tired, he cuts fast. He wants to be challenged, and if you don't challenge him, he'll move on to somebody else who can. Sagittarius rising desires respect and approval, but that's hard to come by for somebody who doesn't always stick around.

A female with Sagittarius rising seeks approval from her father and, if it is not forthcoming, will work to get approval from other males. She doesn't have it easy—femininity doesn't always come naturally to her.

The male rising sign gets bored easily and wants to move on. This gets him in trouble, particularly if he's married, since he usually considers that his wife—not he—is the one who's married, giving him carte blanche to do his own thing.

When afflicted, Sagittarius rising gets sloppy and stops dressing well. He also gets unconcerned about feelings—others' and his own—

and begins a downward, negative streak where he expects perfection from others even when he is less than perfect or unable to cope.

Sagittarius rising is freedom loving and doesn't like to be fenced in. When he starts feeling confined, either physically or emotionally, it takes its toll. He has to work hard to transcend this condition or he will certainly pay the consequences.

CAPRICORN RISING

Whereas most rising signs share the characteristics of their Sun Sign counterparts, Capricorn rising is a bit of an anomaly. A Capricorn Sun is usually tall and extroverted, but on the rising sign, he is short and a little cool and aloof. It's a strange phenomenon, but Saturn's impact on the rising sign diminishes and takes certain things away.

Capricorn rising is more involved with the maturation of the ego than the Sun Sign since the first house/ascendant house is the house of the ego. Some Capricorn risings look and act old in their youth—they're six-year-old little old men and women. They're sweet yet cautious, as though they have knowledge and awareness that belies their age. However, the older they get, the better they get. As Capricorn rising matures, instead of remaining a little old man, the child inside finally begins to emerge; he starts to look and act youthful and develops a wonderful sense of humor. A sixty-year-old Capricorn rising sometimes looks younger and better than a forty-year-old. As he gets older and finer, a freedom comes to Capricorn rising because he has already taken care of all his responsibilities and can simply begin to enjoy life at last.

If afflicted, Capricorn rising loses his self-control and high responsibility level. He can also lead a double life—though a conservative and respectable individual to those around him, when he leaves town, he really lets down his hair and loosens up. As an earth sign, Capricorn rising has a sensuality and a passion that he keeps hidden under the weight of maturity and responsibility because he is afraid of being judged. He won't do anything that he feels violates his code of ethics in his immediate environment—he'll just do it in another environment.

Capricorn rising doesn't want to recognize his own ego and puts a brick wall around it. When he can't get past that brick wall to give out and receive the companionship and love he craves, he gets frustrated, tense, and eventually, ill.

Capricorn rising creates tension because he has to be in control, has to do it himself, and feels that nobody else can be trusted to do it as well as he can. This control issue leads to such symptoms as migraine headaches, sleeping disorders, teeth grinding . . . he's got to let it go and start having faith in the abilities of others.

Capricorn rising needs to be the savior of his family and friends. He is often an enabler as well. Everybody benefits because a Capricorn rising boss will employ everyone he knows, feeling as if he's the only one who can provide support and parenting. If afflicted, his need to have everyone under one roof will be done for the sake of control and manipulation. Sooner or later, this is going to backfire, which will lead to difficult confrontations. If Capricorn rising finds dissension, disloyalty, or loss of control, he will revert back to the one thing he can control—pouring every bit of his energy into work and earning money. He will become the ultimate workaholic. Sadly, this is often triggered by the fact that he doesn't feel loved. He begins to believe that if he works hard and produces more, he'll be well liked. Unfortunately, what happens is that Capricorn rising only winds up feeling betrayed.

With the coming Aquarian Age, it is likely that Capricorn risings are going to see the value of their own serious and philosophical concepts and wind up earning their livings in New Age fields such as astrology, yoga, and the metaphysical sciences.

AQUARIUS RISING

When Aquarius is rising it creates a unique personality. Aquarius is ruled by Uranus, and Uranus is the planet of eccentricity. Uranus demands that you identify yourself with and retain your individuality. Early in life, the child with Aquarius rising is going to be labeled precocious. This child knows exactly what he or she wants. However, if there is an affliction, he will lack identity and will do whatever his friends are doing.

With maturity, the electricity of the Aquarius rising personality comes forth and begins to attract. It takes creativity and work to get and keep the attention of an Aquarius rising—his mind wanders, so you have to be quick, get to the point, or shock him—or you will lose him.

Aquarius rising needs mental freedom. He's a natural storyteller. As a child, he possesses a great imagination and will make up little stories and fantasies. Sometimes he is even falsely accused of lying. He is not lying but merely creating, and he innately knows the difference. If afflicted, he can become a child who, because he lacks identity, doesn't know where he stands or can't relate to his environment, and this will prompt him to speak in half-truths or lies.

The Aquarius rising personality is often misunderstood. He's not easy to understand or accept because of an innate ability to transcend the mundane. An Aquarius rising is out of step with society, sometimes even ahead of it. How can he fit in? Sometimes he has to quiet down his personality and wait for the rest of the world to catch up.

Aquarius rising is prophetic—he can look ahead and see the result of a situation. If he is not honed or polished, he can wind up becoming indiscreet, putting his foot in his mouth, and getting into trouble because of the prematurity of his thoughts and actions.

Aquarius rising is humanitarian, sociable, and well liked. He is happy, entertaining, and enjoys being part of a group. If afflicted, he becomes rebellious and will destroy the status quo just for the heck of it. He will love uprooting traditions and making sure that everyone around him is uncomfortable with what is going on. He'll even set up an argument just to be on the other side of it and create controversy. Even though he is wise, intelligent, and ahead of his time, if he's not careful, he'll wind up running ahead and jumping over the edge.

PISCES RISING

Pisces rising is difficult to decipher. Neptune, the ruler of Pisces, can create an individual with an impenetrable facade, the world's finest actor, and the chameleon of the universe. This is extremely misleading. Pisces is a water sign, the ultimate of water signs, possessing the greatest psychic ability bestowed on any of the constellations.

Pisces rising has a big problem—early in life, he begins picking up the vibes of his surroundings and the emotions of other people. This is problematic because he then has difficulty separating his personal stimulation from that of others. As a result, he is constantly filled with strange sensations that must be separated and put into proper perspective.

An idealist, Pisces rising sees things through rose-colored glasses, giving everyone the benefit of the doubt. His idealism is frequently crushed when he has to face the reality of other people's faults and frailties. He expects others to live up to his expectations, puts people on pedestals, expects the very best, and almost always winds up being crushed. The irony here is that Pisces rising innately knows the reality of others' limitations, but prefers to be romantic and idealistic.

If afflicted, Pisces rising is enormously lazy, never getting up off his butt and doing what has to get done. This is a shame because he is multitalented. When well-aspected, Pisces rising is successful and resourceful—if he can't earn a living one way, he'll earn it in another.

Mood swings are also common to Pisces rising. One moment he's happy, exuding a positiveness to those around him . . . the next moment he's falling into a depression, feeling sorry for himself or accusing others for illusionary things that don't exist or do! Pisces rising can swing between these extreme highs and lows to the point where he loses energy and becomes dependent, moody, demanding, overbearing, and, most of all, afraid.

Pisces rising is a psychic. He can pick up on truths that others are trying to hide. However, he must learn to wait, for truths do eventually surface and prove him correct. Pisces must also learn to trust. In doing so, his mood swings will diminish.

It is advisable for Pisces rising to find an outlet, whether it be through religion or medicine—anything that benefits others. Sooner or later, Pisces rising has to serve and share. If he doesn't, he will wind up drowning in his own misery, drowning in those waters of emotion that cannot serve anyone, including himself. As such, he is like a sponge that has absorbed much too much water and has to be squeezed to get rid of the overflow. As he gives of himself to others, Pisces rising becomes stronger and functions more productively.

Pisces rising's strength lies in his believing what he knows to be true, though others are in denial. Time can be his best ally when he trusts his knowledge.

★

Chapter Six

Planets Through the Signs
and Houses

MOON

The Moon represents mother. Mother is your inheritance factor, the underbelly, representing your subconscious motivations, which can often prevent you from making contact with your emotions. Emotional maturity allows the qualities of the Moon to integrate with the Sun. The Moon has no light of its own; it reflects the Sun.

The Moon takes approximately twenty-nine days to revolve around the Earth, spending two to three days in each constellation. The Moon rules the sign of Cancer and the fourth house, which is the entrance of the soul.

The Moon also represents your body. The Moon and its aspects will influence what you look like, what your health will be, and how you are going to respond emotionally to the world around you.

Moon Through the Signs

MOON IN ARIES

With a Moon in Aries there is the potential for danger. The Moon is the vehicle by which emotion is felt and displayed, and so its placement in this fire sign makes Moon in Aries impulsive. He has a quick temper and often takes things too personally, responding in a reactionary way without thinking. This spontaneity of temper can be foolhardy, exploding like a firecracker. When Moon in Aries senses the slightest intimidation, he is going to react and hit before he gets hit. After he's cooled off, he might be sorry and ask for forgiveness, but one thing is guaranteed—it will happen over and over again.

MOON IN TAURUS

The Moon in Taurus has an ability to hold rages so strongly that one day he'll simply blow up. Moon in Taurus doesn't really know how to handle emotions and must learn to deal with each indignation as it comes up rather than stockpiling them.

Far more than other signs, Moon in Taurus has an enormous interest in money. His emotional security is predicated on finances. Moon in Taurus is hardworking and possesses a stamina, a physical agility, and an energy that makes for a good earner—he's persistent and will stay in there way after everybody else has quit. Financial security provides Moon in Taurus with the ability to enjoy the "good life" he so innately desires.

The emotions of Moon in Taurus are passionate and strong. When well-aspected, he is charming, loves beautiful things, and is sensitive to his surroundings. He has a sexual attractiveness that can belie his physical appearance. Both males and females with Moon in Taurus have a sexual magnetism that others gravitate to. Until you sting a Moon in Taurus, you don't know how ferocious he can be.

MOON IN GEMINI

Moon in Gemini has to work hard for stability because it doesn't come naturally. He is prone to bursts of nervous energy, and his mind and body are in constant conflict—the body holds the emotions when emotions are there to be felt. Moon in Gemini doesn't want to feel, he wants to intellectualize, and so he is caught between the rational and the emotional. Because of this mind-body conflict, Moon in Gemini winds up exhausted. When afflicted, this can be unhealthy and lead to illness.

Moon in Gemini needs to enhance his mind-over-body control through focus, study, and the exploration of self-awareness. Without this, he might self-destruct.

MOON IN CANCER

Moon in Cancer mothers the world and has psychic ability. But Moon in Cancer is also oversensitive, moody, and emotional. He can be easygoing, sociable, and entertaining, but he first needs to be flattered, stroked, and appreciated.

Moon in Cancer is friendly but can also be touchy and prickly. This is a spiteful Moon if afflicted—one that will not forget hurts but just move away and snub you. The Moon in Cancer takes everything personally, often without thinking. He will begin to amass possessions as a way of compensating for his emotional voids.

MOON IN LEO

The Moon in Leo is strong and has a natural agility, energy, and vitality that can't be found anywhere else. His need for prominence—the desire to be noticed—translates into a flair. When he cooks, he cooks with a flair; when he designs, he designs with a flair . . . even if he's making a bed, he'll do that with a flair, too. He is creative and powerful. Moon in Leo is like that regal lion taking care of his den—he'll proudly roam around his domain, making sure everyone is safe.

Moon in Leo is an idealist. Wealth only comes to Leo when he can adjust to the reality of his environment and his source of income. Nothing is as strange or devastating to a Leo as the embarrassment over the fashion in which he earns a living. Money is far more important than he lets on.

If afflicted, since Leo rules the heart, Moon in Leo can be prone to heart conditions. This is a manifestation of his disappointment in his ability to achieve his preconceived level of status.

MOON IN VIRGO

The Moon in Virgo is isolated and reserved. Even when in the midst of others, he is usually quiet. He harbors an inferiority complex, and when that begins to surface, he withdraws emotion and becomes analytical and critical, putting up a cold facade. If you prod, push, or burden him in any way, he's going to respond nastily.

Moon in Virgo is literally born with a deprivation. He's often unable to digest—it's as though he is always hungry and not of a strong constitution. He usually has to deal with illness, all of which stems from the central nervous system, creating intestinal-track difficulties as well as a tendency for allergies, asthma, or even arthritis (this is contingent on the rest of the chart). The Moon in Virgo is so prone to these afflictions that supplements of vitamins and minerals are highly recommended. Taking care of his health should be uppermost to Moon in Virgo.

Moon in Virgo is intellectual but feels put upon when he has to interact with others. This placement is not particularly conducive to being social and fun-loving. This is someone who works better behind the scenes.

MOON IN LIBRA

The Moon in Libra is a rather refined, gentle person who is charming and sympathetic. If afflicted, she can detach completely and give the impression of not being interested or involved when, in fact, she is dependent and feels almost incomplete without a partner.

Moon in Libra is always striving for peace and harmony, particularly in personal relationships, even if it means holding back or controlling emotions to avoid controversy.

MOON IN SCORPIO

Moon in Scorpio is a dominating and aggressive Moon. He tends to get moody and brood and is also terribly jealous. This jealousy leads to possessiveness and stubbornness. He is set in his ways—it's his way or no way—which makes for inequality and a rather archaic attitude, especially in a male toward a female. Moon in Scorpio females, having acquired the courage to display this quality, might dominate their home entirely too much, which is not conducive to a good relationship or equality in a household. It often leads to divorce.

Moon in Scorpio holds grudges and looks to "get even." This brooder, who swings his emotions from one end of the pole to the other, requires controlling. However, when well-aspected, this is a powerful Moon. Under positive circumstances, he can be successful, magnetic, strong, and self-reliant.

MOON IN SAGITTARIUS

In Sagittarius, the Moon combines with Jupiter. Jupiter expands, which makes Moon in Sagittarius yearn for freedom. He needs to be free to speak his mind and hence, his truth, according to his own concepts. While he is friendly and can attract others with his gregariousness and optimistic attitude, don't count on the promises he makes because he's not going to keep them. Moon in Sagittarius is fickle. He makes a good temporary companion, but in a serious relationship, he runs hot and cold.

Should he be afflicted, Moon in Sagittarius might be a liar or overly extravagant.

Moon in Sagittarius is, by nature, a dabbler. Whatever is in mode, whatever is the style, he'll go and sniff it out, but he won't sink his teeth into it or do anything about it because he doesn't have the ability to get involved in anything that would lead to a commitment, either personally or philosophically.

MOON IN CAPRICORN

The emotions of Moon in Capricorn have a wet blanket over them because this is Moon/Saturn and Saturn is authority. Saturn restricts and limits emotional expression so it produces someone who takes himself seriously and is too stringent. This is a child with an old head on his shoulders. While he has strong ambitions, Moon in Capricorn is also looking for security and authority. On the inside, however, he is withdrawn, holding back emotions and coming across as undemonstrative and unsympathetic. If there are other influential and liberating aspects, Moon in Capricorn can be a serious and achievement-oriented individual.

Moon in Capricorn never forgets his beginnings, which are usually humble or restricted. Even if he becomes wealthy, he will always have feelings of deprivation and never take money or possessions for granted.

MOON IN AQUARIUS

Moon in Aquarius is ahead of his time and willing to move into new territories. Since he deals with everything from a mental/intellectual orientation, he does not deal with emotions—he tries to transcend emotions and winds up feeling nothing.

Moon in Aquarius is forgetful—he can't even remember events that were significant or traumatic to him. He doesn't want to remember. Because of this, he'll keep repeating the same patterns or mistakes over and over without learning his lesson.

If afflicted, Moon in Aquarius can be extremely selfish, self-centered, and self-protecting. Or, he might be a butterfly—friendly with everyone but unable to handle the intimacy of close relationships. Very likely, somewhere in his past a bad or betrayed friendship left him scarred, and since he hasn't yet worked it out, he avoids the intimacy of friendship altogether.

MOON IN PISCES

The Moon in Pisces is extremely sensitive. It is not considered a particularly strong Moon, yet, oddly, it has the ability to survive. Whether it means having to drag a broken leg, overcoming obstacles, or dealing with emotional battering, Moon in Pisces has the grit to withstand anything and go on.

Nobody knows the depth of Moon in Pisces. He suffers a great deal and needs to separate from the world every so often to strengthen or energize. Should the rest of the chart be strong, Moon in Pisces can be one of the most sensitive visionaries—a dreamer who, in fact, can carry those dreams to realization. Whatever he feels or senses can eventually be actualized. The Moon in Pisces is also multitalented, so, unless afflicted or lazy, he will most certainly achieve.

Moon Through the Houses

MOON IN THE FIRST HOUSE

The Moon placed within two degrees of the ascendant is considered part of the ascendant. There will be too much vulnerability. The ego becomes entangled by emotions, and reactions are immature at best. It can lead to late maturation and physical endangerment.

MOON IN THE SECOND HOUSE
The handling of money and assets becomes unstable. The attitude swings from generosity to holding money for the sake of security.

MOON IN THE THIRD HOUSE
This Moon placement lacks the consistency needed for a good education. Concentration is easily disturbed causing the loss of thinking power.

MOON IN THE FOURTH HOUSE
This Moon creates an emotional bond with mother that doesn't allow for independence. The need to protect the self takes precedence over all other needs.

MOON IN THE FIFTH HOUSE
This placement produces strong emotions that need creative outlets. This individual can be a great host or cook or a great parent. On the downside, he can seek personal pleasure or satisfactions that will sacrifice others.

MOON IN THE SIXTH HOUSE
In this placement, emotions will register on the body. Diet becomes important since digestion and assimilation will be disturbed. Those with this Moon position can work well in areas of medical care and service to others.

MOON IN THE SEVENTH HOUSE
This Moon shows an emotional need for a mate or partner. A person with this placement feels he can't function alone. He usually draws partners who are sensitive or moody.

MOON IN THE EIGHTH HOUSE

This Moon possesses a powerful sex drive that can replace love and affection. A beneficial quality is a psychic sensitivity toward the feelings or needs of others.

MOON IN THE NINTH HOUSE

The love of travel prevails, whether mentally, as in reading *National Geographic*, or physically, as in trips and explorations. This Moon will maintain and be true to the religion of his parents or acquire his own philosophy and hold fast to it.

MOON IN THE TENTH HOUSE

The Moon indicates what type of reputation will be achieved. Whether famous or infamous, this person will be before the public. The best direction for this placement is to make society's or the world's needs his concern.

MOON IN THE ELEVENTH HOUSE

Attracting friendships is not difficult, but sustaining and taking care of them is. Intimacy is uncomfortable. This Moon doesn't seem to know the difference between use and abuse. Fortunately, its superficiality will do little damage.

MOON IN THE TWELFTH HOUSE

The Moon releases the subconscious. The flow of knowledge is easy. Psychic abilities abound, which can make people with this placement either sensitive or withdrawn to solitude and isolation. The only way through this karma is to serve others without reservation. This also includes the karma with mother.

MERCURY

Mercury revolves around the Sun every eighty-eight days, which means that it goes full circle many times in a year. It is always in one of three positions: before your Sun Sign, in conjunction with (or on top of) your Sun Sign, or past your Sun Sign. It is never more than twenty-seven degrees from the Sun in any direction.

Mercury, which rules the signs of Gemini and Virgo, is the planet of communications. Two types of communication are going on at all times—that which you tell yourself and that which you tell others. You have to be careful of Mercury because, depending on its aspect, it can be the world's greatest liar, superficial to the point of distorting the obvious truth.

Mercury talks to the Sun Sign, telling it what it thinks, whether right or wrong. It represents your mental activity.

MERCURY RETROGRADE

A Mercury retrograde usually occurs every three months, so that there are three or four Mercury retrograde periods per year, each lasting exactly twenty-one days. When Mercury goes retrograde, if you were born during a Mercury retrograde, it is a time to really make contact with yourself. You will be inspired and moved to recognize your ideas and thought processes with clarity.

When a person is born with a Mercury retrograde, he has a communication problem. He can tell you what he thinks, but he can't tell you what he feels. He doesn't make contact with his emotions because Mercury blocks it. There is also difficulty communicating with the self.

Mercury Through the Signs

MERCURY IN ARIES

Mercury in Aries means Mercury is quick. His mind is fast and enthusiastic. Mercury in Aries is flamboyant and childlike and all of those things that are part and parcel to Aries. He has to be careful because he hits and runs. He gathers information quickly but usually does nothing with it.

If afflicted, Mercury in Aries is going to have a bad temper. He is also somebody who likes to talk but who doesn't give the courtesy of listening. He cuts you off before you've finished your sentence, then starts talking about who knows what—not necessarily the subject at hand. Mercury in Aries needs to stabilize and learn control so that he can not only become a better listener but so he can impart better and more complete information to others.

MERCURY IN TAURUS

Mercury in Taurus produces a conservative mind that gives more leeway to others. He is often unsure about his thinking mechanism, so his mind operates in a slow, conservative manner. Don't underestimate it though, because one of the things Mercury in Taurus possesses is the ability to store and recall information. His methodical manner sometimes makes him insecure and feel as if he's not up-to-date on information or as if he has been left behind. Maturity and experience release an artistic side of this Mercury.

MERCURY IN GEMINI

Mercury is ruled by Gemini, so it is comfortable in this placement and knows what to do. It is a keen and alert mind, a restless mind that could become a think tank. The negative side of this is a tendency to overthink to the point of mental exhaustion. This intense thinking can lead to a confusion of the mind, the picking of other people's brains, and, consequently, a jumping to conclusions. When afflicted, Mercury in Gemini lacks the consistency to gather facts or concepts. He cannot master a subject until he learns to stay focused. He must also learn to pace himself to avoid mental exhaustion.

MERCURY IN CANCER

Mercury in Cancer is a Mercury/Moon association. It is a good placement for absorbing information and for producing an excellent memory. Mercury in Cancer also has psychic healing ability—he can listen to, empathize with, and help others. This person would make a good psychologist or therapist or succeed at any career in the healing arts.

This is a sensitive Mercury—almost prickly. He has an underlying need to protect himself and his potent emotions. You cannot deal with a Mercury in Cancer from a rational point of view—he is going to resist and is not going to accept.

MERCURY IN LEO

Mercury in Leo doesn't trust easily. Since he thinks in an idealistic way, he interprets everything as some perversion of his idealism. He holds tough to his opinions and is not going to change—his mind is rigid and unwavering. Forty years from now, he'll still hold the notions and attitudes he has today.

Mercury in Leo has faith only in that which is consistent. That such consistency might lead to his falling behind or becoming out of sync with the rest of the world is something he doesn't seem to fathom or care about. He is going to take everything at his own pace and make progress slowly. He only trusts that which has been proven to him personally. When afflicted, his rigidity leads to extreme stubbornness.

MERCURY IN VIRGO

Mercury in Virgo is stable and staid. Because of that, this mind lends itself well to architects and engineers. This very logical mind sees with an earth-like quality and structure that can make for an exceptionally knowledgeable individual. The problem is that it also makes for somebody who is not necessarily noticing the impact of his words on others. He might be an excellent orator, but that doesn't mean that he will be interested in speaking on a one-to-one, selfless, emotional level.

Mercury in Virgo, with his analytical tendencies, is looking for perfection in everything and everybody. When afflicted, he can be an intellectual snob who deems his mind better than anyone else's. No matter what your education, no matter what techniques you use to prove that you are comparable, he will look for and find some flaw—whether it be in the selection of your words or the fashion in which you acquire or pass on knowledge.

On the positive side, Mercury in Virgo can make an excellent teacher or accountant.

MERCURY IN LIBRA

Mercury plus Libra/Venus gives a finesse—a quality that can lead to speaking in a diplomatic fashion. But it is not necessarily a mind that will speak with substance. She does not speak emphatically or passionately, nor reflect upon what she herself is feeling.

Mercury in Libra wants harmony. Ideally, she wants everyone to have a good time and be nice to one another.

If afflicted, she is either going to speak in a militant fashion, almost making you feel as if you ought to salute her, or she will be wishy-washy, noncommittal, and afraid to step on anyone's toes. Unless sustained by a particular group of stable planets, Mercury in Libra is not even going to remember what she told you. Her communications are often detached and lacking in passion.

MERCURY IN SCORPIO

What a quick and powerful mind this is—it can reach the deepest recesses of the collective unconscious. The only problem with Mercury in Scorpio is that he expects others to be just as bright, quick, and knowledgeable. Scorpio is ruled by Pluto, and as such, he has a power, a directness, and a freedom from inhibition. His mind works quickly and sharply in acquiring information, making him an excellent detective or diagnostician. Pluto is always underneath; it rules the underworld. And so, Mercury in Scorpio has the ability to get under things.

Should it be afflicted, this is going to be a difficult placement for Mercury. His mouth is going to open up and bury you. He will be harsh, cold-blooded, and unconcerned about any feelings you might have.

MERCURY IN SAGITTARIUS

Mercury in Sagittarius doesn't have the barriers that are necessary for concentration. So while the mind is good and alert, it can't concentrate on any one subject to create a goal or objective. This mind goes here and there, touches this and that—but its impatience and inability to hone causes him to expound articulately about an ideal or philosophy without wholeheartedly believing it.

MERCURY IN CAPRICORN

Mercury in Capricorn is a sober thinker. He has a powerful ability to concentrate and an excellent memory. He is structured, detail oriented, and great at remembering little anecdotes. But because of Saturn, he is not witty. Mercury in Capricorn tends to behave like a little old man since Saturn matures him way before his time or chronological age indicates.

Mercury likes security, so, if afflicted, he is always going to be fearful of the things he lacks. Mercury in Capricorn needs to become optimistic, which is difficult to accomplish because, by nature, he is incredibly pessimistic. He is always concerned with what he doesn't have rather than enjoying what he does have. Ironically, he can be an excellent achiever. That is, of course, if his pessimism doesn't get in the way and create psychosomatic illnesses or other neuroses.

MERCURY IN AQUARIUS

This is an excellent position for Mercury. This is a good mind that is resourceful. Uranus is a subconscious planet and gives Aquarius an intuitive quality that borders on prophetic. An affliction, however, can make Mercury in Aquarius opinionated because, since he sees farther down the line and innately knows the outcome, he wants to bring it to the present. While he might be insightful and correct in his opinions and ideas, this prophetic quality can make him untimely in his judgment. If he is working alone, he can be ahead of the crowd and totally dependent on himself. Only when he's dealing with others do his stubbornness and convictions make him difficult to be around.

Mercury in Aquarius is a good position for a writer because it allows him to take his ideas and opinions and run with them successfully. If he becomes sensitive to group dynamics, more timely in his approach, and if those around him are, in fact, willing to accept his innovative, ahead-of-its-time thinking, Mercury in Aquarius can become productive in a group situation.

MERCURY IN PISCES

Mercury in Pisces has the potential to be a psychic visionary, one who is in touch with sensitive and artistic expression. Whenever Pisces appears, there is a multitude of talent, so expressions are made through many artistic forms—writing, poetry, music, or dance.

Mercury in Pisces is not necessarily group oriented. He feels, but cannot always cope, behaving in a moody, negative, and sensitive fashion. Mercury in Pisces picks up everyone else's moods and vibrations, which can be confusing because he can't always distinguish between what he is thinking and feeling versus what everybody else is thinking and feeling. So, depending on the atmosphere, environment, and circumstances, if he has a positive flow, he feels good and expressive. But if the conditions are negative or emotionally difficult, he is going to brood and be moody and unstable. Mercury in Pisces has to be careful to avoid projecting the negativity of his environment or else he can wind up being a victim to, rather than overcoming, his surroundings. If this happens, he will become oversensitive and prickly. The best solution is to withdraw, regenerate, and then reenter that environment with complete self-awareness. Mercury in Pisces must learn to set boundaries and not worry about the "what ifs." If this is accomplished, he can become strong and productive.

Mercury Through the Houses

MERCURY IN THE FIRST HOUSE

This placement performs in a vital and alert manner. However, it also gives the individual the notion that what he thinks is more important than what others think. The thought process is emotionally based, creating nervous reactions.

MERCURY IN THE SECOND HOUSE

Mercury in this house produces speaking or writing ability. In fact, any kind of communication can be mastered. This individual is business minded and an excellent moneymaker.

MERCURY IN THE THIRD HOUSE

This is a good student, curious and intelligent, who can excel as a researcher or investigator. He will have strong ties to his family. If afflicted, he will filter experiences through his intellect and avoid emotion.

MERCURY IN THE FOURTH HOUSE

High-strung thinking can cause high anxiety. The result of this placement is an unstable, erratic home life, which can lead to isolation.

MERCURY IN THE FIFTH HOUSE

This creative mind can excel in writing and lecturing. Communications of all forms are fortified. Difficult aspects can cause an opinionated, fixed mentality.

MERCURY IN THE SIXTH HOUSE

Preoccupation with one's health can result from this placement. Worry, fear, or overwork will take its toll on the body. Proper nutrition, rest, and recreation can revive the central nervous system.

MERCURY IN THE SEVENTH HOUSE

Partnerships or marriage will become an intellectual experience instead of an emotional exchange. This person can spend too much time arguing and squabbling over incidentals.

MERCURY IN THE EIGHTH HOUSE

Communications must be clear. Lending and/or borrowing must be spelled out clearly, investments and contracts taken seriously—this will protect the inheritance of the person with this Mercury.

MERCURY IN THE NINTH HOUSE

Mercurial thinking needs stabilizing before this individual can acquire the religion or philosophy he longs for. Should he not settle down and avoid distractions, he will lose his objectives. In-laws could make his life a misery.

MERCURY IN THE TENTH HOUSE

Saturn extracts from Mercury a seriousness and a disciplined outlook. This individual will be aware that one's honor, reputation, or standing in this world is important. He will be heard unless an affliction prevents him from staying on a straight path.

MERCURY IN THE ELEVENTH HOUSE

Mercury, glib and light, can attract an intellectual entourage rather than friends. Friendships require an emotional investment. To realize a goal takes thought and attention, but, unfortunately, this placement creates delays and interference with plans.

MERCURY IN THE TWELFTH HOUSE

Mercury can tap areas of the individual's psyche that he can't share with others. Information will be available to this individual from a source he can't understand. If there is no affliction, he may make use of it; otherwise he will become afraid of it.

Venus revolves around the Sun every 225 days. Venus rules the signs of Taurus and Libra and is associated with passive and feminine qualities. In a male, the passive quality of Venus is displayed as harmony and devotion—the ability to cooperate with others.

Venus in a chart produces "class." It is associated with refinement and beauty on all levels.

Venus says, "I want." Venus is there to produce self-love, which, kept in balance, is an important quality. On the negative side, however, it can be self-indulgent and self-serving.

VENUS RETROGRADE

If you were born during the time of a Venus retrograde, your inability to appreciate the self is obvious. You are unable to express self-love. You don't know how to get what it is that you want or how to satisfy the self. You must learn not to expect such things from others but, instead, develop them within yourself.

Venus Through the Signs

VENUS IN ARIES

Venus in Aries has a challenge—it's a clashing situation where Venus is going to be worn out by Aries's mode of "action without thinking." Venus in Aries is headed in one direction—the fulfillment of her central desire or ego—and so, she becomes impulsive. There's a tendency to fall in love with love but not to fall in love with the person himself, which makes Venus in Aries often shallow, inconsiderate, and untrustworthy. One day, she can be charming and flirtatious, and the next day she can stomp all over everything until she tears it apart. With one hand she builds and with the other she destroys.

VENUS IN TAURUS

Venus rules Taurus, so she's quite at home here. In Taurus, she possesses a powerful, earthy quality. Her physical, sensual, and emotional responses are going to be emphasized. This is a Venus that wants to stroke and be stroked. She is the comfort-acquiring/comfort-giving Venus who is not going to be sloppy, unconcerned, or even jealous. Unless afflicted, Venus in Taurus will not be competitive nor want to upstage anyone—she recognizes her worth and is comfortable and happy with herself and what she brings to others.

VENUS IN GEMINI

Venus in Gemini is charming and witty but somewhat superficial. Emotions are lacking depth. The Mercurial quality of Gemini produces an inconsistency and a disinterest in experiencing emotions. Her charm attracts many people and she gets along well with her family, but don't try to pin her down. Like a butterfly, she cannot be harnessed. She will entertain you and please you, but will eventually leave you. An affliction to this placement can create a compulsive talker who wants understanding from others but is unable to reciprocate.

VENUS IN CANCER

Venus in Cancer, unfortunately, has a changeable, moody, "today she wants this and tomorrow she doesn't want it" inconsistency. The pleasure response of Venus in Cancer comes more from an emotional than an intellectual base. She is always looking for security. That security might be education, self-sufficiency, or dependence on a mate. Because of the Moon's influence, this person tends to do a lot of mothering and/or smothering. A woman with Venus in Cancer, instead of being a man's equal, plays a "you need me" role, which can prove detrimental to her relationships. In the male, Venus in Cancer can be committed to his family and a good partner to his wife because that feminine side of him is empathetic and sympathetic to those things that are necessary to maintain a home and family. If Venus in Cancer is heavily afflicted, she will always feel that she cannot get what she wants and will wind up feeling empty or deprived.

VENUS IN LEO

When Venus is in Leo, you can actually see the drama—that colorful character is projected through Venus. Everything is a passion. Venus in Leo doesn't just like something, she loves it; she doesn't dislike something, she loathes it. Nothing and nobody in this world can change a Venus in Leo into anything other than what she is, so you might as well leave her alone and accept her.

Venus in Leo is a lover of good things—good wine, good food, good surroundings, good people. If afflicted, she might overindulge herself and be taken in by flattery. She tends to be attractive—Venusian qualities are really emphasized by the influence and vitality of Leo's ruler, the Sun, so this person is, basically, a star. She is going to be methodical and also have a flair. Leo has a majestic quality that shines through Venus, all of which is very attractive, all of which attracts. Venus in Leo really likes attracting—she loves an entourage, loves to have the admiration of others. Even if afflicted, this dramatic Venus in Leo will not suffer or get into trouble—her dignity doesn't seem to fail her. She is thoroughly refined.

VENUS IN VIRGO

Whenever a man has a Venus in Virgo, he is looking for the perfect woman. He winds up having trouble relating to women because he's analyzing instead of simply loving. He breaks his relationships apart to see what love is made of. Sadly, by the time he discovers what love is made of, he's lost it.

In a woman, Venus in Virgo is the proverbial nun—none today and none tomorrow. She is good at serving, maintaining a household, and is quite fastidious, but this is not someone who will hug you. She is not demonstrative or approachable. You'll only hear from a Venus in Virgo when something is wrong. If everything is okay and acceptable, there are no praises. But if there is a problem or flaw—and she will definitely find one—the criticism will begin.

A woman with Venus in Virgo is not likely to attract—she's not charming and doesn't have the feminine softness that is so attractive in Libra or Taurus. She comes across as a difficult person to deal with and will have trouble finding and keeping a mate. Venus doesn't do well placed in Virgo—not for the male or the female.

VENUS IN LIBRA

Venus is comfortable in Libra. She is airy and free to take flight of fantasy. She is intellectual and loves everything that is artistic and refined. Venus in Libra can bring some wonderful qualities or refinement to a person. Her emotions are under control and she doesn't hold a grudge.

If afflicted, however, it is just the reverse—this is somebody who is not going to trust you. If you hurt her once, you'll hurt her again, so she winds up holding a grudge.

Venus in Libra makes a wonderful hostess. She loves to create an atmosphere of total comfort and beauty. However, if there is any upheaval or discord, or if anything gets "out of whack," Venus in Libra's physical well-being, particularly her nervous system, will be affected.

Nevertheless, both men and women with Venus in Libra look for the tranquillity and the joy of all things beautiful and do not want grossness or disruption around them.

VENUS IN SCORPIO

Venus in Scorpio is concerned with all that is physical and carnal. Naturally, Venus resents this because Venus is basically the love principle. What she wants is tranquillity, refinement, and love. Because of Scorpio's water quality, Venus in Scorpio is going to appear sedate and softer than she really is. She is going to appear as if everything is under control when, in fact, she is actually suppressing. A militancy is hidden within this individual because, underneath, Scorpio is active and forward moving—she presents herself with great force and wants others to know exactly what it is that she wants, regardless of whether it might be inopportune or incorrect. She lacks all inhibition and can be rude and crude.

Venus in Scorpio is a detrimental placement because these two planets, Venus and Mars, are in conflict. If afflicted, sexuality takes over, and instead of being "in love," Venus in Scorpio falls "in lust" without understanding the difference between the two.

VENUS IN SAGITTARIUS

Venus in Sagittarius links Venus with Jupiter, the two aspects that are associated with love. This individual is open, affectionate, and kind to others. Venus in Sagittarius has a theoretical mind and wholeheartedly believes that everybody should love one another. While she is affectionate and loving, she cannot necessarily sustain a relationship for the long haul—displaying affection and falling in love are two very different things to her.

If there is an affliction to Venus in Sagittarius, she becomes a hard gambler, obsessed with the idea and thrill of taking risks.

VENUS IN CAPRICORN

Venus combined with Capricorn's ruler, Saturn, can create a rather strange love nature. Venus in Capricorn feels that she must take herself seriously and proceed with caution in all ways—she's an earth sign, and the ego sensitivity that is often associated with Capricorn makes her act with caution in the pursuit of love. Therefore, Venus in Capricorn matures into a passionate and love-oriented individual. In her youth, she is rather restrained and withholding, even afraid. Until she overcomes the fear that keeps her aloof, she will use that restraint as a shield or mask to prevent her from succumbing to love.

If afflicted, this will become the kind of restraint that doesn't allow her to trust another person, feel love, or even feel as if she is genuinely loved by others. Sadly, this is difficult for those close to her to alter. Love is to be felt, and if you don't feel worthy of love, no matter how much someone loves you, it won't make a difference. Venus in Capricorn must learn that she is, in fact, lovable and that she must be open to love for her own loving quality to mature, blossom, and be effective and satisfying.

VENUS IN AQUARIUS

In Aquarius, Venus is not only detached but calm and completely cool. Venus in Aquarius finds it difficult to understand her emotions, her ability to love, and to demonstrate love. She is not always understanding of, or comfortable dealing with, the emotions of others. She intellectualizes love, which is an empty and ultimately lonely circumstance. So Venus in Aquarius must learn one important thing—she must become a friend. Once Venus in Aquarius acquires friendship or a friendliness toward others, she can eventually move on to a loving situation.

What usually happens to Venus in Aquarius is that she develops an ability to love and understand later in life. If not, her relationships and marriage will be unfulfilling and suffer. When detached, Venus in Aquarius functions strictly for the self, which prevents good and enduring interactions with others.

VENUS IN PISCES

What a delight. Venus, which is love, combines with Neptune, which is the deepest of all the constellations. This creates a unique type of love—a willingness to sacrifice, a lack of fear, and a deep-rooted passion. There is, with Venus in Pisces, the ability to touch the soul.

Venus in Pisces is poetic, a lover of art and music, and also extremely psychic. Venus in Pisces can't be fooled—she knows when she's loved, and she also knows when she is not loved. A male with Venus in Pisces has a gentle and feminine side. This is a man who has refinement, who can appreciate a passionate opera or a tear-jerking film without feeling as if his masculinity is threatened.

Venus in Pisces can go beyond the call of duty. If afflicted, this romantic nature, this ability to romanticize everything, is going to backfire. When Venus in Pisces is confronted with the flaws and limitations of other people, she becomes disappointed and disillusioned. When love rules a situation and things go awry, it brings her great unhappiness. This is a hurdle that Venus in Pisces must overcome—she must take off the rose-colored glasses and see the world for what it is.

Venus in Pisces believes everyone deserves love, but she needs to recognize that self-love is of equal importance. She must learn to appreciate the self, foster her one-to-one relationships, and curb her view of universal love.

Venus Through the Houses

VENUS IN THE FIRST HOUSE

Venus will project into this placement an attractive but vain personality. The world will respond in a cooperative manner. Should it be afflicted, this native will be lazy and unconcerned.

VENUS IN THE SECOND HOUSE

This placement brings a keen eye for what is beautiful, which can lead to profitable investments. She will attract all measure of financial wealth or help. Bad aspects to this house can produce excessive spending.

VENUS IN THE THIRD HOUSE

Venus here has a soothing effect on the mind and makes for a pleasant disposition. An interest in music encourages artistic and creative abilities. Aspects will determine if this easygoing manner will turn to laziness.

VENUS IN THE FOURTH HOUSE

This person loves to be home. She will share, entertain, and can handle all aspects of social/political gatherings. If it is not afflicted, there will be a good relationship with mother.

VENUS IN THE FIFTH HOUSE

Love is not wanting for this placement, and she is an attractive and charismatic personality to which the opposite sex will respond. She possesses an ease with children, whether her own or youngsters at large. An affliction can lead to overspeculations.

VENUS IN THE SIXTH HOUSE

There will be a peaceful atmosphere at work or at home. Venus will benefit any work that requires diplomacy. Should there be an affliction to this house, the illnesses that can occur will be caused by excess or some loss of balance. Moderation is the key.

VENUS IN THE SEVENTH HOUSE

Marriages and other legal partnerships will be favored. The love that is attracted by Venus in this house makes for long marriages. If afflicted, there might be more than one marriage but no lack of love.

VENUS IN THE EIGHTH HOUSE

Legacies will be protected, whether they be from a partner or other family members. Inheritances, including those incurred in a past life, are covered. An affliction can create a preoccupation with sex.

VENUS IN THE NINTH HOUSE

The pleasure that is afforded to this native has no boundaries. This is a traveling person who can indulge and appreciate foreign cultures. This individual also actually loves his in-laws. The expansion of consciousness enables one to relate to all philosophies. Should there be an affliction, prejudice takes over and a bad attitude prevails.

VENUS IN THE TENTH HOUSE

The world loves you! If you love the world, it will reward you with all measure of success. In business it will open doors—the reputation alone will be a passport. If afflicted, scandal occurs, which will result in a fall from high office.

VENUS IN THE ELEVENTH HOUSE

The support and cooperation from friends benefits the objectives of this native. The proper use of organizations can lead to a satisfied life. A negative approach from this house can lead to a people abuser who will only be self-serving.

VENUS IN THE TWELFTH HOUSE

How does one get what she wants? This placement doesn't make it easy. One must be clear and direct about what one desires or one will be left behind. If high-minded, the native will seek a spiritual life doing "God's work" on Earth. This is an excellent placement for meditation. If afflicted, the individual will isolate and escape through alcohol and/or drugs.

MARS

Mars revolves around the Sun in 687 days, coming to its original point in a chart once every two years. Mars rules Aries (and before the discovery of Pluto, it ruled Scorpio) and is associated with temperament.

When Mars makes contact with the Sun, it develops an energy that enables you to do. Mars, well-aspected, can move mountains. Negatively aspected, it can be one of the biggest destroyers because it fosters action without thought.

Mars is associated with the initiation of relationships—love affairs, marriages, business partnerships, and so on. Relationships often appear to go through two-year cycles that relate to the orbit of Mars. Whenever Mars comes back to its original position, which is called a Mars return, it frequently creates upheaval in relationships. This upheaval isn't necessarily negative; it is an opportunity to review and assess existing circumstances or, in the worst case, eliminate them.

Careers are also influenced by Mars since the planet is almost always associated with a job—the end of one or the beginning of another.

Mars is a generator. When Mars is cycling, it gets people up and rolling. Since Mars rules muscular structure, it creates an energy that spurs movement. When Mars is in conjunction with any planet, it energizes it.

MARS RETROGRADE

The inability to act is created in a retrograde Mars. It is as though you have been victimized by others simply because you are not using your aggressive qualities correctly—you either don't know how to be aggressive or you fear aggression. You water down your energies. This does not make for a happy person; it creates a person who internalizes his aggressions and anger. This is dangerous because a retrograde Mars can lead to brooding or nursing old wounds and, eventually, to health problems ranging from ulcers to anxiety. Angers that cannot be externalized wind up being internalized, which impacts one's health. Retrograde Mars in a chart indicates the inability to displace its natural energy in a positive or productive manner.

Mars Through the Signs

MARS IN ARIES

Mars in Aries has energy and physical/mental capabilities. He's quick. He's a little firecracker who moves with enthusiasm.

Mars in Aries afflicted is going to be bad tempered and an unstable personality who acts before he thinks. Of course, his intentions are good—he has good ideals—but because he doesn't stop to think, he's bound to get himself into trouble.

When a male demonstrates this type of behavior, it is usually acceptable; but females with this placement are challenged because they develop an aggressive stance that is often viewed as problematic by the outside world. If a female with Mars in Aries begins to experience difficulties, developing a little self-discipline will go a long way.

MARS IN TAURUS

Taurus is ruled by Venus, which has a slow and deliberate quality. So when Mars comes along and shakes it up, it creates a personal push/pull situation. Mars activates Venus in a peculiar way so that instead of being self-loving, it makes him self-centered, giving the individual no other objective than self-gratification. Mars in Taurus will find himself overindulging—in food, drink, sex, and so on.

As a youngster, Mars in Taurus is not allowed to express these self-indulgent qualities, so he winds up being outwardly cool and sedate, while inside, his suppressed qualities are churning. Mars in Taurus is slow to burn, but once he explodes, he's also slow to cool.

If afflicted, that resentment is multiplied; the selfishness becomes central and the need to protect the self becomes overwhelming, prompting him to lash out at anyone who threatens him. An afflicted Mars in Taurus can be dangerous—he's a little spark ready to ignite and can become a great, big fire if the rest of the chart doesn't mitigate or displace this afflicted quality. Self-discipline is necessary and important for Mars in Taurus to master. With self-discipline, he can take this energy and channel it into a productive activity, like sports. Otherwise, his temperament will be his downfall.

MARS IN GEMINI

Mars in Gemini is contradictory. He has the ability to act at two levels—he can be intellectual, witty, chatty, and friendly, but if his innate emotional insecurity kicks in, he can suddenly turn nasty. Mars in Gemini has a quick tongue, and that doesn't necessarily mean keen or alert; it means that he speaks through both sides of his mouth. In essence, he's a pretty good liar. The natural Gemini duality of intellect versus emotion becomes activated and exaggerated by Mars, making it difficult for him to reconcile the two. He wants to be in both places at once, which is impossible and frustrating.

Should Mars in Gemini be afflicted, it will create a nervousness that could result in stuttering or the inability to complete sentences. The mind is going to wear down the body, producing nervous ticks and other psychosomatic illnesses.

MARS IN CANCER

Can you imagine every single emotion that a human being possesses, fired up? That is Mars in Cancer. Talk about extremes—this individual is so emotional, sensitive, and prickly that he's going to wind up full of fear and insecurity. He will, more than likely, spend his life feeling as if somebody kicked him in the stomach. This is a difficult placement for Mars even when the rest of the chart is well-aspected. If there is an affliction, Mars in Cancer will be prone to stomach disorders, bleeding ulcers . . . even too much in the breadbasket. Mars in Cancer must control and/or displace his emotions, rather than swallow them. If kept in the gut, it is a sure bet that those emotions will burn a hole right through the stomach or accelerate all of the digestive juices, making Mars in Cancer hungry all the time. This will result in obesity and many other unpleasant side effects in addition to moodiness and bad feelings.

MARS IN LEO

When Mars joins the Sun, there is no end to the energy—it is overwhelming. Mars in Leo is going to leave everybody else in his dust. He's a born leader who wants to make absolutely sure that he is heard and understood. He wants to be the leader of the pack.

If afflicted, he can become indignant. He is going to challenge authority and be hard to hold down. He'll also wind up getting into lots of trouble. Because he pushes his will as most fire signs do, Mars in Leo is going to insist, no matter how wrong he is, that he is right. He will become quarrelsome and annoying—not the type of person others want to deal with. Mars in Leo will roar; he will become bombastic and melodramatic, feeling as if he hurts more than anybody else. He will start to overdo and his vitality will prove troublesome for him.

Leo rules the heart, so Mars, which produces a bad temper when afflicted, can lead to heart problems. It is important that Mars in Leo learn to cool off and chill out.

MARS IN VIRGO

Mars in Virgo is a tireless worker who loves the labor but has an endless obsession with details. He possesses an energy that, when well structured, is productive and successful. If he comes from the viewpoint of analysis, instead of criticism, he will react to things positively, instead of becoming angry and quarrelsome. Afflictions can produce a critical, demanding, and unfeeling personality. The results, unfortunately, are loneliness and a feeling of rejection that the native doesn't understand. On the other hand, when well-aspected, Mars in Virgo has a self-regulating attitude that can lead to cooperation and productivity.

MARS IN LIBRA

Mars in Libra is easygoing, lazy, and not particularly self-reliant. Though Libra is a militant Sun Sign, with the influence of Mars she becomes more dependent, although she still intends to dominate. The scales of Mars in Libra tip from one side to the other; she can appear smooth and diplomatic, acting with a great deal of finesse . . . but at other times she'll turn into the pushiest, nastiest, "get out of my way" person with an attitude that can be ice-cold.

Mars in Libra makes many plans but can't seem to get them off the drawing board. She sits and vacillates, wondering if she really needs somebody else to help get her plans in order. When afflicted, this is a militant general—demanding, unconcerned, and lacking compassion.

MARS IN SCORPIO

Mars in Scorpio has intense emotions, which are projected without inhibition. This is an overbearing personality that needs to be tempered. He must learn that it is much better to attract with honey and softness than through sheer force. He needs to learn to draw from love rather than fear.

Mars in Scorpio can instill fear in others and intimidate—he's a real bully. Mars in Scorpio needs to recognize that bullying does not come from strength but from weakness or insecurity. While he can be powerful in whatever he undertakes, his pushiness can prove a real turnoff to others.

MARS IN SAGITTARIUS

Something inside Mars in Sagittarius makes him feel he can take chances yet land on his feet. He has an inner knowing, and although it might appear to others as impulsiveness, it is actually behavior that is very directed. It has a source and an intuition that become apparent even before Mars in Sagittarius has taken that action.

Should there be an affliction . . . look out. He cannot be held down to anything. He's unreliable, and the chances he takes are not inspired, they are just plain old gambles. Mars in Sagittarius sees every challenge in life as a gamble. His ultimate desire is to bring the will of the universe into his control—Sagittarius is perhaps the most willful of all the fire signs. Hence, when afflicted, with Mars energizing, it creates a "get out of my way, here I come" attitude. Mars in Sagittarius is so open and up-front that you know way before he arrives that he is going to be there and you're going to have to contend with him. He's going to be blunt and tactless. He can be quite self-righteous and needs to recognize the rights of others.

MARS IN CAPRICORN

This is probably the best Mars placement in the Zodiac, especially if the rest of the chart indicates ambition. Mars in Capricorn is disciplined and capable. As an adult, he thrives. However, as a youngster, he is restricted by Saturn (Capricorn's ruler) and behaves almost like an old person, taking on more responsibility than the average child should bear. That situation really takes the fun out of being a kid. But as Mars in Capricorn matures, a rather strange reversal takes place—Saturn releases him and he becomes self-reliant. He can slowly and methodically reach the top of the mountain. The only way he will fall off it is if he hasn't been ethical.

This strong and capable Mars in Capricorn, if afflicted, becomes someone who is a little slow on the uptake. While methodical and productive, with an affliction pessimism will set in, producing an inability to make use of acquired knowledge. He will be closeted, double-checking himself all the time, and eventually become his own undoer. He can be quarrelsome, challenge authority, and take on a "think what you like" mentality.

MARS IN AQUARIUS

Mars in Aquarius pairs Mars with Uranus, which is a strange combination, one that can lead to trouble. Mars in Aquarius is more than likely going to be out of step with family, peers, business colleagues, and partners.

Mars in Aquarius has an innate desire for freedom and a relentless need to know. This often makes him quarrelsome—he just doesn't let up. When dealing with a Mars in Aquarius who becomes argumentative, don't pick up the issue. Drop it, let it go, and turn your back because he will just continue to argue and force his so-called concepts and ideas upon you.

Mars in Aquarius can be untimely. If he isn't brought under control, he could well be speaking the truth but at the wrong or an inopportune time. He'll blurt out his thoughts and opinions and take over without considering someone else's need to express himself. Mars in Aquarius is capable of bringing down the establishment.

MARS IN PISCES

Mars in Pisces is a control freak. Pisces/Neptune produces fears, and Mars can exaggerate those fears and bring about a personality that is aggressive and domineering, someone who will try to jump over people's heads, acting purely out of fear. Pisces carries subconscious fears or memories from past lives.

The quest for Mars in Pisces is to conquer and overcome his fears. Once that is accomplished, Mars in Pisces becomes calm. Calmness is necessary because it restores vitality. This is important because, if afflicted, the innate fears and aggressions of Mars in Pisces can create illness.

Mars Through the Houses

MARS IN THE FIRST HOUSE

The personality is intense, quick, and brash. There is a physical strength and energy that must be displaced carefully, otherwise the person will find himself in dangerous positions. Self-confidence can turn into egocentricity if afflicted. A bad temper will be his undoing.

MARS IN THE SECOND HOUSE

The resources of this house can be energized, leading to the accumulation of assets. A good education or plain hard work will make for gains. Mars is volatile, and an affliction can lead to loss of all that has been gained.

MARS IN THE THIRD HOUSE

The mental faculties must be kept positive in this placement. Negative thoughts can cause nervous tension and irritability. The quickness of mind can lead to quarrels with all around him. The mental energies can best be displaced by study and higher education.

MARS IN THE FOURTH HOUSE

Mother's attitude is reflected when Mars sits in this house. We live what we are taught, so a constant discipline over the emotions is necessary to avoid chaos. An affliction can create difficulties from birth until death.

MARS IN THE FIFTH HOUSE

The energy of Mars propels this person to seek and reach the limelight. He will display unusual strength and fortitude in the pursuit of his goals. Should this house be afflicted, disappointment and sorrow will surround the children of this native.

MARS IN THE SIXTH HOUSE

This individual should take care not to become a workaholic. To achieve successful relations with coworkers, this person needs space and some degree of solitude. If afflicted, he will revert to an intellectual, cold attitude, which will be troublesome to him.

MARS IN THE SEVENTH HOUSE

Mars doesn't allow partnerships or marriages to succeed. The individual tends to be bad tempered. He feels "his way or no way" is the only solution. If afflicted, the battle will surely lead him to divorce court.

MARS IN THE EIGHTH HOUSE

War will rage over money or legacies. Sexual attitudes or activities will dominate the personality. If afflicted, he will find himself embroiled in the misuse of occult knowledge.

MARS IN THE NINTH HOUSE

This person is off to see the world and to dabble in foreign cultures. He will probably research religion or philosophy. Badly aspected, this placement can turn one into a fanatic.

MARS IN THE TENTH HOUSE

This Mars placement can carry a business or military man to heights of prestige. Discord with dad can make for a runaway. This pattern will cause friction with all authority. A negative attitude will place his reputation at risk.

MARS IN THE ELEVENTH HOUSE

Be careful of whom you call "friend." The need to be sociable can lead to dangerous associations. The lack of integrity for personal advancement can be the undoing of this placement.

MARS IN THE TWELFTH HOUSE

This Mars appears diluted. A person with this placement doesn't always know how to displace his energy. Nevertheless, this quality, if harnessed, can be creative in handling hidden enemies or any other threat. An affliction can lead to explosions of suppressed hostilities.

JUPITER

Jupiter takes approximately twelve years to revolve around the Sun. Jupiter is a wonderful, lucky planet that can provide realization. Jupiter allows you to relate to others and to yourself. It taps into emotions and increases the ability to empathize. Learning to distinguish between what you think and what you feel results in self-awareness.

Jupiter, which rules Sagittarius, expands. It triggers human physical development. It influences the menstrual cycle in females and the onset of puberty in males, both of which usually occur at the age of twelve, exactly the number of years it takes Jupiter to make a full revolution around the Sun. It spends one year in each house.

Jupiter rules the liver, which is the seat of anger. When negatively impacted, it can create physical or hormonal difficulties within an individual.

JUPITER RETROGRADE

A retrograde Jupiter usually leads to an overbearing individual, especially if placed in the fourth house—it is a tyrant in that house. It creates an inability to empathize with others, which results in an insensitive and isolated individual.

Jupiter Through the Signs

JUPITER IN ARIES

Jupiter in Aries produces a fairly good sense of the self and strong self-esteem. He possesses a quick mind and a great deal of strength and energy. When equipped with solid skills and education, Jupiter in Aries has leadership skills and makes a good executive. He's a bit of a risk-taker, too. Whether it is a risk in business, the stock market, or even for the self, with his "I can do that" attitude he will take chances with the highest sense of optimism.

If afflicted, this risk-taking tendency might turn to gambling or lead him to live in the fast lane. By and large, however, Jupiter in Aries does well.

JUPITER IN TAURUS

Love is in the air! Jupiter in Taurus is the ultimate lover of everything. He is fond of luxury, fond of culture and elegance, and fond of an upscale, material-filled environment. He is immersed in sensuality. He has a wonderful appetite for food and a wonderful appetite for sex. Jupiter in Taurus is bent on looking for all of the comforts and joys of life.

You can't push a Jupiter in Taurus—he will stubbornly stick to his guns even more. He's quite content enjoying and smelling the roses and anything else that comes his way. The price he pays comes in later years when those overindulgences turn to overweight.

JUPITER IN GEMINI

Jupiter in Gemini takes his emotion and intellectualizes it so that he winds up not caring. He doesn't want to expend emotion, he'd rather filter it through his head, which doesn't work. This individual has a tendency to be self-centered, which imposes a natural separation and isolation from everyone else. He does not attract friends or wealth.

Jupiter doesn't do well in Gemini. He scatters his energies and avoids listening to his heart. When his forked tongue surfaces, he loses credibility.

JUPITER IN CANCER

Jupiter in Cancer really cares. He has a nurturing and caring instinct that makes for an extremely sensitive and attractive personality. His manner says to others, "I want to take care of you, I want to benefit you." He is one of the most selfless Jupiters of the Zodiac.

A woman with Jupiter in Cancer is a loyal and loving mate because she is the proverbial mama who will make chicken soup and take care of her home, husband, and the children. A man with Jupiter in Cancer is a good provider. He is artistic and senses what others need. He also works well with the public.

Jupiter in Cancer should watch those calories because this placement can lead to weight problems, usually caused by a lack of digestive enzymes.

If afflicted, Jupiter in Cancer is one of the tightest wads going—a crab that battens down all the hatches and goes down under. An afflicted Jupiter in Cancer has an enormous fear of starvation, so he gets overly bossy and wants to rule—the children, the spouse, the dog, the cat—and hangs on to every cent he can get his hands on.

JUPITER IN LEO

Jupiter in Leo is a wonderful and vital placement since Jupiter combines with the power of the Sun. In fact, all through the Zodiac, whenever Jupiter conjuncts the Sun, regardless of the constellation, it means you have a guardian angel. That's because the ability to contact the self, that flow that comes between the conscious and subconscious, is very pronounced in this position.

Jupiter in Leo possesses self-reliance, courage, and loyalty. This individual is magnanimous. He is a true leader and a capable executive. If afflicted, he can be victimized by his pride and desire to impress others so that he is likely to fall prey to anybody who can stroke his ego, usually for their own advantage.

JUPITER IN VIRGO

Here you have expansive Jupiter trying hard to operate in what is probably one of the more insecure signs of the Zodiac. Being practical, intellectual, and critical can restrain Jupiter in Virgo so that instead of expanding and making him optimistic, the opposite occurs—he becomes pessimistic. If afflicted, Jupiter in Virgo relates to others not only from an intellectually critical point of view, but from a condemning point of view as well. He is always looking for the dirty spot. This afflicted quality condemns others so that he can feel better because he suffers from inner condemnation. Jupiter in Virgo, in this stance, is never going to be content nor find anything worthwhile. He is nitpicky, critical, irritable, petty—paying too much attention to little nothings, which make him impossible to deal with. About the only place such characteristics have value is in the field of investigation. Other than that, Jupiter in Virgo has to learn to stop picking away at the little things. He needs to get past the details and take a look at the much bigger picture.

JUPITER IN LIBRA

Jupiter in Libra is friendly and outgoing. A lover of beauty, she can be successful in the arts. Jupiter in Libra is also going to be attracted to law—Libra is the constellation of law, so lawyers and judges often have Libra in this placement (or in other planets in their charts).

An affliction can prove troublesome since Jupiter in Libra might not hold up her end of a partnership. Obviously, this can lead to problems in a marriage or business relationship. She will be looking out for her self-interest and sensuous pleasures rather than being involved with the everyday consistency that is necessary to succeed in any profession, business, or personal relationship.

JUPITER IN SCORPIO

Scorpio can be subtle, covert, and secretive—it is his nature. Jupiter in Scorpio is going to relate to others in a conservative manner, keeping to himself and keeping things close to his vest. This is a person you will usually find in police work. He could also probably excel in engineering or medicine. In the right line of work, he is both practical and successful. Jupiter in Scorpio is analytical and a wonderful diagnostician. He even has the ability to regenerate himself from illness or the mistakes of poor decisions.

If afflicted, his secretiveness becomes almost devious; he might know what can help you but will keep it to himself and avoid getting involved. With this kind of affliction, Jupiter in Scorpio must learn how to care for other people in a loving, positive way and not out of self-interest.

JUPITER IN SAGITTARIUS

Jupiter is in domicile position here since Jupiter rules Sagittarius. It makes him one of the most optimistic, freewheeling, outgoing, and happy individuals around. He enjoys everything, especially those things that take him outdoors—nature, horses, sports, and so on.

Jupiter in Sagittarius is a natural financier. He has an uncanny ability to attract money. If he makes a two-dollar bet, he wins big; if he drops a quarter into a slot machine, dozens pour out of it. This financial success is not gender specific—a woman with Jupiter in Sagittarius can successfully compete with men because she possesses wonderful executive qualities.

Jupiter in Sagittarius has an interesting, almost metaphysical aspect—the ability to bend the will of the universe. If he says he's going to do it, miraculously, through his positive thinking, he will make it happen.

Unfortunately, if afflicted, Jupiter in Sagittarius is going to go haywire. This is your gambler—he's going to make a million and lose a million. His great love of horses will lead to gambling, or his great love of traveling and the outdoors will lead to wanderlust. His love of freedom might make him irresponsible and lead him astray.

JUPITER IN CAPRICORN

The ruler of Capricorn is Saturn, and Saturn and Jupiter contradict each other—when one says, "Go," the other says, "Stop." So Jupiter in Capricorn is in a bad situation. He's just going to plod along. He'll get ahead in the world, but he's going to be overly cautious and pessimistic throughout the journey.

Jupiter is optimistic and Saturn is pessimistic, which gives Jupiter in Capricorn an internal push/pull. This meticulous and careful individual, who is penny wise and pound foolish, is always afraid of losing, so he's certainly not going to take a chance.

As Jupiter in Capricorn matures and learns that no one is out to get him, he can loosen up. He can even make some money if he invests it rather than hangs on to it.

If afflicted, unfortunately, loosening up will be the very thing he can't do. Jupiter in Capricorn afflicted means that this person is going to spend the rest of his life hanging on to everything for fear that he will lose. There's only one bottom line for Jupiter in Capricorn—to stop worrying about losing and to take a chance.

JUPITER IN AQUARIUS

Jupiter in Aquarius is going to be interested in science and groundbreaking projects; he is definitely the reformer. He's the consummate humanist bent on changing the world, ending hunger and poverty—fighting the dragon at every corner.

Jupiter in Aquarius is forward thinking. He's extremely original, although being ahead of his time sometimes makes for an unconventional individual who might or might not succeed. For example, Albert Einstein had Jupiter in Aquarius, and look how far ahead he was—he was exploring concepts and formulas that took years to be accepted.

When afflicted, Jupiter in Aquarius has his foot in his mouth at all times. Instead of being that organizer, that world leader, that person ahead of his time, he is just going to be discontented, always taking things apart for examination. He will be thinking in terms of what you should be doing, what you ought to be doing—he is very theoretical, but, unfortunately, that doesn't mean he knows what is good for you or for himself.

JUPITER IN PISCES

Jupiter in Pisces can relate to others emotionally. He is quiet and interested in nurturing and caring. He has an innate sense of how the other guy feels, how not to step on his toes, and how to encourage him to be the best he can be. That doesn't necessarily mean that Jupiter in Pisces can encourage himself. He doesn't seem to have self-ambition or self-betterment and is not looking for it either. He believes that if he does good for others, somehow or another, good will automatically come to him.

With his great ability to empathize, Jupiter in Pisces is comfortable and successful in any humanistic setting—at the hospital, at a shelter, at a hospice. He thrives tending to children, whether in child care or helping youngsters who are ill or troubled. Jupiter in Pisces can transcend all the limitations that most people have, allowing his rare talents to benefit others.

Afflicted, Jupiter in Pisces has a tremendous fear of pushing the self. He will be a very retiring individual, perhaps even lazy. At times he literally has to stand up and be counted, and Jupiter in Pisces is afraid of just that.

Jupiter Through the Houses

JUPITER IN THE FIRST HOUSE

Jupiter is associated with expansion, or making larger; therefore the ego can create an optimistic individual or a self-indulgent personality. The good fortune of this placement is often seen as a "guardian angel." If there is an affliction, weight will get out of control.

JUPITER IN THE SECOND HOUSE

This position gives financial prowess. The individual has the ability to deal with others' finances and assets while securing an impressive portfolio for himself. However, should an affliction to this house exist, the losses can be great.

JUPITER IN THE THIRD HOUSE

Feel good about yourself! The family will cooperate and responses will be positive. This native can be a good student, usually one who needs a great deal of mental stimulation. With an affliction, there will be restlessness and loss of concentration.

JUPITER IN THE FOURTH HOUSE

The inheritance of the fourth house is displayed by good family relationships. The native will be aware of his soul and create a peaceful and content environment. He will know good fortune until the end.

JUPITER IN THE FIFTH HOUSE

Lucky you! Expression of creativity in all forms is yours. Children will be a blessing, and you will know how to enjoy all good fortune. On the other hand, an affliction is going to force a payback for the neglect in past lives.

JUPITER IN THE SIXTH HOUSE

In this placement, health and the work environment are a pleasure. Hard work and dependability are going to be rewarded. If there is an affliction, health will suffer. Jupiter rules the liver, so temperament and diet can stress that organ and create illness.

JUPITER IN THE SEVENTH HOUSE

What a great catch! Partnerships or marriage will be benefited from all aspects. Plenty of love, money, and social position guaranteed.

JUPITER IN THE EIGHTH HOUSE

A great deal of emotional or sexual energy is released here, coupled with the ability to regenerate the self. Legacies are also covered. If afflicted, poor judgment will lead to extravagances that can be costly.

JUPITER IN THE NINTH HOUSE

Here is the world traveler who is always on the go and off to foreign shores. He will succeed whether philosophizing, writing, or teaching. Afflictions will interfere with the juggling of his personal and professional lives.

JUPITER IN THE TENTH HOUSE

What a climber. Right to the top of the ladder of success, he attracts opportunity and cooperation from others. His place before the public will be assured unless there is an affliction, in which case he will fall from high office in disgrace.

JUPITER IN THE ELEVENTH HOUSE

Choose your friends wisely. The promise of a good social life and help from friends will occur as long as an affliction doesn't produce poor judgment. If afflicted, there will be a downfall of objectives and a life of strife.

JUPITER IN THE TWELFTH HOUSE

The lesson here is that being right is not enough—one must also be timely. This placement allows the native to tap the reservoir where all past-life experiences await. With good judgment, this individual can apply lessons learned to meet the challenges of his life. Hidden enemies will fall by the wayside since a guardian angel is at work. Success can be achieved in the medical field, investigative work, or research. An affliction can produce a person who is quick to judge—not necessarily wrong, just untimely. The native should learn to hold his counsel.

♄ SATURN

Saturn revolves around the Sun approximately every twenty-nine-and-a-half years. Saturn is a somber and serious planet. It deals with the responsibilities you take on and work through. Saturn was feared by the ancients because it was a warning of limitations.

Saturn is the first of the karmic planets, meaning it relates to unfinished business, usually from a past life. Wherever Saturn is placed, it demands that something be accomplished. If you haven't taken care of your responsibilities, Saturn is not going to let you proceed. Saturn is a restrictor; it will confine. It can confine you in numerous ways, from a broken body to the limitations of your finances.

With Saturn, there is a lesson to learn and a lesson to teach. Through Saturn, we grow and develop, both physically and mentally. It is the planet of maturation. Saturn makes absolutely sure that you will reap what you sow. Saturn has been referred to as the "old man of the sky," and it is not going to let you get away with anything that is not part and parcel to your positive development or evolution.

Saturn rules Capricorn, the midheaven, and the tenth house.

SATURN RETROGRADE

Saturn retrograde relates to self-worth. The inability to judge oneself accurately shows up in a retrograde Saturn. Saturn, as a maturation planet, puts your self-worth into proper perspective. People who tend to place more importance on themselves than on others will certainly learn the lesson—Saturn will restrict them until they balance their own worth with the worth of others.

Saturn Through the Signs

SATURN IN ARIES

Saturn is restrictive, and Aries, with its Martian energy, just wants to run amok. So Saturn in Aries is going to be one frustrated individual. Early in life, this child will probably get into trouble—run and then hit the wall. As a result, he begins to develop a suspicion and becomes distrustful and holds back, whereas, ordinarily, Aries runs and jumps without thinking. Saturn in Aries holds an innate fear that the authorities over him—parents, teachers, clergymen—are somehow going to stop him. The fear might even produce guilt, which will make him feel he is doing something wrong and stop him in his tracks.

The problem with Aries, in general, is that he starts but never finishes; but in this placement, Saturn will hold him down and make him finish. As he matures, with Saturn stabilizing the energy of Mars, Saturn in Aries will make slow, productive movement. He will be more successful in his middle to older years. He has mental power, is particularly bright and intelligent, and is always adventurous.

Should Saturn in Aries be afflicted, he will simply hold back and repress. He will suffer from headaches, and his whole body will begin to stagnate. His natural thinking, physical prowess, and fiery, dynamic personality will be dampened.

SATURN IN TAURUS

Saturn in Taurus is going to learn an extremely important lesson in regard to value, cost, and the price we pay. Whether it be an emotional price, a physical price, or a material price is incidental. He needs to understand that what he has acquired and what has been given to him is in no way detrimental; that he should not deny himself what is his honest due.

If Saturn in Taurus gets involved with excesses, he will immediately pay. He needs to learn that material needs are not important—his self-worth is not determined from material but within himself.

If afflicted, Saturn in Taurus is going to learn some hard lessons. There is extremism in Saturn in Taurus that must be brought into balance. It's either complete denial or complete indulgence, neither of which is acceptable or healthy. Saturn in Taurus is afraid that if he doesn't glut himself, he will starve, or if he doesn't amass possessions, he will wind up destitute. It will take a great deal of strength for Saturn in Taurus to come to terms with these extremes and take things in moderation.

SATURN IN GEMINI

Gemini is a particularly intelligent constellation, so when Saturn is in Gemini, it controls that butterfly "hit-and-run" quality that makes Gemini superficial. Instead, Saturn in Gemini is disciplined. He begins to think and does some deep mind-searching about himself and about life. His adaptable nature teaches him how to strike the right balance between his intellect and emotions. With Saturn in Gemini, he stabilizes and his mood swings are not quite as high or as deep.

If Saturn in Gemini is afflicted, instead of stabilizing he will just swing back and forth like a pendulum. He will wind up having either a lot of central nervous disorders or dermatological problems.

SATURN IN CANCER

The Saturn in Cancer personality is predicated on fear. He is frightened and pessimistic and, as a result, hell-bent on protecting himself. Early in life, he looks for his parents to protect him and begins to feel sorry for himself, which creates a selfishness that is always in need of justification. Often, his fears become self-fulfilling prophecies—Saturn in Cancer sometimes feels so darn sorry for himself that nobody wants to be around him. He'll get closed up and involved with the self, which only leads to loneliness and the inability to share, trust, or attract others.

In this loneliness, Saturn in Cancer can become ambitious and shrewd, but he will rarely be generous. If afflicted, he'll just lock himself behind the door, draw the curtains, and not bother with anybody because he's afraid that nobody wants to deal with him. By this time, it's important for Saturn in Cancer to learn how to get out of himself and reach out to others.

SATURN IN LEO

Saturn in Leo might find it difficult to believe that somebody really loves him for himself, and so he walks around puffing out his chest and telling everyone how wonderful he is . . . but that's because he doesn't really believe it.

Saturn in Leo not only gets pompous, but strong willed—he's going to have things his way for fear that he won't get his way at all. It's that old "hit before you get hit" situation. Saturn in Leo carries a chip on his shoulder that doesn't let up.

If afflicted, Saturn in Leo is going to get in trouble with the law. He'll be the boy or girl who gets into trouble in school. He's going to be pushy, demand attention, act up or act out—doing all the disruptive things kids do to get attention. Saturn in Leo needs a lot of positive stroking to reassure him that he is, in fact, important. The healthiest thing Saturn in Leo can do is calm down and give to others the love and respect he wants, because, ultimately, he will get back what he gives. Humility must be learned.

SATURN IN VIRGO

Saturn in Virgo has an orderly, analytical mind that can find or break down all the details, making a good accountant, bookkeeper, researcher, or scientist. Saturn in Virgo feels productive and capable when working alone. He often has difficulty with coworkers because he is so detail oriented that those around him who are not will prove exasperating to him.

Saturn in Virgo has to avoid becoming an intellectual snob. Everyone holds a talent in a different place, so that, collectively, we become great. Saturn in Virgo must learn that he only plays a certain part within the group.

When afflicted, Saturn in Virgo tends to panic. He nags and nitpicks and can wind up wreaking havoc with his central nervous system. He gets flaky, hits the wall, and becomes accusatory and hysterical until things fall into place. Saturn in Virgo has difficulty dealing with the stimulation of other people's thoughts and ideas, desires and needs. That is why he works better alone.

SATURN IN LIBRA

Saturn in Libra takes seriously all of those qualities that Libra represents—equilibrium, partnership, cooperation. This individual really understands the balance between his or her ego and another person's ego. Saturn in Libra develops a certain patience, an understanding and cooperation that appreciates and allows others to explore, explain, do—she doesn't need to jump on their heads or upstage them. Saturn in

Libra innately knows what it takes to keep the wheels rolling so that everybody can move forward.

If afflicted, where partnerships are usually great, they become just the opposite. Instead of cooperating, Saturn in Libra detaches and becomes lazy, afraid, and dependent. This leads to difficulty in all types of relationships, especially in marriage.

SATURN IN SCORPIO

Saturn in Scorpio has a great deal of inner strength, but it requires a great deal of careful handling. He has a strong ego and sense of self-importance. He is a shrewd individual with a strong lust for power who needs to learn discipline and self-control.

If afflicted, Saturn in Scorpio is extremely jealous, possessive, and vindictive. He can love greatly or hate bitterly. He'll imagine that somebody is doing something personally to him—he interprets everything as a personal affront.

If not brought under control, Saturn in Scorpio can overpower the influence of the Sun. This is a difficult aspect that can either positively empower a weak chart or create danger in a strong chart. When afflicted, Saturn in Scorpio can turn into a self-seeking, power-hungry individual who will find himself in great emotional and physical pain as a result of his drives. He needs to watch his gallbladder, which is particularly vulnerable.

Being resourceful, Saturn in Scorpio is out to get what he wants, even if he causes destruction to himself and others. If he can become self-disciplined, it will prevent him from falling prey to his own destructive tendencies.

SATURN IN SAGITTARIUS

Saturn in Sagittarius has a quest for the truth. He looks to understand. He is naturally philosophical, regardless of his religious or philosophical background. An innate quality within Saturn in Sagittarius allows him to be accepting of circumstances and in the know. Because of that, he is outspoken—there is not a fear within him. Even when challenged, he will just shrug his shoulders and remain unfazed. He possesses a well-honed intuition that empowers him with assuredness.

Saturn in Sagittarius is a superb communicator who can take on any mental challenge set before him. His mind is keen, flexible, intelligent, and able to hold its own among peers.

An affliction makes Saturn in Sagittarius careless and indifferent. That seeker of the truth becomes plain old argumentative and wants to challenge for the sake of challenging, which overshadows his respectable mind. You have to turn your back on him because he'll just babble to make a point. He will hone in on what he thinks is your weakest point and attack you right there, even though it might be out of left field. He'll bring in the kitchen sink to win an argument. He'll know where to hurt you, how to deviate from an argument to win, believing that he who shouts the loudest wins.

SATURN IN CAPRICORN

Saturn rules Capricorn, so it is very much at home here. This individual knows what power is in its truest form. It gives him prestige and a strong sense of responsibility toward his family, the neighborhood, or business. He selflessly gives way to the support and concern of others. As Saturn in Capricorn matures, he acquires humility and masters one of his greatest fears—the fear of deprivation.

If afflicted, this goal of power and mastery is going to take over, and Saturn in Capricorn becomes hell-bent on squashing or putting his thumb on other people. He becomes extremely selfish and will wind up alone, brooding, since nobody will want to deal with him. In addition, Saturn in Capricorn could also manifest physical conditions that affect the joints, bones, and entire skeletal structure.

SATURN IN AQUARIUS

Saturn says, "Stay"; Uranus says, "Go." So, Saturn in Aquarius starts out early in life insecure about who he is and what he is about. He always finds himself having to do for others. For the first half of his life, Saturn in Aquarius lives with a continuous and difficult quest for identity. He is forever wondering, "Where do I belong?" Whether it be within the community, country, an identity with his heritage, or whatever, he has to find the answers and integrate them into his personality. He must take responsibility for himself.

Fortunately, as he approaches midlife, he usually discovers who and what he is about. Once Saturn in Aquarius establishes this, he comes to peace at last.

On the other hand, if there is an affliction, there is going to be a great deal of anxiety. His circulatory system comes under pressure, making him uptight and depressed. Saturn in Aquarius will need to go inside himself to establish his sense of belonging.

SATURN IN PISCES

Neptune is a planet without form, and Saturn is a restrictor. So Saturn in Pisces restricts himself. Everything becomes emotionally charged. It is often a negative charge in that he becomes fearful, clinging to the past, worrying and carrying it around on his shoulders, convinced that if something happened before, it will happen again. As a result, Saturn in Pisces is not daring. He is going to tell himself over and over again, "I can't win," and, most certainly, he's not going to win—his fears will become self-fulfilling prophecies. This is an anxiety he must learn to overcome. Saturn in Pisces winds up carrying the world on top of his shoulders.

If afflicted, Saturn in Pisces needs the compassion of others because he really must work hard and diligently to come out of his shell, face the world, face his ghosts, and let go. He must learn to let go of the past.

Saturn Through the Houses

SATURN IN THE FIRST HOUSE

This placement makes for an old personality who will be responsible for everyone. He is working toward approval because he doesn't feel loved. Shy and unassertive, he needs to overcome the feeling that he is not important. If afflicted, selfishness and self-importance will take over and make for an intolerable person.

SATURN IN THE SECOND HOUSE

The poor man's mentality has to be modified. The quest for real estate or hard work without end doesn't make for peace of mind. Saturn can attract inheritances, but the value will be determined by one's attitude.

SATURN IN THE THIRD HOUSE

Education must be taken seriously but will require consistency, the overcoming of interruptions and delays. Family life can be a responsibility that weighs heavily. Depression lurks in this placement, which has a serious and deep mentality.

SATURN IN THE FOURTH HOUSE

The fear of separation from family can lead to unhappiness. Clinging to the past will prevent the independence needed to grow and develop. The stomach will be particularly vulnerable.

SATURN IN THE FIFTH HOUSE

The responsibility for children is prevalent in this placement. Their care and needs will take priority. This could also be the aspect that doesn't allow for reproduction. In this event, the native can resolve this limitation by working as a teacher or in any field that serves children.

SATURN IN THE SIXTH HOUSE

Rewards come only to those who work hard for them. The lack of recognition could push this individual into demanding irrational feats from himself, sacrificing his health in the process. Developing a healthy attitude toward the environment will pay off well.

SATURN IN THE SEVENTH HOUSE

This placement makes for a loner—the one who can do it all by himself but who must also learn to cooperate. He is sensitive and shy but doesn't want anyone to know. He will probably marry for security.

SATURN IN THE EIGHTH HOUSE

The demand in this sector is of restraint, whether it be sex or any other appetite. Striving for balance in all things can regenerate this placement. Financial difficulties are inherited through a marital or business partner.

SATURN IN THE NINTH HOUSE

The continuation of a past-life philosophy or religion takes hold early in life. The individual holds on to his beliefs throughout life and evolves to a higher level. Saturn can, if afflicted, go out of balance and produce a fanatical religious zealot.

SATURN IN THE TENTH HOUSE

Dad might not be there to create an example or image. This placement has to guard against using power incorrectly or a fall is guaranteed. Ambitious and self-reliant, he will climb the ladder of success, but he can't afford to forget service or payback to others.

SATURN IN THE ELEVENTH HOUSE

Discipline is the path necessary to achieve all the goals and objectives of this native. Rewards or achievements will arrive, but only in due time. Patience and honest, hard work will produce a good, mature life. Should the wrong types of association become important, all plans can go awry.

SATURN IN THE TWELFTH HOUSE

Like any other planet placed in the twelfth house, the source of past-life qualities can be tapped. Each emotion faced at the conscious level produces a liberation of the personality. It allows for the dissolution of attitudes produced by negativity. In turn, the native comes forth and reaches out to others.

Uranus takes eighty-four years to revolve around the Sun, spending seven years in each house.

Uranus, which rules Aquarius, is slow moving and slow to impact. What you see in Uranus is usually the tip of the iceberg because it is a subliminal planet, a planet of the subconscious. Uranus deals with your individuality and your personal identity—not as others have told you you are, but who you discover you are. Uranus makes you unique and unconventional.

URANUS RETROGRADE

For those people born with a retrograde Uranus, the action of Uranus, which is slow, becomes even slower. The unique and unconventional quality of Uranus ceases to be because something is underdeveloped or undeveloped that must be caught up with. This creates the late bloomer, one who doesn't readily discover his rare individuality.

Uranus Through the Signs

URANUS IN ARIES

Uranus plus Aries's rulership of Mars is a difficult combination. These two planets will do the unexpected. Uranus in Aries is ready to jump and to pioneer. He possesses a spirit of inquisitiveness that motivates him. He is a real trailblazer.

If it is badly aspected, Uranus in Aries is rebellious. He can really undo himself, trip himself. The results can be loss of a job or physical endangerment. Uranus in Aries has an innate suspicion and fear—the worst fear is of being rejected.

URANUS IN TAURUS

Uranus in Taurus plods along slowly and meticulously. He holds on to all material possessions that he feels can be refurbished and/or salvaged. Uranus in Taurus has a difficult time because Uranus is looking to bring in the new and get rid of the old, while Taurus feels as though everything is being taken out from under him and changing too quickly. Since Taurus is a fixed sign, he likes to take his time. He needs to think and plan and will do wonderful things in his own way and time. When pushed, however, he can never be sure whether he did the right thing.

When afflicted, Uranus in Taurus has difficulties in love affairs—the refined influence of Venus, the ruling planet of Taurus, has no effect, causing partnerships to deteriorate. He will make demands on his partner, many of which are unrealistic. In this placement, negatively afflicted, the innate harmony of Venus will turn to discord. Vulgarity will emerge, and force, rather than love, will motivate his actions.

URANUS IN GEMINI

Gemini is an air sign, a sign that is looking to balance, a sign that wants to be intellectual, use the mind, and communicate. Uranus speeds this up. It makes the mental faculties sharp and quick, and, therefore, the ideas flow. People with Uranus in Gemini succeed in anything having to do with communications (such as radio and television) or with the passing of ideas and concepts (as in teaching or writing).

If afflicted, Uranus in Gemini will create difficulties with those around him, especially relatives. His restlessness will make him tactless.

URANUS IN CANCER

Uranus in Cancer is insecure and often feels sorry for himself. He feels he isn't cared for or loved enough, so he becomes prickly, touchy, and erratic, feeling as if too many demands are placed on him. The underground function of Uranus stirs emotions from a subconscious level. It also makes for a difficult home life, especially in the early years.

Cancer represents home, so Uranus in Cancer is bent on improving the quality of his home life.

URANUS IN LEO

Uranus in Leo is forthright and self-aware. He believes he has control over his destiny. He is bold and adventurous. Should he be high-minded, his intelligence and courage will entice him to accept challenges.

If afflicted, Uranus in Leo is a petty tyrant. He will be vain and destructive and trample on and use people for his own well-being.

URANUS IN VIRGO

Uranus in Virgo has an analytical mind that seeks the truth. He is a reformer and an activist. A civic-minded person, he advocates safety, healthy living, a clean environment, and the like. This person is conscious of what indiscriminate living will produce.

If afflicted, Uranus in Virgo will become a hypochondriac and excessive worrier.

URANUS IN LIBRA

Uranus in Libra deals with the law. The symbol of Libra, the scales, represents justice. The law has a spirit that is often overlooked, so Uranus in Libra will revisit the law.

People born with Uranus in Libra are interested in love, beauty, and harmony, but not in the traditional sense. These people explore the arts. They will look for an independence in marriage that is not traditional.

If afflicted, individuals with this placement should be wary of kidney ailments.

URANUS IN SCORPIO

This is a strong and good placement for Uranus. It produces a powerful individual, someone who possesses a strong will and the persistence to forge ahead in spite of confrontation.

Uranus in Scorpio can thrive in the medical world as a surgeon, healer, psychologist—any area that involves probing, digging deep, looking for causes and cures, trying to get to the bottom of all of the ills of the world.

Uranus in Scorpio is very black or white. He can be an angel or a demon. His energy must find an outlet for better or worse. With Uranus in Scorpio, all emotions surface. If afflicted, this individual can be susceptible to drug abuse or trafficking, cults, and the like.

URANUS IN SAGITTARIUS

Uranus in Sagittarius creates audacity and rebelliousness—especially toward that which is orthodox and conventional. Uranus in Sagittarius supplies the need to expand one's personal horizons and to research and understand various philosophies both for evaluation and application.

Sagittarius rules the thighs and hips, so, unfortunately, if afflicted, Uranus in Sagittarius will have to contend with lower-back problems, especially the sciatic nerve.

URANUS IN CAPRICORN

When well-aspected, Uranus in Capricorn can take a stuffed shirt and turn him into a lighthearted individual who's willing to take a gamble—Capricorn normally never gambles or takes chances. Uranus in Capricorn might undertake politics or some other prestigious undertaking that will allow his need for authority to blossom. If afflicted, he's going to put on cement boots and be as rigid as can be. And rigidity causes the body to suffer—the skeletal system and the digestive system.

Uranus in Capricorn is constantly dealing with the push/pull of "Should I or shouldn't I?" He will have to resolve the home-versus-profession issue. The resolution is this: When he's home, he's wonderful and faithful; when he's out of town, there's no accounting for what he's going to do. The best solution for Uranus in Capricorn is to let go, enjoy, and not be afraid.

URANUS IN AQUARIUS

In Aquarius, Uranus is in domicile position. He is intellectually far ahead and scientific minded. This is the New Age in mentality—to get rid of the old to make way for the new. The problem with this attitude is that Uranus in Aquarius has to develop compassion and understanding to overcome his detached, impersonal attitude. This attitude works fine when dealing with a group, but in a one-on-one situation, it becomes problematic. If afflicted, it makes Uranus in Aquarius downright cruel. He has an indiscriminating mouth that might be correct but nevertheless spits in your face.

Uranus in Aquarius has to learn to develop some compassion and softening up, because he can be a hard person. The way to reach this person is through logic and reason; or perhaps just develop a thick skin.

URANUS IN PISCES

Uranus in Pisces, because of its Neptune rulership, is an uplifting combination. Neptune is a planet that has no form; Pisces deals with old fears and sorrows, and the "what ifs." Uranus in Pisces puts a halt to all that and begins to break up the old patterns. Neptune is an inspiring planet but has a way of slipping through your fingers because it can't be harnessed. But when Uranus is in Pisces, it fences in Neptune and gives it a form. As a result, Neptune begins to reinforce the intuition of Pisces, giving it enormous comprehension, psychic ability, understanding, and sensitivity.

Because of its sensitivity, Uranus in Pisces needs isolation. It must get away from the crowds and overstimulation to relax and recharge its nervous system. When afflicted, the native often escapes through drugs, alcohol, or sex.

Uranus Through the Houses

URANUS IN THE FIRST HOUSE

The ego will undergo changes. It will appear to be erratic and impulsive. The native doesn't know what he wants or how to go about getting what he wants. Uranus will isolate him until he learns how to be cooperative.

URANUS IN THE SECOND HOUSE

There will be feast or famine depending on the rest of the chart. This person must be willing to invent innovative methods of earning his income. This is not a good placement for someone who wants a fixed or predictable income.

URANUS IN THE THIRD HOUSE

The native will feel somewhat isolated and different from the rest of the family, particularly brothers and sisters. If he becomes extremely unconventional, he will suffer. Education will be interrupted unless interest and willingness are maintained.

URANUS IN THE FOURTH HOUSE

Mother may not be dependable, causing emotional difficulties for the native. The home life will repeatedly be upset, whether through moving from place to place or because the family undergoes financial changes.

URANUS IN THE FIFTH HOUSE

Unconventionality displays itself in this house. The children of the native might prove to be exceptional or, if there is little discipline, terribly destructive. Cooperation is of utmost importance or romance will not survive. Creativity is high but can be of an unusual nature.

URANUS IN THE SIXTH HOUSE

An ingenious personality, but this native will need an environment where he can move about. Boredom can lead to psychosomatic illnesses. The central nervous system is vulnerable. Self-control will be his greatest medicine.

URANUS IN THE SEVENTH HOUSE

Partners of this native will be difficult and uncooperative, demanding great discipline from the native. Divorce or separation will most likely be the outcome. Maturity can produce a successful but unconventional union.

URANUS IN THE EIGHTH HOUSE

This placement calls for caution. Uranus and Mars together are always dangerous. Bad tempers can create havoc whether it be with partners or on one's health. Sexual habits will need controlling. Money,

especially inheritances or partners' wealth, can disappear unexpectedly.

URANUS IN THE NINTH HOUSE

The philosophy or religious background of this native may not be
orthodox, leading him through various experiences. He will probably
deal with foreign affairs, which will, in turn, supply him with teaching
or publishing successes.

URANUS IN THE TENTH HOUSE

Uranus's placement here is an indicator of the student of astrology.
It can produce a particularly original and humanistic occultist. This
placement carries a karma that can only be displaced, not altered.

URANUS IN THE ELEVENTH HOUSE

This placement can produce a person who deals with all measures
of people. He could be the social worker who deals with troubled
people or the serious businessman who succeeds through management
of others. This native will most likely "find himself" late in life, as
his goals and objectives are in constant flux.

URANUS IN THE TWELFTH HOUSE

The twelfth house can be a place of confinement or liberation. The
fashion in which the native handles one or the other will surface from
the reservoir of past lives and foster growth. It can allow a multitude
of talent to reveal a new and prosperous path.

NEPTUNE

Neptune, the ruler of Pisces, is the other planet of the subconscious. It takes 165 years to revolve around the Sun, spending fourteen years in each house.

The glyph of Neptune is a three-pronged fork. One side of the fork is illusion and the other side is delusion. The middle prong, which is crossed, takes that illusion/delusion aspect, puts it on the cross of matter, and tests it. This is symbolic of how Neptune operates.

Neptune is elusive and difficult to harness. Neptune is like sand slipping through your fingers. People who have Neptune transiting through certain sectors of their chart are kept from flowering, achieving, and acquiring—that is the reason they are late bloomers. When Neptune moves on, these individuals are finally able to take back control of their lives and be constructive, even if this occurs in later years. There is no deadline as to when one can start over and produce something worthwhile.

Neptune can inspire you to unbelievable and creative things; it is an endless source of information and talent. But Neptune must be conquered, otherwise it produces nothing but fear, which will hold you back.

Neptune is vast and deep. It rules the ocean, fog, and oil. It deals with things that are subliminal, below the level of consciousness, so that many people do not realize until after the fact that Neptune has undone them.

A dangerous planet, Neptune is associated with drug and alcohol abuse. It is a planet not to be messed with. Even when you are handling Neptune, you can never be sure that it is under control. It is difficult to bring to form and to conquer.

NEPTUNE RETROGRADE

Neptune in retrograde is a humdinger. Neptune is a difficult planet, so in retrograde action the negativity of Neptune becomes prominent. Neptune has a depth that can be lifesaving; but when it turns retrograde, it goes underground and doesn't surface. All of the wonderful concepts, ideas, and creative forces that are generally in Neptune when it is well-aspected will produce irrational fears and anxieties when in retrograde position. These fears are considered irrational because they are usually not created within the context of this lifetime, but from past-life issues and unfinished business.

If born with a Neptune retrograde, it is necessary to maintain faith and courage in the face of all challenges.

Neptune Through the Signs*

NEPTUNE IN GEMINI

Neptune in Gemini expands the mind, explores concepts and ideas, and brings about the fulfillment of hopes and ideals. The mind is restless in this placement, looking for development, innovation, and intellectual pursuits.

NEPTUNE IN CANCER

Neptune in Cancer is nostalgic. People with this placement tend to cling to their ancestral heritages because identity, home (and homeland), and family ties are important. Karmic lessons are experienced if there is a lack of compassion.

NEPTUNE IN LEO

This is not a good placement. Neptune clouds judgment, making it unable to see facts and truths clearly. As a generation, those with Neptune in Leo were reared during World War I and were not able to see what was happening politically in Europe during that era. They would be fooled by those infamous, rising dictators.

People born with Neptune in Leo, if afflicted, have trouble giving, receiving, or understanding love.

---

*Since Neptune was not discovered until 1846, its astrological influence before that time can only be reflected upon in retrospect. However, since Neptune entered the signs of Aries and Taurus prior to 1887, no one remains alive today with such placements in his or her chart.

In the same vein, since Neptune in Pisces will not occur until 2012, its placement will not be of influence until that time.

NEPTUNE IN VIRGO

Neptune in Virgo produces tension, fears, and stress. The term *psychosomatic* was coined during this transit, and nervous tension, particularly stress, was observed as a cause of many illnesses.

On the positive side, this transit drives people to serve their fellow man and the world. It can create the true humanitarian.

If afflicted, Neptune in Virgo can be self-centered and self-serving, critical and always looking for flaws.

NEPTUNE IN LIBRA

Neptune in Libra looks for partnerships and alliances. On the negative side, those with this placement can be prone to divorce.

More wars were experienced during this transit than ever before. However, sustaining harmony and love, which is native to Libra, can end conflict.

People with this placement have strong artistic tendencies and will develop new and creative art forms.

NEPTUNE IN SCORPIO

Neptune in Scorpio highlights escapism. Negatively influenced, it can mean escapism through alcohol, sex, and drugs. Positively influenced, it can bring self-awareness through meditation and psychic study.

The children of this generation will contend with the results of their parents' actions, which they will overcome through a sense of discipline their parents didn't have.

NEPTUNE IN SAGITTARIUS

Neptune in Sagittarius brings truth. It is a strong position. Sagittarius has a cognitive ability and an innate knowing that makes it seem lucky. Here is where the seed of truth surfaces. It allows one to decipher, clean up, and rectify. It allows one to look at old or orthodox concepts and see if, in fact, they're still applicable.

During this transit, the world will be in a state of upheaval, prompting natives with this placement to go beyond their personal borders, physically and economically. If afflicted, the native will lack judgment and be indecisive.

NEPTUNE IN CAPRICORN

The century will end as Neptune travels through Capricorn. It will signal the end of karma and the beginning of New Age. As an applicable reality, healing throughout the world will begin.

Neptune in Capricorn brings clarity of thought to the individual.

NEPTUNE IN AQUARIUS

Neptune in Aquarius represents evolution. It can carry on, rectify, turn around, and, most importantly, evolve. This transit will take the world through the next millennium.

Neptune Through the Houses

NEPTUNE IN THE FIRST HOUSE

The ego suffers and the lack of reality surrounding this native is emotionally difficult. He must control and alter attitudes to feel comfortable with his interactions. Although he might know what he wants, he doesn't know if he deserves it. Few people will really know him.

NEPTUNE IN THE SECOND HOUSE

This placement is not going to allow you to keep your resources to yourself. The inability to see clearly how others manipulate or help themselves to your assets will produce losses. The beauty of this aspect is that if you choose to share, there will always be a refill. The flow is not interrupted.

NEPTUNE IN THE THIRD HOUSE

The need to harness and concentrate shows up as a poor student. This placement can create an artistic imagination if supported by the rest of the chart. Brothers and sisters will never be understood due to karmic lessons involved.

NEPTUNE IN THE FOURTH HOUSE

Home and family conditions will never be clear. The native will find himself being sacrificed or surprised by circumstances he can't control. Alcohol or other neurotic afflictions will bring unhappiness until the native moves away from the source.

NEPTUNE IN THE FIFTH HOUSE

This is a great placement for an actor. His drama is played out through many roles. The inability to find a love of his own can lead to affairs or dead-end relationships. There will be great sacrifices yet little rewards. Until they reach adulthood, children can prove to be a burden.

NEPTUNE IN THE SIXTH HOUSE

This person must be his own doctor. He must resort to natural forms of healing. Diagnoses are almost impossible—although the symptoms are evident, the causes are hidden. The sensitivity of this native creates a vulnerability that can prevent him from functioning with others. Isolation is not the best option, yet it is often what saves the native.

NEPTUNE IN THE SEVENTH HOUSE

The romantic aura that surrounds any partnership undertaken can cloud the dependencies or imperfections of the union. Sacrifice, the key note of Neptune, produces fantasies and dreams of the perfect marriage. Though he has been giving his power away, the truth is that the native is stronger and more capable than his partner.

NEPTUNE IN THE EIGHTH HOUSE

Neptune disperses all that would be gained either through a partner or a legacy. This native must not use his strength for his own gain because he owes others. He will be the keeper of others' souls. He could be an excellent financier if he serves the public.

NEPTUNE IN THE NINTH HOUSE

The mind of this individual becomes clouded, rendering him unable to articulate. His thoughts might be high-minded or mystical but not tangible. This person might give the impression that he lacks sympathy because he will indulge in intellectual, theoretical concepts while missing the emotional contact.

NEPTUNE IN THE TENTH HOUSE

This Saturn house extracts a karmic lesson. The native will never receive credit for work done unless he has earned it. Authority in this person's life will have proved irresponsible. He must therefore take the mature role and overcome his obstacles.

NEPTUNE IN THE ELEVENTH HOUSE

All dreams and hopes can be fulfilled if they are defined and supported. This native must be careful of whom he calls friend. He must understand human nature to avoid the deception that surrounds him. Others will want to ride his coattails.

NEPTUNE IN THE TWELFTH HOUSE

Since Neptune rules the twelfth house, we would think all is well. Not true. This placement can be the cause of irrational fears. A feeling of isolation can stress the native until he is ill. Finding a connection to a deity or fellow man can keep this native from suffering.

♇
PLUTO

Pluto is a small, dense planet situated in the outermost position among all the planets.

Pluto, which was discovered in 1930, ushered in extraordinary world changes. The discovery of Pluto precipitated the Great Depression in the United States and the rise of Nazism in Europe.

Pluto takes 248 years to revolve around the Sun, but its course is erratic—since its discovery, it has increased in velocity, spending less and less time in each sign. It has speed, it carries information, it has the ability to awake and shake and bring things to the surface. Pluto rules earthquakes; it rules anything that is subterranean, whether at the physical, emotional, or mental level.

Wherever Pluto is in your chart, it makes enormous demands. It will provide the greatest challenges of your life. Since Pluto moves quickly through each constellation, it produces rapid changes, generational changes. Although there is no permanency with Pluto, it never winds up taking away what you need.

The regenerative powers of Pluto are endless. Enormous strength in the human being is projected through Pluto. Pluto is authentic, but Pluto requires mastery. It will not let you get away with faking it. Pluto is a hard taskmaster, but it will also give you that which no one can take away.

The positive expression through Pluto is a willingness, a grace that you accept, a calmness that allows you to transform and function. It takes you deep inside your soul and subconscious and brings forth that which is already within you. Pluto allows you to make contact with yourself and grow.

The negative expression through Pluto is an intensity that can lead to destruction or death. It can create a loss of balance, getting completely out of kilter and becoming obsessive and willful.

Pluto exemplifies the law of retribution—what you set forth, you are going to receive back in spades. Not just in action but in intent.

PLUTO RETROGRADE

Pluto is generational. During its long revolution, many people will be born within each of its aspects. If Pluto is in retrograde motion, which it is for about six months of the year, half of the population will be born with a retrograde Pluto. This group of people is not necessarily going to act according to the rest of the group. These individuals will, sooner or later, stand out within that generation. They will either be famous or infamous.

Pluto Through the Signs*

PLUTO IN TAURUS

The most memorable and perhaps most important aspect of Pluto in Taurus is that those people born within this era left an important legacy: the birth of psychiatry. During the transit of Pluto in Taurus, the world was influenced by such eminent people as Sigmund Freud and his student Carl Jung.

The word *psychiatry* was invented at that time. The generation born with this evolving concept saw medicine take a new step—the introduction of the body/mind connection. This concept would take many years to be polished and accepted. Nevertheless, generations would eventually be affected by the seed that was planted with Pluto in Taurus.

PLUTO IN GEMINI

Pluto in Gemini is a collector of information. It produces communication and expression. This was an era of communicating, talking about, and introducing.

While Pluto was in Gemini, the world began to shrink. Airplanes were bringing countries closer together, which allowed people to visit other continents. The automobile shortened the distance between towns and states. The world was suddenly as close as our doorstep.

PLUTO IN CANCER

During the transit of Pluto in Cancer, the United States isolated itself from the rest of the world under the guise of "patriotism." The results would be a war that would send men to places and experiences they were ill prepared to face. The United States faced an economic and emotional depression that would unite people in a common cause.

---

*Since Pluto was not discovered until 1930, its astrological influence before that time can only be reflected upon in retrospect, beginning with its placement in Taurus at the turn of the twentieth century.

Pluto's coming transit through the signs of Capricorn, Aquarius, and Pisces—where its influence has yet to be determined—is difficult to speculate upon at this time and, therefore, is omitted. However, as we approach the Aquarian Age, it is likely that Pluto's influence in these remaining signs will be one of transition and increased spiritual development.

Emotions and intuitions are brought to the surface of those with Pluto in Cancer, and they can be either heightened or displaced.

PLUTO IN LEO

When Pluto was in Leo, dictators became prominent and there was a struggle for world power. That was exemplified by two wars: World War II and the Korean War. The sneak attack on Pearl Harbor and the appeasement of European dictators, which allowed them to do as they pleased, illustrate the most negative part of the authoritarian quality of Pluto in Leo.

Individuals with this placement can be either power hungry or ambitious for the good of society.

PLUTO IN VIRGO

During this period, people stopped surrendering themselves to physicians and became interested in vitamins and organic food— the self-help concept was born. Society adopted an attitude of cleanliness, whether at home, in restaurants, hospitals, or cities. New laws and ordinances were instituted to protect food and water. This was an era that advocated purity and all things unadulterated.

Those born with Pluto in Virgo make excellent nurses, doctors, healers, and even chefs and innkeepers. They are careful and meticulous, caught up in all that is soothing and clean, maintaining the beauty in simplicity.

PLUTO IN LIBRA

Pluto in Libra signaled not only a need for equality, symmetry, and balance, but it also dealt with equilibrium. This was very relevant to partnerships. Pluto in Libra made absolutely certain that the egos of the partners in a relationship were, indeed, considered equal, making sure that one did not weaken or overpower. Without respect and trust for a partner, there is no advancement.

During this time, relationships, marriage, and unions came to the forefront. The divorce rate was significantly increasing and society started to believe that it was easier to discard a partner than to work problems out. A differentiation was made between a union created by two people and a simple, interacting relationship in which people communicate. This era demonstrated a lack of truth, a lack of reality, and a lack of solid interpersonal relationships. Marriage suffered the worse for it.

Those born with Pluto in Libra have a need for harmony in their relationships, but they often put their relationships to the test.

PLUTO IN SCORPIO

Pluto rules Scorpio, so for every sunny disposition there is a dark side of the personality that is usually kept hidden.

In the beginning of this transit there was a tension and a falling apart. Everything turned to dust, everything disintegrated. Talent was questioned and the only way to survive was to make sure you were good at what you were doing and not taking it for granted. You had to work hard and hone your craft, talent, or profession, because if you didn't master it, you were going to lose it.

Those born with Pluto in Scorpio are going to carry, in their subconscious, the need to clean up. Not just cleaning up the planet, but cleaning up the inner self. In discovering the power within, in touching the spirit without labeling it, there will be self-esteem and the energy to keep illness at bay.

Pluto in Scorpio is a generation of powerful egos. And *ego* is not a dirty word. Everybody has an ego. Once the ego is recognized, fortified, and overcome, it can be eliminated.

PLUTO IN SAGITTARIUS

This is the time of Pluto in Sagittarius. It's Pluto to Jupiter, and Jupiter deals with relating. Jupiter gives Sagittarius a cognitive ability, and Pluto rules the collective unconscious. Strides will be made over the next few years, certainly with the generation now being born. This generation cares about their fellow man. They can see things from a global perspective, cross cultures, understand and embrace the foreigner. Pluto in Sagittarius is going to formulate a brand-new human community in which the fellow man is understood. The separation of mankind that began 150 years ago with Pluto in Gemini is ready to be altered for the better. It is a small Earth, and man is more powerful, intelligent, and able to deal with people when he can understand and accept all religions, languages, and customs. Respect can finally surface for those things that we don't know or understand. There is no limit to where Pluto in Sagittarius can take us.

Pluto Through the Houses

PLUTO IN THE FIRST HOUSE

This placement calls for the native to become aware of the changes and extremes that his ego will undergo. If he becomes timid and afraid, he will suffer personality wounds. If he becomes overbearing, rejection will destroy his confidence. Balance is the lesson Pluto calls for in this house.

PLUTO IN THE SECOND HOUSE

In this house, Pluto carries the memory and fears of the miser. If the native learns to acquire, share, enjoy, and not hoard, he will keep the flow of prosperity going. If he becomes self-absorbed, he will have to reconstruct his financial life over and over until the correct approach can overcome his negative tactics.

PLUTO IN THE THIRD HOUSE

The house of communication works subtly, but it allows the native to use writing, painting, and other forms of expression to release thoughts from a depth he might not understand. There is an ease of thinking that makes for mental power. The native can displace energy in a healthy fashion or, like a pressure cooker, blow unexpectedly.

PLUTO IN THE FOURTH HOUSE

Pluto destroys the roots, hoping we will reroot. Dependent Cancers with this placement often have a great deal to work out with mother. A home life of peace and tranquillity eludes this person until he has set a foundation of love and selflessness.

PLUTO IN THE FIFTH HOUSE

Ruled by the Sun, this placement becomes a powerhouse. A word of caution—this power requires a great deal of strength to handle. Without restraint, it can lead to all kinds of excesses. Gentle, loving parents can handle unusual children. The rewards acquired by this position are of a grand scale.

PLUTO IN THE SIXTH HOUSE

Pluto's depth allows this position to tap a knowing that is helpful in the care of others. Psychologists or other mental caregivers usually have a strong Mercury/Pluto aspect. The need to serve is present, but it must be as a joyous giver or those around this person will recognize the facade. This position makes for a hardworking individual whose health is dependent on releasing the energies of the central nervous system.

PLUTO IN THE SEVENTH HOUSE

Relationships, of which marriage can be the most important, are difficult as the individual is being asked to withstand the onslaught of partners' thoughts and actions. Knowing what your partner is all about and still loving him might take all the power you possess. Corporate lawyers with this marker can lead mediations and other legal matters successfully as they can see both sides of the coin.

PLUTO IN THE EIGHTH HOUSE

This position has always been associated with death, the ultimate change. The native can really create change with this aspect since only after a rebirth can we progress. The alternative is not to use these energies until one has degenerated into a physical illness or the darkness of the mind. To reach self-mastery is a victory that must be undertaken alone. The rewards are extraordinary strength and a fearless attitude.

PLUTO IN THE NINTH HOUSE

This is the house where the mind can go deep into the subconscious and explore the "source," such as reincarnation and/or other systems. Unfortunately, it can lead to a fear that produces fanatics or people who force their beliefs on others.

PLUTO IN THE TENTH HOUSE

The struggle that is inherent in this position can swing the native from being a recluse to being before the public. The success of the native is attained by hard work and mastery. The willingness to share knowledge, to have patience with others, and to act with diplomacy results in rewards.

PLUTO IN THE ELEVENTH HOUSE

Pluto will attract all measure of help, so be careful of the source. Choosing friends and activities wisely is important or you can find yourself dragged through the mud. The high level of Pluto can produce a much admired and/or followed leader. Objectives and goals are achieved with a little help from friends.

PLUTO IN THE TWELFTH HOUSE

This placement at its best creates a knowing. The native seems to have a beforehand knowledge that can create inspiration or misery. Feelings of confinement can be transcended by serving others as opposed to serving the ego. The talents of past lives can emerge as a source for advancement, regardless of the level of education in this life.

Chapter Seven

Planetary Relationships
and Movement

Aspects

An aspect is the angle formed by two or more planets in relationship to each other. Collectively, the various aspects bring a chart to life.

Aspects are to be looked at simply as opportunities, some of which are difficult, some of which are frustrating, some of which are easy, and some of which are great. An aspect creates a potential—it is energy, and what you choose to do with this energy is entirely up to you; you make it either positive or negative.

There are many different aspects: squares, oppositions, conjunctions, trines, sextiles, quincunx, grand trines, grand crosses, and tee squares. Some of these are hard aspects, meaning that they present challenges but can inevitably produce more powerful or strengthening effects. Some are soft aspects, meaning that their influence is easy and free flowing.

☐ SQUARE

If two planets in your chart are 90 degrees apart, they form a square. A square is a powerful position. Without squares in your chart, you're never going to get off your duff and get anything done. A square is blocked energy, but it also creates a need to work things out. It is a hard aspect, but it has significance in a chart because it is an energizer.

Each square carries within it a quality that must be reconciled. It is the type of quality that makes you better as you get older. If you look at any chart of a successful person, there are sure to be squares.

☍ OPPOSITION

When two planets are 180 degrees apart, they form an opposition. Opposition means just that—two planets opposing each other. It is also a hard aspect.

An opposition has a midpoint where the qualities of these two planets can be reconciled. When planets oppose each other, they are polarizing, each representing the extreme end of the same polarity.

The key word in an opposition is *objectivity*. Objectivity makes us aware of things we are often too close to see in an unbiased fashion. We are usually the worst judges of ourselves. We project ourselves into the world with a certain attitude or set of personal intentions, but the world is often picking up something else. With an opposition, we can begin to gain awareness and understand cause and effect. We are given an objectivity that we don't ordinarily possess.

Three or more oppositions in a chart is considered a medical chart. It usually means there is going to be hell to pay, most likely at the physical level. Too many oppositions make for a sick person. If that is the case in your chart, it's important to work to reconcile these polarities. That can be accomplished with a change of attitude.

☌ CONJUNCTION

A conjunction occurs when two planets come together within a few degrees (up to 10 degrees, depending on the power of the planet). A conjunction is considered a hard aspect.

Conjunctions often occur when two planets are within the same constellation. They can also be in different constellations as long as the distance between those planets is less than 10 degrees.

Because it produces a power, a conjunction demands that you work through these planets at the same time. When a planet transits close to another planet and triggers it, it is called an approach. An approach is a powerful combination because it has a relay or domino effect—the planet that triggers the first, triggers the second. It is a position of power and should be handled.

Conjunctions often produce overbearing or demanding people.

△ TRINE

A trine consists of three planets placed 120 degrees from one another. Trines have always been looked upon as lucky and beneficial. When they occur in a chart, they create a smoothness, a kind of agility in the personality. Learning is easier, projecting is easier, performing is easier—it is as though there is a harmony between intellect and emotion.

A trine indicates that you develop and function with an ease and harmony that produce creativity. In appearance, a trine makes you feel as if things are coming easily to you.

If your chart is full of trines, it can become problematic because it produces laziness. You feel as if you don't have to work for anything. It requires an individual to use those aspects so that laziness can be overcome.

If you combine a trine and a square, it creates a real dynamo. A square is going to give you energy and a trine is going to give you luck—that's a surefire combination for success. It will give you both the energy and creative impetus to get your ideas up off the drawing board.

✳ SEXTILE

A sextile is an aspect created by two planets 60 degrees from each other. This is a soft aspect, not as easy as the trine, but ever so compatible.

What lies in a sextile is a chance. Two planets in a sextile aspect can easily be reconciled to produce opportunity. If you have a sextile in your chart, it is entirely up to you whether you work with the opportunity or ignore it.

Aspect Relationships

When you have a natal chart created professionally or via computer, in addition to the wheel, an aspect grid may also be included (see page

30 for an example). The grid displays aspect relationships at the time of your birth in an easy-to-read format.

Make note of the specific aspect relationships in your own chart and use the following guide to provide an explanation of each aspect.

ASPECTS TO THE SUN

(Given the close proximity of these planets, conjunctions are the only aspects made between Sun/Venus and Sun/Mercury.)

Sun ☌ Moon—A psychological orphan. The native will likely have to deal with the male or the female quality within himself from a personal point of view instead of from the perspective of his parents.

Sun △/⚹ Moon—There was a great deal of harmony between one's parents at the time of conception leading to harmony within this native.

Sun □ Moon—The native was born into a household where mom and dad were jockeying for position or simply didn't get along, causing inner conflict for this individual.

Sun ☍ Moon—Personal harmony must be worked out because it was not found between your parents at the time of your birth.

Sun ☌ Mercury—The native communicates well and listens to himself.

Sun ☌ Venus—Self-love is an important factor in the development of this personality—more than likely, self-love was not taught.

Sun ☌ Mars—The native possesses a great deal of energy and can be impulsive.

Sun △/⚹ Mars—Deliberate and agile, the native works toward success. The energy in this female is attractive to males.

Sun □ Mars—Frustrated and willful, the native works with a violent attitude that can lead to accidents or cruel acts.

Sun ☌° Mars—Irritable and angry, this personality becomes difficult and bossy. The actions of females with this aspect are prone to be competitive.

Sun ☌ Jupiter—This aspect gives the ability to understand and relate to oneself. It also allows an understanding of the law of cause and effect.

Sun △/✳ Jupiter—Naturally attuned to the laws of the universe, the native is basically healthy. A wonderful aspect for those in the medical field.

Sun ☐ Jupiter—Dishonest and willing to ride on the coattails of others, which can create an uncertain and unhealthy atmosphere. Honesty can help release stress and prevent health problems.

Sun ☌° Jupiter—This difficult aspect tends to overinflate self-importance. Could lead to overeating or overspending.

Sun ☌ Saturn—Indicates unfinished business. The native should take his status in the world seriously. Know there is something he must personally do and develop a sense of responsibility for it.

Sun △/✳ Saturn—This native doesn't challenge. He loves to work, does it well, and keeps his goals in sight, no matter how difficult the road may be.

Sun ☐ Saturn—Epitomizes "self-fulfilling prophesy." The native is negative and fearful and, eventually, hardens. He receives what he gives. His body will become rigid and painful.

Sun ☌° Saturn—This aspect gives a native a chance to see what his attitudes can produce. He will attract people who will "do him one better" and force him to deal with his egocentricity.

Sun ☌ Uranus—Prophetic but untimely, the native must learn discretion. His strong will can lead to impulsiveness. The female finds her femininity a handicap.

Sun △/✳ Uranus—The forces of the collective unconscious come to the foreground. The personality is independent, original, and unconventional, but not good for intimacy.

Sun □ **Uranus**—This aspect is very difficult to live with. The native can be impulsive, rude, and rebellious. His life will take sudden changes, some of which will go nowhere.

Sun ☍ **Uranus**—This native's life is subject to unexpected and uncontrollable conditions. He will be a victim of the whims or wills of others. He must learn to roll with the punches.

Sun ☌ **Neptune**—A misunderstood personality. The male appears to be romantic or mystical but is, in fact, lazy. The female comes across as a "whatever you want me to be" type, who still holds to her own agenda.

Sun △/✶ **Neptune**—Whatever talents have been accumulated through past lives will surface. This native is a multitalented person, who can excel in any field and have great staying power.

Sun □ **Neptune**—The native must serve or sacrifice. Past life debts are to be collected.

Sun ☍ **Neptune**—This native "can't see the forest for the trees." Others will bring disappointment through unstable and chaotic situations. The native must learn to let go and avoid obsessive patterns of behavior.

Sun ☌ **Pluto**—Power in the most raw conditions. Negative views will produce infamy but a positive attitude will attain the highest position within one's environment.

Sun △/✶ **Pluto**—Success will come. Strength and self-awareness cut a path toward achieving one's personal goals. The ability to empower others attracts support and admiration.

Sun □ **Pluto**—Negative but strong-willed, this individual can be ruthless and egotistical. He can draw the worst of the underworld.

Sun ☍ **Pluto**—The danger of giving his power away to partners and/or associates is his emotional pitfall. This can lead to a brutality or jealousy that makes him self-destructive.

ASPECTS TO THE MOON

Moon ☌ Mercury—This person "can't hold his tongue." He can be a gossip or engage in condemnation to his own detriment unless he becomes disciplined.

Moon △/✱ Mercury—This native is smooth thinking and an agile communicator. His brain is in gear before he speaks. He thinks on his feet and shows coordination between emotions and logic.

Moon □ Mercury—The objective of this native is to feel and think in harmony. He could bring troubles to himself through the written word.

Moon ☍ Mercury—This native doesn't hold back his opinion—he'll give it whether he's asked to or not. The results are that he will suffer in kind . . . and the payback hurts.

Moon ☌ Venus—Love is in the air—when one love dies, another is waiting in the wings for this individual. The endowed physical beauty gives an opportunity to choose between love and the magnetic attraction of beauty.

Moon △/✱ Venus—Pleasant, sedate, and orderly, this native, in an artistic atmosphere, can acquire financial security.

Moon □ Venus—Sloppy, especially with the feelings of others, this native has little or no knowledge of sisterhood.

Moon ☍ Venus—This aspect brings objectivity to the native. By observing the actions of others, the native realizes what he has brought upon himself. This can help overcome lovelessness.

Moon ☌ Mars—This aspect creates a bad temper and volatile situations. It also means that although a mother might have attended to this child responsibly and well, she might not have bonded as well as she could have.

Moon △/✱ Mars—Energy plus controlled emotions make for an ease of actions and a great lover. Vitality and recuperative powers prove healing.

Moon □ **Mars**—An aggressive, self-centered character who will use the opposite sex for personal gratification. He will carry over into his life what his angry mother provided.

Moon ♂° **Mars**—Use restraint or suffer. This native will attract what he hates most. Emotional upheavals will be constant irritations that can only be overcome by patience and a loving attitude.

Moon ♂ **Jupiter**—A guardian angel is at work—whatever this native touches turns to gold. There is a protection bestowed upon him that makes for a safe life. The native must not allow food to be his companion.

Moon △/✱ **Jupiter**—The ability to believe in oneself brings success. This, coupled with the assistance of others, makes for a shared joy. The environment supports all endeavors.

Moon □ **Jupiter**—Control over diet or other indulgences is a must. Relating to others can overcome the narcissistic attitude of the native.

Moon ♂° **Jupiter**—The law of cause and effect is at work here. The native attracts what he projects even when he is not conscious of the action. His secret heart is revealed.

Moon ♂ **Saturn**—This difficult and frustrating aspect has the native in the grip of payback. Feeling sorry for himself will find him alone. Mother did little or no nurturing so he must be careful not to make others pay for this.

Moon △/✱ **Saturn**—Responsibility for accomplishments is key in this aspect. The native will take his family, job, and public duty seriously. He can withstand aloneness while serving others.

Moon □ **Saturn**—This aspect signifies a cold, difficult relationship with mother. To overcome inherent fear and depression, this native needs to cultivate as much love as he can.

Moon ♂° **Saturn**—This aspect provides a chance to overcome the rigidity that Saturn imposes. Materialism is exciting and can provide many things as long as it is not handled in a cold and unresponsive way.

Moon ♂ Uranus—This aspect has difficulty relating to mother, therefore early training is not accepted. If lucky, intuition will prevent the native from creating more problems than he can handle. If not, the body pays.

Moon △/✳ Uranus—Potential for genius. Mental capacities and intuition combine to produce a creative and far-reaching individual who can adapt to sudden changes.

Moon □ Uranus—Unstable and willful, this person can create impossible relationships. Not successful at parenting, since nurturing requires calm, consistent, and loving acts that are difficult for this native to perform.

Moon ♂° Uranus—This ambitious and energetic native has to be careful of his goals and who he enlists in his pursuits. The wrong people can influence him or support his willfulness, which can result in sorrow.

Moon ♂ Neptune—This sensitive and emotionally responsive native can overload. Diagnosis of his health is unclear as he seldom shows symptoms. Drugs are a problem as he poisons easily. The best medicine is sleep.

Moon △/✳ Neptune—Psychic abilities abound. The native must learn to protect himself since he cannot tolerate friction and chaos. Music, drama, and writing release a creative side of this personality.

Moon □ Neptune—The family, particularly mother, may suffer from many afflictions leaving this native with many insecurities and limitations. Until this personality develops a willingness to act, he will not acquire self-confidence.

Moon ♂° Neptune—This person must take a leap of faith to conquer the fears that cause his limitations. He must keep his head on straight and overcome the doubts that surface whenever he "overthinks" things.

Moon ♂ Pluto—This powerful aspect requires discipline to prevent takeovers. Mother, while influential, is a presence that has to be diminished for a while so that this native can discover himself. This is a great aspect for a psychologist, since it allows this person to become attuned to the needs of others.

Moon △/✳ Pluto—This aspect brings a sense of survival that overcomes any event. This native can rise above the impossible. This comes not from luck, but from strength.

Moon ☐ Pluto—Patience and tolerance must be learned from others or else this individual will find himself alone and unsupported. Emotional upheavals will be part of his life.

Moon ☍ Pluto—An attraction to a powerful partner will have many ramifications whether good or bad. Emotional ties can lead to unorthodox liaisons. Even when misunderstood, this native attracts others to him.

ASPECTS TO MERCURY

(Note: Given the close proximity of these planets, the only aspects made between Mercury and Venus are conjunction and sextile.)

Mercury ☌ Venus—Charming and mannered, this refined and artistic individual will be offended by coarse or crass communications.

Mercury ✳ Venus—There is just enough ability for this native to be friendly, sociable, and pleasant . . . but don't expect much more.

Mercury ☌ Mars—Mentally aggressive, this native can become argumentative, sarcastic, and blunt, which, unless tempered by thought, will turn off many people.

Mercury △/✳ Mars—A clever fellow with a quick mind and wit. His sense of reason and mental dexterity makes for a fine student of any abstract subject.

Mercury ☐ Mars—A bad temper needs to be overcome or accidents will occur. Irritability will affect the nervous system of this native and the body will pay the price with muscle spasms.

Mercury ☍ Mars—If he uses his energies well, this native can persevere and reach his goals. If not, he will find himself a victim of bad press.

Mercury ☌ Jupiter—A philosophical mind and a generous soul. This native will be paid in kind. If he is not lazy or stubborn, he will enjoy abundance.

Mercury △/✳ Jupiter—Good judgment and awareness of possibilities will help this native to cope with even the most difficult of circumstances. He keeps the faith and reaps the benefits of positive thinking.

Mercury ☐ Jupiter—The native with this aspect cannot keep his promises. His intentions are good, but he bites off more than he can chew. He can procrastinate and become physically ill when his goals are not reached.

Mercury ☍ Jupiter—Depending on the polarities, this aspect can produce stubbornness and unbiased opinions or good judgment and cooperation.

Mercury ☌ Saturn—A serious personality whose hard work, coupled with ambition, can lead to success but cost him the joys of life.

Mercury △/✳ Saturn—This native takes the responsibility of education seriously. He has an excellent memory and practical attitudes that result in success in his profession. He will make sure his portfolio is up to date.

Mercury ☐ Saturn—Negative thinking is easy but causes depression. This native must work to clear his mind of the negative to avoid and overcome the psychosomatic conditions that can afflict him.

Mercury ☍ Saturn—Separation seems to plague this life. Loneliness becomes the result of distrust and suspicion. This can be overcome by efforts to reach out.

Mercury ☌ Uranus—When the energies of this aspect are harnessed, it creates a superior mind. But let those same energies run wild and it will bring destruction.

Mercury △/✳ Uranus—This aspect is quick and ahead of the pack, but can lose patience with those who are not similarly endowed. Individuality can be well expressed through writing.

Mercury □ **Uranus**—The mental forces are strong, intuitive, and prophetic here but this native is seldom understood. He will not be taken seriously unless he harnesses his mental energies and develops tact.

Mercury ⚹ **Uranus**—Thoughts are erratic and difficult to explain. This native will display impatience, which compounds his nervousness and sometimes confusing communications.

Mercury ☌ **Neptune**—Neptune creates inaccuracies in mental function. The objective is to focus on the tried and true and harden to external stimuli.

Mercury △/✳ **Neptune**—This aspect introduces options that can formulate dreams, visions, and the creative mind with which to implement them. The native enters the void and returns inspired.

Mercury □ **Neptune**—This position creates an illusion that will eventually undress the native. He must take seriously, and depend on, his own mental faculties as opposed to picking someone else's mind.

Mercury ⚹ **Neptune**—What we don't see in ourselves, others do. There is a great deal of suffering from the reactions of others to a "wishy-washy" attitude.

Mercury ☌ **Pluto**—This aspect is the signature of psychologists, psychiatrists, and anyone else who deals with the collective unconscious.

Mercury △/✳ **Pluto**—This agile mind can absorb and retain information to everyone's surprise. He can move groups with his logic and influence with his emotions.

Mercury □ **Pluto**—This powerful aspect requires tempering as it can lead to workaholic types. This is a person whose intensity will burn him out.

Mercury ⚹ **Pluto**—Insight and inner strength help to smooth a conflict that is ever present in this native. The world will see him as a rock while he longs for tender love.

ASPECTS TO VENUS

Venus ☌ Mars—Love or lust . . . which is it? This aspect will challenge the native until he can distinguish between the two and act accordingly.

Venus △/✳ Mars—One hand washes the other. Cooperation, love, and kindness add up to tranquillity. The success will be seen in matters of love and money.

Venus □ Mars—The responses of this native tend to feed cruel and violent acts. He must learn to control himself or he will be battered.

Venus ☍ Mars—This native has to be aware of the mood swings that trigger his responses. Practicing self-control is his best ally.

Venus ☌ Jupiter—The grace bestowed on this aspect takes the native far both socially and professionally. This aspect can also produce a detached but cultured personality.

Venus △/✳ Jupiter—This position gives the native a softer approach to others. He will be aware of others' needs, and while he prospers in all areas, he will also share.

Venus □ Jupiter—The need for controlling what would ordinarily be considered good fortune shows up in this aspect. This abundance can lead to over-indulgences that will be manifested in the body.

Venus ☍ Jupiter—This native must not indulge in vanity or wastefulness at the cost of future security.

Venus ☌ Saturn—This conjunction brings a fear that can prohibit love from others or the ability to give love. It will take courage to open up.

Venus △/✳ Saturn—This native has the insight to endure whatever life brings without losing faith. Maturity will reward this individual with caring people and solid relationships.

Venus □ **Saturn**—This aspect brings the inability to understand the meaning of self-love, which results in disappointments in relationships and an eventual sense of loneliness.

Venus ♂° **Saturn**—This aspect is hard to live with but if one can give love to those who are unloving, this karma can be overcome.

Venus ♂ **Uranus**—There are other fish in the ocean, so this native goes looking for them. He can't tell the difference between independence and indifference.

Venus △/✶ **Uranus**—This magnet has to be discreet. He can attract all measure of money and exciting love affairs. He can also find himself starting over . . . not to worry, he can!

Venus □ **Uranus**—Take one step at a time and be willing to redirect. Uranus is a magnet but, in this aspect, there is no guarantee that what is caught has longevity or is beneficial.

Venus ♂° **Uranus**—Don't fence anyone in or they will leave—business or marital partners and/or children. Watch finances.

Venus ♂ **Neptune**—This position creates an instability in love affairs. While reality is not as romantic as love, on a higher plane, reality is more reliable.

Venus △/✶ **Neptune**—The good bestowed upon the native is not easily recognized. The sensitive nature of this individual loves music and tranquil surroundings. He doesn't do well in the corporate world.

Venus □ **Neptune**—This aspect can be overcome by being loving toward all in a universal sense. It does not work well on a one-to-one basis. Care must be given to financial resources or others will help themselves.

Venus ♂° **Neptune**—Doing the unpopular thing for the right reasons can put this native on the road to sacrifice. He needs to take off the rose-colored glasses and strengthen his resolve. Being alone can sometimes lead to insight.

Venus ☌ **Pluto**—This aspect brings a power and strength to the love nature that can result in insatiable lust at any cost. The positive side is a nature that transcends all superficial barriers.

Venus △/✳ **Pluto**—The quiet but powerful magnetism of Pluto ensures the abundance of money, love, respect, opportunities, or whatever else the native might need to succeed.

Venus □ **Pluto**—This aspect can produce an unethical personality who will eventually be exposed. Loneliness will be his companion until he learns to respect and love others.

Venus ☍ **Pluto**—This native can find himself in a love triangle . . . and he will lose. Loving without vested interest will be far more rewarding and safe.

ASPECTS TO MARS

Mars ☌ **Jupiter**—The energy produced by this combination can be either dangerous or inspired. If not disciplined, it's merely risk-taking. If controlled, physical stress can be avoided.

Mars △/✳ **Jupiter**—The expansion of Jupiter can bring an abundance of energy to the athlete or mental prowess to the philosophical mind. The ease of this combination allows for completion of all tasks.

Mars □ **Jupiter**—Depending on the rest of the chart, this aspect can undo the native. He either wants too much of everything or acts in a "hit and run" manner. This aspect requires pondering and self-awareness to make profitable use of these energies.

Mars ☍ **Jupiter**—One can lose sight of what and when is enough, which can be physically damaging or financially dangerous. The intolerance toward others makes for a lonely path.

Mars ☌ **Saturn**—This aspect creates frustration and the inability to push forward no matter how much energy is spent. Power will elude the native.

Mars △/✶ Saturn—Success in business and a willingness to work for it produce good results. The discipline of Mars leads to a steady and fruitful life.

Mars ☐ Saturn—Frustration and a dampening of energy is created by this aspect.

Mars ☍ Saturn—The push/pull of energy quiets the antagonism. Conquer and complete the "unfinished business" brought by Saturn and karmic debts will be paid.

Mars ☌ Uranus—The temperament of this native can lead to his demise. While he appears fearless, his impatience makes him dangerous. The most beneficial undertaking for this native is to care for others tirelessly.

Mars △/✶ Uranus—The correct use of this aspect makes for an exciting, adventurous character. He will be on the move looking for what's new in the world.

Mars ☐ Uranus—This aspect will quickly show the results of unwise decisions. The sudden violence that can erupt will leave no time for regrets. Through recklessness, the native draws and courts disaster.

Mars ☍ Uranus—This native will be faced with having to control the disruptive and bad-tempered people drawn to him. The situation can be diffused by learning not to react.

Mars ☌ Neptune—Neptune waters down the energies of Mars, leaving a frightened and sometimes disruptive personality. Self-actualization can bring about a responsible, disciplined, and advanced individual.

Mars △/✶ Neptune—An active but hidden guardian angel is at work. Dreams are fulfilled, while distractions are ineffective.

Mars ☐ Neptune—Clear, direct, and honest communications are a must. Actions backed by good motives are the way to avoid difficulties. Alcohol is detrimental to mind and body.

Mars ☍ Neptune—This native can be taken by others. Deception and deceit must be avoided. Making sacrifices for others can be of benefit.

Mars ☌ Pluto—Gentle, loving actions succeed where bullish destructive actions fail.

Mars △/✷ Pluto—This self-reliant and self-motivated athlete or corporate head achieves. This aspect also shows occult abilities.

Mars □ Pluto—Controlling the tiger within can avoid a violent, internal struggle. Be careful!

Mars ☍ Pluto—The native must be alert to the influences of others or he will fall into a path of destruction.

ASPECTS TO JUPITER

Jupiter ☌ Saturn—This native can be effective when wise enough to get the hang of his life's expanding path.

Jupiter △/✷ Saturn—This aspect doesn't let you kid yourself. The native works for what he desires and achieves.

Jupiter □ Saturn—This aspect calls for the native to face his responsibilities. In not doing so, he can flitter away his talents and opportunities.

Jupiter ☍ Saturn—Reclusive or outgoing? The choice will be made through the maturation process.

Jupiter ☌ Uranus—The ability to couple strong intuition with creative powers makes this combination forceful if not unconventional.

Jupiter △/✷ Uranus—Whatever the native pursues is attained. Good fortune allows him to capitalize on all opportunities.

Jupiter □ Uranus—Patience will calm the irritability of this aspect. The mind is fast and follow-through is spontaneous.

Jupiter ☍ Uranus—Religious pursuit will cause this native to challenge the dogma of established institutions. Judgment must be checked to see if it is trustworthy.

Jupiter ☌ Neptune—The emotions are on a roller-coaster ride. This aspect can have the native paying lip service when his courage fails.

Jupiter △/✳ Neptune—The chance to put together thought and action results in a sedate, kind, and almost mystical personality.

Jupiter ☐ Neptune—Constrict thoughts and actions or fall into the hands of unscrupulous people.

Jupiter ☍ Neptune—Watch the body—it will pay for all lack of control. Stop depending on others; heal thyself.

Jupiter ☌ Pluto—A leader must attain self-mastery. Only then can he achieve with ease the recognition, admiration, and cooperation of others.

Jupiter △/✳ Pluto—This native has the strength to succeed no matter what. He must help himself as well as others.

Jupiter ☐ Pluto—This aspect doesn't assure one's power, which leads to constant testing. This can be a waste of time, bringing only self-deception.

Jupiter ☍ Pluto—The instability with which this native operates is testimony to his anxieties about his self-importance.

ASPECTS TO SATURN

Saturn ☌ Uranus—This native usually shows only the tip of the iceberg. The danger lies in an unexpected reaction that can destroy all of his accomplishments.

Saturn △/✳ Uranus—This native can sort the value of the old from the outmoded. He grows toward the new without offending.

Saturn ☐ Uranus—The way to freedom is to face responsibilities. When that is done, Uranus will drive this native.

Saturn ⚷ Uranus—Security drawn from what is tried and true can lead to boredom. Avoid impulsive acts for they will not remedy this situation. There could be many losses.

Saturn ☌ Neptune—Neptune can deepen fears, and depression can lead to withdrawal. Facing limitations will lead to forward movement.

Saturn △/✶ Neptune—Psychic abilities can produce tangible results.

Saturn □ Neptune—Perhaps the hardest of aspects, this native endures irrational fears. Safety lies in acquiring a God-oriented philosophy.

Saturn ⚷ Neptune—Striking a balance between spirituality and materialism can benefit this native. He will find himself having to choose constantly.

Saturn ☌ Pluto—This native cannot handle superficial people or acts. His seriousness about life leads him to sort out what is truly important.

Saturn △/✶ Pluto—This slow, methodical, and trustworthy native will succeed in his endeavors but must not expect others to function as he does.

Saturn □ Pluto—The need to express individuality may cause pain and upheaval. Lessons will be passed on for the use of future generations.

Saturn ⚷ Pluto—What is brought by this aspect to the native can be the greatest challenge of his life. To hang on, no matter how unfair, difficult, or trying, is to conquer the fear of all vulnerability.

ASPECTS TO URANUS

Uranus ☌ Neptune—There is an insecurity about personal freedom. Reform of social or personal conditions will be made. New drugs on the market might have adverse effects.

Uranus △/✶ Neptune—The realization that one has a spirit and the desire to express it occurs with this aspect. Those around might not understand or see the value. Go for it.

Uranus □ **Neptune**—Keep the mind healthy, whether by good nutrition or a positive attitude. Avoid joining strange groups without investigating carefully. What is new is not necessarily good.

Uranus ☍ **Neptune**—Putting a handle on what this aspect can bring will require a great deal of grounding. The opportunity to rise above a boring life can lead to strange encounters. Be careful.

Uranus ☌ **Pluto**—This aspect prompts changes. It brings cleansing and healing of the environment, medicine, or one's psyche.

Uranus △/✳ **Pluto**—There will be a slow but methodical exploration of one's life. The result will be changes, growth, and transformation. Karmic debts are being paid.

Uranus □ **Pluto**—This native is prone to upheaval and will not be able to stay put. Regeneration of the self becomes a must for survival.

Uranus ☍ **Pluto**—Life is filled with deception and upheaval. One must learn to take it in stride.

ASPECTS TO NEPTUNE

Neptune ☌ **Pluto**—Adventurous personality with unusual ideas and objectives.

Neptune △/✳ **Pluto**—Justice in all endeavors is key.

Neptune □ **Pluto**—Persevering, knowing what is right, and gently letting go of what is not, will prevent falling into the wrong hands.

Neptune ☍ **Pluto**—It's time to clean closets and unload material or mental/psychological debris. Lighten the load and live.

⚻ QUINCUNX

A quincunx is a 150-degree angle between two planets. Since this aspect is 30 degrees short of being an opposition, it leaves you flapping in the breeze.

A quincunx creates a difficulty, an irritation, or a lack of harmony. It is called a neurotic genius aspect, which is not a bad thing. Oriental philosophy says that to polish a gem, there must be friction. In a quincunx, there is enormous friction. If you are grumpy, crabby, and not working out or reconciling your feelings, that's all you're ever going to be and you will get stuck in your tracks. But if you use a quincunx well, the byproduct of friction and discord will be harmony.

GRAND TRINE

When the three Sun Signs of each element (fire, earth, air, or water) are all in trine position to each other, it is called a grand trine. Although trines are considered lucky, a grand trine is basically equated with laziness and a lackadaisical attitude.

GRAND CROSS

A grand cross is created by the four signs of any quadruplicity being in a square to one another. The "cross" is formed by the two sets of oppositions that intersect in the chart. A grand cross influences the mind/body connection of a chart. This is a difficult aspect to handle because, although it can be dynamic, it is also hard to keep this energy in balance. As they say, what doesn't kill you will make you stronger.

There are three types of grand crosses, each emphasizing the unique quality of either cardinal, fixed, or mutable:

Cardinal Grand Cross—The cardinal grand cross represents initiation and action, powerful energies that can destroy or create. It is will versus soul, reflecting where you have taken your soul, where you stand, and your status in this world.

Fixed Grand Cross—In the fixed grand cross, the strength of body and mind will be challenged. To know oneself, be disciplined, and give to others requires a trust that individuals with this cross do not naturally possess. This is the embodiment of the paradox of "what you hold, you will lose; what you give, you will have."

Mutable Grand Cross—The mutable grand cross creates a nervous tension that is calling for change. One must give up, change, or release uncertainty. It is time to review, not criticize.

TEE SQUARE

Suppose one of the four planets was missing from a grand cross—you have an opposition and two squares, but there's an empty leg. So, instead of having four planets in square positions to one another, you only have three. That is what is called a tee square. And it is really going to throw you out of kilter.

The tee square can only be reconciled by the empty leg. The empty leg creates the ability to reconcile the other three planets, but not with ease. It is always a difficult situation when you have a tee square. It brings a lot of energy, but you must learn to use and direct that energy in a way that is advantageous to yourself and for the benefit of others. Although tee squares are difficult, they can, ultimately, show you the way. They keep your strength up. They are necessary to accomplish.

TRANSITS

The day, hour, and place of your birth create your natal chart. That's a frozen moment of time that will not change. However, all the planets represented in your chart at the time of your birth have now moved on, each according to its own velocity. That movement is called a separation aspect. This is important because maturation occurs through the impact of planets as they continue to move—to transit.

That frozen moment of your birth is a recording of your innate and inherited traits, personality, and potential. The natal chart and its aspects are important because they form your foundation. To understand what can be developed out of that foundation and how you handle this maturation will be influenced by transits.

To find out past, present, and future transits, you can consult the following resources:

- an ephemeris
- one of many astrological Internet sites
- daily newspaper horoscopes (transits are often mentioned)
- a monthly astrology periodical or annual horoscope/forecast book

RETROGRADE TRANSITS

A retrograde is an apparent backward motion—a loss of velocity in comparison to the Earth. The highest level of tension will occur at the point where the planet appears to be stationary before retrograding. Each planet will carry its own message and will affect your chart accordingly.

Mercury Retrograde—This happens three times a year, always in a different constellation; therefore, some will be easy to handle and others will be difficult. Communications will be delayed or lost. Signing of contracts or other commitments will be unclear. You will have wished you read the small print. Luckily, this retrograde lasts for only three weeks.

Venus Retrograde—Venus will be retrograding for six weeks, during which time there will be an effect on women at large. Diplomacy will more than likely get us what we need even during this difficult time.

Mars Retrograde—This occurs for ten weeks every two years. This cycle gives us a chance to review our jobs or love affairs. If all is well, a direct Mars will not destroy the relationship. We will probably stay on the job but look toward a promotion.

Jupiter Retrograde—Jupiter spends two and a half months retrograding. The point of retrograde varies from year to year, but the effects are important to the chart. It is an opportunity to see if you are aware of how you relate to others. The retrograde will give feedback on the effects.

Saturn Retrograde—Saturn retrogrades for about four and a half months. You can be sure you will note it because it takes your energy and forces you to be patient. It asks that you sort out your responsibilities and apply yourself to worthwhile endeavors.

Uranus Retrograde—Uranus retrogrades for about five months. It will give you the opportunity to review that new idea you thought was great. Will it work out? Build a better mousetrap or work with time. This retrograde forces a closer look at unconventionalites.

Neptune Retrograde—Neptune retrogrades for about five months. Because it is in each house for fourteen years, it is important to understand the house in which it is retrograding. The fear that can surface during a Neptune retrograde can destroy the positive creativity of the individual.

Pluto Retrograde—Pluto retrogrades for about six months. Its travel is slow and eccentric, causing great stress for the house it is occupying. The opportunity to rectify your goals is present, as Pluto provides a wealth of information.

Appendix

Glossary

affliction: An unfavorable aspect to a planet in an astrological chart.

air signs: The three Sun Signs associated with mentality—Gemini, Libra, and Aquarius.

ascendant: The sign of the Zodiac rising over the eastern horizon at the time of birth. Also referred to as the rising sign.

aspect: The relationship between planets measured in degrees.

astrological chart: A diagram of the placement of planets in signs and houses of a pivotal, timed moment of inception such as a birth, marriage, start of a business, and so on.

astrology: The art and science of analyzing human development and events by the effects of the position and movement of zodiacal signs and planets.

birth chart: A diagram of the placement of planets in signs and houses at a person's date and time of birth.

cardinal cross: A group of four signs—Aries, Cancer, Libra, and Capricorn—that are positioned in opposition to one another in the natural Zodiac and share similar characteristics of initiative and action.

collective unconscious: Term coined by psychologist Carl Jung that refers to the concept of a universal field or bank of knowledge that can be tapped by those who are psychically evolved.

conjunction: Two planets that occupy the same position or degree or are in close proximity to each other.

constellation: A band of stars in the universe. Twelve of these bands represent the twelve signs of the Zodiac.

cross: Four planets in opposition to each other that share certain dynamic qualities. There are three crosses—cardinal, fixed, and mutable. Also referred to as quadruplicity or mode.

cusp: The dividing line at which an astrological sign or house begins.

decanate: One of three 10-degree segments of a 30-degree zodiacal Sun Sign.

descendant: The opposition point of the ascendant in an astrological chart occurring on the western horizon. Equal to the seventh house or sunset part of a day.

Dragon's Head/Dragon's Tail: See MOON NODES.

earth signs: The three Sun Signs associated with practicality and groundedness—Taurus, Virgo, and Capricorn.

ecliptic: The orbit of the Earth and the apparent orbit of the Sun.

elements: Four elements—fire, earth, air, and water—each consisting of three signs that share similar characteristics. Also referred to as triplicities.

ephemeris: A reference guide that shows exact planetary positions for any day, month, or year.

esoteric astrology: The study of the symbolic meaning of the planets and signs.

fire signs: The three Sun Signs associated with enthusiasm and impulsiveness—Aries, Leo, and Sagittarius.

fixed cross: A group of four signs—Taurus, Leo, Scorpio, and Aquarius—that are positioned in opposition to one another in the natural Zodiac and share similar characteristics of determination and rigidity.

geocentric: The astrological perspective placing the Earth rather than the Sun at the center of planetary movement.

glyph: A symbol that represents an astrological sign, planet, or aspect.

grand trine: A triangle formed by three planets positioned 120 degrees from one another.

horoscope: See ASTROLOGICAL CHART.

houses: The twelve segments of an astrological chart.

imum coeli (IC): See NADIR.

karma: The results that a person's actions bring upon himself during the whole of his existence.

mandala: The birth chart or horoscope.

medium coeli (MC): See MIDHEAVEN.

midheaven: The upper meridian or noon position in an astrological chart. Occurs in the tenth house.

mode: See CROSS.

Moon Nodes: The north and south points on the ecliptic where the Moon crosses it. The North Node is also referred to as the Dragon's Head; the South Node is also referred to as the Dragon's Tail.

mutable cross: A group of four signs—Gemini, Virgo, Sagittarius, and Pisces—that are positioned in opposition to one another in the natural Zodiac and share similar characteristics of adaptability and flexibility.

nadir: The lower meridian of an astrological chart or the fourth house (also called IC).

natal chart: See BIRTH CHART.

native: The person for whom a horoscope is made.

North Node: See MOON NODES. Also referred to as the Dragon's Head.

opposition: Two planets that are in a 180-degree aspect to each other or opposing each other.

planets: The ten celestial bodies that influence astrology. The Sun (a star) and the Moon (a satellite of Earth) are considered planets for the purposes of astrology.

polarity: Signs in opposition to each other within the Zodiac.

quadruplicity: See CROSS.

quincunx: Two planets that are in a 150-degree aspect to each other.

retrograde: The loss of velocity of a planet that makes it appear to be traveling backward.

rising sign: See ASCENDANT.

sextile: Two planets that are in a 60-degree aspect to each other.

sign: The zodiacal constellation that any planet falls into in an astrological chart.

South Node: See MOON NODES. Also referred to as the Dragon's Tail.

square: Two planets that are in a 90-degree aspect to each other. Indicative of a difficulty that needs to be overcome.

Sun Sign: One of the twelve signs of the Zodiac, each embodying unique personality characteristics.

transit: The movement of a planet through a sign, or house, or over another planet.

trine: Two planets in a 120-degree aspect to each other. Usually indicates a harmonious situation.

triplicity: See ELEMENTS.

water signs: The three Sun Signs that are associated with emotion and sensitivity—Cancer, Scorpio, and Pisces.

Zodiac: A belt of fixed stars that circles the Earth, divided into twelve sections representing the constellations of Aries, Taurus, Gemini, Cancer, Leo, Virgo, Libra, Scorpio, Sagittarius, Capricorn, Aquarius, and Pisces.

Planet Finder

How to Use This Section

The purpose of the Planet Finder is to easily and readily help you determine the placement of the planets (by sign) at the time of your birth. Please note that many of these listings are approximations and do not guarantee total accuracy. For a more accurate and thorough depiction of your birth chart, it is recommended you have your birth information calculated by a professional astrologer, a computer software program, or astrological chart service.

Once you have looked up your planets, you can log this information onto the worksheet at the back of this book, or just refer to the corresponding section in the preceding chapters.

Rising Signs

The following calculations are only valid if you were born in North America, and they are only approximations. If the rising sign listed feels inappropriate, move back to the previous sign or ahead to the next sign and see if these ascendant descriptions are more a reflection of your outward persona.

Sign	JANUARY	FEBRUARY	MARCH	APRIL	MAY	JUNE
ARIES	11:00A–12:15P	9:00–10:15A	7:00–8:15A	5:00–6:15A	3:00–4:15A	1:00–2:15A
TAURUS	12:15–2:00P	10:15A–12:00P	8:15–10:00A	6:15–8:00A	4:15–6:00A	2:15–4:00A
GEMINI	2:00–4:00P	12:00–2:00P	10:00A–12:00P	8:00–10:00A	6:00–8:00A	4:00–6:00A
CANCER	4:00–6:30P	2:00–4:30P	12:00–2:30P	10:00A–12:30P	8:00–10:30A	6:00–8:30A
LEO	6:30–9:00P	4:30–7:00P	2:30–5:00P	12:30–3:00P	10:30–1:00P	8:30–11:00A
VIRGO	9:00–11:30P	7:00–9:30P	5:00–7:30P	3:00–5:30P	1:00–3:30P	11:00A–1:30P
LIBRA	11:30P–2:00A	9:30P–12:00A	7:30–10:00P	5:30–8:00P	3:30–6:00P	1:30–4:00P
SCORPIO	2:00–4:30A	12:00–2:30A	10:00P–12:30A	8:00–10:30P	6:00–7:15P	4:00–6:30P
SAGITTARIUS	4:30–6:45A	2:30–4:45A	12:30–2:45A	10:30P–12:30A	7:15–10:45P	6:30–9:00P
CAPRICORN	6:45–8:30A	4:45–6:30A	2:45–4:30A	12:30–2:30A	10:45P–12:30A	9:00–10:30P
AQUARIUS	8:30–9:45A	6:30–7:45A	4:30–5:45A	2:30–3:45A	12:30–1:45A	10:30–11:45P
PISCES	9:45–11:00A	7:45–9:00A	5:45–7:00A	3:45–5:00A	1:45–3:00A	11:45P–1:00A

Sign	JULY	AUGUST	SEPTEMBER	OCTOBER	NOVEMBER	DECEMBER
ARIES	11:00A–12:15A	9:00–10:15P	7:00–8:15P	5:00–6:15P	3:00–4:15P	1:00–2:15P
TAURUS	12:15–2:00A	10:15P–12:00A	8:15–10:00P	6:15–8:00P	4:15–6:00P	2:15–4:00P
GEMINI	2:00–4:00A	12:00–2:00A	10:00P–12:00A	8:00–10:00P	6:00–8:00P	4:00–6:00P
CANCER	4:00–6:30A	2:00–4:30A	12:00–2:30A	10:00P–12:30A	8:00–10:30P	6:00–8:30P
LEO	6:30–9:00A	4:30–7:00A	2:30–5:00A	12:30–3:00A	10:30P–1:00A	8:30–11:00P
VIRGO	9:00–11:30A	7:00–9:30A	5:00–7:30A	3:00–5:30A	1:00–3:30A	11:00P–1:30A
LIBRA	11:30A–2:00P	9:30A–12:00P	7:30–10:00A	5:30–8:00A	3:30–6:00A	1:30–4:00A
SCORPIO	2:00–4:30P	12:00–2:30P	10:00A–12:30P	8:00–10:30A	6:00–8:30A	4:00–6:30A
SAGITTARIUS	4:30–7:00P	2:30–5:00P	12:30–3:00P	10:30A–1:00P	8:30–11:00A	6:30–9:00A
CAPRICORN	7:00–8:30P	5:00–6:30P	3:00–4:30P	1:00–2:30P	11:00A–12:30P	9:00–10:30A
AQUARIUS	8:30–9:45P	6:30–7:45P	4:30–5:45P	2:30–3:45P	12:30–1:45P	10:30–11:45A
PISCES	9:45–11:00P	7:45–9:00P	5:45–7:00P	3:45–5:00P	1:45–3:00P	11:45A–1:00P

Moon

The following tables show Moon sign changes through the years. To locate the placement of your Moon, look for the year of your birth and then look across the column for your birth date. If your actual birth date is not listed, refer to the date *before* your date of birth and note the sign listed. This will be your Moon sign.

1925

JAN—**1** ARI **3** TAU **5** GEM **8** CAN **10** LEO **13** VIR **15** LIB **17** SCO **20** SAG **22** CAP **24** AQU **26** PIS **28** ARI **30** TAU
FEB—**2** GEM **4** CAN **7** LEO **9** VIR **11** LIB **14** SCO **16** SAG **18** CAP **20** AQU **22** PIS **24** ARI **26** TAU
MAR—**1** GEM **3** CAN **6** LEO **8** VIR **11** LIB **13** SCO **15** SAG **17** CAP **19** AQU **21** PIS **24** ARI **26** TAU **28** GEM **31** CAN
APR—**2** LEO **5** VIR **7** LIB **9** SCO **11** SAG **13** CAP **16** AQU **18** PIS **20** ARI **22** TAU **25** GEM **27** CAN **30** LEO
MAY—**2** VIR **4** LIB **7** SCO **9** SAG **11** CAP **13** AQU **15** PIS **17** ARI **19** TAU **22** GEM **24** CAN **27** LEO **29** VIR
JUN—**1** LIB **3** SCO **5** SAG **7** CAP **9** AQU **11** PIS **13** ARI **16** TAU **18** GEM **21** CAN **23** LEO **26** VIR **28** LIB **30** SCO
JUL—**3** SAG **5** CAP **7** AQU **9** PIS **11** ARI **13** TAU **15** GEM **18** CAN **20** LEO **23** VIR **25** LIB **28** SCO **30** SAG
AUG—**1** CAP **3** AQU **5** PIS **7** ARI **9** TAU **12** GEM **14** CAN **17** LEO **19** VIR **22** LIB **24** SCO **26** SAG **28** CAP **30** AQU
SEP—**1** PIS **4** ARI **6** TAU **8** GEM **10** CAN **13** LEO **15** VIR **18** LIB **20** SCO **22** SAG **25** CAP **27** AQU **29** PIS
OCT—**1** ARI **3** TAU **5** GEM **8** CAN **10** LEO **13** VIR **15** LIB **18** SCO **20** SAG **22** CAP **24** AQU **26** PIS **28** ARI **30** TAU
NOV—**2** GEM **4** CAN **7** LEO **9** VIR **12** LIB **14** SCO **16** SAG **18** CAP **20** AQU **22** PIS **25** ARI **27** TAU **29** GEM
DEC—**1** CAN **4** LEO **6** VIR **9** LIB **11** SCO **13** SAG **16** CAP **18** AQU **20** PIS **22** ARI **24** TAU **26** GEM **29** CAN **31** LEO

1926

JAN—**1** LEO **3** VIR **5** LIB **8** SCO **10** SAG **12** CAP **14** AQU **16** PIS **18** ARI **20** TAU **23** GEM **25** CAN **27** LEO **30** VIR
FEB—**2** LIB **4** SCO **6** SAG **8** CAP **10** AQU **12** PIS **14** ARI **17** TAU **19** GEM **21** CAN **24** LEO **26** VIR
MAR—**1** LIB **3** SCO **6** SAG **8** CAP **10** AQU **12** PIS **14** ARI **16** TAU **18** GEM **21** CAN **23** LEO **26** VIR **28** LIB **30** SCO
APR—**2** SAG **4** CAP **6** AQU **8** PIS **10** ARI **12** TAU **15** GEM **17** CAN **19** LEO **22** VIR **24** LIB **27** SCO **29** SAG
MAY—**1** CAP **3** AQU **6** PIS **8** ARI **10** TAU **12** GEM **14** CAN **17** LEO **19** VIR **22** LIB **24** SCO **26** SAG **29** CAP **31** AQU
JUN—**2** PIS **4** ARI **6** TAU **8** GEM **11** CAN **13** LEO **16** VIR **18** LIB **20** SCO **23** SAG **25** CAP **27** AQU **29** PIS
JUL—**1** ARI **3** TAU **6** GEM **8** CAN **10** LEO **13** VIR **15** LIB **18** SCO **20** SAG **22** CAP **24** AQU **26** PIS **28** ARI **31** TAU
AUG—**2** GEM **4** CAN **7** LEO **9** VIR **12** LIB **14** SCO **17** SAG **19** CAP **21** AQU **23** PIS **25** ARI **27** TAU **29** GEM **31** CAN
SEP—**3** LEO **5** VIR **8** LIB **10** SCO **13** SAG **15** CAP **17** AQU **19** PIS **21** ARI **23** TAU **25** GEM **28** CAN **30** LEO
OCT—**3** VIR **5** LIB **8** SCO **10** SAG **12** CAP **15** AQU **17** PIS **19** ARI **21** TAU **23** GEM **25** CAN **27** LEO **30** VIR
NOV—**1** LIB **4** SCO **6** SAG **9** CAP **11** AQU **13** PIS **15** ARI **17** TAU **19** GEM **21** CAN **24** LEO **26** VIR **29** LIB
DEC—**1** SCO **4** SAG **6** CAP **8** AQU **10** PIS **12** ARI **14** TAU **17** GEM **19** CAN **21** LEO **24** VIR **26** LIB **29** SCO **31** SAG

1927

JAN—**1** SAG **2** CAP **4** AQU **6** PIS **9** ARI **11** TAU **13** GEM **15** CAN **17** LEO **20** VIR **22** LIB **25** SCO **27** SAG **30** CAP
FEB—**1** AQU **3** PIS **5** ARI **7** TAU **9** GEM **11** CAN **14** LEO **16** VIR **19** LIB **21** SCO **24** SAG **26** CAP **28** AQU
MAR—**2** PIS **4** ARI **6** TAU **8** GEM **11** CAN **13** LEO **15** VIR **18** LIB **21** SCO **23** SAG **25** CAP **28** AQU **30** PIS
APR—**1** ARI **3** TAU **5** GEM **7** CAN **9** LEO **12** VIR **14** LIB **17** SCO **19** SAG **22** CAP **24** AQU **26** PIS **28** ARI **30** TAU
MAY—**2** GEM **4** CAN **7** LEO **9** VIR **12** LIB **14** SCO **16** SAG **19** CAP **21** AQU **23** PIS **25** ARI **28** TAU **30** GEM
JUN—**1** CAN **3** LEO **5** VIR **8** LIB **10** SCO **13** SAG **15** CAP **17** AQU **20** PIS **22** ARI **24** TAU **26** GEM **28** CAN **30** LEO
JUL—**3** VIR **5** LIB **8** SCO **10** SAG **13** CAP **15** AQU **17** PIS **19** ARI **21** TAU **23** GEM **25** CAN **28** LEO **30** VIR
AUG—**1** LIB **4** SCO **7** SAG **9** CAP **11** AQU **13** PIS **15** ARI **17** TAU **19** GEM **22** CAN **24** LEO **26** VIR **29** LIB **31** SCO
SEP—**3** SAG **5** CAP **8** AQU **10** PIS **12** ARI **14** TAU **16** GEM **18** CAN **20** LEO **23** VIR **25** LIB **28** SCO **30** SAG
OCT—**3** CAP **5** AQU **7** PIS **9** ARI **11** TAU **13** GEM **15** CAN **17** LEO **20** VIR **22** LIB **25** SCO **27** SAG **30** CAP
NOV—**1** AQU **3** PIS **6** ARI **8** TAU **10** GEM **12** CAN **14** LEO **16** VIR **19** LIB **21** SCO **24** SAG **26** CAP **28** AQU
DEC—**1** PIS **3** ARI **5** TAU **7** GEM **9** CAN **11** LEO **13** VIR **16** LIB **18** SCO **21** SAG **23** CAP **26** AQU **28** PIS **30** ARI

1928

JAN—**1** TAU **3** GEM **5** CAN **8** LEO **10** VIR **12** LIB **15** SCO **17** SAG **20** CAP **22** AQU **24** PIS **26** ARI **28** TAU **31** GEM
FEB—**2** CAN **4** LEO **6** VIR **9** LIB **11** SCO **14** SAG **16** CAP **18** AQU **21** PIS **23** ARI **25** TAU **27** GEM **29** CAN
MAR—**2** LEO **5** VIR **7** LIB **9** SCO **12** SAG **14** CAP **17** AQU **19** PIS **21** ARI **23** TAU **25** GEM **27** CAN **29** LEO
APR—**1** VIR **3** LIB **6** SCO **8** SAG **11** CAP **13** AQU **15** PIS **18** ARI **20** TAU **22** GEM **24** CAN **26** LEO **28** VIR **30** LIB
MAY—**3** SCO **5** SAG **8** CAP **10** AQU **13** PIS **15** ARI **17** TAU **19** GEM **21** CAN **23** LEO **25** VIR **28** LIB **30** SCO
JUN—**2** SAG **4** CAP **7** AQU **9** PIS **11** ARI **13** TAU **15** GEM **17** CAN **19** LEO **22** VIR **24** LIB **26** SCO **29** SAG
JUL—**2** CAP **4** AQU **6** PIS **9** ARI **11** TAU **13** GEM **15** CAN **17** LEO **19** VIR **21** LIB **24** SCO **26** SAG **29** CAP **31** AQU
AUG—**3** PIS **5** ARI **7** TAU **9** GEM **11** CAN **13** LEO **15** VIR **18** LIB **20** SCO **23** SAG **25** CAP **28** AQU **30** PIS
SEP—**1** ARI **3** TAU **5** GEM **7** CAN **10** LEO **12** VIR **14** LIB **16** SCO **19** SAG **22** CAP **24** AQU **26** PIS **28** ARI **30** TAU
OCT—**3** GEM **5** CAN **7** LEO **9** VIR **11** LIB **14** SCO **16** SAG **19** CAP **21** AQU **24** PIS **26** ARI **28** TAU **30** GEM
NOV—**1** CAN **3** LEO **5** VIR **8** LIB **10** SCO **13** SAG **15** CAP **18** AQU **20** PIS **22** ARI **24** TAU **26** GEM **28** CAN **30** LEO
DEC—**3** VIR **5** LIB **7** SCO **10** SAG **12** CAP **15** AQU **17** PIS **20** ARI **22** TAU **24** GEM **26** CAN **28** LEO **30** VIR

1929

JAN—**1** LIB **4** SCO **6** SAG **9** CAP **11** AQU **14** PIS **16** ARI **18** TAU **20** GEM **22** CAN **24** LEO **26** VIR **29** LIB **31** SCO
FEB—**2** SAG **5** CAP **7** AQU **10** PIS **12** ARI **14** TAU **16** GEM **19** CAN **21** LEO **23** VIR **25** LIB **27** SCO
MAR—**2** SAG **4** CAP **7** AQU **9** PIS **11** ARI **14** TAU **16** GEM **18** CAN **20** LEO **22** VIR **24** LIB **27** SCO **29** SAG
APR—**1** CAP **3** AQU **5** PIS **8** ARI **10** TAU **12** GEM **14** CAN **16** LEO **18** VIR **21** LIB **23** SCO **25** SAG **28** CAP **30** AQU
MAY—**3** PIS **5** ARI **7** TAU **9** GEM **11** CAN **13** LEO **16** VIR **18** LIB **20** SCO **23** SAG **25** CAP **28** AQU **30** PIS
JUN—**2** ARI **4** TAU **6** GEM **8** CAN **10** LEO **12** VIR **14** LIB **16** SCO **19** SAG **21** CAP **24** AQU **26** PIS **29** ARI
JUL—**1** TAU **3** GEM **5** CAN **7** LEO **9** VIR **11** LIB **14** SCO **16** SAG **19** CAP **21** AQU **24** PIS **26** ARI **28** TAU **31** GEM
AUG—**2** CAN **4** LEO **6** VIR **8** LIB **10** SCO **12** SAG **15** CAP **17** AQU **20** PIS **22** ARI **25** TAU **27** GEM **29** CAN **31** LEO
SEP—**2** VIR **4** LIB **6** SCO **9** SAG **11** CAP **14** AQU **16** PIS **19** ARI **21** TAU **23** GEM **25** CAN **27** LEO **29** VIR
OCT—**2** LIB **4** SCO **6** SAG **9** CAP **11** AQU **14** PIS **16** ARI **18** TAU **20** GEM **22** CAN **25** LEO **27** VIR **29** LIB **31** SCO
NOV—**2** SAG **5** CAP **7** AQU **10** PIS **12** ARI **15** TAU **17** GEM **19** CAN **21** LEO **23** VIR **25** LIB **27** SCO **30** SAG
DEC—**2** CAP **5** AQU **7** PIS **10** ARI **12** TAU **14** GEM **16** CAN **18** LEO **20** VIR **22** LIB **25** SCO **27** SAG **30** CAP

1930

JAN—**1** AQU **4** PIS **6** ARI **8** TAU **11** GEM **13** CAN **15** LEO **17** VIR **19** LIB **21** SCO **23** SAG **26** CAP **28** AQU **31** PIS
FEB—**2** ARI **5** TAU **7** GEM **9** CAN **11** LEO **13** VIR **15** LIB **17** SCO **20** SAG **22** CAP **25** AQU **27** PIS
MAR—**2** ARI **4** TAU **6** GEM **8** CAN **10** LEO **12** VIR **15** LIB **17** SCO **19** SAG **21** CAP **24** AQU **26** PIS **29** ARI **31** TAU
APR—**2** GEM **5** CAN **7** LEO **9** VIR **11** LIB **13** SCO **15** SAG **18** CAP **20** AQU **23** PIS **25** ARI **28** TAU **30** GEM
MAY—**2** CAN **4** LEO **6** VIR **8** LIB **10** SCO **13** SAG **15** CAP **18** AQU **20** PIS **23** ARI **25** TAU **27** GEM **29** CAN **31** LEO
JUN—**2** VIR **4** LIB **7** SCO **9** SAG **11** CAP **14** AQU **16** PIS **19** ARI **21** TAU **24** GEM **26** CAN **28** LEO **30** VIR
JUL—**2** LIB **4** SCO **6** SAG **9** CAP **11** AQU **14** PIS **16** ARI **19** TAU **21** GEM **23** CAN **25** LEO **27** VIR **29** LIB **31** SCO
AUG—**2** SAG **5** CAP **7** AQU **10** PIS **12** ARI **15** TAU **17** GEM **19** CAN **21** LEO **23** VIR **25** LIB **28** SCO **30** SAG
SEP—**1** CAP **4** AQU **6** PIS **9** ARI **11** TAU **14** GEM **16** CAN **18** LEO **20** VIR **22** LIB **24** SCO **26** SAG **28** CAP
OCT—**1** AQU **3** PIS **6** ARI **8** TAU **11** GEM **13** CAN **15** LEO **17** VIR **19** LIB **21** SCO **24** SAG **26** CAP **28** AQU **31** PIS
NOV—**2** ARI **5** TAU **7** GEM **9** CAN **11** LEO **13** VIR **16** LIB **18** SCO **20** SAG **22** CAP **25** AQU **27** PIS **30** ARI
DEC—**2** TAU **4** GEM **7** CAN **9** LEO **11** VIR **13** LIB **15** SCO **17** SAG **20** CAP **22** AQU **24** PIS **27** ARI **29** TAU

1931

JAN—**1** GEM **3** CAN **5** LEO **7** VIR **9** LIB **11** SCO **13** SAG **16** CAP **18** AQU **21** PIS **23** ARI **26** TAU **28** GEM **30** CAN
FEB—**1** LEO **3** VIR **5** LIB **8** SCO **10** SAG **12** CAP **15** AQU **17** PIS **20** ARI **22** TAU **25** GEM **27** CAN
MAR—**1** LEO **3** VIR **5** LIB **7** SCO **9** SAG **11** CAP **14** AQU **16** PIS **19** ARI **21** TAU **24** GEM **26** CAN **28** LEO **30** VIR
APR—**1** LIB **3** SCO **5** SAG **8** CAP **10** AQU **13** PIS **15** ARI **18** TAU **20** GEM **22** CAN **25** LEO **27** VIR **29** LIB
MAY—**1** SCO **3** SAG **5** CAP **7** AQU **10** PIS **12** ARI **15** TAU **17** GEM **20** CAN **22** LEO **24** VIR **26** LIB **28** SCO **30** SAG
JUN—**1** CAP **4** AQU **6** PIS **9** ARI **11** TAU **14** GEM **16** CAN **18** LEO **20** VIR **22** LIB **24** SCO **27** SAG **29** CAP
JUL—**1** AQU **4** PIS **6** ARI **9** TAU **11** GEM **13** CAN **15** LEO **17** VIR **20** LIB **22** SCO **24** SAG **26** CAP **28** AQU **31** PIS
AUG—**2** ARI **5** TAU **7** GEM **10** CAN **12** LEO **14** VIR **16** LIB **18** SCO **20** SAG **22** CAP **25** AQU **27** PIS **30** ARI
SEP—**1** TAU **4** GEM **6** CAN **8** LEO **10** VIR **12** LIB **14** SCO **16** SAG **19** CAP **21** AQU **23** PIS **26** ARI **28** TAU
OCT—**1** GEM **3** CAN **6** LEO **8** VIR **10** LIB **12** SCO **14** SAG **16** CAP **18** AQU **21** PIS **23** ARI **26** TAU **28** GEM **31** CAN
NOV—**2** LEO **4** VIR **6** LIB **8** SCO **10** SAG **12** CAP **14** AQU **17** PIS **19** ARI **22** TAU **24** GEM **27** CAN **29** LEO
DEC—**1** VIR **3** LIB **6** SCO **8** SAG **10** CAP **12** AQU **14** PIS **17** ARI **19** TAU **22** GEM **24** CAN **26** LEO **29** VIR **31** LIB

1932

JAN—**1** LIB **2** SCO **4** SAG **6** CAP **8** AQU **11** PIS **13** ARI **16** TAU **18** GEM **20** CAN **23** LEO **25** VIR **27** LIB **29** SCO **31** SAG
FEB—**2** CAP **5** AQU **7** PIS **9** ARI **12** TAU **14** GEM **17** CAN **19** LEO **21** VIR **23** LIB **25** SCO **27** SAG
MAR—**1** CAP **3** AQU **5** PIS **8** ARI **10** TAU **13** GEM **15** CAN **18** LEO **20** VIR **22** LIB **24** SCO **26** SAG **28** CAP **30** AQU
APR—**2** PIS **4** ARI **7** TAU **9** GEM **12** CAN **14** LEO **16** VIR **18** LIB **20** SCO **22** SAG **24** CAP **26** AQU **29** PIS
MAY—**1** ARI **4** TAU **6** GEM **9** CAN **11** LEO **13** VIR **16** LIB **18** SCO **20** SAG **22** CAP **24** AQU **26** PIS **29** ARI **31** TAU
JUN—**3** GEM **5** CAN **7** LEO **10** VIR **12** LIB **14** SCO **16** SAG **18** CAP **20** AQU **22** PIS **25** ARI **27** TAU **30** GEM
JUL—**2** CAN **5** LEO **7** VIR **9** LIB **11** SCO **13** SAG **15** CAP **18** AQU **20** PIS **22** ARI **25** TAU **27** GEM **30** CAN
AUG—**1** LEO **3** VIR **5** LIB **7** SCO **10** SAG **12** CAP **14** AQU **16** PIS **19** ARI **21** TAU **24** GEM **26** CAN **28** LEO **31** VIR
SEP—**2** LIB **4** SCO **6** SAG **8** CAP **10** AQU **12** PIS **15** ARI **17** TAU **20** GEM **22** CAN **25** LEO **27** VIR **29** LIB
OCT—**1** SCO **3** SAG **5** CAP **7** AQU **10** PIS **12** ARI **15** TAU **17** GEM **20** CAN **22** LEO **24** VIR **27** LIB **29** SCO **31** SAG
NOV—**2** CAP **4** AQU **6** PIS **8** ARI **11** TAU **13** GEM **16** CAN **18** LEO **21** VIR **23** LIB **25** SCO **27** SAG **29** CAP
DEC—**1** AQU **3** PIS **6** ARI **8** TAU **11** GEM **13** CAN **16** LEO **18** VIR **20** LIB **22** SCO **24** SAG **26** CAP **28** AQU **31** PIS

1933

JAN—**1** PIS **2** ARI **4** TAU **7** GEM **9** CAN **12** LEO **14** VIR **16** LIB **19** SCO **21** SAG **23** CAP **25** AQU **27** PIS **29** ARI
FEB—**1** TAU **3** GEM **6** CAN **8** LEO **10** VIR **13** LIB **15** SCO **17** SAG **19** CAP **21** AQU **23** PIS **26** ARI **28** TAU
MAR—**3** GEM **5** CAN **8** LEO **10** VIR **12** LIB **14** SCO **16** SAG **18** CAP **20** AQU **23** PIS **25** ARI **27** TAU **30** GEM
APR—**1** CAN **4** LEO **6** VIR **8** LIB **11** SCO **13** SAG **15** CAP **17** AQU **19** PIS **21** ARI **24** TAU **26** GEM **29** CAN
MAY—**1** LEO **4** VIR **6** LIB **8** SCO **10** SAG **12** CAP **14** AQU **16** PIS **19** ARI **21** TAU **23** GEM **26** CAN **29** LEO **31** VIR
JUN—**2** LIB **4** SCO **6** SAG **8** CAP **10** AQU **12** PIS **15** ARI **17** TAU **20** GEM **22** CAN **25** LEO **27** VIR **30** LIB
JUL—**2** SCO **4** SAG **6** CAP **8** AQU **10** PIS **12** ARI **14** TAU **17** GEM **20** CAN **22** LEO **24** VIR **27** LIB **29** SCO **31** SAG
AUG—**2** CAP **4** AQU **6** PIS **8** ARI **11** TAU **13** GEM **16** CAN **18** LEO **21** VIR **23** LIB **25** SCO **27** SAG **29** CAP
SEP—**1** AQU **3** PIS **5** ARI **7** TAU **10** GEM **12** CAN **15** LEO **17** VIR **19** LIB **21** SCO **24** SAG **26** CAP **28** AQU **30** PIS
OCT—**2** ARI **5** TAU **7** GEM **9** CAN **12** LEO **14** VIR **17** LIB **19** SCO **21** SAG **23** CAP **25** AQU **27** PIS **30** ARI
NOV—**1** TAU **3** GEM **6** CAN **8** LEO **11** VIR **13** LIB **15** SCO **17** SAG **19** CAP **21** AQU **23** PIS **26** ARI **28** TAU
DEC—**1** GEM **3** CAN **6** LEO **8** VIR **11** LIB **13** SCO **15** SAG **17** CAP **19** AQU **21** PIS **23** ARI **25** TAU **28** GEM **30** CAN

1934

JAN—**1** CAN **2** LEO **4** VIR **7** LIB **2** SCO **11** SAG **13** CAP **15** AQU **17** PIS **19** ARI **22** TAU **24** GEM **27** CAN **29** LEO
FEB—**1** VIR **3** LIB **5** SCO **8** SAG **10** CAP **12** AQU **14** PIS **16** ARI **18** TAU **20** GEM **23** CAN **25** LEO **28** VIR
MAR—**2** LIB **5** SCO **7** SAG **9** CAP **11** AQU **13** PIS **15** ARI **17** TAU **20** GEM **22** CAN **25** LEO **27** VIR **30** LIB
APR—**1** SCO **3** SAG **5** CAP **7** AQU **9** PIS **12** ARI **14** TAU **16** GEM **19** CAN **21** LEO **24** VIR **26** LIB **28** SCO **30** SAG
MAY—**2** CAP **5** AQU **7** PIS **9** ARI **11** TAU **13** GEM **16** CAN **18** LEO **21** VIR **23** LIB **26** SCO **28** SAG **30** CAP
JUN—**1** AQU **3** PIS **5** ARI **7** TAU **10** GEM **12** CAN **15** LEO **17** VIR **20** LIB **22** SCO **24** SAG **26** CAP **28** AQU **30** PIS
JUL—**2** ARI **5** TAU **7** GEM **9** CAN **12** LEO **15** VIR **17** LIB **19** SCO **22** SAG **24** CAP **26** AQU **28** PIS **30** ARI
AUG—**1** TAU **3** GEM **6** CAN **8** LEO **11** VIR **13** LIB **16** SCO **18** SAG **20** CAP **22** AQU **24** PIS **26** ARI **28** TAU **30** GEM
SEP—**2** CAN **4** LEO **7** VIR **9** LIB **12** SCO **14** SAG **16** CAP **18** AQU **20** PIS **23** ARI **25** TAU **27** GEM **29** CAN
OCT—**2** LEO **4** VIR **7** LIB **9** SCO **11** SAG **14** CAP **16** AQU **18** PIS **20** ARI **22** TAU **24** GEM **27** CAN **29** LEO
NOV—**1** VIR **3** LIB **5** SCO **8** SAG **10** CAP **12** AQU **14** PIS **16** ARI **18** TAU **21** GEM **23** CAN **25** LEO **28** VIR **30** LIB
DEC—**3** SCO **5** SAG **7** CAP **9** AQU **11** PIS **13** ARI **16** TAU **18** GEM **20** CAN **23** LEO **25** VIR **28** LIB **30** SCO

1935

JAN—**1** SAG **4** CAP **6** AQU **8** PIS **10** ARI **12** TAU **14** GEM **17** CAN **19** LEO **22** VIR **24** LIB **27** SCO **29** SAG **31** CAP
FEB—**2** AQU **4** PIS **6** ARI **8** TAU **10** GEM **13** CAN **15** LEO **18** VIR **20** LIB **23** SCO **25** SAG **27** CAP
MAR—**2** AQU **4** PIS **6** ARI **8** TAU **10** GEM **12** CAN **15** LEO **17** VIR **20** LIB **22** SCO **24** SAG **27** CAP **29** AQU **31** PIS
APR—**2** ARI **4** TAU **6** GEM **8** CAN **11** LEO **13** VIR **16** LIB **18** SCO **21** SAG **23** CAP **25** AQU **27** PIS **29** ARI
MAY—**1** TAU **4** GEM **6** CAN **8** LEO **11** VIR **13** LIB **16** SCO **18** SAG **20** CAP **22** AQU **24** PIS **27** ARI **29** TAU **31** GEM
JUN—**2** CAN **5** LEO **7** VIR **10** LIB **12** SCO **14** SAG **17** CAP **19** AQU **21** PIS **23** ARI **25** TAU **27** GEM **29** CAN
JUL—**2** LEO **4** VIR **7** LIB **9** SCO **12** SAG **14** CAP **16** AQU **18** PIS **20** ARI **22** TAU **24** GEM **27** CAN **29** LEO
AUG—**1** VIR **3** LIB **6** SCO **8** SAG **10** CAP **12** AQU **14** PIS **16** ARI **18** TAU **21** GEM **23** CAN **25** LEO **28** VIR **30** LIB
SEP—**2** SCO **4** SAG **7** CAP **9** AQU **11** PIS **13** ARI **15** TAU **17** GEM **19** CAN **22** LEO **24** VIR **27** LIB **29** SCO
OCT—**2** SAG **4** CAP **6** AQU **8** PIS **10** ARI **12** TAU **14** GEM **17** CAN **19** LEO **21** VIR **24** LIB **26** SCO **29** SAG **31** CAP
NOV—**2** AQU **5** PIS **7** ARI **9** TAU **11** GEM **13** CAN **15** LEO **18** VIR **20** LIB **23** SCO **25** SAG **27** CAP **30** AQU
DEC—**2** PIS **4** ARI **6** TAU **8** GEM **10** CAN **13** LEO **15** VIR **18** LIB **20** SCO **23** SAG **25** CAP **27** AQU **29** PIS **31** ARI

1936

JAN—**1** ARI **2** TAU **5** GEM **7** CAN **9** LEO **11** VIR **14** LIB **16** SCO **19** SAG **21** CAP **23** AQU **25** PIS **27** ARI **30** TAU
FEB—**1** GEM **3** CAN **5** LEO **8** VIR **10** LIB **13** SCO **15** SAG **18** CAP **20** AQU **22** PIS **24** ARI **26** TAU **28** GEM
MAR—**1** CAN **4** LEO **6** VIR **9** LIB **11** SCO **14** SAG **16** CAP **18** AQU **20** PIS **22** ARI **24** TAU **26** GEM **28** CAN **31** LEO
APR—**2** VIR **5** LIB **7** SCO **10** SAG **12** CAP **15** AQU **17** PIS **19** ARI **21** TAU **23** GEM **25** CAN **27** LEO **30** VIR
MAY—**2** LIB **5** SCO **7** SAG **9** CAP **12** AQU **14** PIS **16** ARI **18** TAU **20** GEM **22** CAN **24** LEO **27** VIR **29** LIB
JUN—**1** SCO **3** SAG **6** CAP **8** AQU **10** PIS **12** ARI **14** TAU **17** GEM **19** CAN **21** LEO **23** VIR **26** LIB **28** SCO
JUL—**1** SAG **3** CAP **5** AQU **8** PIS **10** ARI **12** TAU **14** GEM **16** CAN **18** LEO **21** VIR **23** LIB **26** SCO **28** SAG **30** CAP
AUG—**2** AQU **4** PIS **6** ARI **8** TAU **10** GEM **12** CAN **15** LEO **17** VIR **19** LIB **22** SCO **24** SAG **27** CAP **29** AQU **31** PIS
SEP—**2** ARI **4** TAU **6** GEM **9** CAN **11** LEO **13** VIR **16** LIB **18** SCO **21** SAG **23** CAP **25** AQU **28** PIS **30** ARI
OCT—**2** TAU **4** GEM **6** CAN **8** LEO **10** VIR **13** LIB **15** SCO **18** SAG **20** CAP **23** AQU **25** PIS **27** ARI **29** TAU **31** GEM
NOV—**2** CAN **4** LEO **7** VIR **9** LIB **12** SCO **14** SAG **17** CAP **19** AQU **21** PIS **24** ARI **26** TAU **28** GEM **30** CAN
DEC—**2** LEO **4** VIR **6** LIB **9** SCO **11** SAG **14** CAP **16** AQU **19** PIS **21** ARI **23** TAU **25** GEM **27** CAN **29** LEO **31** VIR

1937

JAN—**1** VIR **3** LIB **5** SCO **8** SAG **10** CAP **13** AQU **15** PIS **17** ARI **19** TAU **21** GEM **23** CAN **26** LEO **28** VIR **30** LIB
FEB—**2** SCO **4** SAG **7** CAP **9** AQU **11** PIS **13** ARI **15** TAU **18** GEM **20** CAN **22** LEO **24** VIR **26** LIB
MAR—**1** SCO **3** SAG **6** CAP **8** AQU **11** PIS **13** ARI **15** TAU **17** GEM **19** CAN **21** LEO **23** VIR **26** LIB **28** SCO **31** SAG
APR—**2** CAP **5** AQU **7** PIS **9** ARI **11** TAU **13** GEM **15** CAN **17** LEO **20** VIR **22** LIB **25** SCO **27** SAG **30** CAP
MAY—**2** AQU **4** PIS **7** ARI **9** TAU **11** GEM **13** CAN **15** LEO **17** VIR **19** LIB **22** SCO **24** SAG **27** CAP **29** AQU
JUN—**1** PIS **3** ARI **5** TAU **7** GEM **9** CAN **11** LEO **13** VIR **16** LIB **18** SCO **21** SAG **23** CAP **26** AQU **28** PIS **30** ARI
JUL—**2** TAU **4** GEM **6** CAN **8** LEO **11** VIR **13** LIB **15** SCO **18** SAG **20** CAP **23** AQU **25** PIS **27** ARI **30** TAU
AUG—**1** GEM **3** CAN **5** LEO **7** VIR **9** LIB **12** SCO **14** SAG **17** CAP **19** AQU **21** PIS **24** ARI **26** TAU **28** GEM **30** CAN
SEP—**1** LEO **3** VIR **6** LIB **8** SCO **11** SAG **13** CAP **15** AQU **18** PIS **20** ARI **22** TAU **24** GEM **26** CAN **28** LEO
OCT—**1** VIR **3** LIB **5** SCO **8** SAG **10** CAP **13** AQU **15** PIS **17** ARI **19** TAU **21** GEM **24** CAN **26** LEO **28** VIR **30** LIB
NOV—**2** SCO **4** SAG **7** CAP **9** AQU **12** PIS **14** ARI **16** TAU **18** GEM **20** CAN **22** LEO **24** VIR **26** LIB **29** SCO
DEC—**1** SAG **4** CAP **6** AQU **9** PIS **11** ARI **13** TAU **15** GEM **17** CAN **19** LEO **21** VIR **24** LIB **26** SCO **29** SAG **31** CAP

1938

JAN—**1** CAP **3** AQU **5** PIS **7** ARI **10** TAU **12** GEM **14** CAN **16** LEO **18** VIR **20** LIB **22** SCO **25** SAG **27** CAP **30** AQU
FEB—**1** PIS **4** ARI **6** TAU **8** GEM **10** CAN **12** LEO **14** VIR **16** LIB **19** SCO **21** SAG **24** CAP **26** AQU
MAR—**1** PIS **3** ARI **5** TAU **7** GEM **9** CAN **12** LEO **14** VIR **16** LIB **18** SCO **21** SAG **23** CAP **26** AQU **28** PIS **30** ARI
APR—**1** TAU **4** GEM **6** CAN **8** LEO **10** VIR **12** LIB **15** SCO **17** SAG **19** CAP **22** AQU **24** PIS **27** ARI **29** TAU
MAY—**1** GEM **3** CAN **5** LEO **7** VIR **9** LIB **12** SCO **14** SAG **17** CAP **19** AQU **22** PIS **24** ARI **26** TAU **28** GEM **30** CAN
JUN—**1** LEO **3** VIR **6** LIB **8** SCO **10** SAG **13** CAP **16** AQU **18** PIS **20** ARI **23** TAU **25** GEM **27** CAN **29** LEO
JUL—**1** VIR **3** LIB **5** SCO **8** SAG **10** CAP **13** AQU **15** PIS **18** ARI **20** TAU **22** GEM **24** CAN **26** LEO **28** VIR **30** LIB
AUG—**2** SCO **4** SAG **7** CAP **9** AQU **12** PIS **14** ARI **16** TAU **18** GEM **21** CAN **23** LEO **25** VIR **27** LIB **29** SCO **31** SAG
SEP—**3** CAP **5** AQU **8** PIS **10** ARI **12** TAU **15** GEM **17** CAN **19** LEO **21** VIR **23** LIB **25** SCO **28** SAG **30** CAP
OCT—**3** AQU **5** PIS **8** ARI **10** TAU **12** GEM **14** CAN **16** LEO **18** VIR **20** LIB **23** SCO **25** SAG **27** CAP **30** AQU
NOV—**2** PIS **4** ARI **6** TAU **8** GEM **10** CAN **12** LEO **15** VIR **17** LIB **19** SCO **21** SAG **24** CAP **26** AQU **29** PIS
DEC—**1** ARI **4** TAU **6** GEM **8** CAN **10** LEO **12** VIR **14** LIB **16** SCO **19** SAG **21** CAP **24** AQU **26** PIS **29** ARI **31** TAU

1939

JAN—1 TAU 2 GEM 4 CAN 6 LEO 8 VIR 10 LIB 12 SCO 15 SAG 17 CAP 20 AQU 22 PIS 25 ARI 27 TAU 30 GEM
FEB—1 CAN 3 LEO 5 VIR 7 LIB 9 SCO 11 SAG 14 CAP 16 AQU 19 PIS 21 ARI 24 TAU 26 GEM 28 CAN
MAR—2 LEO 4 VIR 6 LIB 8 SCO 10 SAG 13 CAP 15 AQU 18 PIS 20 ARI 23 TAU 25 GEM 27 CAN 29 LEO 31 VIR
APR—3 LIB 5 SCO 7 SAG 9 CAP 12 AQU 14 PIS 17 ARI 19 TAU 21 GEM 24 CAN 26 LEO 28 VIR 30 LIB
MAY—2 SCO 4 SAG 7 CAP 9 AQU 12 PIS 14 ARI 16 TAU 19 GEM 21 CAN 23 LEO 25 VIR 27 LIB 29 SCO
JUN—1 SAG 3 CAP 5 AQU 8 PIS 10 ARI 13 TAU 15 GEM 17 CAN 19 LEO 21 VIR 23 LIB 26 SCO 28 SAG 30 CAP
JUL—3 AQU 5 PIS 8 ARI 10 TAU 12 GEM 15 CAN 17 LEO 19 VIR 21 LIB 23 SCO 25 SAG 27 CAP 30 AQU
AUG—1 PIS 4 ARI 6 TAU 9 GEM 11 CAN 13 LEO 15 VIR 17 LIB 19 SCO 21 SAG 24 CAP 26 AQU 29 PIS 31 ARI
SEP—3 TAU 5 GEM 7 CAN 9 LEO 11 VIR 13 LIB 15 SCO 18 SAG 20 CAP 22 AQU 25 PIS 28 ARI 30 TAU
OCT—2 GEM 5 CAN 7 LEO 9 VIR 11 LIB 13 SCO 15 SAG 17 CAP 20 AQU 22 PIS 25 ARI 27 TAU 30 GEM
NOV—1 CAN 3 LEO 5 VIR 7 LIB 9 SCO 11 SAG 14 CAP 16 AQU 19 PIS 21 ARI 24 TAU 26 GEM 28 CAN 30 LEO
DEC—2 VIR 5 LIB 7 SCO 9 SAG 11 CAP 13 AQU 16 PIS 19 ARI 21 TAU 23 GEM 26 CAN 28 LEO 30 VIR

1940

JAN—1 LIB 3 SCO 5 SAG 7 CAP 10 AQU 12 PIS 15 ARI 17 TAU 20 GEM 22 CAN 24 LEO 26 VIR 28 LIB 30 SCO
FEB—1 SAG 4 CAP 6 AQU 9 PIS 11 ARI 14 TAU 16 GEM 18 CAN 20 LEO 22 VIR 24 LIB 26 SCO 29 SAG
MAR—2 CAP 4 AQU 7 PIS 9 ARI 12 TAU 14 GEM 17 CAN 19 LEO 21 VIR 23 LIB 25 SCO 27 SAG 29 CAP
APR—1 AQU 3 PIS 6 ARI 8 TAU 11 GEM 13 CAN 15 LEO 17 VIR 19 LIB 21 SCO 23 SAG 26 CAP 28 AQU 30 PIS
MAY—3 ARI 5 TAU 8 GEM 10 CAN 12 LEO 15 VIR 17 LIB 19 SCO 21 SAG 23 CAP 25 AQU 28 PIS 30 ARI
JUN—2 TAU 4 GEM 6 CAN 9 LEO 11 VIR 13 LIB 15 SCO 17 SAG 19 CAP 22 AQU 24 PIS 27 ARI 29 TAU
JUL—2 GEM 4 CAN 6 LEO 8 VIR 10 LIB 12 SCO 14 SAG 17 CAP 19 AQU 21 PIS 24 ARI 26 TAU 29 GEM 31 CAN
AUG—2 LEO 4 VIR 6 LIB 9 SCO 11 SAG 13 CAP 15 AQU 18 PIS 20 ARI 23 TAU 25 GEM 28 CAN 30 LEO
SEP—1 VIR 3 LIB 5 SCO 7 SAG 9 CAP 11 AQU 14 PIS 16 ARI 19 TAU 22 GEM 24 CAN 26 LEO 28 VIR 30 LIB
OCT—2 SCO 4 SAG 6 CAP 9 AQU 11 PIS 14 ARI 16 TAU 19 GEM 21 CAN 23 LEO 26 VIR 28 LIB 30 SCO
NOV—1 SAG 3 CAP 5 AQU 7 PIS 10 ARI 13 TAU 15 GEM 17 CAN 20 LEO 22 VIR 24 LIB 26 SCO 28 SAG 30 CAP
DEC—2 AQU 5 PIS 7 ARI 10 TAU 12 GEM 15 CAN 17 LEO 19 VIR 21 LIB 23 SCO 26 SAG 28 CAP 30 AQU

1941

JAN—1 PIS 4 ARI 6 TAU 9 GEM 11 CAN 13 LEO 15 VIR 18 LIB 20 SCO 22 SAG 24 CAP 26 AQU 29 PIS 31 ARI
FEB—2 TAU 5 GEM 7 CAN 10 LEO 12 VIR 14 LIB 16 SCO 18 SAG 20 CAP 23 AQU 25 PIS 27 ARI
MAR—2 TAU 4 GEM 7 CAN 9 LEO 11 VIR 13 LIB 15 SCO 17 SAG 19 CAP 22 AQU 24 PIS 27 ARI 29 TAU
APR—1 GEM 3 CAN 5 LEO 8 VIR 10 LIB 12 SCO 14 SAG 16 CAP 18 AQU 20 PIS 23 ARI 25 TAU 28 GEM 30 CAN
MAY—3 LEO 5 VIR 7 LIB 9 SCO 11 SAG 13 CAP 15 AQU 18 PIS 20 ARI 23 TAU 25 GEM 28 CAN 30 LEO
JUN—1 VIR 4 LIB 6 SCO 8 SAG 10 CAP 12 AQU 14 PIS 16 ARI 19 TAU 21 GEM 24 CAN 26 LEO 29 VIR
JUL—1 LIB 3 SCO 5 SAG 7 CAP 9 AQU 11 PIS 14 ARI 16 TAU 19 GEM 21 CAN 24 LEO 26 VIR 28 LIB 30 SCO
AUG—1 SAG 3 CAP 5 AQU 8 PIS 10 ARI 13 TAU 15 GEM 18 CAN 20 LEO 22 VIR 24 LIB 26 SCO 28 SAG 31 CAP
SEP—2 AQU 4 PIS 6 ARI 9 TAU 11 GEM 14 CAN 16 LEO 19 VIR 21 LIB 23 SCO 25 SAG 27 CAP 29 AQU
OCT—1 PIS 4 ARI 6 TAU 9 GEM 11 CAN 14 LEO 16 VIR 18 LIB 20 SCO 22 SAG 24 CAP 26 AQU 29 PIS 31 ARI
NOV—2 TAU 5 GEM 7 CAN 10 LEO 12 VIR 15 LIB 17 SCO 19 SAG 21 CAP 23 AQU 25 PIS 27 ARI 30 TAU
DEC—2 GEM 5 CAN 7 LEO 10 VIR 12 LIB 14 SCO 16 SAG 18 CAP 20 AQU 22 PIS 24 ARI 27 TAU 29 GEM

1942

JAN—**1** CAN **3** LEO **6** VIR **8** LIB **10** SCO **12** SAG **14** CAP **16** AQU **19** PIS **21** ARI **23** TAU **26** GEM **28** CAN **31** LEO
FEB—**2** VIR **4** LIB **7** SCO **9** SAG **11** CAP **13** AQU **15** PIS **17** ARI **20** TAU **22** GEM **25** CAN **27** LEO
MAR—**1** VIR **4** LIB **6** SCO **8** SAG **10** CAP **12** AQU **14** PIS **17** ARI **19** TAU **21** GEM **24** CAN **26** LEO **29** VIR **31** LIB
APR—**2** SCO **4** SAG **6** CAP **8** AQU **11** PIS **13** ARI **15** TAU **18** GEM **20** CAN **23** LEO **25** VIR **27** LIB **30** SCO
MAY—**2** SAG **4** CAP **6** AQU **8** PIS **10** ARI **13** TAU **15** GEM **18** CAN **20** LEO **23** VIR **25** LIB **27** SCO **29** SAG **31** CAP
JUN—**2** AQU **4** PIS **6** ARI **9** TAU **11** GEM **14** CAN **16** LEO **19** VIR **21** LIB **23** SCO **25** SAG **27** CAP **29** AQU
JUL—**1** PIS **4** ARI **6** TAU **9** GEM **11** CAN **14** LEO **16** VIR **18** LIB **21** SCO **23** SAG **25** CAP **27** AQU **29** PIS **31** ARI
AUG—**2** TAU **5** GEM **7** CAN **10** LEO **12** VIR **15** LIB **17** SCO **19** SAG **21** CAP **23** AQU **25** PIS **27** ARI **30** TAU
SEP—**1** GEM **4** CAN **6** LEO **9** VIR **11** LIB **13** SCO **15** SAG **17** CAP **20** AQU **22** PIS **24** ARI **26** TAU **29** GEM
OCT—**1** CAN **4** LEO **6** VIR **8** LIB **10** SCO **13** SAG **15** CAP **17** AQU **19** PIS **21** ARI **23** TAU **26** GEM **28** CAN **31** LEO
NOV—**2** VIR **5** LIB **7** SCO **9** SAG **11** CAP **13** AQU **15** PIS **17** ARI **20** TAU **22** GEM **25** CAN **27** LEO **30** VIR
DEC—**2** LIB **4** SCO **6** SAG **8** CAP **10** AQU **12** PIS **15** ARI **17** TAU **19** GEM **22** CAN **24** LEO **27** VIR **29** LIB

1943

JAN—**1** SCO **3** SAG **5** CAP **7** AQU **9** PIS **11** ARI **13** TAU **16** GEM **18** CAN **21** LEO **23** VIR **26** LIB **28** SCO **30** SAG
FEB—**1** CAP **3** AQU **5** PIS **7** ARI **10** TAU **12** GEM **14** CAN **17** LEO **19** VIR **22** LIB **24** SCO **26** SAG
MAR—**1** CAP **3** AQU **5** PIS **7** ARI **9** TAU **11** GEM **14** CAN **16** LEO **19** VIR **21** LIB **23** SCO **26** SAG **28** CAP **30** AQU
APR—**1** PIS **3** ARI **5** TAU **8** GEM **10** CAN **13** LEO **15** VIR **18** LIB **20** SCO **22** SAG **24** CAP **26** AQU **28** PIS **30** ARI
MAY—**3** TAU **5** GEM **7** CAN **10** LEO **12** VIR **15** LIB **17** SCO **19** SAG **21** CAP **23** AQU **26** PIS **28** ARI **30** TAU
JUN—**1** GEM **4** CAN **6** LEO **9** VIR **11** LIB **14** SCO **16** SAG **18** CAP **20** AQU **22** PIS **24** ARI **26** TAU **29** GEM
JUL—**1** CAN **4** LEO **6** VIR **9** LIB **11** SCO **13** SAG **15** CAP **17** AQU **19** PIS **21** ARI **23** TAU **26** GEM **28** CAN **31** LEO
AUG—**2** VIR **5** LIB **7** SCO **10** SAG **12** CAP **14** AQU **16** PIS **18** ARI **20** TAU **22** GEM **25** CAN **27** LEO **30** VIR
SEP—**1** LIB **3** SCO **6** SAG **8** CAP **10** AQU **12** PIS **14** ARI **16** TAU **18** GEM **21** CAN **23** LEO **26** VIR **28** LIB
OCT—**1** SCO **3** SAG **5** CAP **7** AQU **9** PIS **12** ARI **14** TAU **16** GEM **18** CAN **21** LEO **23** VIR **26** LIB **28** SCO **30** SAG
NOV—**1** CAP **4** AQU **6** PIS **8** ARI **10** TAU **12** GEM **15** CAN **17** LEO **20** VIR **22** LIB **24** SCO **27** SAG **29** CAP
DEC—**1** AQU **3** PIS **5** ARI **7** TAU **10** GEM **12** CAN **14** LEO **17** VIR **19** LIB **22** SCO **24** SAG **26** CAP **28** AQU **30** PIS

1944

JAN—**1** ARI **3** TAU **6** GEM **8** CAN **11** LEO **13** VIR **16** LIB **18** SCO **20** SAG **23** CAP **25** AQU **27** PIS **29** ARI **31** TAU
FEB—**2** GEM **4** CAN **7** LEO **9** VIR **12** LIB **14** SCO **17** SAG **19** CAP **21** AQU **23** PIS **25** ARI **27** TAU **29** GEM
MAR—**3** CAN **5** LEO **8** VIR **10** LIB **13** SCO **15** SAG **17** CAP **19** AQU **22** PIS **24** ARI **26** TAU **28** GEM **30** CAN
APR—**1** LEO **4** VIR **6** LIB **9** SCO **11** SAG **14** CAP **16** AQU **18** PIS **20** ARI **22** TAU **24** GEM **26** CAN **29** LEO
MAY—**1** VIR **4** LIB **6** SCO **9** SAG **11** CAP **13** AQU **15** PIS **17** ARI **19** TAU **21** GEM **24** CAN **26** LEO **29** VIR **31** LIB
JUN—**3** SCO **5** SAG **7** CAP **9** AQU **11** PIS **13** ARI **16** TAU **18** GEM **20** CAN **22** LEO **25** VIR **27** LIB **30** SCO
JUL—**2** SAG **4** CAP **7** AQU **9** PIS **11** ARI **13** TAU **15** GEM **17** CAN **20** LEO **22** VIR **25** LIB **27** SCO **30** SAG
AUG—**1** CAP **3** AQU **5** PIS **7** ARI **9** TAU **11** GEM **14** CAN **16** LEO **18** VIR **21** LIB **24** SCO **26** SAG **28** CAP **30** AQU
SEP—**1** PIS **3** ARI **5** TAU **8** GEM **10** CAN **12** LEO **15** VIR **17** LIB **20** SCO **22** SAG **25** CAP **27** AQU **29** PIS
OCT—**1** ARI **3** TAU **5** GEM **7** CAN **10** LEO **12** VIR **15** LIB **17** SCO **19** SAG **22** CAP **24** AQU **26** PIS **28** ARI **30** TAU
NOV—**1** GEM **4** CAN **6** LEO **8** VIR **11** LIB **13** SCO **16** SAG **18** CAP **20** AQU **23** PIS **25** ARI **27** TAU **29** GEM
DEC—**1** CAN **3** LEO **6** VIR **8** LIB **11** SCO **13** SAG **15** CAP **18** AQU **20** PIS **22** ARI **24** TAU **26** GEM **28** CAN **31** LEO

1945

JAN—1 LEO 2 VIR 4 LIB 7 SCO 9 SAG 12 CAP 14 AQU 16 PIS 18 ARI 20 TAU 22 GEM 25 CAN 27 LEO 29 VIR
FEB—1 LIB 3 SCO 6 SAG 8 CAP 10 AQU 12 PIS 14 ARI 17 TAU 19 GEM 21 CAN 23 LEO 26 VIR 28 LIB
MAR—3 SCO 5 SAG 8 CAP 10 AQU 12 PIS 14 ARI 16 TAU 18 GEM 20 CAN 22 LEO 25 VIR 27 LIB 30 SCO
APR—1 SAG 4 CAP 6 AQU 8 PIS 10 ARI 12 TAU 14 GEM 16 CAN 19 LEO 21 VIR 24 LIB 26 SCO 29 SAG
MAY—1 CAP 3 AQU 6 PIS 8 ARI 10 TAU 12 GEM 14 CAN 16 LEO 18 VIR 21 LIB 23 SCO 26 SAG 28 CAP 31 AQU
JUN—2 PIS 4 ARI 6 TAU 8 GEM 10 CAN 12 LEO 15 VIR 17 LIB 20 SCO 22 SAG 25 CAP 27 AQU 29 PIS
JUL—1 ARI 3 TAU 6 GEM 8 CAN 10 LEO 12 VIR 15 LIB 17 SCO 20 SAG 22 CAP 24 AQU 26 PIS 29 ARI 31 TAU
AUG—2 GEM 4 CAN 6 LEO 8 VIR 11 LIB 13 SCO 16 SAG 18 CAP 21 AQU 23 PIS 25 ARI 27 TAU 29 GEM 31 CAN
SEP—2 LEO 5 VIR 7 LIB 10 SCO 12 SAG 15 CAP 17 AQU 19 PIS 21 ARI 23 TAU 25 GEM 27 CAN 30 LEO
OCT—2 VIR 4 LIB 7 SCO 10 SAG 12 CAP 14 AQU 17 PIS 19 ARI 21 TAU 23 GEM 25 CAN 27 LEO 29 VIR
NOV—1 LIB 3 SCO 6 SAG 8 CAP 11 AQU 13 PIS 15 ARI 17 TAU 19 GEM 21 CAN 23 LEO 26 VIR 28 LIB 30 SCO
DEC—3 SAG 6 CAP 8 AQU 10 PIS 12 ARI 15 TAU 17 GEM 19 CAN 21 LEO 23 VIR 25 LIB 28 SCO 30 SAG

1946

JAN—1 SAG 2 CAP 4 AQU 6 PIS 9 ARI 11 TAU 13 GEM 15 CAN 17 LEO 19 VIR 22 LIB 24 SCO 27 SAG 29 CAP
FEB—1 AQU 3 PIS 5 ARI 7 TAU 9 GEM 11 CAN 13 LEO 16 VIR 18 LIB 20 SCO 23 SAG 26 CAP 28 AQU
MAR—2 PIS 4 ARI 6 TAU 8 GEM 11 CAN 13 LEO 15 VIR 17 LIB 20 SCO 22 SAG 25 CAP 27 AQU 30 PIS
APR—1 ARI 3 TAU 5 GEM 7 CAN 9 LEO 11 VIR 14 LIB 16 SCO 19 SAG 21 CAP 24 AQU 26 PIS 28 ARI 30 TAU
MAY—2 GEM 4 CAN 6 LEO 8 VIR 11 LIB 13 SCO 16 SAG 18 CAP 21 AQU 23 PIS 26 ARI 28 TAU 30 GEM
JUN—1 CAN 3 LEO 5 VIR 7 LIB 10 SCO 12 SAG 15 CAP 17 AQU 20 PIS 22 ARI 24 TAU 26 GEM 28 CAN 30 LEO
JUL—2 VIR 4 LIB 7 SCO 9 SAG 12 CAP 14 AQU 17 PIS 19 ARI 21 TAU 23 GEM 25 CAN 27 LEO 30 VIR
AUG—1 LIB 3 SCO 6 SAG 8 CAP 11 AQU 13 PIS 15 ARI 17 TAU 20 GEM 22 CAN 24 LEO 26 VIR 28 LIB 31 SCO
SEP—2 SAG 5 CAP 7 AQU 9 PIS 12 ARI 14 TAU 16 GEM 18 CAN 20 LEO 22 VIR 25 LIB 27 SCO 29 SAG
OCT—2 CAP 4 AQU 7 PIS 9 ARI 11 TAU 13 GEM 15 CAN 17 LEO 20 VIR 22 LIB 24 SCO 27 SAG 29 CAP
NOV—1 AQU 3 PIS 5 ARI 7 TAU 10 GEM 12 CAN 14 LEO 16 VIR 18 LIB 20 SCO 23 SAG 25 CAP 28 AQU 30 PIS
DEC—3 ARI 5 TAU 7 GEM 9 CAN 11 LEO 13 VIR 15 LIB 18 SCO 20 SAG 23 CAP 25 AQU 28 PIS 30 ARI

1947

JAN—1 TAU 3 GEM 5 CAN 7 LEO 9 VIR 12 LIB 14 SCO 16 SAG 19 CAP 22 AQU 24 PIS 26 ARI 29 TAU 31 GEM
FEB—2 CAN 4 LEO 6 VIR 8 LIB 10 SCO 13 SAG 15 CAP 18 AQU 20 PIS 23 ARI 25 TAU 27 GEM
MAR—1 CAN 3 LEO 5 VIR 7 LIB 10 SCO 12 SAG 15 CAP 17 AQU 20 PIS 22 ARI 24 TAU 26 GEM 28 CAN 31 LEO
APR—2 VIR 4 LIB 6 SCO 8 SAG 11 CAP 13 AQU 16 PIS 18 ARI 20 TAU 23 GEM 25 CAN 27 LEO 29 VIR
MAY—1 LIB 3 SCO 6 SAG 8 CAP 11 AQU 13 PIS 16 ARI 18 TAU 20 GEM 22 CAN 24 LEO 26 VIR 28 LIB 31 SCO
JUN—2 SAG 5 CAP 7 AQU 10 PIS 12 ARI 14 TAU 16 GEM 18 CAN 20 LEO 22 VIR 25 LIB 27 SCO 29 SAG
JUL—2 CAP 4 AQU 7 PIS 9 ARI 12 TAU 14 GEM 16 CAN 18 LEO 20 VIR 22 LIB 24 SCO 27 SAG 29 CAP
AUG—1 AQU 3 PIS 6 ARI 8 TAU 10 GEM 12 CAN 14 LEO 16 VIR 18 LIB 20 SCO 23 SAG 25 CAP 28 AQU 30 PIS
SEP—2 ARI 4 TAU 6 GEM 9 CAN 11 LEO 13 VIR 15 LIB 17 SCO 19 SAG 22 CAP 24 AQU 27 PIS 29 ARI
OCT—1 TAU 4 GEM 6 CAN 8 LEO 10 VIR 12 LIB 14 SCO 17 SAG 19 CAP 22 AQU 24 PIS 26 ARI 29 TAU 31 GEM
NOV—2 CAN 4 LEO 6 VIR 8 LIB 11 SCO 13 SAG 15 CAP 18 AQU 20 PIS 23 ARI 25 TAU 27 GEM 29 CAN
DEC—1 LEO 3 VIR 6 LIB 8 SCO 10 SAG 13 CAP 15 AQU 18 PIS 20 ARI 23 TAU 25 GEM 27 CAN 29 LEO 31 VIR

1948

JAN—**1** VIR **2** LIB **4** SCO **6** SAG **9** CAP **11** AQU **14** PIS **16** ARI **19** TAU **21** GEM **23** CAN **25** LEO **27** VIR **29** LIB **31** SCO
FEB—**3** SAG **5** CAP **8** AQU **10** PIS **13** ARI **15** TAU **17** GEM **20** CAN **22** LEO **24** VIR **26** LIB **28** SCO
MAR—**1** SAG **3** CAP **6** AQU **8** PIS **11** ARI **13** TAU **16** GEM **18** CAN **20** LEO **22** VIR **24** LIB **26** SCO **28** SAG **31** CAP
APR—**2** AQU **5** PIS **7** ARI **10** TAU **12** GEM **14** CAN **16** LEO **18** VIR **21** LIB **23** SCO **25** SAG **27** CAP **30** AQU
MAY—**2** PIS **5** ARI **7** TAU **9** GEM **11** CAN **14** LEO **16** VIR **18** LIB **20** SCO **22** SAG **25** CAP **27** AQU **29** PIS
JUN—**1** ARI **3** TAU **6** GEM **8** CAN **10** LEO **12** VIR **14** LIB **16** SCO **18** SAG **21** CAP **23** AQU **26** PIS **28** ARI
JUL—**1** TAU **3** GEM **5** CAN **7** LEO **9** VIR **11** LIB **13** SCO **16** SAG **18** CAP **21** AQU **23** PIS **26** ARI **28** TAU **30** GEM
AUG—**2** CAN **4** LEO **6** VIR **8** LIB **10** SCO **12** SAG **14** CAP **17** AQU **19** PIS **22** ARI **24** TAU **27** GEM **29** CAN **31** LEO
SEP—**2** VIR **4** LIB **6** SCO **8** SAG **11** CAP **13** AQU **16** PIS **18** ARI **21** TAU **23** GEM **25** CAN **27** LEO **29** VIR
OCT—**1** LIB **3** SCO **6** SAG **8** CAP **10** AQU **13** PIS **15** ARI **18** TAU **20** GEM **23** CAN **25** LEO **27** VIR **29** LIB **31** SCO
NOV—**2** SAG **4** CAP **7** AQU **9** PIS **12** ARI **14** TAU **17** GEM **19** CAN **21** LEO **23** VIR **25** LIB **27** SCO **29** SAG
DEC—**2** CAP **4** AQU **6** PIS **9** ARI **12** TAU **14** GEM **16** CAN **18** LEO **20** VIR **22** LIB **25** SCO **27** SAG **29** CAP **31** AQU

1949

JAN—**1** AQU **3** PIS **5** ARI **8** TAU **10** GEM **12** CAN **15** LEO **17** VIR **19** LIB **21** SCO **23** SAG **25** CAP **28** AQU **30** PIS
FEB—**2** ARI **4** TAU **7** GEM **9** CAN **11** LEO **13** VIR **15** LIB **17** SCO **19** SAG **22** CAP **24** AQU **26** PIS
MAR—**1** ARI **3** TAU **6** GEM **8** CAN **10** LEO **13** VIR **15** LIB **17** SCO **19** SAG **21** CAP **23** AQU **26** PIS **28** ARI **31** TAU
APR—**2** GEM **5** CAN **7** LEO **9** VIR **11** LIB **13** SCO **15** SAG **17** CAP **19** AQU **22** PIS **24** ARI **27** TAU **29** GEM
MAY—**2** CAN **4** LEO **6** VIR **8** LIB **10** SCO **12** SAG **15** CAP **17** AQU **19** PIS **22** ARI **24** TAU **27** GEM **29** CAN **31** LEO
JUN—**2** VIR **5** LIB **7** SCO **9** SAG **11** CAP **13** AQU **16** PIS **18** ARI **21** TAU **23** GEM **25** CAN **28** LEO **30** VIR
JUL—**2** LIB **4** SCO **6** SAG **8** CAP **11** AQU **13** PIS **15** ARI **18** TAU **20** GEM **23** CAN **25** LEO **27** VIR **29** LIB **31** SCO
AUG—**2** SAG **5** CAP **7** AQU **9** PIS **12** ARI **14** TAU **17** GEM **19** CAN **21** LEO **23** VIR **25** LIB **27** SCO **30** SAG
SEP—**1** CAP **3** AQU **6** PIS **8** ARI **11** TAU **13** GEM **15** CAN **18** LEO **20** VIR **22** LIB **24** SCO **26** SAG **28** CAP **30** AQU
OCT—**3** PIS **5** ARI **8** TAU **10** GEM **13** CAN **15** LEO **17** VIR **19** LIB **21** SCO **23** SAG **25** CAP **28** AQU **30** PIS
NOV—**2** ARI **4** TAU **7** GEM **9** CAN **11** LEO **14** VIR **16** LIB **18** SCO **20** SAG **22** CAP **24** AQU **26** PIS **29** ARI
DEC—**1** TAU **4** GEM **6** CAN **9** LEO **11** VIR **13** LIB **15** SCO **17** SAG **19** CAP **21** AQU **24** PIS **26** ARI **29** TAU **31** GEM

1950

JAN—**1** GEM **3** CAN **5** LEO **7** VIR **9** LIB **11** SCO **14** SAG **16** CAP **18** AQU **20** PIS **22** ARI **25** TAU **28** GEM **30** CAN
FEB—**1** LEO **3** VIR **6** LIB **8** SCO **10** SAG **12** CAP **14** AQU **16** PIS **19** ARI **21** TAU **24** GEM **26** CAN
MAR—**1** LEO **3** VIR **5** LIB **7** SCO **9** SAG **11** CAP **13** AQU **16** PIS **18** ARI **21** TAU **23** GEM **26** CAN **28** LEO **30** VIR
APR—**1** LIB **3** SCO **5** SAG **7** CAP **10** AQU **12** PIS **14** ARI **17** TAU **19** GEM **22** CAN **24** LEO **27** VIR **29** LIB
MAY—**1** SCO **3** SAG **5** CAP **7** AQU **9** PIS **12** ARI **14** TAU **17** GEM **19** CAN **22** LEO **24** VIR **26** LIB **28** SCO **30** SAG
JUN—**1** CAP **3** AQU **5** PIS **8** ARI **10** TAU **13** GEM **15** CAN **18** LEO **20** VIR **22** LIB **25** SCO **27** SAG **29** CAP
JUL—**1** AQU **3** PIS **5** ARI **8** TAU **10** GEM **13** CAN **15** LEO **17** VIR **20** LIB **22** SCO **24** SAG **26** CAP **28** AQU **30** PIS
AUG—**2** ARI **4** TAU **7** GEM **9** CAN **11** LEO **14** VIR **16** LIB **18** SCO **20** SAG **22** CAP **24** AQU **27** PIS **29** ARI **31** TAU
SEP—**3** GEM **5** CAN **8** LEO **10** VIR **12** LIB **14** SCO **16** SAG **18** CAP **21** AQU **23** PIS **25** ARI **28** TAU **30** GEM
OCT—**3** CAN **5** LEO **7** VIR **10** LIB **12** SCO **14** SAG **16** CAP **18** AQU **20** PIS **23** ARI **25** TAU **28** GEM **30** CAN
NOV—**2** LEO **4** VIR **6** LIB **8** SCO **10** SAG **12** CAP **14** AQU **16** PIS **19** ARI **21** TAU **24** GEM **26** CAN **29** LEO
DEC—**1** VIR **3** LIB **6** SCO **8** SAG **10** CAP **12** AQU **14** PIS **16** ARI **19** TAU **21** GEM **24** CAN **26** LEO **28** VIR **31** LIB

1951

JAN—**1** LIB **2** SCO **4** SAG **6** CAP **8** AQU **10** PIS **12** ARI **15** TAU **17** GEM **20** CAN **22** LEO **25** VIR **27** LIB **29** SCO **31** SAG
FEB—**2** CAP **4** AQU **7** PIS **9** ARI **11** TAU **14** GEM **16** CAN **19** LEO **21** VIR **23** LIB **25** SCO **28** SAG
MAR—**2** CAP **4** AQU **6** PIS **8** ARI **11** TAU **13** GEM **16** CAN **18** LEO **20** VIR **23** LIB **25** SCO **27** SAG **29** CAP **31** AQU
APR—**2** PIS **5** ARI **7** TAU **9** GEM **12** CAN **14** LEO **17** VIR **19** LIB **21** SCO **23** SAG **25** CAP **27** AQU **29** PIS
MAY—**2** ARI **4** TAU **7** GEM **9** CAN **12** LEO **14** VIR **16** LIB **19** SCO **21** SAG **23** CAP **25** AQU **27** PIS **29** ARI **31** TAU
JUN—**3** GEM **5** CAN **8** LEO **10** VIR **13** LIB **15** SCO **17** SAG **19** CAP **21** AQU **23** PIS **25** ARI **28** TAU **30** GEM
JUL—**3** CAN **5** LEO **8** VIR **10** LIB **12** SCO **14** SAG **16** CAP **18** AQU **20** PIS **23** ARI **25** TAU **27** GEM **30** CAN
AUG—**1** LEO **4** VIR **6** LIB **9** SCO **11** SAG **13** CAP **15** AQU **17** PIS **19** ARI **21** TAU **24** GEM **26** CAN **29** LEO **31** VIR
SEP—**3** LIB **5** SCO **7** SAG **9** CAP **11** AQU **13** PIS **15** ARI **18** TAU **20** GEM **23** CAN **25** LEO **28** VIR **30** LIB
OCT—**2** SCO **4** SAG **6** CAP **8** AQU **11** PIS **13** ARI **15** TAU **17** GEM **20** CAN **22** LEO **25** VIR **27** LIB **29** SCO
NOV—**1** SAG **3** CAP **5** AQU **7** PIS **9** ARI **11** TAU **14** GEM **16** CAN **19** LEO **21** VIR **24** LIB **26** SCO **28** SAG **30** CAP
DEC—**2** AQU **4** PIS **6** ARI **9** TAU **11** GEM **13** CAN **16** LEO **19** VIR **21** LIB **23** SCO **25** SAG **27** CAP **29** AQU **31** PIS

1952

JAN—**1** PIS **3** ARI **5** TAU **7** GEM **10** CAN **12** LEO **15** VIR **17** LIB **20** SCO **22** SAG **24** CAP **26** AQU **28** PIS **30** ARI
FEB—**1** TAU **3** GEM **6** CAN **9** LEO **11** VIR **14** LIB **16** SCO **18** SAG **20** CAP **22** AQU **24** PIS **26** ARI **29** TAU
MAR—**2** GEM **4** CAN **7** LEO **9** VIR **12** LIB **14** SCO **16** SAG **19** CAP **21** AQU **23** PIS **25** ARI **27** TAU **29** GEM
APR—**1** CAN **3** LEO **6** VIR **8** LIB **10** SCO **13** SAG **15** CAP **17** AQU **19** PIS **21** ARI **23** TAU **26** GEM **28** CAN **30** LEO
MAY—**3** VIR **5** LIB **8** SCO **10** SAG **12** CAP **14** AQU **16** PIS **18** ARI **21** TAU **23** GEM **25** CAN **28** LEO **30** VIR
JUN—**1** LIB **4** SCO **6** SAG **8** CAP **10** AQU **12** PIS **15** ARI **17** TAU **19** GEM **22** CAN **24** LEO **27** VIR **29** LIB
JUL—**2** SCO **4** SAG **6** CAP **8** AQU **10** PIS **12** ARI **14** TAU **16** GEM **19** CAN **21** LEO **24** VIR **26** LIB **29** SCO **31** SAG
AUG—**2** CAP **4** AQU **6** PIS **8** ARI **10** TAU **13** GEM **15** CAN **18** LEO **20** VIR **23** LIB **25** SCO **27** SAG **30** CAP
SEP—**1** AQU **3** PIS **5** ARI **7** TAU **9** GEM **11** CAN **14** LEO **16** VIR **19** LIB **21** SCO **24** SAG **26** CAP **28** AQU **30** PIS
OCT—**2** ARI **4** TAU **6** GEM **9** CAN **11** LEO **14** VIR **16** LIB **19** SCO **21** SAG **23** CAP **25** AQU **27** PIS **29** ARI
NOV—**1** TAU **3** GEM **5** CAN **7** LEO **10** VIR **13** LIB **15** SCO **17** SAG **19** CAP **21** AQU **24** PIS **26** ARI **28** TAU **30** GEM
DEC—**2** CAN **5** LEO **7** VIR **10** LIB **12** SCO **15** SAG **17** CAP **19** AQU **21** PIS **23** ARI **25** TAU **27** GEM **30** CAN

1953

JAN—**1** LEO **4** VIR **6** LIB **9** SCO **11** SAG **13** CAP **15** AQU **17** PIS **19** ARI **21** TAU **24** GEM **26** CAN **28** LEO **31** VIR
FEB—**3** LIB **5** SCO **7** SAG **10** CAP **12** AQU **14** PIS **16** ARI **18** TAU **20** GEM **22** CAN **25** LEO **27** VIR
MAR—**2** LIB **4** SCO **7** SAG **9** CAP **11** AQU **13** PIS **15** ARI **17** TAU **19** GEM **22** CAN **24** LEO **27** VIR **29** LIB
APR—**1** SCO **3** SAG **5** CAP **7** AQU **10** PIS **12** ARI **14** TAU **16** GEM **18** CAN **20** LEO **23** VIR **25** LIB **28** SCO **30** SAG
MAY—**2** CAP **5** AQU **7** PIS **9** ARI **11** TAU **13** GEM **15** CAN **18** LEO **20** VIR **23** LIB **25** SCO **27** SAG **30** CAP
JUN—**1** AQU **3** PIS **5** ARI **7** TAU **9** GEM **12** CAN **14** LEO **16** VIR **19** LIB **21** SCO **24** SAG **26** CAP **28** AQU **30** PIS
JUL—**2** ARI **5** TAU **7** GEM **9** CAN **11** LEO **14** VIR **16** LIB **19** SCO **21** SAG **23** CAP **26** AQU **28** PIS **30** ARI
AUG—**1** TAU **3** GEM **5** CAN **8** LEO **10** VIR **13** LIB **15** SCO **18** SAG **20** CAP **22** AQU **24** PIS **26** ARI **28** TAU **30** GEM
SEP—**1** CAN **4** LEO **6** VIR **9** LIB **11** SCO **14** SAG **16** CAP **18** AQU **21** PIS **23** ARI **25** TAU **27** GEM **29** CAN
OCT—**1** LEO **4** VIR **6** LIB **9** SCO **11** SAG **13** CAP **16** AQU **18** PIS **20** ARI **22** TAU **24** GEM **26** CAN **28** LEO **31** VIR
NOV—**2** LIB **5** SCO **7** SAG **10** CAP **12** AQU **14** PIS **16** ARI **18** TAU **20** GEM **22** CAN **25** LEO **27** VIR **30** LIB
DEC—**2** SCO **5** SAG **7** CAP **9** AQU **11** PIS **14** ARI **16** TAU **18** GEM **20** CAN **22** LEO **25** VIR **27** LIB **30** SCO

1954

JAN—**1** SAG **3** CAP **6** AQU **8** PIS **10** ARI **12** TAU **14** GEM **16** CAN **19** LEO **21** VIR **23** LIB **26** SCO **28** SAG **31** CAP
FEB—**2** AQU **4** PIS **6** ARI **8** TAU **10** GEM **13** CAN **15** LEO **17** VIR **20** LIB **22** SCO **25** SAG **27** CAP
MAR—**1** AQU **3** PIS **5** ARI **7** TAU **10** GEM **12** CAN **14** LEO **16** VIR **19** LIB **21** SCO **24** SAG **26** CAP **29** AQU **31** PIS
APR—**2** ARI **4** TAU **6** GEM **8** CAN **10** LEO **13** VIR **15** LIB **18** SCO **20** SAG **23** CAP **25** AQU **27** PIS **29** ARI
MAY—**1** TAU **3** GEM **5** CAN **8** LEO **10** VIR **12** LIB **15** SCO **17** SAG **20** CAP **22** AQU **25** PIS **27** ARI **29** TAU **31** GEM
JUN—**2** CAN **4** LEO **6** VIR **9** LIB **11** SCO **14** SAG **16** CAP **19** AQU **21** PIS **23** ARI **25** TAU **27** GEM **29** CAN
JUL—**1** LEO **4** VIR **6** LIB **9** SCO **11** SAG **14** CAP **16** AQU **18** PIS **20** ARI **22** TAU **24** GEM **27** CAN **29** LEO **31** VIR
AUG—**2** LIB **5** SCO **7** SAG **10** CAP **12** AQU **14** PIS **16** ARI **19** TAU **21** GEM **23** CAN **25** LEO **27** VIR **30** LIB
SEP—**1** SCO **4** SAG **6** CAP **9** AQU **11** PIS **13** ARI **15** TAU **17** GEM **19** CAN **21** LEO **24** VIR **26** LIB **29** SCO
OCT—**1** SAG **4** CAP **6** AQU **8** PIS **10** ARI **12** TAU **14** GEM **16** CAN **19** LEO **21** VIR **23** LIB **26** SCO **28** SAG **31** CAP
NOV—**2** AQU **5** PIS **7** ARI **9** TAU **11** GEM **13** CAN **15** LEO **17** VIR **20** LIB **22** SCO **25** SAG **27** CAP **30** AQU
DEC—**2** PIS **4** ARI **6** TAU **8** GEM **10** CAN **12** LEO **14** VIR **17** LIB **19** SCO **22** SAG **24** CAP **27** AQU **29** PIS **31** ARI

1955

JAN—**1** ARI **3** TAU **5** GEM **7** CAN **9** LEO **11** VIR **13** LIB **16** SCO **18** SAG **21** CAP **23** AQU **25** PIS **28** ARI **30** TAU
FEB—**1** GEM **3** CAN **5** LEO **7** VIR **10** LIB **12** SCO **15** SAG **17** CAP **19** AQU **22** PIS **24** ARI **26** TAU **28** GEM
MAR—**2** CAN **4** LEO **7** VIR **9** LIB **11** SCO **14** SAG **16** CAP **19** AQU **21** PIS **23** ARI **25** TAU **27** GEM **29** CAN
APR—**1** LEO **3** VIR **5** LIB **8** SCO **10** SAG **13** CAP **15** AQU **18** PIS **20** ARI **22** TAU **24** GEM **26** CAN **28** LEO **30** VIR
MAY—**2** LIB **5** SCO **7** SAG **10** CAP **12** AQU **15** PIS **17** ARI **19** TAU **21** GEM **23** CAN **25** LEO **27** VIR **30** LIB
JUN—**1** SCO **4** SAG **6** CAP **9** AQU **11** PIS **13** ARI **16** TAU **18** GEM **20** CAN **22** LEO **24** VIR **26** LIB **28** SCO
JUL—**1** SAG **3** CAP **6** AQU **8** PIS **11** ARI **13** TAU **15** GEM **17** CAN **19** LEO **21** VIR **23** LIB **26** SCO **28** SAG **31** CAP
AUG—**2** AQU **5** PIS **7** ARI **9** TAU **11** GEM **13** CAN **15** LEO **18** VIR **20** LIB **22** SCO **25** SAG **27** CAP **30** AQU
SEP—**1** PIS **3** ARI **5** TAU **8** GEM **10** CAN **12** LEO **14** VIR **16** LIB **18** SCO **21** SAG **23** CAP **26** AQU **28** PIS
OCT—**1** ARI **3** TAU **5** GEM **7** CAN **9** LEO **11** VIR **13** LIB **16** SCO **18** SAG **21** CAP **23** AQU **26** PIS **28** ARI **30** TAU
NOV—**1** GEM **3** CAN **5** LEO **7** VIR **10** LIB **12** SCO **15** SAG **17** CAP **20** AQU **22** PIS **24** ARI **27** TAU **29** GEM
DEC—**1** CAN **3** LEO **5** VIR **7** LIB **9** SCO **12** SAG **14** CAP **17** AQU **19** PIS **22** ARI **24** TAU **26** GEM **28** CAN **30** LEO

1956

JAN—**1** VIR **3** LIB **6** SCO **8** SAG **11** CAP **13** AQU **16** PIS **18** ARI **20** TAU **22** GEM **24** CAN **26** LEO **28** VIR **31** LIB
FEB—**2** SCO **4** SAG **7** CAP **9** AQU **12** PIS **14** ARI **16** TAU **19** GEM **21** CAN **23** LEO **25** VIR **27** LIB **29** SCO
MAR—**3** SAG **5** CAP **8** AQU **10** PIS **12** ARI **15** TAU **17** GEM **19** CAN **21** LEO **23** VIR **25** LIB **28** SCO **30** SAG
APR—**1** CAP **4** AQU **6** PIS **9** ARI **11** TAU **13** GEM **15** CAN **17** LEO **20** VIR **22** LIB **24** SCO **26** SAG **29** CAP
MAY—**1** AQU **4** PIS **6** ARI **8** TAU **11** GEM **13** CAN **15** LEO **17** VIR **19** LIB **21** SCO **24** SAG **26** CAP **29** AQU **31** PIS
JUN—**3** ARI **5** TAU **7** GEM **9** CAN **11** LEO **13** VIR **15** LIB **18** SCO **20** SAG **22** CAP **25** AQU **27** PIS **30** ARI
JUL—**2** TAU **4** GEM **6** CAN **8** LEO **10** VIR **12** LIB **15** SCO **17** SAG **20** CAP **22** AQU **25** PIS **27** ARI **30** TAU
AUG—**1** GEM **3** CAN **5** LEO **7** VIR **9** LIB **11** SCO **13** SAG **16** CAP **18** AQU **21** PIS **23** ARI **26** TAU **28** GEM **30** CAN
SEP—**1** LEO **3** VIR **5** LIB **7** SCO **10** SAG **12** CAP **15** AQU **17** PIS **20** ARI **22** TAU **24** GEM **26** CAN **29** LEO
OCT—**1** VIR **3** LIB **5** SCO **7** SAG **10** CAP **12** AQU **15** PIS **17** ARI **19** TAU **22** GEM **24** CAN **26** LEO **28** VIR **30** LIB
NOV—**1** SCO **3** SAG **6** CAP **8** AQU **11** PIS **13** ARI **16** TAU **18** GEM **20** CAN **22** LEO **24** VIR **26** LIB **29** SCO
DEC—**1** SAG **3** CAP **6** AQU **8** PIS **11** ARI **13** TAU **15** GEM **17** CAN **19** LEO **21** VIR **24** LIB **26** SCO **28** SAG **31** CAP

1957

JAN—**1** CAP **2** AQU **5** PIS **7** ARI **9** TAU **12** GEM **14** CAN **16** LEO **18** VIR **20** LIB **22** SCO **24** SAG **27** CAP **29** AQU
FEB—**1** PIS **3** ARI **6** TAU **8** GEM **10** CAN **12** LEO **14** VIR **16** LIB **18** SCO **21** SAG **23** CAP **26** AQU **28** PIS
MAR—**3** ARI **5** TAU **7** GEM **10** CAN **12** LEO **14** VIR **16** LIB **18** SCO **20** SAG **22** CAP **25** AQU **27** PIS **30** ARI
APR—**1** TAU **4** GEM **6** CAN **8** LEO **10** VIR **12** LIB **14** SCO **16** SAG **19** CAP **21** AQU **24** PIS **26** ARI **29** TAU
MAY—**1** GEM **3** CAN **5** LEO **7** VIR **9** LIB **12** SCO **14** SAG **16** CAP **18** AQU **21** PIS **23** ARI **26** TAU **28** GEM **30** CAN
JUN—**1** LEO **4** VIR **6** LIB **8** SCO **10** SAG **12** CAP **15** AQU **17** PIS **20** ARI **22** TAU **25** GEM **27** CAN **29** LEO
JUL—**1** VIR **3** LIB **5** SCO **7** SAG **10** CAP **12** AQU **15** PIS **17** ARI **20** TAU **22** GEM **24** CAN **26** LEO **28** VIR **30** LIB
AUG—**1** SCO **4** SAG **6** CAP **8** AQU **11** PIS **13** ARI **16** TAU **18** GEM **21** CAN **23** LEO **25** VIR **27** LIB **29** SCO **31** SAG
SEP—**2** CAP **5** AQU **7** PIS **10** ARI **12** TAU **15** GEM **17** CAN **19** LEO **21** VIR **23** LIB **25** SCO **27** SAG **29** CAP
OCT—**2** AQU **4** PIS **7** ARI **9** TAU **12** GEM **14** CAN **16** LEO **18** VIR **21** LIB **23** SCO **25** SAG **27** CAP **29** AQU
NOV—**1** PIS **3** ARI **6** TAU **8** GEM **10** CAN **13** LEO **15** VIR **17** LIB **19** SCO **21** SAG **23** CAP **26** AQU **28** PIS
DEC—**1** ARI **3** TAU **5** GEM **8** CAN **10** LEO **12** VIR **14** LIB **16** SCO **18** SAG **21** CAP **23** AQU **25** PIS **28** ARI **30** TAU

1958

JAN—**1** TAU **2** GEM **4** CAN **6** LEO **8** VIR **10** LIB **12** SCO **15** SAG **17** CAP **19** AQU **22** PIS **24** ARI **27** TAU **29** GEM **31** CAN
FEB—**3** LEO **5** VIR **7** LIB **9** SCO **11** SAG **13** CAP **16** AQU **18** PIS **21** ARI **23** TAU **26** GEM **28** CAN
MAR—**2** LEO **4** VIR **6** LIB **8** SCO **10** SAG **12** CAP **15** AQU **17** PIS **20** ARI **22** TAU **25** GEM **27** CAN **29** LEO
APR—**1** VIR **3** LIB **5** SCO **7** SAG **9** CAP **11** AQU **13** PIS **16** ARI **19** TAU **21** GEM **23** CAN **26** LEO **28** VIR **30** LIB
MAY—**2** SCO **4** SAG **6** CAP **8** AQU **11** PIS **13** ARI **16** TAU **18** GEM **21** CAN **23** LEO **25** VIR **27** LIB **29** SCO **31** SAG
JUN—**3** CAP **5** AQU **7** PIS **10** ARI **12** TAU **15** GEM **17** CAN **19** LEO **21** VIR **24** LIB **26** SCO **28** SAG **30** CAP
JUL—**2** AQU **4** PIS **7** ARI **9** TAU **12** GEM **14** CAN **17** LEO **19** VIR **21** LIB **23** SCO **25** SAG **27** CAP **29** AQU
AUG—**1** PIS **3** ARI **6** TAU **8** GEM **11** CAN **13** LEO **15** VIR **17** LIB **19** SCO **21** SAG **23** CAP **26** AQU **28** PIS **31** ARI
SEP—**2** TAU **5** GEM **7** CAN **9** LEO **11** VIR **13** LIB **15** SCO **18** SAG **20** CAP **22** AQU **24** PIS **27** ARI **29** TAU
OCT—**2** GEM **4** CAN **7** LEO **9** VIR **11** LIB **13** SCO **15** SAG **17** CAP **19** AQU **22** PIS **24** ARI **27** TAU **29** GEM
NOV—**1** CAN **3** LEO **5** VIR **7** LIB **9** SCO **11** SAG **13** CAP **16** AQU **18** PIS **20** ARI **23** TAU **25** GEM **28** CAN **30** LEO
DEC—**3** VIR **5** LIB **7** SCO **9** SAG **11** CAP **13** AQU **15** PIS **18** ARI **20** TAU **23** GEM **25** CAN **27** LEO **30** VIR

1959

JAN—**1** LIB **3** SCO **5** SAG **7** CAP **9** AQU **12** PIS **14** ARI **17** TAU **19** GEM **21** CAN **24** LEO **26** VIR **28** LIB **30** SCO
FEB—**1** SAG **4** CAP **6** AQU **8** PIS **10** ARI **13** TAU **15** GEM **18** CAN **20** LEO **22** VIR **24** LIB **27** SCO
MAR—**1** SAG **3** CAP **5** AQU **7** PIS **10** ARI **12** TAU **15** GEM **17** CAN **20** LEO **22** VIR **24** LIB **26** SCO **28** SAG **30** CAP
APR—**1** AQU **4** PIS **6** ARI **8** TAU **11** GEM **14** CAN **16** LEO **18** VIR **20** LIB **22** SCO **24** SAG **26** CAP **28** AQU
MAY—**1** PIS **3** ARI **6** TAU **8** GEM **11** CAN **13** LEO **16** VIR **18** LIB **20** SCO **22** SAG **24** CAP **26** AQU **28** PIS **30** ARI
JUN—**2** TAU **5** GEM **7** CAN **9** LEO **12** VIR **14** LIB **16** SCO **18** SAG **20** CAP **22** AQU **24** PIS **27** ARI **29** TAU
JUL—**2** GEM **4** CAN **7** LEO **9** VIR **11** LIB **13** SCO **16** SAG **18** CAP **20** AQU **22** PIS **24** ARI **27** TAU **29** GEM
AUG—**1** CAN **3** LEO **5** VIR **8** LIB **10** SCO **12** SAG **14** CAP **16** AQU **18** PIS **20** ARI **23** TAU **25** GEM **28** CAN **30** LEO
SEP—**2** VIR **4** LIB **6** SCO **8** SAG **10** CAP **12** AQU **15** PIS **17** ARI **19** TAU **22** GEM **24** CAN **27** LEO **29** VIR
OCT—**1** LIB **3** SCO **5** SAG **7** CAP **10** AQU **12** PIS **14** ARI **17** TAU **19** GEM **22** CAN **24** LEO **26** VIR **29** LIB **31** SCO
NOV—**2** SAG **4** CAP **6** AQU **8** PIS **10** ARI **13** TAU **15** GEM **18** CAN **20** LEO **23** VIR **25** LIB **27** SCO **29** SAG
DEC—**1** CAP **3** AQU **5** PIS **8** ARI **10** TAU **13** GEM **15** CAN **18** LEO **20** VIR **22** LIB **25** SCO **27** SAG **29** CAP **31** AQU

1960

JAN—**1** AQU **2** PIS **4** ARI **6** TAU **9** GEM **11** CAN **14** LEO **16** VIR **19** LIB **21** SCO **23** SAG **25** CAP **27** AQU **29** PIS **31** ARI
FEB—**3** TAU **5** GEM **8** CAN **10** LEO **13** VIR **15** LIB **17** SCO **19** SAG **21** CAP **23** AQU **26** PIS **28** ARI
MAR—**1** TAU **4** GEM **6** CAN **9** LEO **11** VIR **13** LIB **15** SCO **17** SAG **20** CAP **22** AQU **24** PIS **26** ARI **28** TAU **31** GEM
APR—**2** CAN **5** LEO **7** VIR **10** LIB **12** SCO **14** SAG **16** CAP **18** AQU **20** PIS **22** ARI **25** TAU **27** GEM **30** CAN
MAY—**2** LEO **5** VIR **7** LIB **9** SCO **11** SAG **13** CAP **15** AQU **17** PIS **20** ARI **22** TAU **24** GEM **27** CAN **29** LEO
JUN—**1** VIR **3** LIB **6** SCO **8** SAG **10** CAP **12** AQU **14** PIS **16** ARI **18** TAU **21** GEM **23** CAN **26** LEO **28** VIR
JUL—**1** LIB **3** SCO **5** SAG **7** CAP **9** AQU **11** PIS **13** ARI **15** TAU **18** GEM **20** CAN **23** LEO **25** VIR **28** LIB **30** SCO
AUG—**1** SAG **3** CAP **5** AQU **7** PIS **10** ARI **12** TAU **14** GEM **17** CAN **19** LEO **22** VIR **24** LIB **26** SCO **29** SAG **31** CAP
SEP—**2** AQU **4** PIS **6** ARI **8** TAU **11** GEM **13** CAN **16** LEO **18** VIR **20** LIB **23** SCO **25** SAG **27** CAP **29** AQU
OCT—**1** PIS **3** ARI **6** TAU **8** GEM **10** CAN **13** LEO **15** VIR **18** LIB **20** SCO **22** SAG **24** CAP **26** AQU **28** PIS **31** ARI
NOV—**2** TAU **4** GEM **7** CAN **9** LEO **12** VIR **14** LIB **16** SCO **19** SAG **21** CAP **23** AQU **25** PIS **27** ARI **29** TAU
DEC—**2** GEM **4** CAN **7** LEO **9** VIR **12** LIB **14** SCO **16** SAG **18** CAP **20** AQU **22** PIS **24** ARI **26** TAU **29** GEM **31** CAN

1961

JAN—**1** CAN **3** LEO **5** VIR **8** LIB **10** SCO **12** SAG **14** CAP **16** AQU **18** PIS **20** ARI **23** TAU **25** GEM **28** CAN **30** LEO
FEB—**2** VIR **4** LIB **6** SCO **9** SAG **11** CAP **13** AQU **15** PIS **17** ARI **19** TAU **21** GEM **24** CAN **26** LEO
MAR—**1** VIR **3** LIB **6** SCO **8** SAG **10** CAP **12** AQU **14** PIS **16** ARI **18** TAU **21** GEM **23** CAN **26** LEO **28** VIR **31** LIB
APR—**2** SCO **4** SAG **6** CAP **9** AQU **11** PIS **13** ARI **15** TAU **17** GEM **19** CAN **22** LEO **25** VIR **27** LIB **29** SCO
MAY—**2** SAG **4** CAP **6** AQU **8** PIS **10** ARI **12** TAU **14** GEM **17** CAN **19** LEO **22** VIR **24** LIB **27** SCO **29** SAG **31** CAP
JUN—**2** AQU **4** PIS **6** ARI **8** TAU **11** GEM **13** CAN **16** LEO **18** VIR **21** LIB **23** SCO **25** SAG **27** CAP **29** AQU
JUL—**1** PIS **4** ARI **6** TAU **8** GEM **10** CAN **13** LEO **15** VIR **18** LIB **20** SCO **23** SAG **25** CAP **27** AQU **29** PIS **31** ARI
AUG—**2** TAU **4** GEM **7** CAN **9** LEO **12** VIR **14** LIB **17** SCO **19** SAG **21** CAP **23** AQU **25** PIS **27** ARI **29** TAU
SEP—**1** GEM **3** CAN **5** LEO **8** VIR **10** LIB **13** SCO **15** SAG **18** CAP **20** AQU **22** PIS **24** ARI **26** TAU **28** GEM **30** CAN
OCT—**3** LEO **5** VIR **8** LIB **10** SCO **13** SAG **15** CAP **17** AQU **19** PIS **21** ARI **23** TAU **25** GEM **28** CAN **30** LEO
NOV—**2** VIR **4** LIB **6** SCO **9** SAG **11** CAP **13** AQU **15** PIS **17** ARI **20** TAU **22** GEM **24** CAN **26** LEO **29** VIR
DEC—**1** LIB **4** SCO **6** SAG **8** CAP **10** AQU **13** PIS **15** ARI **17** TAU **19** GEM **21** CAN **24** LEO **26** VIR **29** LIB **31** SCO

1962

JAN—**1** SCO **3** SAG **5** CAP **7** AQU **9** PIS **11** ARI **13** TAU **15** GEM **18** CAN **20** LEO **23** VIR **25** LIB **28** SCO **30** SAG
FEB—**1** CAP **3** AQU **5** PIS **7** ARI **9** TAU **12** GEM **14** CAN **16** LEO **19** VIR **21** LIB **24** SCO **26** SAG
MAR—**1** CAP **3** AQU **5** PIS **7** ARI **9** TAU **11** GEM **13** CAN **16** LEO **18** VIR **21** LIB **23** SCO **26** SAG **28** CAP **30** AQU
APR—**1** PIS **3** ARI **5** TAU **7** GEM **9** CAN **12** LEO **14** VIR **17** LIB **19** SCO **22** SAG **24** CAP **26** AQU **28** PIS
MAY—**1** ARI **3** TAU **5** GEM **7** CAN **9** LEO **12** VIR **14** LIB **17** SCO **19** SAG **21** CAP **24** AQU **26** PIS **28** ARI **30** TAU
JUN—**1** GEM **3** CAN **6** LEO **8** VIR **10** LIB **13** SCO **15** SAG **18** CAP **20** AQU **22** PIS **24** ARI **26** TAU **28** GEM
JUL—**1** CAN **3** LEO **5** VIR **8** LIB **10** SCO **13** SAG **15** CAP **17** AQU **19** PIS **21** ARI **23** TAU **26** GEM **28** CAN **30** LEO
AUG—**2** VIR **4** LIB **7** SCO **9** SAG **11** CAP **14** AQU **16** PIS **18** ARI **20** TAU **22** GEM **24** CAN **26** LEO **29** VIR **31** LIB
SEP—**3** SCO **5** SAG **8** CAP **10** AQU **12** PIS **14** ARI **16** TAU **18** GEM **20** CAN **23** LEO **25** VIR **28** LIB **30** SCO
OCT—**3** SAG **5** CAP **7** AQU **10** PIS **12** ARI **14** TAU **16** GEM **18** CAN **20** LEO **22** VIR **25** LIB **27** SCO **30** SAG
NOV—**1** CAP **4** AQU **6** PIS **8** ARI **10** TAU **12** GEM **14** CAN **16** LEO **19** VIR **21** LIB **24** SCO **26** SAG **29** CAP
DEC—**1** AQU **3** PIS **5** ARI **7** TAU **9** GEM **11** CAN **14** LEO **16** VIR **19** LIB **21** SCO **24** SAG **26** CAP **28** AQU **30** PIS

1963

JAN—**1** ARI **4** TAU **6** GEM **8** CAN **10** LEO **12** VIR **15** LIB **17** SCO **20** SAG **22** CAP **25** AQU **27** PIS **29** ARI **31** TAU
FEB—**2** GEM **4** CAN **6** LEO **9** VIR **11** LIB **14** SCO **16** SAG **19** CAP **21** AQU **23** PIS **25** ARI **27** TAU
MAR—**1** GEM **3** CAN **6** LEO **8** VIR **11** LIB **13** SCO **16** SAG **18** CAP **20** AQU **23** PIS **25** ARI **27** TAU **29** GEM **31** CAN
APR—**2** LEO **4** VIR **7** LIB **9** SCO **12** SAG **14** CAP **17** AQU **19** PIS **21** ARI **23** TAU **25** GEM **27** CAN **29** LEO
MAY—**2** VIR **4** LIB **7** SCO **9** SAG **12** CAP **14** AQU **16** PIS **18** ARI **20** TAU **22** GEM **24** CAN **27** LEO **29** VIR **31** LIB
JUN—**3** SCO **5** SAG **8** CAP **10** AQU **12** PIS **15** ARI **17** TAU **19** GEM **21** CAN **23** LEO **25** VIR **28** LIB **30** SCO
JUL—**3** SAG **5** CAP **7** AQU **10** PIS **12** ARI **14** TAU **16** GEM **18** CAN **20** LEO **23** VIR **25** LIB **27** SCO **30** SAG
AUG—**1** CAP **4** AQU **6** PIS **8** ARI **10** TAU **12** GEM **14** CAN **17** LEO **19** VIR **21** LIB **24** SCO **26** SAG **29** CAP **31** AQU
SEP—**2** PIS **4** ARI **7** TAU **9** GEM **11** CAN **13** LEO **15** VIR **18** LIB **20** SCO **23** SAG **25** CAP **28** AQU **30** PIS
OCT—**2** ARI **4** TAU **6** GEM **8** CAN **10** LEO **12** VIR **15** LIB **17** SCO **20** SAG **22** CAP **25** AQU **27** PIS **29** ARI **31** TAU
NOV—**2** GEM **4** CAN **6** LEO **9** VIR **11** LIB **14** SCO **16** SAG **19** CAP **21** AQU **24** PIS **26** ARI **28** TAU **30** GEM
DEC—**2** CAN **4** LEO **6** VIR **8** LIB **11** SCO **13** SAG **16** CAP **18** AQU **21** PIS **23** ARI **25** TAU **27** GEM **29** CAN **31** LEO

1964

JAN—**1** LEO **2** VIR **5** LIB **7** SCO **10** SAG **12** CAP **15** AQU **17** PIS **19** ARI **21** TAU **24** GEM **26** CAN **28** LEO **30** VIR
FEB—**1** LIB **4** SCO **6** SAG **9** CAP **11** AQU **13** PIS **16** ARI **18** TAU **20** GEM **22** CAN **24** LEO **26** VIR **28** LIB
MAR—**2** SCO **4** SAG **7** CAP **9** AQU **12** PIS **14** ARI **16** TAU **18** GEM **20** CAN **22** LEO **25** VIR **27** LIB **29** SCO
APR—**1** SAG **3** CAP **6** AQU **8** PIS **10** ARI **12** TAU **14** GEM **16** CAN **19** LEO **21** VIR **23** LIB **26** SCO **28** SAG
MAY—**1** CAP **3** AQU **5** PIS **8** ARI **10** TAU **12** GEM **14** CAN **16** LEO **18** VIR **20** LIB **23** SCO **25** SAG **28** CAP **30** AQU
JUN—**2** PIS **4** ARI **6** TAU **8** GEM **10** CAN **12** LEO **14** VIR **17** LIB **19** SCO **22** SAG **24** CAP **27** AQU **29** PIS
JUL—**1** ARI **4** TAU **6** GEM **8** CAN **10** LEO **12** VIR **14** LIB **16** SCO **19** SAG **21** CAP **24** AQU **26** PIS **29** ARI **31** TAU
AUG—**2** GEM **4** CAN **6** LEO **8** VIR **10** LIB **13** SCO **15** SAG **18** CAP **20** AQU **23** PIS **25** ARI **27** TAU **29** GEM **31** CAN
SEP—**2** LEO **5** VIR **7** LIB **9** SCO **11** SAG **14** CAP **16** AQU **19** PIS **21** ARI **23** TAU **25** GEM **28** CAN **30** LEO
OCT—**2** VIR **4** LIB **6** SCO **9** SAG **11** CAP **14** AQU **16** PIS **19** ARI **21** TAU **23** GEM **25** CAN **27** LEO **29** VIR **31** LIB
NOV—**3** SCO **5** SAG **8** CAP **10** AQU **13** PIS **15** ARI **17** TAU **19** GEM **21** CAN **23** LEO **25** VIR **28** LIB **30** SCO
DEC—**2** SAG **5** CAP **7** AQU **10** PIS **12** ARI **15** TAU **17** GEM **19** CAN **21** LEO **23** VIR **25** LIB **27** SCO **30** SAG

1965

JAN—**1** CAP **4** AQU **6** PIS **9** ARI **11** TAU **13** GEM **15** CAN **17** LEO **19** VIR **21** LIB **23** SCO **26** SAG **28** CAP **31** AQU
FEB—**2** PIS **5** ARI **7** TAU **9** GEM **11** CAN **13** LEO **16** VIR **18** LIB **20** SCO **22** SAG **25** CAP **27** AQU
MAR—**2** PIS **4** ARI **6** TAU **9** GEM **11** CAN **13** LEO **15** VIR **17** LIB **19** SCO **22** SAG **24** CAP **27** AQU **29** PIS **31** ARI
APR—**3** TAU **5** GEM **7** CAN **9** LEO **11** VIR **13** LIB **16** SCO **18** SAG **20** CAP **23** AQU **25** PIS **28** ARI **30** TAU
MAY—**2** GEM **4** CAN **6** LEO **8** VIR **11** LIB **13** SCO **15** SAG **18** CAP **20** AQU **23** PIS **25** ARI **27** TAU **30** GEM
JUN—**1** CAN **3** LEO **5** VIR **7** LIB **9** SCO **12** SAG **14** CAP **16** AQU **19** PIS **21** ARI **24** TAU **26** GEM **28** CAN **30** LEO
JUL—**2** VIR **4** LIB **6** SCO **9** SAG **11** CAP **14** AQU **16** PIS **19** ARI **21** TAU **23** GEM **25** CAN **27** LEO **29** VIR **31** LIB
AUG—**3** SCO **5** SAG **7** CAP **10** AQU **13** PIS **15** ARI **17** TAU **20** GEM **22** CAN **24** LEO **26** VIR **28** LIB **30** SCO
SEP—**1** SAG **4** CAP **6** AQU **9** PIS **11** ARI **14** TAU **16** GEM **18** CAN **20** LEO **22** VIR **24** LIB **26** SCO **29** SAG
OCT—**1** CAP **4** AQU **6** PIS **9** ARI **11** TAU **13** GEM **15** CAN **17** LEO **20** VIR **22** LIB **24** SCO **26** SAG **28** CAP **31** AQU
NOV—**2** PIS **5** ARI **7** TAU **9** GEM **12** CAN **14** LEO **16** VIR **18** LIB **20** SCO **22** SAG **25** CAP **27** AQU **30** PIS
DEC—**2** ARI **5** TAU **7** GEM **9** CAN **11** LEO **13** VIR **15** LIB **17** SCO **20** SAG **22** CAP **25** AQU **27** PIS **30** ARI

1966

JAN—**1** TAU **3** GEM **5** CAN **7** LEO **9** VIR **11** LIB **14** SCO **16** SAG **18** CAP **21** AQU **23** PIS **26** ARI **28** TAU **31** GEM
FEB—**2** CAN **4** LEO **6** VIR **8** LIB **10** SCO **12** SAG **5** CAP **17** AQU **20** PIS **22** ARI **25** TAU **27** GEM
MAR—**1** CAN **3** LEO **5** VIR **7** LIB **9** SCO **12** SAG **14** CAP **16** AQU **19** PIS **21** ARI **24** TAU **26** GEM **29** CAN **31** LEO
APR—**2** VIR **4** LIB **6** SCO **8** SAG **10** CAP **13** AQU **15** PIS **18** ARI **20** TAU **22** GEM **25** CAN **27** LEO **29** VIR
MAY—**1** LIB **3** SCO **5** SAG **8** CAP **10** AQU **12** PIS **15** ARI **17** TAU **20** GEM **22** CAN **24** LEO **26** VIR **28** LIB **31** SCO
JUN—**2** SAG **4** CAP **6** AQU **9** PIS **11** ARI **14** TAU **16** GEM **18** CAN **20** LEO **23** VIR **25** LIB **27** SCO **29** SAG
JUL—**1** CAP **4** AQU **6** PIS **9** ARI **11** TAU **14** GEM **16** CAN **18** LEO **20** VIR **22** LIB **24** SCO **26** SAG **29** CAP **31** AQU
AUG—**2** PIS **5** ARI **7** TAU **10** GEM **12** CAN **14** LEO **16** VIR **18** LIB **20** SCO **22** SAG **25** CAP **27** AQU **30** PIS
SEP—**1** ARI **4** TAU **6** GEM **9** CAN **11** LEO **13** VIR **15** LIB **17** SCO **19** SAG **21** CAP **23** AQU **26** PIS **28** ARI
OCT—**1** TAU **3** GEM **6** CAN **8** LEO **10** VIR **12** LIB **14** SCO **16** SAG **18** CAP **21** AQU **23** PIS **26** ARI **28** TAU **31** GEM
NOV—**2** CAN **4** LEO **6** VIR **8** LIB **11** SCO **13** SAG **15** CAP **17** AQU **20** PIS **22** ARI **25** TAU **27** GEM **29** CAN
DEC—**2** LEO **4** VIR **6** LIB **8** SCO **10** SAG **12** CAP **14** AQU **17** PIS **19** ARI **22** TAU **24** GEM **27** CAN **29** LEO **31** VIR

1967

JAN—**1** VIR **2** LIB **4** SCO **6** SAG **9** CAP **11** AQU **13** PIS **16** ARI **18** TAU **21** GEM **23** CAN **25** LEO **27** VIR **29** LIB **31** SCO
FEB—**3** SAG **5** CAP **7** AQU **10** PIS **12** ARI **15** TAU **17** GEM **19** CAN **22** LEO **24** VIR **26** LIB **28** SCO
MAR—**2** SAG **4** CAP **6** AQU **9** PIS **11** ARI **14** TAU **16** GEM **19** CAN **21** LEO **23** VIR **25** LIB **27** SCO **29** SAG **31** CAP
APR—**3** AQU **5** PIS **8** ARI **10** TAU **13** GEM **15** CAN **17** LEO **20** VIR **22** LIB **24** SCO **26** SAG **28** CAP **30** AQU
MAY—**2** PIS **5** ARI **7** TAU **10** GEM **12** CAN **15** LEO **17** VIR **19** LIB **21** SCO **23** SAG **25** CAP **27** AQU **30** PIS
JUN—**1** ARI **4** TAU **6** GEM **9** CAN **11** LEO **13** VIR **15** LIB **17** SCO **19** SAG **21** CAP **24** AQU **26** PIS **28** ARI
JUL—**1** TAU **3** GEM **6** CAN **8** LEO **10** VIR **12** LIB **15** SCO **17** SAG **19** CAP **21** AQU **23** PIS **26** ARI **28** TAU **31** GEM
AUG—**2** CAN **4** LEO **7** VIR **9** LIB **11** SCO **13** SAG **15** CAP **17** AQU **20** PIS **22** ARI **25** TAU **27** GEM **30** CAN
SEP—**1** LEO **3** VIR **5** LIB **7** SCO **9** SAG **11** CAP **14** AQU **16** PIS **18** ARI **21** TAU **23** GEM **26** CAN **28** LEO **30** VIR
OCT—**2** LIB **4** SCO **6** SAG **9** CAP **11** AQU **13** PIS **16** ARI **18** TAU **21** GEM **23** CAN **26** LEO **28** VIR **30** LIB
NOV—**1** SCO **3** SAG **5** CAP **7** AQU **9** PIS **12** ARI **14** TAU **17** GEM **19** CAN **22** LEO **24** VIR **26** LIB **28** SCO **30** SAG
DEC—**2** CAP **4** AQU **7** PIS **9** ARI **12** TAU **14** GEM **17** CAN **19** LEO **21** VIR **24** LIB **26** SCO **28** SAG **30** CAP

1968

JAN—**1** AQU **3** PIS **6** ARI **8** TAU **11** GEM **13** CAN **15** LEO **18** VIR **20** LIB **22** SCO **24** SAG **26** CAP **28** AQU **31** PIS
FEB—**2** ARI **4** TAU **7** GEM **9** CAN **12** LEO **14** VIR **16** LIB **18** SCO **20** SAG **22** CAP **25** AQU **27** PIS **29** ARI
MAR—**3** TAU **5** GEM **8** CAN **10** LEO **12** VIR **14** LIB **17** SCO **19** SAG **21** CAP **23** AQU **25** PIS **28** ARI **30** TAU
APR—**2** GEM **4** CAN **7** LEO **9** VIR **11** LIB **13** SCO **15** SAG **17** CAP **19** AQU **21** PIS **24** ARI **26** TAU **29** GEM
MAY—**1** CAN **4** LEO **6** VIR **8** LIB **10** SCO **12** SAG **14** CAP **16** AQU **19** PIS **21** ARI **24** TAU **26** GEM **29** CAN **31** LEO
JUN—**2** VIR **5** LIB **7** SCO **9** SAG **11** CAP **13** AQU **15** PIS **17** ARI **20** TAU **22** GEM **25** CAN **27** LEO **30** VIR
JUL—**2** LIB **4** SCO **6** SAG **8** CAP **10** AQU **12** PIS **15** ARI **17** TAU **20** GEM **22** CAN **25** LEO **27** VIR **29** LIB **31** SCO
AUG—**3** SAG **5** CAP **7** AQU **9** PIS **11** ARI **13** TAU **16** GEM **18** CAN **21** LEO **23** VIR **25** LIB **28** SCO **30** SAG
SEP—**1** CAP **3** AQU **5** PIS **7** ARI **10** TAU **12** GEM **15** CAN **17** LEO **20** VIR **22** LIB **24** SCO **26** SAG **28** CAP **30** AQU
OCT—**2** PIS **5** ARI **7** TAU **10** GEM **12** CAN **15** LEO **17** VIR **19** LIB **21** SCO **23** SAG **25** CAP **27** AQU **30** PIS
NOV—**1** ARI **3** TAU **6** GEM **8** CAN **11** LEO **13** VIR **16** LIB **18** SCO **20** SAG **22** CAP **24** AQU **26** PIS **28** ARI
DEC—**1** TAU **3** GEM **6** CAN **8** LEO **11** VIR **13** LIB **15** SCO **17** SAG **19** CAP **21** AQU **23** PIS **26** ARI **28** TAU **30** GEM

1969

JAN—**1** GEM **2** CAN **4** LEO **7** VIR **9** LIB **12** SCO **14** SAG **16** CAP **18** AQU **20** PIS **22** ARI **24** TAU **27** GEM **29** CAN
FEB—**1** LEO **3** VIR **6** LIB **8** SCO **10** SAG **12** CAP **14** AQU **16** PIS **18** ARI **21** TAU **23** GEM **26** CAN **28** LEO
MAR—**2** VIR **5** LIB **7** SCO **9** SAG **11** CAP **13** AQU **16** PIS **18** ARI **20** TAU **22** GEM **25** CAN **27** LEO **30** VIR
APR—**1** LIB **3** SCO **5** SAG **8** CAP **10** AQU **12** PIS **14** ARI **16** TAU **19** GEM **21** CAN **24** LEO **26** VIR **29** LIB
MAY—**1** SCO **3** SAG **5** CAP **7** AQU **9** PIS **11** ARI **14** TAU **16** GEM **19** CAN **21** LEO **24** VIR **26** LIB **28** SCO **30** SAG
JUN—**1** CAP **3** AQU **5** PIS **7** ARI **10** TAU **12** GEM **15** CAN **17** LEO **20** VIR **22** LIB **25** SCO **27** SAG **29** CAP
JUL—**1** AQU **3** PIS **5** ARI **7** TAU **10** GEM **12** CAN **15** LEO **17** VIR **20** LIB **22** SCO **24** SAG **26** CAP **28** AQU **30** PIS
AUG—**1** ARI **3** TAU **6** GEM **8** CAN **11** LEO **13** VIR **16** LIB **18** SCO **20** SAG **22** CAP **24** AQU **26** PIS **29** ARI **31** TAU
SEP—**2** GEM **5** CAN **7** LEO **10** VIR **12** LIB **14** SCO **17** SAG **19** CAP **21** AQU **23** PIS **25** ARI **27** TAU **29** GEM
OCT—**2** CAN **4** LEO **7** VIR **9** LIB **12** SCO **14** SAG **16** CAP **18** AQU **20** PIS **22** ARI **25** TAU **27** GEM **29** CAN
NOV—**1** LEO **3** VIR **6** LIB **8** SCO **10** SAG **12** CAP **14** AQU **16** PIS **19** ARI **21** TAU **23** GEM **26** CAN **28** LEO
DEC—**1** VIR **3** LIB **5** SCO **8** SAG **10** CAP **12** AQU **14** PIS **16** ARI **18** TAU **20** GEM **23** CAN **25** LEO **28** VIR **30** LIB

1970

JAN—**1** LIB **2** SCO **4** SAG **6** CAP **8** AQU **10** PIS **12** ARI **14** TAU **17** GEM **19** CAN **22** LEO **24** VIR **27** LIB **29** SCO
     31 SAG
FEB—**2** CAP **4** AQU **6** PIS **8** ARI **11** TAU **13** GEM **15** CAN **18** LEO **20** VIR **23** LIB **25** SCO **28** SAG
MAR—**2** CAP **4** AQU **6** PIS **8** ARI **10** TAU **12** GEM **15** CAN **17** LEO **20** VIR **22** LIB **25** SCO **27** SAG **29** CAP **31** AQU
APR—**2** PIS **4** ARI **6** TAU **9** GEM **11** CAN **14** LEO **16** VIR **19** LIB **21** SCO **23** SAG **25** CAP **27** AQU **30** PIS
MAY—**2** ARI **4** TAU **6** GEM **8** CAN **11** LEO **13** VIR **16** LIB **18** SCO **20** SAG **23** CAP **25** AQU **27** PIS **29** ARI **31** TAU
JUN—**2** GEM **5** CAN **7** LEO **10** VIR **12** LIB **15** SCO **17** SAG **19** CAP **21** AQU **23** PIS **25** ARI **27** TAU **30** GEM
JUL—**2** CAN **4** LEO **7** VIR **10** LIB **12** SCO **14** SAG **16** CAP **18** AQU **20** PIS **22** ARI **25** TAU **27** GEM **29** CAN
AUG—**1** LEO **3** VIR **6** LIB **8** SCO **11** SAG **13** CAP **15** AQU **17** PIS **19** ARI **21** TAU **23** GEM **26** CAN **28** LEO **31** VIR
SEP—**2** LIB **5** SCO **7** SAG **9** CAP **11** AQU **13** PIS **15** ARI **17** TAU **19** GEM **22** CAN **24** LEO **27** VIR **29** LIB
OCT—**2** SCO **4** SAG **6** CAP **9** AQU **11** PIS **13** ARI **15** TAU **17** GEM **19** CAN **22** LEO **24** VIR **27** LIB **29** SCO **31** SAG
NOV—**3** CAP **5** AQU **7** PIS **9** ARI **11** TAU **13** GEM **16** CAN **18** LEO **20** VIR **23** LIB **25** SCO **28** SAG **30** CAP
DEC—**2** AQU **4** PIS **6** ARI **8** TAU **11** GEM **13** CAN **15** LEO **18** VIR **20** LIB **23** SCO **25** SAG **27** CAP **29** AQU **31** PIS

1971

JAN—**1** PIS **3** ARI **5** TAU **7** GEM **9** CAN **12** LEO **14** VIR **17** LIB **19** SCO **22** SAG **24** CAP **26** AQU **28** PIS **30** ARI
FEB—**1** TAU **3** GEM **5** CAN **8** LEO **10** VIR **13** LIB **15** SCO **18** SAG **20** CAP **22** AQU **24** PIS **26** ARI **28** TAU
MAR—**2** GEM **5** CAN **7** LEO **10** VIR **12** LIB **15** SCO **17** SAG **19** CAP **22** AQU **24** PIS **26** ARI **28** TAU **30** GEM
APR—**1** CAN **3** LEO **6** VIR **8** LIB **11** SCO **13** SAG **16** CAP **18** AQU **20** PIS **22** ARI **24** TAU **26** GEM **28** CAN
MAY—**1** LEO **3** VIR **6** LIB **8** SCO **11** SAG **13** CAP **15** AQU **17** PIS **20** ARI **22** TAU **24** GEM **26** CAN **28** LEO **30** VIR
JUN—**2** LIB **5** SCO **7** SAG **9** CAP **11** AQU **14** PIS **16** ARI **18** TAU **20** GEM **22** CAN **24** LEO **27** VIR **29** LIB
JUL—**2** SCO **4** SAG **7** CAP **9** AQU **11** PIS **13** ARI **15** TAU **17** GEM **19** CAN **22** LEO **24** VIR **27** LIB **29** SCO
AUG—**1** SAG **3** CAP **5** AQU **7** PIS **9** ARI **11** TAU **13** GEM **16** CAN **18** LEO **20** VIR **23** LIB **26** SCO **28** SAG **30** CAP
SEP—**2** AQU **4** PIS **6** ARI **8** TAU **10** GEM **12** CAN **14** LEO **17** VIR **19** LIB **22** SCO **24** SAG **27** CAP **29** AQU
OCT—**1** PIS **3** ARI **5** TAU **7** GEM **9** CAN **12** LEO **14** VIR **16** LIB **19** SCO **22** SAG **24** CAP **26** AQU **29** PIS **31** ARI
NOV—**2** TAU **4** GEM **6** CAN **8** LEO **10** VIR **13** LIB **15** SCO **18** SAG **20** CAP **23** AQU **25** PIS **27** ARI **29** TAU
DEC—**1** GEM **3** CAN **5** LEO **8** VIR **10** LIB **13** SCO **15** SAG **17** CAP **20** AQU **22** PIS **24** ARI **26** TAU **28** GEM **30** CAN

1972

JAN—**1** CAN **2** LEO **4** VIR **6** LIB **9** SCO **11** SAG **14** CAP **16** AQU **18** PIS **20** ARI **23** TAU **25** GEM **27** CAN **29** LEO
31 VIR
FEB—**3** LIB **5** SCO **8** SAG **10** CAP **12** AQU **15** PIS **17** ARI **19** TAU **21** GEM **23** CAN **25** LEO **28** VIR
MAR—**1** LIB **4** SCO **6** SAG **9** CAP **11** AQU **13** PIS **15** ARI **17** TAU **19** GEM **21** CAN **24** LEO **26** VIR **28** LIB **31** SCO
APR—**2** SAG **5** CAP **7** AQU **10** PIS **12** ARI **14** TAU **16** GEM **18** CAN **20** LEO **22** VIR **25** LIB **27** SCO **30** SAG
MAY—**2** CAP **5** AQU **7** PIS **9** ARI **11** TAU **13** GEM **15** CAN **17** LEO **19** VIR **22** LIB **24** SCO **27** SAG **30** CAP
JUN—**1** AQU **3** PIS **5** ARI **7** TAU **9** GEM **11** CAN **14** LEO **16** VIR **18** LIB **21** SCO **23** SAG **26** CAP **28** AQU **30** PIS
JUL—**3** ARI **5** TAU **7** GEM **9** CAN **11** LEO **13** VIR **15** LIB **18** SCO **20** SAG **23** CAP **25** AQU **28** PIS **30** ARI
AUG—**1** TAU **3** GEM **5** CAN **7** LEO **10** VIR **12** LIB **14** SCO **17** SAG **19** CAP **22** AQU **24** PIS **26** ARI **28** TAU **30** GEM
SEP—**1** CAN **4** LEO **6** VIR **8** LIB **11** SCO **13** SAG **16** CAP **18** AQU **20** PIS **22** ARI **24** TAU **27** GEM **29** CAN
OCT—**1** LEO **3** VIR **5** LIB **8** SCO **10** SAG **13** CAP **15** AQU **18** PIS **20** ARI **22** TAU **24** GEM **26** CAN **28** LEO **30** VIR
NOV—**2** LIB **4** SCO **7** SAG **9** CAP **12** AQU **14** PIS **16** ARI **18** TAU **20** GEM **22** CAN **24** LEO **27** VIR **29** LIB
DEC—**1** SCO **4** SAG **7** CAP **9** AQU **11** PIS **14** ARI **16** TAU **18** GEM **20** CAN **22** LEO **24** VIR **26** LIB **29** SCO **31** SAG

1973

JAN—**1** SAG **3** CAP **5** AQU **8** PIS **10** ARI **12** TAU **14** GEM **16** CAN **18** LEO **20** VIR **23** LIB **25** SCO **28** SAG **30** CAP
FEB—**2** AQU **4** PIS **6** ARI **8** TAU **10** GEM **13** CAN **15** LEO **17** VIR **19** LIB **21** SCO **24** SAG **26** CAP
MAR—**1** AQU **3** PIS **5** ARI **8** TAU **10** GEM **12** CAN **14** LEO **16** VIR **18** LIB **21** SCO **23** SAG **26** CAP **28** AQU **31** PIS
APR—**2** ARI **4** TAU **6** GEM **8** CAN **10** LEO **12** VIR **15** LIB **17** SCO **20** SAG **22** CAP **25** AQU **27** PIS **29** ARI
MAY—**1** TAU **3** GEM **5** CAN **7** LEO **10** VIR **12** LIB **14** SCO **17** SAG **19** CAP **22** AQU **24** PIS **27** ARI **29** TAU **31** GEM
JUN—**2** CAN **4** LEO **6** VIR **8** LIB **11** SCO **13** SAG **16** CAP **18** AQU **21** PIS **23** ARI **25** TAU **27** GEM **29** CAN
JUL—**1** LEO **3** VIR **5** LIB **8** SCO **10** SAG **13** CAP **15** AQU **18** PIS **20** ARI **22** TAU **25** GEM **27** CAN **29** LEO **31** VIR
AUG—**2** LIB **4** SCO **7** SAG **9** CAP **12** AQU **14** PIS **16** ARI **19** TAU **21** GEM **23** CAN **25** LEO **27** VIR **29** LIB
SEP—**1** SCO **3** SAG **5** CAP **8** AQU **10** PIS **13** ARI **15** TAU **17** GEM **19** CAN **21** LEO **23** VIR **26** LIB **28** SCO **30** SAG
OCT—**3** CAP **5** AQU **8** PIS **10** ARI **12** TAU **14** GEM **16** CAN **19** LEO **21** VIR **23** LIB **25** SCO **28** SAG **30** CAP
NOV—**2** AQU **4** PIS **6** ARI **9** TAU **11** GEM **13** CAN **15** LEO **17** VIR **19** LIB **22** SCO **24** SAG **26** CAP **29** AQU
DEC—**1** PIS **4** ARI **6** TAU **8** GEM **10** CAN **12** LEO **14** VIR **16** LIB **19** SCO **21** SAG **24** CAP **26** AQU **29** PIS **31** ARI

1974

JAN—**1** ARI **2** TAU **5** GEM **7** CAN **9** LEO **11** VIR **13** LIB **15** SCO **17** SAG **20** CAP **22** AQU **25** PIS **27** ARI **30** TAU
FEB—**1** GEM **3** CAN **5** LEO **7** VIR **9** LIB **11** SCO **14** SAG **16** CAP **19** AQU **21** PIS **24** ARI **26** TAU **28** GEM
MAR—**2** CAN **4** LEO **7** VIR **9** LIB **11** SCO **13** SAG **16** CAP **18** AQU **21** PIS **23** ARI **25** TAU **27** GEM **30** CAN
APR—**1** LEO **3** VIR **5** LIB **7** SCO **9** SAG **12** CAP **14** AQU **17** PIS **19** ARI **22** TAU **24** GEM **26** CAN **28** LEO **30** VIR
MAY—**2** LIB **4** SCO **7** SAG **9** CAP **12** AQU **14** PIS **17** ARI **19** TAU **21** GEM **23** CAN **25** LEO **27** VIR **30** LIB
JUN—**1** SCO **3** SAG **6** CAP **8** AQU **11** PIS **13** ARI **15** TAU **18** GEM **20** CAN **22** LEO **24** VIR **26** LIB **28** SCO **30** SAG
JUL—**3** CAP **5** AQU **8** PIS **10** ARI **13** TAU **15** GEM **17** CAN **19** LEO **21** VIR **23** LIB **25** SCO **28** SAG **30** CAP
AUG—**2** AQU **4** PIS **7** ARI **9** TAU **11** GEM **13** CAN **15** LEO **17** VIR **19** LIB **22** SCO **24** SAG **26** CAP **29** AQU **31** PIS
SEP—**3** ARI **5** TAU **8** GEM **10** CAN **12** LEO **14** VIR **16** LIB **18** SCO **20** SAG **23** CAP **25** AQU **28** PIS **30** ARI
OCT—**2** TAU **5** GEM **7** CAN **9** LEO **11** VIR **13** LIB **15** SCO **18** SAG **20** CAP **22** AQU **25** PIS **27** ARI **30** TAU
NOV—**1** GEM **3** CAN **5** LEO **8** VIR **10** LIB **12** SCO **14** SAG **16** CAP **19** AQU **21** PIS **24** ARI **26** TAU **28** GEM
DEC—**1** CAN **3** LEO **5** VIR **7** LIB **9** SCO **11** SAG **14** CAP **16** AQU **19** PIS **21** ARI **24** TAU **26** GEM **28** CAN **30** LEO

1975

JAN—1 VIR 3 LIB 5 SCO 8 SAG 10 CAP 12 AQU 15 PIS 17 ARI 20 TAU 22 GEM 24 CAN 26 LEO 28 VIR 30 LIB
FEB—2 SCO 4 SAG 6 CAP 9 AQU 11 PIS 14 ARI 16 TAU 19 GEM 21 CAN 23 LEO 25 VIR 27 LIB
MAR—1 SCO 3 SAG 5 CAP 8 AQU 10 PIS 13 ARI 15 TAU 18 GEM 20 CAN 22 LEO 24 VIR 26 LIB 28 SCO 30 SAG
APR—2 CAP 4 AQU 7 PIS 9 ARI 12 TAU 14 GEM 16 CAN 19 LEO 21 VIR 23 LIB 25 SCO 27 SAG 29 CAP
MAY—2 AQU 4 PIS 7 ARI 9 TAU 11 GEM 14 CAN 16 LEO 18 VIR 20 LIB 22 SCO 24 SAG 27 CAP 29 AQU 31 PIS
JUN—3 ARI 5 TAU 8 GEM 10 CAN 12 LEO 14 VIR 16 LIB 18 SCO 21 SAG 23 CAP 25 AQU 28 PIS 30 ARI
JUL—3 TAU 5 GEM 7 CAN 9 LEO 11 VIR 14 LIB 16 SCO 18 SAG 20 CAP 23 AQU 25 PIS 28 ARI 30 TAU
AUG—1 GEM 4 CAN 6 LEO 8 VIR 10 LIB 12 SCO 14 SAG 16 CAP 19 AQU 21 PIS 24 ARI 26 TAU 29 GEM 31 CAN
SEP—2 LEO 4 VIR 6 LIB 8 SCO 10 SAG 13 CAP 15 AQU 18 PIS 20 ARI 23 TAU 25 GEM 27 CAN 30 LEO
OCT—2 VIR 4 LIB 6 SCO 8 SAG 10 CAP 12 AQU 15 PIS 17 ARI 20 TAU 22 GEM 25 CAN 27 LEO 29 VIR 31 LIB
NOV—2 SCO 4 SAG 6 CAP 9 AQU 11 PIS 14 ARI 16 TAU 19 GEM 21 CAN 23 LEO 25 VIR 27 LIB 30 SCO
DEC—2 SAG 4 CAP 6 AQU 8 PIS 11 ARI 13 TAU 16 GEM 18 CAN 20 LEO 23 VIR 25 LIB 27 SCO 29 SAG 31 CAP

1976

JAN—1 CAP 2 AQU 5 PIS 7 ARI 10 TAU 12 GEM 15 CAN 17 LEO 19 VIR 21 LIB 23 SCO 25 SAG 27 CAP 30 AQU
FEB—1 PIS 4 ARI 6 TAU 9 GEM 11 CAN 13 LEO 15 VIR 17 LIB 19 SCO 21 SAG 24 CAP 26 AQU 28 PIS
MAR—2 ARI 4 TAU 7 GEM 9 CAN 12 LEO 14 VIR 16 LIB 18 SCO 20 SAG 22 CAP 24 AQU 27 PIS 29 ARI
APR—1 TAU 3 GEM 6 CAN 8 LEO 10 VIR 12 LIB 14 SCO 16 SAG 18 CAP 20 AQU 23 PIS 25 ARI 28 TAU 30 GEM
MAY—3 CAN 5 LEO 7 VIR 10 LIB 12 SCO 14 SAG 16 CAP 18 AQU 20 PIS 23 ARI 25 TAU 28 GEM 30 CAN
JUN—1 LEO 4 VIR 6 LIB 8 SCO 10 SAG 12 CAP 14 AQU 17 PIS 19 ARI 22 TAU 24 GEM 26 CAN 29 LEO
JUL—1 VIR 3 LIB 5 SCO 7 SAG 9 CAP 12 AQU 14 PIS 16 ARI 19 TAU 21 GEM 24 CAN 26 LEO 28 VIR 30 LIB
AUG—1 SCO 4 SAG 6 CAP 8 AQU 10 PIS 13 ARI 15 TAU 18 GEM 20 CAN 22 LEO 25 VIR 27 LIB 29 SCO 31 SAG
SEP—2 CAP 4 AQU 7 PIS 9 ARI 11 TAU 14 GEM 17 CAN 19 LEO 21 VIR 23 LIB 25 SCO 27 SAG 29 CAP
OCT—1 AQU 4 PIS 6 ARI 9 TAU 11 GEM 14 CAN 16 LEO 18 VIR 21 LIB 23 SCO 25 SAG 27 CAP 29 AQU 31 PIS
NOV—2 ARI 5 TAU 8 GEM 10 CAN 12 LEO 15 VIR 17 LIB 19 SCO 21 SAG 23 CAP 25 AQU 27 PIS 30 ARI
DEC—2 TAU 5 GEM 7 CAN 10 LEO 12 VIR 14 LIB 16 SCO 18 SAG 20 CAP 22 AQU 25 PIS 27 ARI 30 TAU

1977

JAN—1 GEM 4 CAN 6 LEO 8 VIR 10 LIB 13 SCO 15 SAG 17 CAP 19 AQU 21 PIS 23 ARI 26 TAU 28 GEM 31 CAN
FEB—2 LEO 5 VIR 7 LIB 9 SCO 11 SAG 13 CAP 15 AQU 17 PIS 20 ARI 22 TAU 25 GEM 27 CAN
MAR—2 LEO 4 VIR 6 LIB 8 SCO 10 SAG 12 CAP 15 AQU 17 PIS 19 ARI 22 TAU 24 GEM 27 CAN 29 LEO 31 VIR
APR—2 LIB 5 SCO 7 SAG 9 CAP 11 AQU 13 PIS 15 ARI 18 TAU 20 GEM 23 CAN 25 LEO 28 VIR 30 LIB
MAY—2 SCO 4 SAG 6 CAP 8 AQU 10 PIS 13 ARI 15 TAU 18 GEM 20 CAN 23 LEO 25 VIR 27 LIB 29 SCO 31 SAG
JUN—2 CAP 4 AQU 7 PIS 9 ARI 11 TAU 14 GEM 16 CAN 19 LEO 21 VIR 24 LIB 26 SCO 28 SAG 30 CAP
JUL—2 AQU 4 PIS 6 ARI 9 TAU 11 GEM 14 CAN 16 LEO 19 VIR 21 LIB 23 SCO 25 SAG 27 CAP 29 AQU 31 PIS
AUG—3 ARI 5 TAU 7 GEM 10 CAN 12 LEO 15 VIR 17 LIB 19 SCO 21 SAG 24 CAP 26 AQU 28 PIS 30 ARI
SEP—1 TAU 4 GEM 6 CAN 9 LEO 11 VIR 13 LIB 16 SCO 18 SAG 20 CAP 22 AQU 24 PIS 26 ARI 29 TAU
OCT—1 GEM 4 CAN 6 LEO 9 VIR 11 LIB 13 SCO 15 SAG 17 CAP 19 AQU 21 PIS 24 ARI 26 TAU 28 GEM 31 CAN
NOV—3 LEO 5 VIR 7 LIB 9 SCO 11 SAG 13 CAP 15 AQU 18 PIS 20 ARI 22 TAU 25 GEM 27 CAN 30 LEO
DEC—2 VIR 5 LIB 7 SCO 9 SAG 11 CAP 13 AQU 15 PIS 17 ARI 19 TAU 22 GEM 25 CAN 27 LEO 30 VIR

1978

JAN—**1** LIB **3** SCO **5** SAG **7** CAP **9** AQU **11** PIS **13** ARI **16** TAU **18** GEM **21** CAN **23** LEO **26** VIR **28** LIB **30** SCO
FEB—**2** SAG **4** CAP **6** AQU **8** PIS **10** ARI **12** TAU **15** GEM **17** CAN **20** LEO **22** VIR **24** LIB **27** SCO
MAR—**1** SAG **3** CAP **5** AQU **7** PIS **9** ARI **12** TAU **14** GEM **16** CAN **19** LEO **21** VIR **24** LIB **26** SCO **28** SAG **30** CAP
APR—**1** AQU **3** PIS **6** ARI **8** TAU **10** GEM **13** CAN **15** LEO **18** VIR **20** LIB **22** SCO **24** SAG **26** CAP **29** AQU
MAY—**1** PIS **3** ARI **5** TAU **8** GEM **10** CAN **13** LEO **15** VIR **17** LIB **20** SCO **22** SAG **24** CAP **26** AQU **28** PIS **30** ARI
JUN—**1** TAU **4** GEM **6** CAN **9** LEO **11** VIR **14** LIB **16** SCO **18** SAG **20** CAP **22** AQU **24** PIS **26** ARI **29** TAU
JUL—**1** GEM **4** CAN **6** LEO **9** VIR **11** LIB **13** SCO **16** SAG **18** CAP **20** AQU **22** PIS **24** ARI **26** TAU **38** GEM **31** CAN
AUG—**2** LEO **5** VIR **7** LIB **10** SCO **12** SAG **14** CAP **16** AQU **18** PIS **20** ARI **22** TAU **25** GEM **27** CAN **30** LEO
SEP—**1** VIR **4** LIB **6** SCO **8** SAG **10** CAP **12** AQU **14** PIS **17** ARI **19** TAU **21** GEM **23** CAN **26** LEO **28** VIR
OCT—**1** LIB **3** SCO **5** SAG **8** CAP **10** AQU **12** PIS **14** ARI **16** TAU **18** GEM **21** CAN **23** LEO **26** VIR **28** LIB **31** SCO
NOV—**2** SAG **4** CAP **6** AQU **8** PIS **10** ARI **12** TAU **15** GEM **17** CAN **20** LEO **22** VIR **25** LIB **27** SCO **29** SAG
DEC—**1** CAP **3** AQU **5** PIS **7** ARI **10** TAU **12** GEM **14** CAN **17** LEO **19** VIR **22** LIB **24** SCO **27** SAG **29** CAP **31** AQU

1979

JAN—**1** AQU **2** PIS **4** ARI **6** TAU **8** GEM **11** CAN **13** LEO **16** VIR **18** LIB **21** SCO **23** SAG **25** CAP **27** AQU **29** PIS **31** ARI
FEB—**2** TAU **5** GEM **7** CAN **9** LEO **12** VIR **15** LIB **17** SCO **19** SAG **21** CAP **24** AQU **26** PIS **28** ARI
MAR—**2** TAU **4** GEM **6** CAN **9** LEO **11** VIR **14** LIB **16** SCO **19** SAG **21** CAP **23** AQU **25** PIS **27** ARI **29** TAU **31** GEM
APR—**3** CAN **5** LEO **8** VIR **10** LIB **12** SCO **15** SAG **17** CAP **19** AQU **21** PIS **23** ARI **25** TAU **28** GEM **30** CAN
MAY—**2** LEO **5** VIR **7** LIB **10** SCO **12** SAG **14** CAP **16** AQU **18** PIS **21** ARI **23** TAU **25** GEM **27** CAN **30** LEO
JUN—**1** VIR **4** LIB **6** SCO **8** SAG **11** CAP **13** AQU **15** PIS **17** ARI **19** TAU **21** GEM **24** CAN **26** LEO **29** VIR
JUL—**1** LIB **4** SCO **6** SAG **8** CAP **10** AQU **12** PIS **14** ARI **16** TAU **19** GEM **21** CAN **23** LEO **26** VIR **28** LIB **31** SCO
AUG—**2** SAG **4** CAP **6** AQU **8** PIS **10** ARI **13** TAU **15** GEM **17** CAN **20** LEO **22** VIR **25** LIB **27** SCO **30** SAG
SEP—**1** CAP **3** AQU **5** PIS **7** ARI **9** TAU **11** GEM **13** CAN **16** LEO **18** VIR **21** LIB **23** SCO **26** SAG **28** CAP **30** AQU
OCT—**2** PIS **4** ARI **6** TAU **8** GEM **11** CAN **13** LEO **16** VIR **18** LIB **21** SCO **23** SAG **25** CAP **28** AQU **30** PIS
NOV—**1** ARI **3** TAU **5** GEM **7** CAN **9** LEO **12** VIR **14** LIB **17** SCO **19** SAG **22** CAP **24** AQU **26** PIS **28** ARI **30** TAU
DEC—**2** GEM **4** CAN **7** LEO **9** VIR **12** LIB **14** SCO **17** SAG **19** CAP **21** AQU **23** PIS **25** ARI **27** TAU **30** GEM

1980

JAN—**1** CAN **3** LEO **6** VIR **8** LIB **11** SCO **13** SAG **15** CAP **17** AQU **19** PIS **21** ARI **24** TAU **26** GEM **28** CAN **30** LEO
FEB—**2** VIR **4** LIB **7** SCO **9** SAG **12** CAP **14** AQU **16** PIS **18** ARI **20** TAU **22** GEM **24** CAN **27** LEO **29** VIR
MAR—**3** LIB **5** SCO **8** SAG **10** CAP **12** AQU **14** PIS **16** ARI **18** TAU **20** GEM **23** CAN **25** LEO **27** VIR **30** LIB
APR—**2** SCO **4** SAG **6** CAP **9** AQU **11** PIS **13** ARI **15** TAU **17** GEM **19** CAN **21** LEO **24** VIR **26** LIB **29** SCO
MAY—**1** SAG **4** CAP **6** AQU **8** PIS **10** ARI **12** TAU **14** GEM **16** CAN **19** LEO **221** VIR **24** LIB **26** SCO **29** SAG **31** CAP
JUN—**2** AQU **4** PIS **6** ARI **9** TAU **11** GEM **13** CAN **15** LEO **17** VIR **20** LIB **22** SCO **25** SAG **27** CAP **29** AQU
JUL—**2** PIS **4** ARI **6** TAU **8** GEM **10** CAN **12** LEO **15** VIR **17** LIB **20** SCO **22** SAG **25** CAP **27** AQU **29** PIS **31** ARI
AUG—**2** TAU **4** GEM **6** CAN **9** LEO **11** VIR **14** LIB **16** SCO **19** SAG **21** CAP **23** AQU **25** PIS **27** ARI **29** TAU **31** GEM
SEP—**3** CAN **5** LEO **7** VIR **10** LIB **12** SCO **15** SAG **17** CAP **20** AQU **22** PIS **24** ARI **26** TAU **28** GEM **30** CAN
OCT—**2** LEO **5** VIR **7** LIB **10** SCO **12** SAG **15** CAP **17** AQU **19** PIS **21** ARI **23** TAU **25** GEM **27** CAN **29** LEO
NOV—**1** VIR **3** LIB **6** SCO **8** SAG **11** CAP **13** AQU **15** PIS **18** ARI **20** TAU **22** GEM **24** CAN **26** LEO **28** VIR
DEC—**1** LIB **3** SCO **6** SAG **8** CAP **10** AQU **13** PIS **15** ARI **17** TAU **19** GEM **21** CAN **23** LEO **25** VIR **28** LIB **30** SCO

1981

JAN—**1** SCO **2** SAG **4** CAP **7** AQU **9** PIS **11** ARI **13** TAU **15** GEM **17** CAN **20** LEO **22** VIR **24** LIB **27** SCO **29** SAG
FEB—**1** CAP **3** AQU **5** PIS **7** ARI **9** TAU **12** GEM **14** CAN **16** LEO **18** VIR **21** LIB **23** SCO **26** SAG **28** CAP
MAR—**2** AQU **5** PIS **7** ARI **9** TAU **11** GEM **13** CAN **15** LEO **18** VIR **20** LIB **22** SCO **25** SAG **27** CAP **30** AQU
APR—**1** PIS **3** ARI **5** TAU **7** GEM **9** CAN **11** LEO **14** VIR **16** LIB **19** SCO **21** SAG **24** CAP **26** AQU **28** PIS
MAY—**1** ARI **3** TAU **5** GEM **7** CAN **9** LEO **11** VIR **13** LIB **16** SCO **18** SAG **21** CAP **23** AQU **26** PIS **28** ARI **30** TAU
JUN—**1** GEM **3** CAN **5** LEO **7** VIR **10** LIB **12** SCO **15** SAG **17** CAP **20** AQU **22** PIS **24** ARI **26** TAU **28** GEM **30** CAN
JUL—**2** LEO **5** VIR **7** LIB **10** SCO **12** SAG **15** CAP **17** AQU **19** PIS **21** ARI **24** TAU **26** GEM **28** CAN **30** LEO
AUG—**1** VIR **3** LIB **6** SCO **8** SAG **11** CAP **13** AQU **16** PIS **18** ARI **20** TAU **22** GEM **24** CAN **26** LEO **28** VIR **31** LIB
SEP—**2** SCO **5** SAG **7** CAP **10** AQU **12** PIS **14** ARI **16** TAU **18** GEM **20** CAN **22** LEO **25** VIR **27** LIB **29** SCO
OCT—**2** SAG **5** CAP **7** AQU **9** PIS **11** ARI **13** TAU **15** GEM **18** CAN **20** LEO **22** VIR **24** LIB **27** SCO **29** SAG
NOV—**1** CAP **3** AQU **6** PIS **8** ARI **10** TAU **12** GEM **14** CAN **16** LEO **18** VIR **21** LIB **23** SCO **26** SAG **28** CAP
DEC—**1** AQU **3** PIS **5** ARI **7** TAU **9** GEM **11** CAN **13** LEO **16** VIR **18** LIB **20** SCO **23** SAG **25** CAP **28** AQU **30** PIS

1982

JAN—**1** PIS **2** ARI **4** TAU **6** GEM **8** CAN **10** LEO **12** VIR **14** LIB **17** SCO **19** SAG **22** CAP **24** AQU **26** PIS **29** ARI **31** TAU
FEB—**2** GEM **4** CAN **6** LEO **8** VIR **11** LIB **13** SCO **15** SAG **18** CAP **20** AQU **23** PIS **25** ARI **27** TAU
MAR—**1** GEM **3** CAN **6** LEO **8** VIR **10** LIB **12** SCO **15** SAG **17** CAP **20** AQU **22** PIS **24** ARI **27** TAU **29** GEM **31** CAN
APR—**2** LEO **4** VIR **6** LIB **9** SCO **11** SAG **14** CAP **16** AQU **19** PIS **21** ARI **23** TAU **25** GEM **27** CAN **29** LEO
MAY—**1** VIR **4** LIB **6** SCO **8** SAG **11** CAP **13** AQU **16** PIS **18** ARI **20** TAU **22** GEM **24** CAN **26** LEO **29** VIR **31** LIB
JUN—**2** SCO **5** SAG **7** CAP **10** AQU **12** PIS **15** ARI **17** TAU **19** GEM **21** CAN **23** LEO **25** VIR **27** LIB **29** SCO
JUL—**2** SAG **4** CAP **7** AQU **9** PIS **12** ARI **14** TAU **16** GEM **18** CAN **20** LEO **22** VIR **24** LIB **27** SCO **29** SAG
AUG—**1** CAP **3** AQU **6** PIS **8** ARI **10** TAU **13** GEM **15** CAN **17** LEO **19** VIR **21** LIB **23** SCO **25** SAG **28** CAP **31** AQU
SEP—**2** PIS **4** ARI **7** TAU **9** GEM **11** CAN **13** LEO **15** VIR **17** LIB **19** SCO **22** SAG **24** CAP **27** AQU **29** PIS
OCT—**2** ARI **4** TAU **6** GEM **8** CAN **10** LEO **12** VIR **15** LIB **17** SCO **19** SAG **22** CAP **24** AQU **27** PIS **29** ARI **31** TAU
NOV—**2** GEM **4** CAN **6** LEO **9** VIR **11** LIB **13** SCO **15** SAG **18** CAP **21** AQU **23** PIS **25** ARI **28** TAU **30** GEM
DEC—**2** CAN **4** LEO **6** VIR **8** LIB **10** SCO **13** SAG **15** CAP **18** AQU **20** PIS **23** ARI **25** TAU **27** GEM **29** CAN **31** LEO

1983

JAN—**1** LEO **2** VIR **4** LIB **7** SCO **9** SAG **12** CAP **14** AQU **17** PIS **19** ARI **21** TAU **24** GEM **26** CAN **28** LEO **30** VIR
FEB—**1** LIB **3** SCO **5** SAG **8** CAP **10** AQU **13** PIS **15** ARI **18** TAU **20** GEM **22** CAN **24** LEO **26** VIR **28** LIB
MAR—**2** SCO **5** SAG **7** CAP **10** AQU **12** PIS **15** ARI **17** TAU **19** GEM **21** CAN **23** LEO **26** VIR **28** LIB **30** SCO
APR—**1** SAG **3** CAP **6** AQU **8** PIS **11** ARI **13** TAU **15** GEM **18** CAN **20** LEO **22** VIR **24** LIB **26** SCO **28** SAG
MAY—**1** CAP **3** AQU **6** PIS **8** ARI **11** TAU **13** GEM **15** CAN **17** LEO **19** VIR **21** LIB **23** SCO **26** SAG **28** CAP **31** AQU
JUN—**2** PIS **5** ARI **7** TAU **9** GEM **11** CAN **13** LEO **15** VIR **17** LIB **20** SCO **22** SAG **24** CAP **27** AQU **29** PIS
JUL—**2** ARI **4** TAU **7** GEM **9** CAN **11** LEO **13** VIR **15** LIB **17** SCO **19** SAG **22** CAP **24** AQU **27** PIS **29** ARI
AUG—**1** TAU **3** GEM **5** CAN **7** LEO **9** VIR **11** LIB **13** SCO **15** SAG **18** CAP **20** AQU **23** PIS **25** ARI **28** TAU **30** GEM
SEP—**1** CAN **3** LEO **5** VIR **7** LIB **10** SCO **12** SAG **14** CAP **17** AQU **19** PIS **22** ARI **24** TAU **26** GEM **29** CAN
OCT—**1** LEO **3** VIR **5** LIB **7** SCO **9** SAG **11** CAP **14** AQU **16** PIS **19** ARI **21** TAU **24** GEM **26** CAN **28** LEO **30** VIR
NOV—**1** LIB **3** SCO **6** SAG **8** CAP **10** AQU **13** PIS **15** ARI **18** TAU **20** GEM **22** CAN **24** LEO **26** VIR **29** LIB
DEC—**1** SCO **3** SAG **5** CAP **8** AQU **10** PIS **13** ARI **15** TAU **17** GEM **20** CAN **22** LEO **24** VIR **26** LIB **28** SCO **30** SAG

1984

JAN—**1** SAG **2** CAP **4** AQU **6** PIS **9** ARI **11** TAU **14** GEM **16** CAN **18** LEO **20** VIR **22** LIB **24** SCO **26** SAG **29** CAP **31** AQU
FEB—**3** PIS **5** ARI **8** TAU **10** GEM **12** CAN **15** LEO **17** VIR **19** LIB **21** SCO **23** SAG **25** CAP **28** AQU
MAR—**1** PIS **4** ARI **6** TAU **8** GEM **11** CAN **13** LEO **15** VIR **17** LIB **19** SCO **21** SAG **23** CAP **26** AQU **28** PIS **31** ARI
APR—**2** TAU **5** GEM **7** CAN **9** LEO **11** VIR **13** LIB **15** SCO **17** SAG **20** CAP **22** AQU **25** PIS **27** ARI **30** TAU
MAY—**2** GEM **4** CAN **6** LEO **9** VIR **11** LIB **13** SCO **15** SAG **17** CAP **19** AQU **22** PIS **24** ARI **27** TAU **29** GEM
JUN—**1** CAN **3** LEO **5** VIR **7** LIB **9** SCO **11** SAG **13** CAP **16** AQU **18** PIS **21** ARI **23** TAU **26** GEM **28** CAN **30** LEO
JUL—**2** VIR **4** LIB **6** SCO **9** SAG **11** CAP **13** AQU **16** PIS **18** ARI **21** TAU **23** GEM **25** CAN **27** LEO **29** VIR **31** LIB
AUG—**3** SCO **5** SAG **7** CAP **9** AQU **12** PIS **14** ARI **17** TAU **19** GEM **22** CAN **24** LEO **26** VIR **28** LIB **30** SCO
SEP—**1** SAG **3** CAP **6** AQU **8** PIS **11** ARI **13** TAU **16** GEM **18** CAN **20** LEO **22** VIR **24** LIB **26** SCO **28** SAG
OCT—**1** CAP **3** AQU **5** PIS **8** ARI **10** TAU **13** GEM **15** CAN **18** LEO **20** VIR **22** LIB **24** SCO **26** SAG **28** CAP **30** AQU
NOV—**2** PIS **4** ARI **7** TAU **9** GEM **12** CAN **14** LEO **16** VIR **18** LIB **20** SCO **22** SAG **24** CAP **27** AQU **29** PIS
DEC—**1** ARI **4** TAU **6** GEM **9** CAN **11** LEO **13** VIR **15** LIB **17** SCO **20** SAG **22** CAP **24** AQU **26** PIS **29** ARI **31** TAU

1985

JAN—**1** TAU **3** GEM **5** CAN **7** LEO **9** VIR **12** LIB **14** SCO **16** SAG **18** CAP **20** AQU **23** PIS **25** ARI **28** TAU **30** GEM
FEB—**2** CAN **4** LEO **6** VIR **8** LIB **10** SCO **12** SAG **14** CAP **17** AQU **19** PIS **21** ARI **24** TAU **27** GEM
MAR—**1** CAN **3** LEO **5** VIR **7** LIB **9** SCO **11** SAG **14** CAP **16** AQU **18** PIS **21** ARI **23** TAU **26** GEM **28** CAN **31** LEO
APR—**2** VIR **4** LIB **6** SCO **8** SAG **10** CAP **12** AQU **14** PIS **17** ARI **20** TAU **22** GEM **25** CAN **27** LEO **29** VIR
MAY—**1** LIB **3** SCO **5** SAG **7** CAP **9** AQU **12** PIS **14** ARI **17** TAU **19** GEM **22** CAN **24** LEO **26** VIR **29** LIB **31** SCO
JUN—**2** SAG **4** CAP **6** AQU **8** PIS **11** ARI **13** TAU **16** GEM **18** CAN **20** LEO **23** VIR **25** LIB **27** SCO **29** SAG
JUL—**1** CAP **3** AQU **5** PIS **8** ARI **10** TAU **13** GEM **15** CAN **18** LEO **20** VIR **22** LIB **24** SCO **26** SAG **28** CAP **31** AQU
AUG—**2** PIS **4** ARI **7** TAU **9** GEM **12** CAN **14** LEO **16** VIR **18** LIB **20** SCO **22** SAG **25** CAP **27** AQU **29** PIS
SEP—**1** ARI **3** TAU **6** GEM **8** CAN **10** LEO **13** VIR **15** LIB **17** SCO **19** SAG **21** CAP **23** AQU **25** PIS **28** ARI **30** TAU
OCT—**3** GEM **5** CAN **8** LEO **10** VIR **12** LIB **14** SCO **16** SAG **18** CAP **20** AQU **23** PIS **25** ARI **28** TAU **30** GEM
NOV—**2** CAN **4** LEO **6** VIR **9** LIB **11** SCO **13** SAG **15** CAP **17** AQU **19** PIS **21** ARI **24** TAU **26** GEM **29** CAN
DEC—**1** LEO **4** VIR **6** LIB **8** CAN **10** SAG **12** CAP **14** AQU **16** PIS **19** ARI **21** TAU **24** GEM **26** CAN **29** LEO **31** VIR

1986

JAN—**1** VIR **2** LIB **4** SCO **6** SAG **8** CAP **11** AQU **13** PIS **15** ARI **17** TAU **20** GEM **22** CAN **25** LEO **27** VIR **29** LIB
FEB—**1** SCO **3** SAG **5** CAP **7** AQU **9** PIS **11** ARI **14** TAU **16** GEM **19** CAN **21** LEO **24** VIR **26** LIB **28** SCO
MAR—**2** SAG **4** CAP **6** AQU **8** PIS **11** ARI **13** TAU **16** GEM **18** CAN **21** LEO **23** VIR **25** LIB **27** SCO **29** SAG **31** CAP
APR—**2** AQU **5** PIS **7** ARI **9** TAU **12** GEM **14** CAN **17** LEO **19** VIR **21** LIB **24** SCO **26** SAG **28** CAP **30** AQU
MAY—**2** PIS **4** ARI **7** TAU **9** GEM **12** CAN **14** LEO **17** VIR **19** LIB **21** SCO **23** SAG **25** CAP **27** AQU **29** PIS **31** ARI
JUN—**3** TAU **5** GEM **8** CAN **11** LEO **13** VIR **15** LIB **17** SCO **19** SAG **21** CAP **23** AQU **26** PIS **28** ARI **30** TAU
JUL—**3** GEM **5** CAN **8** LEO **10** VIR **12** LIB **15** SCO **17** SAG **19** CAP **21** AQU **23** PIS **25** ARI **28** TAU **30** GEM
AUG—**2** CAN **4** LEO **6** VIR **9** LIB **11** SCO **13** SAG **15** CAP **17** AQU **19** PIS **22** ARI **24** TAU **26** GEM **29** CAN **31** LEO
SEP—**3** VIR **5** LIB **7** SCO **9** SAG **11** CAP **14** AQU **16** PIS **18** ARI **20** TAU **23** GEM **25** CAN **28** LEO **30** VIR
OCT—**2** LIB **4** SCO **7** SAG **9** CAP **11** AQU **13** PIS **15** ARI **18** TAU **20** GEM **23** CAN **25** LEO **27** VIR **30** LIB
NOV—**1** SCO **3** SAG **5** CAP **7** AQU **9** PIS **11** ARI **14** TAU **16** GEM **19** CAN **21** LEO **24** VIR **26** LIB **28** SCO **30** SAG
DEC—**2** CAP **4** AQU **6** PIS **9** ARI **11** TAU **14** GEM **16** CAN **19** LEO **21** VIR **24** LIB **26** SCO **28** SAG **30** CAP

1987

JAN—1 AQU 3 PIS 5 ARI 7 TAU 10 GEM 12 CAN 15 LEO 17 VIR 20 LIB 22 SCO 24 SAG 26 CAP 28 AQU 30 PIS
FEB—1 ARI 4 TAU 6 GEM 9 CAN 11 LEO 14 VIR 16 LIB 18 SCO 21 SAG 23 CAP 25 AQU 27 PIS
MAR—1 ARI 3 TAU 5 GEM 8 CAN 10 LEO 13 VIR 15 LIB 18 SCO 20 SAG 22 CAP 24 AQU 26 PIS 28 ARI 30 TAU
APR—2 GEM 4 CAN 7 LEO 9 VIR 12 LIB 14 SCO 16 SAG 18 CAP 20 AQU 22 PIS 25 ARI 27 TAU 29 GEM
MAY—2 CAN 4 LEO 7 VIR 9 LIB 11 SCO 13 SAG 15 CAP 17 AQU 20 PIS 22 ARI 24 TAU 26 GEM 29 CAN 31 LEO
JUN—3 VIR 5 LIB 8 SCO 10 SAG 12 CAP 14 AQU 16 PIS 18 ARI 20 TAU 23 GEM 25 CAN 28 LEO 30 VIR
JUL—3 LIB 5 SCO 7 SAG 9 CAP 11 AQU 13 PIS 15 ARI 18 TAU 20 GEM 22 CAN 25 LEO 27 VIR 30 LIB
AUG—1 SCO 4 SAG 6 CAP 8 AQU 10 PIS 12 ARI 14 TAU 16 GEM 19 CAN 21 LEO 24 VIR 26 LIB 29 SCO 31 SAG
SEP—2 CAP 4 AQU 6 PIS 8 ARI 10 TAU 13 GEM 15 CAN 17 LEO 20 VIR 22 LIB 25 SCO 27 SAG 29 CAP
OCT—1 AQU 3 PIS 6 ARI 8 TAU 10 GEM 12 CAN 15 LEO 17 VIR 20 LIB 22 SCO 24 SAG 26 CAP 29 AQU 31 PIS
NOV—2 ARI 4 TAU 6 GEM 9 CAN 11 LEO 14 VIR 16 LIB 18 SCO 21 SAG 23 CAP 25 AQU 27 PIS 29 ARI
DEC—1 TAU 4 GEM 6 CAN 8 LEO 11 VIR 14 LIB 16 SCO 18 SAG 20 CAP 22 AQU 24 PIS 26 ARI 29 TAU 31 GEM

1988

JAN—1 GEM 2 CAN 5 LEO 7 VIR 10 LIB 12 SCO 15 SAG 17 CAP 19 AQU 21 PIS 23 ARI 25 TAU 27 GEM 30 CAN
FEB—1 LEO 4 VIR 6 LIB 9 SCO 11 SAG 13 CAP 15 AQU 17 PIS 19 ARI 21 TAU 23 GEM 26 CAN 28 LEO
MAR—2 VIR 4 LIB 7 SCO 9 SAG 11 CAP 14 AQU 16 PIS 18 ARI 20 TAU 22 GEM 24 CAN 27 LEO 29 VIR
APR—1 LIB 3 SCO 5 SAG 8 CAP 10 AQU 12 PIS 14 ARI 16 TAU 18 GEM 20 CAN 23 LEO 25 VIR 28 LIB 30 SCO
MAY—3 SAG 5 CAP 7 AQU 9 PIS 11 ARI 13 TAU 16 GEM 18 CAN 20 LEO 23 VIR 25 LIB 28 SCO 30 SAG
JUN—1 CAP 3 AQU 5 PIS 8 ARI 10 TAU 12 GEM 14 CAN 17 LEO 19 VIR 22 LIB 24 SCO 26 SAG 29 CAP
JUL—1 AQU 3 PIS 5 ARI 7 TAU 9 GEM 11 CAN 14 LEO 16 VIR 19 LIB 21 SCO 24 SAG 26 CAP 28 AQU 30 PIS
AUG—1 ARI 3 TAU 5 GEM 8 CAN 10 LEO 13 VIR 15 LIB 18 SCO 20 SAG 22 CAP 24 AQU 26 PIS 28 ARI 30 TAU
SEP—2 GEM 4 CAN 6 LEO 9 VIR 11 LIB 14 SCO 16 SAG 19 CAP 21 AQU 23 PIS 25 ARI 27 TAU 29 GEM
OCT—1 CAN 4 LEO 6 VIR 9 LIB 11 SCO 14 SAG 16 CAP 18 AQU 20 PIS 22 ARI 24 TAU 26 GEM 29 CAN 31 LEO
NOV—2 VIR 5 LIB 7 SCO 10 SAG 12 CAP 14 AQU 17 PIS 19 ARI 21 TAU 23 GEM 25 CAN 27 LEO 30 VIR
DEC—2 LIB 5 SCO 7 SAG 9 CAP 12 AQU 14 PIS 16 ARI 18 TAU 20 GEM 22 CAN 25 LEO 27 VIR 30 LIB

1989

JAN—1 SCO 4 SAG 6 CAP 8 AQU 10 PIS 12 ARI 14 TAU 16 GEM 19 CAN 21 LEO 23 VIR 26 LIB 29 SCO 31 SAG
FEB—2 CAP 4 AQU 6 PIS 8 ARI 11 TAU 13 GEM 15 CAN 17 LEO 20 VIR 22 LIB 25 SCO 27 SAG
MAR—2 CAP 4 AQU 6 PIS 8 ARI 10 TAU 12 GEM 14 CAN 17 LEO 19 VIR 22 LIB 24 SCO 27 SAG 29 CAP 31 AQU
APR—2 PIS 4 ARI 6 TAU 8 GEM 11 CAN 13 LEO 15 VIR 18 LIB 20 SCO 23 SAG 25 CAP 28 AQU 30 PIS
MAY—2 ARI 4 TAU 6 GEM 8 CAN 10 LEO 13 VIR 15 LIB 18 SCO 20 SAG 22 CAP 25 AQU 27 PIS 29 ARI 31 TAU
JUN—2 GEM CAN 7 LEO 9 VIR 11 LIB 14 SCO 16 SAG 19 CAP 21 AQU 23 PIS 25 ARI 27 TAU 30 GEM
JUL—2 CAN 4 LEO 6 VIR 9 LIB 11 SCO 14 SAG 16 CAP 18 AQU 20 PIS 23 ARI 25 TAU 27 GEM 29 CAN 31 LEO
AUG—3 VIR 5 LIB 8 SCO 10 SAG 12 CAP 15 AQU 17 PIS 19 ARI 21 TAU 23 GEM 25 CAN 28 LEO 30 VIR
SEP—1 LIB 4 SCO 6 SAG 9 CAP 11 AQU 13 PIS 15 ARI 17 TAU 19 GEM 21 CAN 24 LEO 26 VIR 29 LIB
OCT—1 SCO 4 SAG 6 CAP 9 AQU 11 PIS 13 ARI 15 TAU 17 GEM 19 CAN 21 LEO 23 VIR 26 LIB 28 SCO 31 SAG
NOV—2 CAP 5 AQU 7 PIS 9 ARI 11 TAU 13 GEM 15 CAN 17 LEO 20 VIR 22 LIB 25 SCO 27 SAG 30 CAP
DEC—2 AQU 4 PIS 7 ARI 9 TAU 11 GEM 13 CAN 15 LEO 17 VIR 19 LIB 22 SCO 24 SAG 27 CAP 29 AQU

1990

JAN—**1** PIS **3** ARI **5** TAU **7** GEM **9** CAN **11** LEO **13** VIR **16** LIB **18** SCO **21** SAG **23** CAP **26** AQU **28** PIS **30** ARI
FEB—**1** TAU **3** GEM **5** CAN **8** LEO **10** VIR **12** LIB **15** SCO **17** SAG **20** CAP **22** AQU **24** PIS **26** ARI **28** TAU
MAR—**2** GEM **5** CAN **7** LEO **9** VIR **12** LIB **14** SCO **16** SAG **19** CAP **21** AQU **24** PIS **26** ARI **28** TAU **30** GEM
APR—**1** CAN **3** LEO **5** VIR **8** LIB **10** SCO **13** SAG **15** CAP **18** AQU **20** PIS **22** ARI **24** TAU **26** GEM **28** CAN **30** LEO
MAY—**3** VIR **5** LIB **8** SCO **10** SAG **13** CAP **15** AQU **17** PIS **20** ARI **22** TAU **24** GEM **26** CAN **28** LEO **30** VIR
JUN—**1** LIB **4** SCO **6** SAG **9** CAP **11** AQU **14** PIS **16** ARI **18** TAU **20** GEM **22** CAN **24** LEO **26** VIR **29** LIB
JUL—**1** SCO **4** SAG **6** CAP **9** AQU **11** PIS **13** ARI **15** TAU **17** GEM **19** CAN **21** LEO **24** VIR **26** LIB **28** SCO **31** SAG
AUG—**2** CAP **5** AQU **7** PIS **9** ARI **12** TAU **14** GEM **16** CAN **18** LEO **20** VIR **22** LIB **25** SCO **27** SAG **30** CAP
SEP—**1** AQU **3** PIS **6** ARI **8** TAU **10** GEM **12** CAN **14** LEO **16** VIR **19** LIB **21** SCO **24** SAG **26** CAP **29** AQU
OCT—**1** PIS **3** ARI **5** TAU **7** GEM **9** CAN **11** LEO **14** VIR **16** LIB **18** SCO **21** SAG **23** CAP **26** AQU **28** PIS **30** ARI
NOV—**2** TAU **4** GEM **6** CAN **8** LEO **10** VIR **112** LIB **15** SCO **17** SAG **20** CAP **22** AQU **25** PIS **27** ARI **29** TAU
DEC—**1** GEM **3** CAN **5** LEO **7** VIR **9** LIB **12** SCO **14** SAG **17** CAP **19** AQU **22** PIS **24** ARI **26** TAU **28** GEM **30** CAN

1991

JAN—**1** LEO **4** VIR **6** LIB **8** SCO **11** SAG **13** CAP **16** AQU **18** PIS **20** ARI **23** TAU **25** GEM **27** CAN **29** LEO **31** VIR
FEB—**2** LIB **4** SCO **7** SAG **9** CAP **12** AQU **14** PIS **17** ARI **19** TAU **21** GEM **23** CAN **25** LEO **27** VIR
MAR—**2** LIB **4** SCO **6** SAG **9** CAP **11** AQU **14** PIS **16** ARI **18** TAU **20** GEM **22** CAN **25** LEO **27** VIR **29** LIB **31** SCO
APR—**3** SAG **5** CAP **8** AQU **10** PIS **12** ARI **15** TAU **17** GEM **19** CAN **21** LEO **23** VIR **25** LIB **28** SCO **30** SAG
MAY—**2** CAP **5** AQU **7** PIS **10** ARI **12** TAU **14** GEM **16** CAN **18** LEO **20** VIR **22** LIB **25** SCO **27** SAG **30** CAP
JUN—**1** AQU **4** PIS **6** ARI **8** TAU **10** GEM **12** CAN **14** LEO **16** VIR **19** LIB **21** SCO **23** SAG **26** CAP **29** AQU
JUL—**1** PIS **3** ARI **6** TAU **8** GEM **10** CAN **12** LEO **14** VIR **16** LIB **18** SCO **21** SAG **23** CAP **26** AQU **28** PIS **31** ARI
AUG—**2** TAU **4** GEM **6** CAN **8** LEO **10** VIR **12** LIB **15** SCO **17** SAG **20** CAP **22** AQU **25** PIS **27** ARI **29** TAU **31** GEM
SEP—**3** CAN **5** LEO **7** VIR **9** LIB **11** SCO **13** SAG **16** CAP **18** AQU **21** PIS **23** ARI **25** TAU **28** GEM **30** CAN
OCT—**2** LEO **4** VIR **6** LIB **8** SCO **11** SAG **13** CAP **16** AQU **18** PIS **21** ARI **23** TAU **25** GEM **27** CAN **29** LEO **31** VIR
NOV—**2** LIB **5** SCO **7** SAG **10** CAP **12** AQU **15** PIS **17** ARI **19** TAU **21** GEM **23** CAN **25** LEO **28** VIR **30** LIB
DEC—**2** SCO **4** SAG **7** CAP **9** AQU **12** PIS **14** ARI **17** TAU **19** GEM **21** CAN **23** LEO **25** VIR **27** LIB **29** SCO

1992

JAN—**1** SAG **3** CAP **6** AQU **8** PIS **11** ARI **13** TAU **15** GEM **17** CAN **19** LEO **21** VIR **23** LIB **25** SCO **28** SAG **30** CAP
FEB—**2** AQU **4** PIS **7** ARI **9** TAU **12** GEM **14** CAN **16** LEO **18** VIR **20** LIB **22** SCO **24** SAG **27** CAP **29** AQU
MAR—**3** PIS **5** ARI **8** TAU **10** GEM **12** CAN **14** LEO **16** VIR **18** LIB **20** SCO **23** SAG **25** CAP **27** AQU **30** PIS
APR—**1** ARI **4** TAU **6** GEM **8** CAN **10** LEO **12** VIR **15** LIB **17** SCO **19** SAG **21** CAP **24** AQU **26** PIS **29** ARI
MAY—**1** TAU **3** GEM **5** CAN **8** LEO **10** VIR **12** LIB **14** SCO **16** SAG **19** CAP **21** AQU **24** PIS **26** ARI **28** TAU **31** GEM
JUN—**2** CAN **4** LEO **6** VIR **9** LIB **10** SCO **13** SAG **15** CAP **17** AQU **20** PIS **22** ARI **25** TAU **27** GEM **29** CAN
JUL—**1** LEO **3** VIR **5** LIB **7** SCO **10** SAG **12** CAP **15** AQU **17** PIS **20** ARI **22** TAU **24** GEM **27** CAN **29** LEO **31** VIR
AUG—**2** LIB **4** SCO **6** SAG **8** CAP **11** AQU **13** PIS **16** ARI **18** TAU **21** GEM **23** CAN **25** LEO **27** VIR **29** LIB **31** SCO
SEP—**2** SAG **5** CAP **7** AQU **10** PIS **12** ARI **15** TAU **17** GEM **19** CAN **21** LEO **24** VIR **26** LIB **28** SCO **30** SAG
OCT—**2** CAP **5** AQU **7** PIS **10** ARI **12** TAU **14** GEM **17** CAN **19** LEO **21** VIR **23** LIB **25** SCO **27** SAG **29** CAP
NOV—**1** AQU **3** PIS **6** ARI **8** TAU **11** GEM **13** CAN **15** LEO **17** VIR **13** LIB **21** SCO **24** SAG **26** CAP **28** AQU
DEC—**1** PIS **3** ARI **6** TAU **8** GEM **10** CAN **12** LEO **14** VIR **16** LIB **19** SCO **21** SAG **23** CAP **26** AQU **28** PIS **31** ARI

1993

JAN—**1** ARI **2** TAU **4** GEM **7** CAN **9** LEO **11** VIR **13** LIB **15** SCO **17** SSAG **19** CAP **22** AQU **24** PIS **27** ARI **29** TAU
FEB—**1** GEM **3** CAN **5** LEO **7** VIR **9** LIB **11** SCO **13** SAG **16** CAP **18** AQU **21** PIS **23** ARI **26** TAU **28** GEM
MAR—**2** CAN **5** LEO **7** VIR **9** LIB **11** SCO **13** SAG **15** CAP **17** AQU **20** PIS **22** ARI **25** TAU **27** GEM **30** CAN
APR—**1** LEO **3** VIR **5** LIB **7** SCO **9** SAG **11** CAP **14** AQU **16** PIS **19** ARI **21** TAU **24** GEM **26** CAN **28** LEO **30** VIR
MAY—**2** LIB **4** SCO **6** SAG **9** CAP **11** AQU **13** PIS **16** ARI **18** TAU **21** GEM **23** CAN **25** LEO **28** VIR **30** LIB
JUN—**1** SCO **3** SAG **5** CAP **7** AQU **10** PIS **12** ARI **15** TAU **17** GEM **19** CAN **22** LEO **24** VIR **26** LIB **28** SCO **30** SAG
JUL—**2** CAP **5** AQU **7** PIS **10** ARI **12** TAU **15** GEM **17** CAN **19** LEO **21** VIR **23** LIB **25** SCO **27** SAG **30** CAP
AUG—**1** AQU **3** PIS **6** ARI **8** TAU **11** GEM **13** CAN **15** LEO **17** VIR **19** LIB **21** SCO **24** SAG **26** CAP **28** AQU **31** PIS
SEP—**2** ARI **5** TAU **7** GEM **10** CAN **12** LEO **14** VIR **16** LIB **18** SCO **20** SAG **22** CAP **24** AQU **27** PIS **29** ARI
OCT—**2** TAU **4** GEM **7** CAN **9** LEO **11** VIR **13** LIB **15** SCO **17** SAG **19** CAP **22** AQU **24** PIS **27** ARI **29** TAU
NOV—**1** GEM **3** CAN **5** LEO **8** VIR **10** LIB **12** SCO **14** SAG **16** CAP **18** AQU **20** PIS **23** ARI **26** TAU **28** GEM **30** CAN
DEC—**3** LEO **5** VIR **7** LIB **9** SCO **11** SAG **13** CAP **15** AQU **18** PIS **20** ARI **23** TAU **25** GEM **28** CAN **30** LEO

1994

JAN—**1** VIR **3** LIB **5** SCO **8** SAG **10** CAP **12** AQU **14** PIS **17** ARI **19** TAU **22** GEM **24** CAN **26** LEO **28** VIR **31** LIB
FEB—**2** SCO **4** SAG **6** CAP **8** AQU **11** PIS **13** ARI **16** TAU **18** GEM **20** CAN **23** LEO **25** VIR **27** LIB
MAR—**1** SCO **3** SAG **5** CAP **7** AQU **10** PIS **12** ARI **15** TAU **17** GEM **20** CAN **22** LEO **24** VIR **26** LIB **28** SCO **30** SAG
APR—**1** CAP **4** AQU **6** PIS **9** ARI **11** TAU **14** GEM **16** CAN **18** LEO **21** VIR **23** LIB **25** SCO **27** SAG **29** CAP
MAY—**1** AQU **3** PIS **6** ARI **8** TAU **11** GEM **13** CAN **16** LEO **18** VIR **20** LIB **22** SCO **24** SAG **26** CAP **28** AQU **31** PIS
JUN—**2** ARI **5** TAU **7** GEM **10** CAN **12** LEO **14** VIR **16** LIB **19** SCO **21** SAG **23** CAP **25** AQU **27** PIS **29** ARI
JUL—**2** TAU **4** GEM **7** CAN **9** LEO **11** VIR **14** LIB **16** SCO **18** SAG **20** CAP **22** AQU **24** PIS **27** ARI **29** TAU
AUG—**1** GEM **3** CAN **6** LEO **8** VIR **10** LIB **12** SCO **14** SAG **16** CAP **18** AQU **21** PIS **23** ARI **26** TAU **28** GEM **31** CAN
SEP—**2** LEO **4** VIR **6** LIB **8** SCO **10** SAG **13** CAP **15** AQU **17** PIS **19** ARI **22** TAU **24** GEM **27** CAN **29** LEO
OCT—**2** VIR **4** LIB **6** SCO **8** SAG **10** CAP **12** AQU **14** PIS **17** ARI **19** TAU **22** GEM **24** CAN **27** LEO **29** VIR **31** LIB
NOV—**2** SCO **4** SAG **6** CAP **8** AQU **11** PIS **13** ARI **15** TAU **18** GEM **20** CAN **23** LEO **25** VIR **28** LIB **30** SCO
DEC—**2** SAG **4** CAP **6** AQU **8** PIS **10** ARI **13** TAU **15** GEM **18** CAN **20** LEO **23** VIR **25** LIB **27** SCO **29** SAG **31** CAP

1995

JAN—**1** CAP **2** AQU **4** PIS **7** ARI **9** TAU **12** GEM **14** CAN **16** LEO **19** VIR **21** LIB **23** SCO **25** SAG **27** CAP **30** AQU
FEB—**1** PIS **3** ARI **5** TAU **8** GEM **10** CAN **13** LEO **15** VIR **17** LIB **19** SCO **22** SAG **24** CAP **26** AQU **28** PIS
MAR—**2** ARI **5** TAU **7** GEM **10** CAN **12** LEO **14** VIR **17** LIB **19** SCO **21** SAG **23** CAP **25** AQU **27** PIS **30** ARI
APR—**1** TAU **3** GEM **6** CAN **9** LEO **11** VIR **13** LIB **15** SCO **17** SAG **19** CAP **21** AQU **24** PIS **26** ARI **28** TAU
MAY—**1** GEM **3** CAN **6** LEO **8** VIR **10** LIB **13** SCO **15** SAG **17** CAP **19** AQU **21** PIS **23** ARI **26** TAU **28** GEM **31** CAN
JUN—**2** LEO **5** VIR **7** LIB **9** SCO **11** SAG **13** CAP **15** AQU **17** PIS **19** ARI **22** TAU **24** GEM **27** CAN **29** LEO
JUL—**2** VIR **4** LIB **6** SCO **8** SAG **10** CAP **12** AQU **14** PIS **17** ARI **19** TAU **22** GEM **24** CAN **27** LEO **29** VIR **31** LIB
AUG—**3** SCO **5** SAG **7** CAP **9** AQU **11** PIS **13** ARI **15** TAU **18** GEM **20** CAN **23** LEO **25** VIR **28** LIB **30** SCO
SEP—**1** SAG **3** CAP **5** AQU **7** PIS **9** ARI **12** TAU **14** GEM **17** CAN **19** LEO **22** VIR **24** LIB **26** SCO **28** SAG **30** CAP
OCT—**2** AQU **5** PIS **7** ARI **9** TAU **12** GEM **14** CAN **17** LEO **19** VIR **21** LIB **23** SCO **26** SAG **28** CAP **30** AQU
NOV—**1** PIS **3** ARI **5** TAU **8** GEM **10** CAN **13** LEO **15** VIR **18** LIB **20** SCO **22** SAG **24** CAP **26** AQU **28** PIS **30** ARI
DEC—**3** TAU **5** GEM **8** CAN **10** LEO **13** VIR **15** LIB **17** SCO **19** SAG **21** CAP **23** AQU **25** PIS **28** ARI **30** TAU

1996

JAN—**1** GEM **4** CAN **6** LEO **9** VIR **11** LIB **14** SCO **16** SAG **18** CAP **20** AQU **22** PIS **24** ARI **26** TAU **29** GEM **31** CAN
FEB—**3** LEO **5** VIR **8** LIB **10** SCO **12** SAG **14** CAP **16** AQU **18** PIS **20** ARI **23** TAU **25** GEM **27** CAN
MAR—**1** LEO **3** VIR **6** LIB **8** SCO **10** SAG **13** CAP **15** AQU **17** PIS **19** ARI **21** TAU **23** GEM **26** CAN **28** LEO **31** VIR
APR—**2** LIB **4** SCO **7** SAG **9** CAP **11** AQU **13** PIS **15** ARI **17** TAU **20** GEM **22** CAN **25** LEO **27** VIR **30** LIB
MAY—**2** SCO **4** SAG **6** CAP **8** AQU **10** PIS **12** ARI **15** TAU **17** GEM **19** CAN **22** LEO **25** VIR **27** LIB **29** SCO **31** SAG
JUN—**2** CAP **4** AQU **6** PIS **9** ARI **11** TAU **13** GEM **16** CAN **18** LEO **21** VIR **23** LIB **26** SCO **28** SAG **30** CAP
JUL—**2** AQU **4** PIS **6** ARI **8** TAU **11** GEM **13** CAN **16** LEO **18** VIR **21** LIB **23** SCO **25** SAG **27** CAP **29** AQU **31** PIS
AUG—**2** ARI **4** TAU **7** GEM **9** CAN **12** LEO **14** VIR **17** LIB **19** SCO **21** SAG **24** CAP **26** AQU **28** PIS **30** ARI
SEP—**1** TAU **3** GEM **6** CAN **8** LEO **11** VIR **13** LIB **15** SCO **18** SAG **20** CAP **22** AQU **24** PIS **26** ARI **28** TAU **30** GEM
OCT—**3** CAN **5** LEO **8** VIR **10** LIB **13** SCO **15** SAG **17** CAP **19** AQU **21** PIS **23** ARI **26** TAU **28** GEM **30** CAN
NOV—**2** LEO **4** VIR **7** LIB **9** SCO **11** SAG **13** CAP **16** AQU **18** PIS **20** ARI **22** TAU **24** GEM **27** CAN **29** LEO
DEC—**2** VIR **4** LIB **6** SCO **9** SAG **11** CAP **13** AQU **15** PIS **17** ARI **19** TAU **22** GEM **24** CAN **26** LEO **29** VIR **31** LIB

1997

JAN—**1** LIB **3** SCO **5** SAG **7** CAP **9** AQU **11** PIS **13** ARI **15** TAU **18** GEM **20** CAN **23** LEO **25** VIR **28** LIB **30** SCO
FEB—**1** SAG **4** CAP **6** AQU **8** PIS **10** ARI **12** TAU **14** GEM **16** CAN **19** LEO **21** VIR **24** LIB **26** SCO
MAR—**1** SAG **3** CAP **5** AQU **7** PIS **9** ARI **11** TAU **13** GEM **16** CAN **18** LEO **21** VIR **23** LIB **26** SCO **28** SAG **30** CAP
APR—**1** AQU **4** PIS **6** ARI **8** TAU **10** GEM **12** CAN **14** LEO **17** VIR **19** LIB **22** SCO **24** SAG **27** CAP **29** AQU
MAY—**1** PIS **3** ARI **5** TAU **7** GEM **9** CAN **12** LEO **14** VIR **17** LIB **19** SCO **22** SAG **24** CAP **26** AQU **28** PIS **30** ARI
JUN—**1** TAU **4** GEM **6** CAN **8** LEO **11** VIR **13** LIB **16** SCO **18** SAG **20** CAP **22** AQU **24** PIS **26** ARI **29** TAU
JUL—**1** GEM **3** CAN **5** LEO **8** VIR **10** LIB **13** SCO **15** SAG **18** CAP **20** AQU **22** PIS **24** ARI **26** TAU **28** GEM **30** CAN
AUG—**2** LEO **4** VIR **7** LIB **9** SCO **12** SAG **14** CAP **16** AQU **18** PIS **20** ARI **22** TAU **24** GEM **27** CAN **29** LEO **31** VIR
SEP—**3** LIB **6** SCO **8** SAG **10** CAP **12** AQU **15** PIS **17** ARI **19** TAU **21** GEM **23** CAN **25** LEO **28** VIR **30** LIB
OCT—**3** SCO **5** SAG **8** CAP **10** AQU **12** PIS **14** ARI **16** TAU **18** GEM **20** CAN **23** LEO **25** VIR **28** LIB **30** SCO
NOV—**1** SAG **4** CAP **6** AQU **8** PIS **10** ARI **12** TAU **14** GEM **17** CAN **19** LEO **21** VIR **26** SCO **29** SAG
DEC—**1** CAP **3** AQU **5** PIS **8** ARI **10** TAU **12** GEM **14** CAN **16** LEO **19** VIR **21** LIB **24** SCO **26** SAG **28** CAP **31** AQU

1998

JAN—**1** AQU **2** PIS **4** ARI **6** TAU **8** GEM **10** CAN **13** LEO **15** VIR **18** LIB **20** SCO **23** SAG **25** CAP **27** AQU **29** PIS **31** ARI
FEB—**2** TAU **4** GEM **7** CAN **9** LEO **11** VIR **14** LIB **16** SCO **19** SAG **21** CAP **23** AQU **25** PIS **27** ARI
MAR—**2** TAU **4** GEM **6** CAN **8** LEO **11** VIR **13** LIB **16** SCO **18** SAG **21** CAP **23** AQU **25** PIS **27** ARI **29** TAU **31** GEM
APR—**2** CAN **4** LEO **7** VIR **9** LIB **12** SCO **14** SAG **17** CAP **19** AQU **21** PIS **23** ARI **25** TAU **27** GEM **29** CAN
MAY—**2** LEO **4** VIR **7** LIB **9** SCO **12** SAG **14** CAP **16** AQU **19** PIS **21** ARI **23** TAU **25** GEM **27** CAN **29** LEO **31** VIR
JUN—**3** LIB **5** SCO **8** SAG **10** CAP **13** AQU **15** PIS **17** ARI **19** TAU **21** GEM **23** CAN **25** LEO **28** VIR **30** LIB
JUL—**3** SCO **5** SAG **8** CAP **10** AQU **12** PIS **14** ARI **16** TAU **18** GEM **21** CAN **23** LEO **25** VIR **28** LIB **30** SCO
AUG—**2** SAG **4** CAP **6** AQU **8** PIS **11** ARI **13** TAU **15** GEM **17** CAN **19** LEO **21** VIR **24** LIB **26** SCO **29** SAG **31** CAP
SEP—**3** AQU **5** PIS **7** ARI **9** TAU **11** GEM **13** CAN **15** LEO **18** VIR **20** LIB **23** SCO **25** SAG **28** CAP **30** AQU
OCT—**2** PIS **4** ARI **6** TAU **8** GEM **10** CAN **13** LEO **15** VIR **17** LIB **20** SCO **23** SAG **25** CAP **27** AQU **30** PIS
NOV—**1** ARI **3** TAU **5** GEM **7** CAN **9** LEO **11** VIR **14** LIB **16** SCO **19** SAG **21** CAP **24** AQU **26** PIS **28** ARI **30** TAU
DEC—**2** GEM **4** CAN **6** LEO **9** VIR **11** LIB **14** SCO **16** SAG **19** CAP **21** AQU **23** PIS **25** ARI **28** TAU **30** GEM

1999

JAN—**1** CAN **3** LEO **5** VIR **7** LIB **10** SCO **12** SAG **15** CAP **17** AQU **19** PIS **22** ARI **24** TAU **26** GEM **28** CAN **30** LEO
FEB—**1** VIR **4** LIB **6** SCO **9** SAG **11** CAP **14** AQU **16** PIS **18** ARI **20** TAU **22** GEM **24** CAN **26** LEO
MAR—**1** VIR **3** LIB **6** SCO **8** SAG **11** CAP **13** AQU **15** PIS **17** ARI **19** TAU **21** GEM **23** CAN **26** LEO **28** VIR **30** LIB
APR—**2** SCO **4** SAG **7** CAP **9** AQU **12** PIS **14** ARI **16** TAU **18** GEM **20** CAN **22** LEO **24** VIR **27** LIB **29** SCO
MAY—**2** SAG **4** CAP **7** AQU **9** PIS **11** ARI **13** TAU **15** GEM **17** CAN **19** LEO **21** VIR **24** LIB **26** SCO **29** SAG **31** CAP
JUN—**3** AQU **5** PIS **8** ARI **10** TAU **12** GEM **14** CAN **16** LEO **18** VIR **20** LIB **23** SCO **25** SAG **28** CAP **30** AQU
JUL—**2** PIS **5** ARI **7** TAU **9** GEM **11** CAN **13** LEO **15** VIR **17** LIB **20** SCO **22** SAG **25** CAP **27** AQU **30** PIS
AUG—**1** ARI **3** TAU **5** GEM **7** CAN **9** LEO **12** VIR **14** LIB **16** SCO **19** SAG **21** CAP **24** AQU **26** PIS **28** ARI **30** TAU
SEP—**2** GEM **4** CAN **6** LEO **8** VIR **10** LIB **13** SCO **15** SAG **18** CAP **20** AQU **22** PIS **25** ARI **27** TAU **29** GEM
OCT—**1** CAN **3** LEO **5** VIR **8** LIB **10** SCO **12** SAG **15** CAP **17** AQU **20** PIS **22** ARI **24** TAU **26** GEM **28** CAN **30** LEO
NOV—**1** VIR **4** LIB **6** SCO **9** SAG **11** CAP **14** AQU **16** PIS **18** ARI **21** TAU **23** GEM **25** CAN **27** LEO **29** VIR
DEC—**1** LIB **3** SCO **6** SAG **8** CAP **11** AQU **13** PIS **16** ARI **18** TAU **20** GEM **22** CAN **24** LEO **26** VIR **28** LIB **31** SCO

2000

JAN—**1** SCO **3** SAG **5** CAP **7** AQU **10** PIS **12** ARI **14** TAU **16** GEM **18** CAN **20** LEO **23** VIR **25** LIB **27** SCO **29** SAG
FEB—**1** CAP **4** AQU **6** PIS **8** ARI **11** TAU **13** GEM **15** CAN **17** LEO **19** VIR **21** LIB **23** SCO **26** SAG **28** CAP
MAR—**2** AQU **4** PIS **7** ARI **9** TAU **11** GEM **13** CAN **15** LEO **17** VIR **20** LIB **22** SCO **24** SAG **27** CAP **29** AQU
APR—**1** PIS **3** ARI **5** TAU **7** GEM **9** CAN **11** LEO **14** VIR **16** LIB **18** SCO **21** SAG **23** CAP **26** AQU **28** PIS **30** ARI
MAY—**3** TAU **5** GEM **7** CAN **9** LEO **11** VIR **13** LIB **15** SCO **18** SAG **20** CAP **23** AQU **25** PIS **28** ARI **30** TAU
JUN—**1** GEM **3** CAN **5** LEO **7** VIR **9** LIB **12** SCO **14** SAG **17** CAP **19** AQU **22** PIS **24** ARI **26** TAU **28** GEM **30** CAN
JUL—**2** LEO **4** VIR **7** LIB **9** SCO **11** SAG **14** CAP **16** AQU **19** PIS **21** ARI **24** TAU **26** GEM **28** CAN **30** LEO
AUG—**1** VIR **3** LIB **5** SCO **8** SAG **10** CAP **13** AQU **15** PIS **18** ARI **20** TAU **22** GEM **24** CAN **26** LEO **28** VIR **30** LIB
SEP—**2** SCO **4** SAG **6** CAP **9** AQU **11** PIS **14** ARI **16** TAU **18** GEM **20** CAN **23** LEO **25** VIR **27** LIB **29** SCO
OCT—**1** SAG **4** CAP **6** AQU **9** PIS **11** ARI **13** TAU **16** GEM **18** CAN **20** LEO **22** VIR **24** LIB **26** SCO **29** SAG **31** CAP
NOV—**3** AQU **5** PIS **8** ARI **10** TAU **12** GEM **14** CAN **16** LEO **18** VIR **20** LIB **23** SCO **25** SAG **27** CAP **30** AQU
DEC—**2** PIS **5** ARI **7** TAU **9** GEM **11** CAN **13** LEO **15** VIR **18** LIB **20** SCO **22** SAG **25** CAP **27** AQU **30** PIS

Mercury

1925

January 1–14	Sagittarius
January 15–February 7	Capricorn
February 8–25	Aquarius
February 26–March 13	Pisces
March 14–April 1	Aries
April 2–15	Taurus
April 16–May 17	Aries
May 18–June 6	Taurus
June 7–20	Gemini
June 21–July 5	Cancer
July 6–26	Leo
July 27–August 27	Virgo
August 28–September 29	Leo
September 30–October 17	Libra
October 18–November 5	Scorpio
November 6–December 31	Sagittarius

1926

January 1–11	Sagittarius
January 12–31	Capricorn
February 1–17	Aquarius
February 18–March 6	Pisces
March 7–May 13	Aries
May 14–29	Taurus
May 30–June 12	Gemini
June 13–29	Cancer
June 30–September 5	Leo
September 6–21	Virgo
September 22–October 9	Libra
October 10–31	Scorpio
November 1–28	Sagittarius
November 29–December 13	Scorpio
December 14–31	Sagittarius

1927

January 1–5	Sagittarius
January 6–24	Capricorn
January 25–February 10	Aquarius
February 11–April 17	Pisces
April 18–May 6	Aries
May 7–20	Taurus
May 21–June 4	Gemini
June 5–28	Cancer
June 29–July 14	Leo
July 15–August 12	Cancer
August 13–28	Leo
August 29–September 14	Virgo
September 15–October 3	Libra
October 4–December 9	Scorpio
December 10–29	Sagittarius
December 30–31	Capricorn

1928

January 1–16	Capricorn
January 17–February 3	Aquarius
February 4–29	Pisces
March 1–18	Aquarius
March 19–April 11	Pisces
April 12–27	Aries
April 28–May 11	Taurus
May 12–28	Gemini
May 29–August 4	Cancer
August 5–19	Leo
August 20–September 5	Virgo
September 6–27	Libra
September 28–October 24	Scorpio
October 25–November 11	Libra
November 12–December 1	Scorpio
December 2–20	Sagittarius
December 21–31	Capricorn

1929

January 1–8	Capricorn
January 9–March 16	Aquarius
March 17–April 3	Pisces
April 4–19	Aries
April 20–May 3	Taurus
May 4–July 11	Gemini
July 12–27	Cancer
July 28–August 11	Leo
August 12–30	Virgo
August 31–November 5	Libra
November 6–24	Scorpio
November 25–December 13	Sagittarius
December 14–31	Capricorn

1930

January 1–2	Capricorn
January 3–23	Aquarius
January 24–February 15	Capricorn
February 16–March 9	Aquarius
March 10–25	Pisces
March 26–April 10	Aries
April 11–May 1	Taurus
May 2–16	Gemini
May 17–June 14	Taurus
June 15–July 4	Gemini
July 5–19	Cancer
July 20–August 4	Leo
August 5–26	Virgo
August 27–September 20	Libra
September 21–October 11	Virgo
October 12–29	Libra
October 30–November 17	Scorpio
November 18–December 6	Sagittarius
December 7–31	Capricorn

1931

January 1–February 11	Capricorn
February 12–March 2	Aquarius
March 3–18	Pisces
March 19–April 3	Aries
April 4–June 11	Taurus
June 12–26	Gemini
June 27–July 10	Cancer
July 11–28	Leo
July 29–October 4	Virgo
October 5–22	Libra
October 23–November 11	Scorpio
November 12–December 1	Sagittarius
December 2–20	Capricorn
December 21–31	Sagittarius

1932

January 1–14	Sagittarius
January 15–February 5	Capricorn
February 6–23	Aquarius
February 24–March 9	Pisces
March 10–May 15	Aries
May 16–June 2	Taurus
June 3–16	Gemini
June 17–July 2	Cancer
July 3–27	Leo
July 28–August 10	Virgo
August 11–September 9	Leo
September 10–26	Virgo
September 27–October 13	Libra
October 14–November 2	Scorpio
November 3–December 31	Sagittarius

1933

January 1–8	Sagittarius
January 9–27	Capricorn
January 28–February 14	Aquarius
February 15–March 3	Pisces
March 4–27	Aries
March 28–April 17	Pisces
April 18–May 10	Aries
May 11–25	Taurus
May 26–June 8	Gemini
June 9–27	Cancer
June 28–September 2	Leo
September 3–17	Virgo
September 18–October 6	Libra
October 7–30	Scorpio
October 31–November 16	Sagittarius
November 17–December 12	Scorpio
December 13–31	Sagittarius

1934

January 1	Sagittarius
January 2–20	Capricorn
January 21–February 6	Aquarius
February 7–April 15	Pisces
April 16–May 2	Aries
May 3–16	Taurus
May 17–June 1	Gemini
June 2–August 9	Cancer
August 10–25	Leo
August 26–September 10	Virgo
September 11–31	Libra
October 1–December 6	Scorpio
December 7–25	Sagittarius
December 26–31	Capricorn

1935

January 1–13	Capricorn
January 14–February 1	Aquarius
February 2–15	Pisces
February 16–March 18	Aquarius
March 19–April 8	Pisces
April 9–24	Aries
April 25–May 8	Taurus
May 9–30	Gemini
May 31–June 20	Cancer
June 21–July 13	Gemini
July 14–August 2	Cancer
August 3–16	Leo
August 17–September 3	Virgo
September 4–28	Libra
September 29–October 12	Scorpio
October 13–November 10	Libra
November 11–28	Scorpio
November 29–December 18	Sagittarius
December 19–31	Capricorn

1936

January 1–6	Capricorn
January 7–March 13	Aquarius
March 14–31	Pisces
April 1–15	Aries
April 16–May 1	Taurus
May 2–July 8	Gemini
July 9–23	Cancer
July 24–August 7	Leo
August 8–27	Virgo
August 28–November 2	Libra
November 3–21	Scorpio
November 22–December 10	Sagittarius
December 11–31	Capricorn

1937

January 1	Capricorn
January 2–9	Aquarius
January 10–February 14	Capricorn
February 15–March 6	Aquarius
March 7–23	Pisces
March 24–April 7	Aries
April 8–June 13	Taurus
June 14–July 15	Gemini
July 16–31	Leo
August 1–October 8	Virgo
October 9–26	Libra
October 27–November 13	Scorpio
November 14–December 3	Sagittarius
December 4–31	Capricorn

1938

January 1–6	Capricorn
January 7–12	Sagittarius
January 13–February 8	Capricorn
February 9–27	Aquarius
February 28–March 14	Pisces
March 15–April 1	Aries
April 2–23	Taurus
April 24–May 16	Aries
May 17–June 8	Taurus
June 9–21	Gemini
June 22–July 7	Cancer
July 8–26	Leo
July 27–September 3	Virgo
September 4–10	Leo
September 11–October 1	Virgo
October 2–18	Libra
October 19–November 6	Scorpio
November 7–December 31	Sagittarius

1939

January 1–12	Sagittarius
January 13–February 1	Capricorn
February 2–19	Aquarius
February 20–March 7	Pisces
March 8–May 14	Aries
May 15–31	Taurus
June 1–13	Gemini
June 14–31	Cancer
July 1–September 7	Leo
September 8–23	Virgo
September 24–October 11	Libra
October 12–November 1	Scorpio
November 2–December 3	Sagittarius
December 4–13	Scorpio
December 14–31	Sagittarius

1940

January 1–6	Sagittarius
January 7–25	Capricorn
January 26–February 11	Aquarius
February 12–March 4	Pisces
March 5–8	Aries
March 9–April 17	Pisces
April 18–May 6	Aries
May 7–21	Taurus
May 22–June 4	Gemini
June 5–26	Cancer
June 27–July 21	Leo
July 22–August 11	Cancer
August 12–29	Leo
August 30–September 14	Virgo
September 15–October 3	Libra
October 4–December 9	Scorpio
December 10–29	Sagittarius
December 30–31	Capricorn

1941

January 1–16	Capricorn
January 17–February 3	Aquarius
February 4–March 7	Pisces
March 8–16	Aquarius
March 17–April 12	Pisces
April 13–28	Aries
April 29–May 13	Taurus
May 14–29	Gemini
May 30–August 6	Cancer
August 7–21	Leo
August 22–September 6	Virgo
September 7–28	Libra
September 29–October 29	Scorpio
October 30–November 11	Libra
November 12–December 2	Scorpio
December 3–22	Sagittarius
December 23–31	Capricorn

1942

January 1–9	Capricorn
January 10–March 16	Aquarius
March 17–April 5	Pisces
April 6–20	Aries
April 21–May 5	Taurus
May 6–July 12	Gemini
July 13–29	Cancer
July 30–August 13	Leo
August 14–31	Virgo
September 1–November 7	Libra
November 8–25	Scorpio
November 26–December 14	Sagittarius
December 15–31	Capricorn

1943

January 1–3	Capricorn
January 4–27	Aquarius
January 28–February 15	Capricorn
February 16–March 11	Aquarius
March 12–28	Pisces
March 29–April 12	Aries
April 13–30	Taurus
May 1–26	Gemini
May 27–June 14	Taurus
June 15–July 6	Gemini
July 7–20	Cancer
July 21–August 5	Leo
August 6–27	Virgo
August 28–September 25	Libra
September 26–October 11	Virgo
October 12–30	Libra
October 31–November 18	Scorpio
November 19–December 8	Sagittarius
December 9–31	Capricorn

1944

January 1–February 12	Capricorn
February 13–March 3	Aquarius
March 4–19	Pisces
March 20–April 3	Aries
April 4–June 11	Taurus
June 12–27	Gemini
June 28–July 11	Cancer
July 12–28	Leo
July 29–October 5	Virgo
October 6–22	Libra
October 23–November 10	Scorpio
November 11–December 1	Sagittarius
December 2–23	Capricorn
December 24–31	Sagittarius

1945

January 1–14	Sagittarius
January 15–February 5	Capricorn
February 6–23	Aquarius
February 24–March 11	Pisces
March 12–May 16	Aries
May 17–June 4	Taurus
June 5–18	Gemini
June 19–July 3	Cancer
July 4–26	Leo
July 27–August 17	Virgo
August 18–September 10	Leo
September 11–27	Virgo
September 28–October 15	Libra
October 16–November 3	Scorpio
November 4–December 31	Sagittarius

1946

January 1–9	Sagittarius
January 10–29	Capricorn
January 30–February 15	Aquarius
February 16–March 4	Pisces
March 5–April 1	Aries
April 2–16	Pisces
April 17–May 11	Aries
May 12–27	Taurus
May 28–June 10	Gemini
June 11–27	Cancer
June 28–September 3	Leo
September 4–19	Virgo
September 20–October 7	Libra
October 8–30	Scorpio
October 31–November 20	Sagittarius
November 21–December 12	Scorpio
December 13–31	Sagittarius

1947

January 1–3	Sagittarius
January 4–21	Capricorn
January 22–February 8	Aquarius
February 9–April 16	Pisces
April 17–May 4	Aries
May 5–18	Taurus
May 19–June 2	Gemini
June 3–August 10	Cancer
August 11–26	Leo
August 27–September 11	Virgo
September 12–October 1	Libra
October 2–December 7	Scorpio
December 8–26	Sagittarius
December 27–31	Capricorn

1948

January 1–14	Capricorn
January 15–February 2	Aquarius
February 3–20	Pisces
February 21–March 18	Aquarius
March 19–April 9	Pisces
April 10–27	Aries
April 28–May 9	Taurus
May 10–28	Gemini
May 29–June 28	Cancer
June 29–July 11	Gemini
July 12–August 2	Cancer
August 3–17	Leo
August 18–September 3	Virgo
September 4–27	Libra
September 28–October 17	Scorpio
October 18–November 10	Libra
November 11–29	Scorpio
November 30–December 18	Sagittarius
December 19–31	Capricorn

1949

January 1–6	Capricorn
January 7–March 14	Aquarius
March 15–April 1	Pisces
April 2–16	Aries
April 17–May 2	Taurus
May 3–July 10	Gemini
July 11–25	Cancer
July 26–August 9	Leo
August 10–28	Virgo
August 29–November 3	Libra
November 4–22	Scorpio
November 23–December 11	Sagittarius
December 12–31	Capricorn

1950

January 1	Capricorn
January 2–15	Aquarius
January 16–February 14	Capricorn
February 15–March 7	Aquarius
March 8–June 14	Taurus
June 15–July 2	Gemini
July 3–16	Cancer
July 17–August 2	Leo
August 3–27	Virgo
August 28–September 10	Libra
September 11–October 9	Virgo
October 10–27	Libra
October 28–November 15	Scorpio
November 16–December 5	Sagittarius
December 6–31	Capricorn

1951

January 1–February 9	Capricorn
February 10–28	Aquarius
March 1–16	Pisces
March 17–April 2	Aries
April 3–May 1	Taurus
May 2–15	Aries
May 16–June 9	Taurus
June 10–24	Gemini
June 25–July 8	Cancer
July 9–27	Leo
July 28–October 2	Virgo
October 3–19	Libra
October 20–November 8	Scorpio
November 9–December 1	Sagittarius
December 2–12	Capricorn
December 13–31	Sagittarius

1952

January 1–13	Sagittarius
January 14–February 3	Capricorn
February 4–20	Aquarius
February 21–March 7	Pisces
March 8–May 14	Aries
May 15–31	Taurus
June 1–14	Gemini
June 15–30	Cancer
July 1–September 7	Leo
September 8–23	Virgo
September 24–October 11	Libra
October 12–November 1	Scorpio
November 2–December 31	Sagittarius

1953

January 1–6	Sagittarius
January 7–25	Capricorn
January 26–February 11	Aquarius
February 12–March 2	Pisces
March 3–15	Aries
March 16–April 17	Pisces
April 18–May 9	Aries
May 10–23	Taurus
May 24–June 6	Gemini
June 7–26	Cancer
June 27–July 28	Leo
July 29–August 11	Cancer
August 12–30	Leo
August 31–September 15	Virgo
September 16–October 4	Libra
October 5–31	Scorpio
November 1–6	Sagittarius
November 7–December 10	Scorpio
December 11–30	Sagittarius
December 31	Capricorn

1954

January 1–18	Capricorn
January 19–February 4	Aquarius
February 5–April 13	Pisces
April 14–30	Aries
May 1–14	Taurus
May 15–30	Gemini
May 31–August 7	Cancer
August 8–22	Leo
August 23–September 8	Virgo
September 9–29	Libra
September 30–November 4	Scorpio
November 5–11	Libra
November 12–December 4	Scorpio
December 5–23	Sagittarius
December 24–31	Capricorn

1955

January 1–10	Capricorn
January 11–March 17	Aquarius
March 18–April 6	Pisces
April 7–22	Aries
April 23–May 6	Taurus
May 7–July 13	Gemini
July 14–30	Cancer
July 31–August 14	Leo
August 15–September 1	Virgo
September 2–November 8	Libra
November 9–27	Scorpio
November 28–December 16	Sagittarius
December 17–31	Capricorn

1957

January 1–February 12	Capricorn
February 13–March 4	Aquarius
March 5–20	Pisces
March 21–April 4	Aries
April 5–June 12	Taurus
June 13–27	Gemini
June 28–July 12	Cancer
July 13–30	Leo
July 31–October 6	Virgo
October 7–23	Libra
October 24–November 11	Scorpio
November 12–December 2	Sagittarius
December 3–28	Capricorn
December 29–31	Sagittarius

1956

January 1–4	Capricorn
January 5–February 2	Aquarius
February 3–15	Capricorn
February 16–March 11	Aquarius
March 12–28	Pisces
March 29–April 12	Aries
April 13–29	Taurus
April 30–July 6	Gemini
July 7–21	Cancer
July 22–August 5	Leo
August 6–26	Virgo
August 27–September 29	Libra
September 30–October 11	Virgo
October 12–31	Libra
November 1–18	Scorpio
November 19–December 8	Sagittarius
December 9–31	Capricorn

1958

January 1–14	Sagittarius
January 15–February 6	Capricorn
February 7–24	Aquarius
February 25–March 12	Pisces
March 13–April 2	Aries
April 3–10	Taurus
April 11–May 17	Aries
May 18–June 20	Taurus
June 21–July 4	Cancer
July 5–26	Leo
July 27–August 23	Virgo
August 24–September 11	Leo
September 12–28	Virgo
September 29–October 16	Libra
October 17–November 5	Scorpio
November 6–December 31	Sagittarius

1959

January 1–10	Sagittarius
January 11–30	Capricorn
January 31–February 17	Aquarius
February 18–March 5	Pisces
March 6–May 12	Aries
May 13–28	Taurus
May 29–June 11	Gemini
June 12–28	Cancer
June 29–September 5	Leo
September 6–21	Virgo
September 22–October 9	Libra
October 10–November 1	Scorpio
November 2–25	Sagittarius
November 26–December 13	Scorpio
December 14–31	Sagittarius

1960

January 1–4	Sagittarius
January 5–23	Capricorn
January 24–February 9	Aquarius
February 10–April 16	Pisces
April 17–May 4	Aries
May 5–19	Taurus
May 20–June 2	Gemini
June 3–July 1	Cancer
July 2–6	Leo
July 7–August 10	Cancer
August 11–27	Leo
August 28–September 12	Virgo
September 13–October 1	Libra
October 2–December 7	Scorpio
December 8–27	Sagittarius
December 28–31	Capricorn

1961

January 1–14	Capricorn
January 15–February 1	Aquarius
February 2–24	Pisces
February 25–March 18	Aquarius
March 19–April 10	Pisces
April 11–26	Aries
April 27–May 10	Taurus
May 11–28	Gemini
May 29–August 4	Cancer
August 5–18	Leo
August 19–September 4	Virgo
September 5–27	Libra
September 28–October 22	Scorpio
October 23–November 10	Libra
November 11–30	Scorpio
December 1–20	Sagittarius
December 21–31	Capricorn

1962

January 1–7	Capricorn
January 8–March 15	Aquarius
March 16–April 3	Pisces
April 4–18	Aries
April 19–May 3	Taurus
May 4–July 11	Gemini
July 12–26	Cancer
July 27–August 10	Leo
August 11–29	Virgo
August 30–November 5	Libra
November 6–23	Scorpio
November 24–December 12	Sagittarius
December 13–31	Capricorn

1963

January 1–2	Capricorn
January 3–20	Aquarius
January 21–February 15	Capricorn
February 16–March 9	Aquarius
March 10–26	Pisces
March 27–April 9	Aries
April 10–May 3	Taurus
May 4–10	Gemini
May 11–June 14	Taurus
June 15–July 4	Gemini
July 5–18	Cancer
July 19–August 3	Leo
August 4–26	Virgo
August 27–September 16	Libra
September 17–October 10	Virgo
October 11–28	Libra
October 29–November 16	Scorpio
November 17–December 6	Sagittarius
December 7–31	Capricorn

1964

January 1–February 10	Capricorn
February 11–29	Aquarius
March 1–16	Pisces
March 17–April 2	Aries
April 3–June 9	Taurus
June 10–24	Gemini
June 25–July 9	Cancer
July 10–27	Leo
July 28–October 2	Virgo
October 3–20	Libra
October 21–November 8	Scorpio
November 9–30	Sagittarius
December 1–16	Capricorn
December 17–31	Sagittarius

1965

January 1–13	Sagittarius
January 14–February 3	Capricorn
February 4–21	Aquarius
February 22–March 9	Pisces
March 10–May 15	Aries
May 16–June 2	Taurus
June 3–16	Gemini
June 17–July 1	Cancer
July 2–31	Leo
August 1–3	Virgo
August 4–September 8	Leo
September 9–25	Virgo
September 26–October 12	Libra
October 13–November 2	Scorpio
November 3–December 31	Sagittarius

1966

January 1–7	Sagittarius
January 8–27	Capricorn
January 28–February 13	Aquarius
February 14–March 3	Pisces
March 4–22	Aries
March 23–April 17	Pisces
April 18–May 9	Aries
May 10–24	Taurus
May 25–June 7	Gemini
June 8–26	Cancer
June 27–September 1	Leo
September 2–17	Virgo
September 18–October 5	Libra
October 6–30	Scorpio
October 31–November 13	Sagittarius
November 14–December 11	Scorpio
December 12–31	Sagittarius

1967

January 1	Sagittarius
January 2–19	Capricorn
January 20–February 6	Aquarius
February 7–April 14	Pisces
April 15–May 1	Aries
May 2–16	Taurus
May 17–31	Gemini
June 1–August 8	Cancer
August 9–24	Leo
August 25–September 9	Virgo
September 10–30	Libra
October 1–December 5	Scorpio
December 6–24	Sagittarius
December 25–31	Capricorn

1969

January 1–4	Capricorn
January 5–March 12	Aquarius
March 13–30	Pisces
March 31–April 14	Aries
April 15–30	Taurus
May 1–July 8	Gemini
July 9–22	Cancer
July 23–August 7	Leo
August 8–October 7	Libra
October 8–9	Virgo
October 10–November 1	Libra
November 2–20	Scorpio
November 21–December 9	Sagittarius
December 10–31	Capricorn

1968

January 1–12	Capricorn
January 13–February 1	Aquarius
February 2–11	Pisces
February 12–March 17	Aquarius
March 18–April 7	Pisces
April 8–22	Aries
April 23–May 6	Taurus
May 7–29	Gemini
May 30–June 13	Cancer
June 14–July 13	Gemini
July 14–31	Cancer
August 1–15	Leo
August 16–September 1	Virgo
September 2–28	Libra
September 29–October 7	Scorpio
October 8–November 8	Libra
November 9–27	Scorpio
November 28–December 16	Sagittarius
December 17–31	Capricorn

1970

January 1–February 13	Capricorn
February 14–March 5	Aquarius
March 6–22	Pisces
March 23–April 6	Aries
April 7–June 13	Taurus
June 14–30	Gemini
July 1–14	Cancer
July 15–31	Leo
August 1–October 7	Virgo
October 8–25	Libra
October 26–November 13	Scorpio
November 14–December 3	Sagittarius
December 4–31	Capricorn

1971

January 1–2	Capricorn
January 3–14	Sagittarius
January 15–February 7	Capricorn
February 8–26	Aquarius
February 27–March 14	Pisces
March 15–April 1	Aries
April 2–18	Taurus
April 19–May 31	Aries
June 1–7	Taurus
June 8–21	Gemini
June 22–July 6	Cancer
July 7–26	Leo
July 27–August 29	Virgo
August 30–September 11	Leo
September 12–30	Virgo
October 1–17	Libra
October 18–November 6	Scorpio
November 7–December 31	Sagittarius

1972

January 1–11	Sagittarius
January 12–31	Capricorn
February 1–18	Aquarius
February 19–March 5	Pisces
March 6–May 12	Aries
May 13–29	Taurus
May 30–June 12	Gemini
June 13–28	Cancer
June 29–September 5	Leo
September 6–21	Virgo
September 22–October 9	Libra
October 10–30	Scorpio
October 31–November 29	Sagittarius
November 30–December 12	Scorpio
December 13–31	Sagittarius

1973

January 1–4	Sagittarius
January 5–23	Capricorn
January 24–February 9	Aquarius
February 10–April 16	Pisces
April 17–May 6	Aries
May 7–20	Taurus
May 21–June 4	Gemini
June 5–25	Cancer
June 26–July 16	Leo
July 17–August 11	Cancer
August 12–28	Leo
August 29–September 13	Virgo
September 14–October 2	Libra
October 3–December 8	Scorpio
December 9–28	Sagittarius
December 29–31	Capricorn

1974

January 1–16	Capricorn
January 17–February 2	Aquarius
February 3–March 2	Pisces
March 3–17	Aquarius
March 18–April 11	Pisces
April 12–28	Aries
April 29–May 12	Taurus
May 13–29	Gemini
May 30–August 5	Cancer
August 6–25	Leo
August 26–September 6	Virgo
September 7–28	Libra
September 29–October 26	Scorpio
October 27–November 11	Libra
November 12–December 2	Scorpio
December 3–21	Sagittarius
December 22–31	Capricorn

1975

January 1–8	Capricorn
January 9–March 16	Aquarius
March 17–April 4	Pisces
April 5–19	Aries
April 20–May 4	Taurus
May 5–July 12	Gemini
July 13–28	Cancer
July 29–August 12	Leo
August 13–30	Virgo
August 31–November 6	Libra
November 7–25	Scorpio
November 26–December 14	Sagittarius
December 15–31	Capricorn

1976

January 1–2	Capricorn
January 3–25	Aquarius
January 26–February 15	Capricorn
February 16–March 9	Aquarius
March 10–26	Pisces
March 27–April 10	Aries
April 11–29	Taurus
April 30–May 19	Gemini
May 20–June 13	Taurus
June 14–July 4	Gemini
July 5–18	Cancer
July 19–August 3	Leo
August 4–25	Virgo
August 26–September 21	Libra
September 22–October 10	Virgo
October 11–29	Libra
October 30–November 16	Scorpio
November 17–December 6	Sagittarius
December 7–31	Capricorn

1977

January 1–February 10	Capricorn
February 11–March 2	Aquarius
March 3–18	Pisces
March 19–April 3	Aries
April 4–June 10	Taurus
June 11–26	Gemini
June 27–July 10	Cancer
July 11–28	Leo
July 29–October 4	Virgo
October 5–21	Libra
October 22–November 9	Scorpio
November 10–December 1	Sagittarius
December 2–21	Capricorn
December 22–31	Sagittarius

1978

January 1–13	Sagittarius
January 14–February 4	Capricorn
February 5–22	Aquarius
February 23–March 10	Pisces
March 11–May 16	Aries
May 17–June 3	Taurus
June 4–17	Gemini
June 18–July 2	Cancer
July 3–27	Leo
July 28–August 13	Virgo
August 14–September 9	Leo
September 10–26	Virgo
September 27–October 14	Libra
October 15–November 3	Scorpio
November 4–December 31	Sagittarius

1979

January 1–8	Sagittarius
January 9–28	Capricorn
January 29–February 14	Aquarius
February 15–March 3	Pisces
March 4–28	Aries
March 29–April 17	Pisces
April 18–May 10	Aries
May 11–26	Taurus
May 27–June 9	Gemini
June 10–27	Cancer
June 28–September 2	Leo
September 3–18	Virgo
September 19–October 7	Libra
October 8–30	Scorpio
October 31–November 18	Sagittarius
November 19–December 12	Scorpio
December 13–31	Sagittarius

1980

January 1–2	Sagittarius
January 3–21	Capricorn
January 22–February 7	Aquarius
February 8–April 14	Pisces
April 15–May 2	Aries
May 3–16	Taurus
May 17–31	Gemini
June 1–August 9	Cancer
August 10–24	Leo
August 25–September 10	Virgo
September 11–31	Libra
October 1–December 5	Scorpio
December 6–25	Sagittarius
December 26–31	Capricorn

1981

January 1–12	Capricorn
January 13–31	Aquarius
February 1–16	Pisces
February 17–March 18	Aquarius
March 19–April 8	Pisces
April 9–24	Aries
April 25–May 8	Taurus
May 9–28	Gemini
May 29–June 22	Cancer
June 23–July 12	Gemini
July 13–August 1	Cancer
August 2–16	Leo
August 17–September 2	Virgo
September 3–27	Libra
September 28–October 14	Scorpio
October 15–November 9	Libra
November 10–28	Scorpio
November 29–December 17	Sagittarius
December 18–31	Capricorn

1982

January 1–5	Capricorn
January 6–March 13	Aquarius
March 14–31	Pisces
April 1–15	Aries
April 16–May 1	Taurus
May 2–July 9	Gemini
July 10–24	Cancer
July 25–August 8	Leo
August 9–28	Virgo
August 29–November 3	Libra
November 4–21	Scorpio
November 22–December 10	Sagittarius
December 11–31	Capricorn

1983

Date	Sign
January 1	Capricorn
January 2–12	Aquarius
January 13–February 14	Capricorn
February 15–March 7	Aquarius
March 8–23	Pisces
March 24–April 7	Aries
April 8–June 14	Taurus
June 15–July 15	Gemini
July 16–August 1	Leo
August 2–29	Virgo
August 30–September 6	Libra
September 7–October 8	Virgo
October 9–26	Libra
October 27–November 14	Scorpio
November 15–December 4	Sagittarius
December 5–31	Capricorn

1984

Date	Sign
January 1–February 9	Capricorn
February 10–27	Aquarius
February 28–March 14	Pisces
March 15–31	Aries
April 1–25	Taurus
April 26–May 15	Aries
May 16–June 7	Taurus
June 8–22	Gemini
June 23–July 6	Cancer
July 7–26	Leo
July 27–September 30	Virgo
October 1–18	Libra
October 19–November 6	Scorpio
November 7–December 1	Sagittarius
December 2–7	Capricorn
December 8–31	Sagittarius

1985

Date	Sign
January 1–11	Sagittarius
January 12–February 1	Capricorn
February 2–18	Aquarius
February 19–March 6	Pisces
March 7–May 14	Aries
May 15–30	Taurus
May 31–June 13	Gemini
June 14–29	Cancer
June 30–September 6	Leo
September 7–22	Virgo
September 23–October 10	Libra
October 11–31	Scorpio
November 1–December 4	Sagittarius
December 5–12	Scorpio
December 13–31	Sagittarius

1986

Date	Sign
January 1–5	Sagittarius
January 6–25	Capricorn
January 26–February 11	Aquarius
February 12–March 3	Pisces
March 4–11	Aries
March 12–April 17	Pisces
April 18–May 7	Aries
May 8–22	Taurus
May 23–June 5	Gemini
June 6–26	Cancer
June 27–July 23	Leo
July 24–August 11	Cancer
August 12–30	Leo
August 31–September 15	Virgo
September 16–October 4	Libra
October 5–December 10	Scorpio
December 11–29	Sagittarius
December 30–31	Capricorn

1987

January 1–17	Capricorn
January 18–February 4	Aquarius
February 5–March 11	Pisces
March 12–13	Aquarius
March 14–April 12	Pisces
April 13–29	Aries
April 30–May 13	Taurus
May 14–30	Gemini
May 31–August 6	Cancer
August 7–21	Leo
August 22–September 7	Virgo
September 8–28	Libra
September 29–November 1	Scorpio
November 2–11	Libra
November 12–December 3	Scorpio
December 4–22	Sagittarius
December 23–31	Capricorn

1988

January 1–10	Capricorn
January 11–March 16	Aquarius
March 17–April 4	Pisces
April 5–20	Aries
April 21–May 4	Taurus
May 5–July 12	Gemini
July 13–28	Cancer
July 29–August 12	Leo
August 13–30	Virgo
August 31–November 6	Libra
November 7–25	Scorpio
November 26–December 14	Sagittarius
December 15–31	Capricorn

1989

January 1–2	Capricorn
January 3–29	Aquarius
January 30–February 14	Capricorn
February 15–March 10	Aquarius
March 11–28	Pisces
March 29–April 11	Aries
April 12–29	Taurus
April 30–May 28	Gemini
May 29–June 12	Taurus
June 13–July 6	Gemini
July 7–20	Cancer
July 21–August 6	Leo
August 7–21	Virgo
August 22–September 26	Libra
September 27–October 11	Scorpio
October 12–30	Libra
October 31–November 18	Scorpio
November 19–December 7	Sagittarius
December 8–31	Capricorn

1990

January 1–February 12	Capricorn
February 13–March 3	Aquarius
March 4–19	Pisces
March 20–April 4	Aries
April 5–June 12	Taurus
June 13–27	Gemini
June 28–July 11	Cancer
July 12–29	Leo
July 30–October 5	Virgo
October 6–23	Libra
October 24–November 10	Scorpio
November 11–December 2	Sagittarius
December 3–25	Capricorn
December 26–31	Sagittarius

1991

January 1–14	Sagittarius
January 15–February 5	Capricorn
February 6–19	Aquarius
February 20–March 11	Pisces
March 12–May 16	Aries
May 17–June 5	Taurus
June 6–19	Gemini
June 20–July 4	Cancer
July 5–26	Leo
July 27–August 19	Virgo
August 20–September 10	Leo
September 11–28	Virgo
September 29–October 15	Libra
October 16–November 4	Scorpio
November 5–December 31	Sagittarius

1992

January 1–10	Sagittarius
January 11–29	Capricorn
January 30–February 16	Aquarius
February 17–March 3	Pisces
March 4–April 3	Aries
April 4–14	Pisces
April 15–May 11	Aries
May 12–26	Taurus
May 27–June 9	Gemini
June 10–27	Cancer
June 28–September 3	Leo
September 4–19	Virgo
September 20–October 7	Libra
October 8–29	Scorpio
October 30–November 21	Sagittarius
November 22–December 12	Scorpio
December 13–31	Sagittarius

1993

January 1–2	Sagittarius
January 3–21	Capricorn
January 22–February 7	Aquarius
February 8–April 15	Pisces
April 16–May 3	Aries
May 4–18	Taurus
May 19–June 2	Gemini
June 3–August 10	Cancer
August 11–26	Leo
August 27–September 11	Virgo
September 12–October 1	Libra
October 2–December 7	Scorpio
December 8–26	Sagittarius
December 27–31	Capricorn

1994

January 1–14	Capricorn
January 15–February 1	Aquarius
February 2–21	Pisces
February 22–March 18	Aquarius
March 19–April 9	Pisces
April 10–25	Aries
April 26–May 9	Taurus
May 10–28	Gemini
May 29–July 2	Cancer
July 3–10	Gemini
July 11–August 3	Cancer
August 4–18	Leo
August 19–September 4	Virgo
September 5–27	Libra
September 28–October 19	Scorpio
October 20–November 10	Libra
November 11–30	Scorpio
December 1–20	Sagittarius
December 21–31	Capricorn

1995

January 1–6	Capricorn
January 7–March 14	Aquarius
March 15–April 2	Pisces
April 3–17	Aries
April 18–May 2	Taurus
May 3–July 10	Gemini
July 11–25	Cancer
July 26–August 10	Leo
August 11–29	Virgo
August 30–November 4	Libra
November 5–22	Scorpio
November 23–December 13	Sagittarius
December 14–31	Capricorn

1996

January 1	Capricorn
January 2–17	Aquarius
January 18–February 15	Capricorn
February 16–March 7	Aquarius
March 8–24	Pisces
March 25–April 8	Aries
April 9–June 13	Taurus
June 14–July 2	Gemini
July 3–16	Cancer
July 17–August 1	Leo
August 2–26	Virgo
August 27–September 12	Libra
September 13–October 9	Virgo
October 10–27	Libra
October 28–November 14	Scorpio
November 15–December 4	Sagittarius
December 5–31	Capricorn

1997

January 1–February 9	Capricorn
February 10–28	Aquarius
March 1–16	Pisces
March 17–April 1	Aries
April 2–May 5	Taurus
May 6–12	Aries
May 13–June 8	Taurus
June 9–23	Gemini
June 24–July 8	Cancer
July 9–27	Leo
July 28–October 2	Virgo
October 3–19	Libra
October 20–November 7	Scorpio
November 8–30	Sagittarius
December 1–13	Capricorn
December 14–31	Sagittarius

1998

January 1–12	Sagittarius
January 13–February 2	Capricorn
February 3–20	Aquarius
February 21–March 8	Pisces
March 9–May 15	Aries
May 16–June 1	Taurus
June 2–15	Gemini
June 16–30	Cancer
July 1–September 8	Leo
September 9–24	Virgo
September 25–October 12	Libra
October 13–November 1	Scorpio
November 2–December 31	Sagittarius

1999

January 1–7	Sagittarius
January 8–26	Capricorn
January 27–February 12	Aquarius
February 13–March 2	Pisces
March 3–18	Aries
March 19–April 17	Pisces
April 18–May 8	Aries
May 9–23	Taurus
May 24–June 7	Gemini
June 8–26	Cancer
June 27–July 31	Leo
August 1–11	Cancer
August 12–31	Leo
September 1–16	Virgo
September 17–October 5	Libra
October 6–30	Scorpio
October 31–November 9	Sagittarius
November 10–December 11	Scorpio
December 12–31	Sagittarius

2000

January 1–18	Capricorn
January 19–February 5	Aquarius
February 6–April 13	Pisces
April 14–30	Aries
May 1–14	Taurus
May 15–30	Gemini
May 31–August 7	Cancer
August 8–22	Leo
August 23–September 7	Virgo
September 8–28	Libra
September 29–November 7	Virgo
November 8	Libra
November 9–December 3	Scorpio
December 4–23	Sagittarius
December 24–31	Capricorn

Venus

1925

January 1–14	Sagittarius
January 15–February 7	Capricorn
February 8–March 3	Aquarius
March 4–27	Pisces
March 28–April 20	Aries
April 21–May 15	Taurus
May 16–June 8	Gemini
June 9–July 3	Cancer
July 4–27	Leo
July 28–August 21	Virgo
August 22–September 15	Libra
September 16–October 11	Scorpio
October 12–November 16	Sagittarius
November 17–December 5	Capricorn
December 6–31	Aquarius

1927

January 1–9	Capricorn
January 10–February 1	Aquarius
February 2–26	Pisces
February 27–March 22	Aries
March 23–April 16	Taurus
April 17–May 11	Gemini
May 12–June 7	Cancer
June 8–July 7	Leo
July 8–November 9	Virgo
November 10–December 8	Libra
December 9–31	Scorpio

1926

January 1–April 5	Aquarius
April 6–May 6	Pisces
May 7–June 2	Aries
June 3–28	Taurus
June 29–July 23	Gemini
July 24–August 17	Cancer
August 18–September 11	Leo
September 12–October 5	Virgo
October 6–29	Libra
October 30–November 22	Scorpio
November 23–December 16	Sagittarius
December 17–31	Capricorn

1928

January 1–3	Scorpio
January 4–28	Sagittarius
January 29–February 22	Capricorn
February 23–March 17	Aquarius
March 18–April 11	Pisces
April 12–May 5	Aries
May 6–29	Taurus
May 30–June 23	Gemini
June 24–July 17	Cancer
July 18–August 11	Leo
August 12–September 4	Virgo
September 5–28	Libra
September 29–October 23	Scorpio
October 24–November 16	Sagittarius
November 17–December 11	Capricorn
December 12–31	Aquarius

1929

January 1–5	Aquarius
January 6–February 2	Pisces
February 3–March 7	Aries
March 8–April 19	Taurus
April 20–June 2	Aries
June 3–July 7	Taurus
July 8–August 4	Gemini
August 5–30	Cancer
August 31–September 25	Leo
September 26–October 19	Virgo
October 20–November 12	Libra
November 13–December 6	Scorpio
December 7–30	Sagittarius
December 31	Capricorn

1930

January 1–23	Capricorn
January 24–February 16	Aquarius
February 17–March 12	Pisces
March 13–April 5	Aries
April 6–30	Taurus
May 1–24	Gemini
May 25–June 18	Cancer
June 19–July 14	Leo
July 15–August 9	Virgo
August 10–September 6	Libra
September 7–October 11	Scorpio
October 12–November 21	Sagittarius
November 22–December 31	Scorpio

1931

January 1–3	Scorpio
January 4–February 6	Sagittarius
February 7–March 4	Capricorn
March 5–31	Aquarius
April 1–25	Pisces
April 26–May 20	Aries
May 21–June 13	Taurus
June 14–July 8	Gemini
July 9–August 2	Cancer
August 3–26	Leo
August 27–September 19	Virgo
September 20–October 13	Libra
October 14–November 6	Scorpio
November 7–30	Sagittarius
December 1–24	Capricorn
December 25–31	Aquarius

1932

January 1–18	Aquarius
January 19–February 11	Pisces
February 12–March 8	Aries
March 9–April 3	Taurus
April 4–May 5	Gemini
May 6–July 12	Cancer
July 13–27	Gemini
July 28–September 8	Cancer
September 9–October 6	Leo
October 7–November 1	Virgo
November 2–25	Libra
November 26–December 20	Scorpio
December 21–31	Sagittarius

1933

January 1–13	Sagittarius
January 14–February 6	Capricorn
February 7–March 2	Aquarius
March 3–26	Pisces
March 27–April 19	Aries
April 20–May 28	Taurus
May 29–June 8	Gemini
June 9–July 2	Cancer
July 3–26	Leo
July 27–August 20	Virgo
August 21–September 14	Libra
September 15–October 10	Scorpio
October 11–November 15	Sagittarius
November 16–December 4	Capricorn
December 5–31	Aquarius

1934

January 1–April 5	Aquarius
April 6–May 5	Pisces
May 6–June 1	Aries
June 2–27	Taurus
June 28–July 22	Gemini
July 23–August 16	Cancer
August 17–September 10	Leo
September 11–October 4	Virgo
October 5–28	Libra
October 29–November 21	Scorpio
November 22–December 15	Sagittarius
December 16–31	Capricorn

1935

January 1–7	Capricorn
January 8–31	Aquarius
February 1–25	Pisces
February 26–March 21	Aries
March 22–April 15	Taurus
April 16–May 10	Gemini
May 11–June 6	Cancer
June 7–July 6	Leo
July 7–November 8	Virgo
November 9–December 7	Libra
December 8–31	Scorpio

1936

January 1–2	Scorpio
January 3–27	Sagittarius
January 28–February 21	Capricorn
February 22–March 16	Aquarius
March 17–April 10	Pisces
April 11–May 4	Aries
May 5–28	Taurus
May 29–June 22	Gemini
June 23–July 16	Cancer
July 17–August 10	Leo
August 11–September 4	Virgo
September 5–27	Libra
September 28–October 22	Scorpio
October 23–November 15	Sagittarius
November 16–December 10	Capricorn
December 11–31	Aquarius

1937

January 1–5	Aquarius
January 6–February 1	Pisces
February 2–March 8	Aries
March 9–April 13	Taurus
April 14–June 3	Aries
June 4–July 6	Taurus
July 7–August 3	Gemini
August 4–29	Cancer
August 30–September 24	Leo
September 25–October 18	Virgo
October 19–November 11	Libra
November 12–December 5	Scorpio
December 6–29	Sagittarius
December 30–31	Capricorn

1938

January 1–22	Capricorn
January 23–February 15	Aquarius
February 16–March 11	Pisces
March 12–April 4	Aries
April 5–28	Taurus
April 29–May 23	Gemini
May 24–June 18	Cancer
June 19–July 13	Leo
July 14–August 8	Virgo
August 9–September 6	Libra
September 7–October 13	Scorpio
October 14–November 14	Sagittarius
November 15–December 31	Scorpio

1939

January 1–3	Scorpio
January 4–February 5	Sagittarius
February 6–March 4	Capricorn
March 5–30	Aquarius
March 31–April 24	Pisces
April 25–May 19	Aries
May 20–June 13	Taurus
June 14–July 8	Gemini
July 9–August 1	Cancer
August 2–25	Leo
August 26–September 19	Virgo
September 20–October 13	Libra
October 14–November 6	Scorpio
November 7–30	Sagittarius
December 1–24	Capricorn
December 25–31	Aquarius

1940

January 1–18	Aquarius
January 19–February 11	Pisces
February 12–March 7	Aries
March 8–April 3	Taurus
April 4–May 5	Gemini
May 6–July 4	Cancer
July 5–31	Gemini
August 1–September 8	Cancer
September 9–October 5	Leo
October 6–31	Virgo
November 1–25	Libra
November 26–December 19	Scorpio
December 20–31	Sagittarius

1942

January 1–April 5	Aquarius
April 6–May 5	Pisces
May 6–June 1	Aries
June 2–26	Taurus
June 27–July 22	Gemini
July 23–August 16	Cancer
August 17–September 9	Leo
September 10–October 3	Virgo
October 4–27	Libra
October 28–November 20	Scorpio
November 21–December 14	Sagittarius
December 15–31	Capricorn

1943

January 1–7	Capricorn
January 8–31	Aquarius
February 1–24	Pisces
February 25–March 20	Aries
March 21–April 14	Taurus
April 15–May 10	Gemini
May 11–June 6	Cancer
June 7–July 6	Leo
July 7–November 8	Virgo
November 9–December 7	Libra
December 8–31	Scorpio

1941

January 1–12	Sagittarius
January 13–February 5	Capricorn
February 6–March 1	Aquarius
March 2–26	Pisces
March 27–April 19	Aries
April 20–May 13	Taurus
May 14–June 6	Gemini
June 7–July 1	Cancer
July 2–26	Leo
July 27–August 20	Virgo
August 21–September 14	Libra
September 15–October 9	Scorpio
October 10–November 5	Sagittarius
November 6–December 4	Capricorn
December 5–31	Aquarius

1944

January 1–2	Scorpio
January 3–27	Sagittarius
January 28–February 20	Capricorn
February 21–March 16	Aquarius
March 17–April 9	Pisces
April 10–May 3	Aries
May 4–28	Taurus
May 29–June 21	Gemini
June 22–July 16	Cancer
July 17–August 9	Leo
August 10–September 2	Virgo
September 3–27	Libra
September 28–October 21	Scorpio
October 22–November 15	Sagittarius
November 16–December 10	Capricorn
December 11–31	Aquarius

1945

January 1–4	Aquarius
January 5–February 1	Pisces
February 2–March 10	Aries
March 11–April 6	Taurus
April 7–June 3	Aries
June 4–July 6	Taurus
July 7–August 3	Gemini
August 4–29	Cancer
August 30–September 23	Leo
September 24–October 18	Virgo
October 19–November 11	Libra
November 12–December 5	Scorpio
December 6–29	Sagittarius
December 30–31	Capricorn

1946

January 1–21	Capricorn
January 22–February 14	Aquarius
February 15–March 10	Pisces
March 11–April 4	Aries
April 5–28	Taurus
April 29–May 23	Gemini
May 24–June 17	Cancer
June 18–July 12	Leo
July 13–August 8	Virgo
August 9–September 6	Libra
September 7–October 15	Scorpio
October 16–November 7	Sagittarius
November 8–December 31	Scorpio

1947

January 1–4	Scorpio
January 5–February 5	Sagittarius
February 6–March 4	Capricorn
March 5–29	Aquarius
March 30–April 24	Pisces
April 25–May 19	Aries
May 20–June 12	Taurus
June 13–July 7	Gemini
July 8–August 1	Cancer
August 2–25	Leo
August 26–September 18	Virgo
September 19–October 12	Libra
October 13–November 5	Scorpio
November 6–29	Sagittarius
November 30–December 23	Capricorn
December 24–31	Aquarius

1948

January 1–17	Aquarius
January 18–February 10	Pisces
February 11–March 7	Aries
March 8–April 3	Taurus
April 4–May 6	Gemini
May 7–June 28	Cancer
June 29–August 2	Leo
August 3–September 7	Cancer
September 8–October 5	Leo
October 6–31	Virgo
November 1–25	Libra
November 26–December 19	Scorpio
December 20–31	Sagittarius

1950

January 1–April 5	Aquarius
April 6–May 4	Pisces
May 5–31	Aries
June 1–26	Taurus
June 27–July 21	Gemini
July 22–August 15	Cancer
August 16–September 9	Leo
September 10–October 3	Virgo
October 4–27	Libra
October 28–November 20	Scorpio
November 21–December 13	Sagittarius
December 14–31	Capricorn

1949

January 1–12	Sagittarius
January 13–February 5	Capricorn
February 6–March 1	Aquarius
March 2–25	Pisces
March 26–April 19	Aries
April 20–May 13	Taurus
May 14–June 6	Gemini
June 7–30	Cancer
July 1–25	Leo
July 26–August 19	Virgo
August 20–September 14	Libra
September 15–October 9	Scorpio
October 10–November 5	Sagittarius
November 6–December 5	Capricorn
December 6–31	Aquarius

1951

January 1–7	Capricorn
January 8–31	Aquarius
February 1–24	Pisces
February 25–March 21	Aries
March 22–April 15	Taurus
April 16–May 10	Gemini
May 11–June 6	Cancer
June 7–July 7	Leo
July 8–November 9	Virgo
November 10–December 7	Libra
December 8–31	Scorpio

1952

January 1–2	Scorpio
January 3–27	Sagittarius
January 28–February 20	Capricorn
February 21–March 16	Aquarius
March 17–April 9	Pisces
April 10–May 4	Aries
May 5–28	Taurus
May 29–June 21	Gemini
June 22–July 16	Cancer
July 17–August 9	Leo
August 10–September 3	Virgo
September 4–27	Libra
September 28–October 21	Scorpio
October 22–November 15	Sagittarius
November 16–December 10	Capricorn
December 11–31	Aquarius

1953

January 1–5	Aquarius
January 6–February 1	Pisces
February 2–March 13	Aries
March 14–31	Taurus
April 1–June 5	Aries
June 6–July 7	Taurus
July 8–August 3	Gemini
August 4–29	Cancer
August 30–September 24	Leo
September 25–October 18	Virgo
October 19–November 11	Libra
November 12–December 5	Scorpio
December 6–29	Sagittarius
December 30–31	Capricorn

1954

January 1–22	Capricorn
January 23–February 15	Aquarius
February 16–March 11	Pisces
March 12–April 4	Aries
April 5–28	Taurus
April 29–May 23	Gemini
May 24–June 17	Cancer
June 18–July 13	Leo
July 14–August 8	Virgo
August 9–September 6	Libra
September 7–October 22	Scorpio
October 23–27	Sagittarius
October 28–December 31	Scorpio

1955

January 1–6	Scorpio
January 7–February 5	Sagittarius
February 6–March 4	Capricorn
March 5–30	Aquarius
March 31–April 24	Pisces
April 25–May 19	Aries
May 20–June 13	Taurus
June 14–July 7	Gemini
July 8–August 1	Cancer
August 2–25	Leo
August 26–September 18	Virgo
September 19–October 13	Libra
October 14–November 5	Scorpio
November 6–30	Sagittarius
December 1–24	Capricorn
December 25–31	Aquarius

1956

January 1–17	Aquarius
January 18–February 11	Pisces
February 12–March 7	Aries
March 8–April 4	Taurus
April 5–May 7	Gemini
May 8–June 23	Cancer
June 24–August 4	Gemini
August 5–September 8	Cancer
September 9–October 5	Leo
October 6–31	Virgo
November 1–25	Libra
November 26–December 19	Scorpio
December 20–31	Sagittarius

1957

January 1–12	Sagittarius
January 13–February 5	Capricorn
February 6–March 1	Aquarius
March 2–25	Pisces
March 26–April 19	Aries
April 20–May 13	Taurus
May 14–June 6	Gemini
June 7–July 1	Cancer
July 2–26	Leo
July 27–August 19	Virgo
August 20–September 14	Libra
September 15–October 19	Scorpio
October 20–November 5	Sagittarius
November 6–December 6	Capricorn
December 7–31	Aquarius

1958

January 1–April 6	Aquarius
April 7–May 5	Pisces
May 6–31	Aries
June 1–26	Taurus
June 27–July 22	Gemini
July 23–August 15	Cancer
August 16–September 9	Leo
September 10–October 3	Virgo
October 4–27	Libra
October 28–November 20	Scorpio
November 21–December 14	Sagittarius
December 15–31	Capricorn

1959

January 1–7	Capricorn
January 8–31	Aquarius
February 1–24	Pisces
February 25–March 20	Aries
March 21–April 14	Taurus
April 15–May 10	Gemini
May 11–June 6	Cancer
June 7–July 8	Leo
July 9–September 20	Virgo
September 21–24	Leo
September 25–November 9	Virgo
November 10–December 7	Libra
December 8–31	Scorpio

1960

January 1–2	Scorpio
January 3–27	Sagittarius
January 28–February 20	Capricorn
February 21–March 15	Aquarius
March 16–April 9	Pisces
April 10–May 5	Aries
May 6–28	Taurus
May 29–June 21	Gemini
June 22–July 15	Cancer
July 16–August 9	Leo
August 10–September 2	Virgo
September 3–26	Libra
September 27–October 21	Scorpio
October 22–November 15	Sagittarius
November 16–December 10	Capricorn
December 11–31	Aquarius

1961

January 1–5	Aquarius
January 6–February 2	Pisces
February 3–June 5	Aries
June 6–July 7	Taurus
July 8–August 3	Gemini
August 4–29	Cancer
August 30–September 23	Leo
September 24–October 17	Virgo
October 18–November 11	Libra
November 12–December 4	Scorpio
December 5–28	Sagittarius
December 29–31	Capricorn

1962

January 1–21	Capricorn
January 22–February 14	Aquarius
February 15–March 10	Pisces
March 11–April 3	Aries
April 4–28	Taurus
April 29–May 22	Gemini
May 23–June 17	Cancer
June 18–July 12	Leo
July 13–August 8	Virgo
August 9–September 6	Libra
September 7–December 31	Scorpio

1963

January 1–6	Scorpio
January 7–February 5	Sagittarius
February 6–March 4	Capricorn
March 5–29	Aquarius
March 30–April 23	Pisces
April 24–May 18	Aries
May 19–June 12	Taurus
June 13–July 7	Gemini
July 8–31	Cancer
August 1–25	Leo
August 26–September 18	Virgo
September 19–October 12	Libra
October 13–November 5	Scorpio
November 6–29	Sagittarius
November 30–December 23	Capricorn
December 24–31	Aquarius

1964

January 1–16	Aquarius
January 17–February 10	Pisces
February 11–March 7	Aries
March 8–April 4	Taurus
April 5–May 9	Gemini
May 10–June 17	Cancer
June 18–August 5	Gemini
August 6–September 8	Cancer
September 9–October 5	Leo
October 6–31	Virgo
November 1–24	Libra
November 25–December 19	Scorpio
December 20–31	Sagittarius

1966

January 1–February 6	Aquarius
February 7–25	Capricorn
February 26–April 6	Aquarius
April 7–May 5	Pisces
May 6–31	Aries
June 1–26	Taurus
June 27–July 21	Gemini
July 22–August 15	Cancer
August 16–September 8	Leo
September 9–October 2	Virgo
October 3–26	Libra
October 27–November 19	Scorpio
November 20–December 13	Sagittarius
December 14–31	Capricorn

1965

January 1–12	Sagittarius
January 13–February 5	Capricorn
February 6–March 1	Aquarius
March 2–25	Pisces
March 26–April 18	Aries
April 19–May 12	Taurus
May 13–June 6	Gemini
June 7–30	Cancer
July 1–25	Leo
July 26–August 19	Virgo
August 20–September 13	Libra
September 14–October 9	Scorpio
October 10–November 5	Sagittarius
November 6–December 7	Capricorn
December 8–31	Aquarius

1967

January 1–6	Capricorn
January 7–30	Aquarius
January 31–February 23	Pisces
February 24–March 20	Aries
March 21–April 14	Taurus
April 15–May 10	Gemini
May 11–June 6	Cancer
June 7–July 8	Leo
July 9–September 9	Virgo
September 10–October 1	Leo
October 2–November 9	Virgo
November 10–December 7	Libra
December 8–31	Scorpio

1968

January 1	Scorpio
January 2–26	Sagittarius
January 27–February 20	Capricorn
February 21–March 15	Aquarius
March 16–April 8	Pisces
April 9–May 3	Aries
May 4–27	Taurus
May 28–June 20	Gemini
June 21–July 15	Cancer
July 16–August 8	Leo
August 9–September 2	Virgo
September 3–26	Libra
September 27–October 21	Scorpio
October 22–November 14	Sagittarius
November 15–December 9	Capricorn
December 10–31	Aquarius

1969

January 1–4	Aquarius
January 5–February 2	Pisces
February 3–June 6	Aries
June 7–July 6	Taurus
July 7–August 3	Gemini
August 4–28	Cancer
August 29–September 22	Leo
September 23–October 17	Virgo
October 18–November 10	Libra
November 11–December 4	Scorpio
December 5–28	Sagittarius
December 29–31	Capricorn

1970

January 1–21	Capricorn
January 22–February 14	Aquarius
February 15–March 10	Pisces
March 11–April 3	Aries
April 4–27	Taurus
April 28–May 22	Gemini
May 23–June 16	Cancer
June 17–July 12	Leo
July 13–August 8	Virgo
August 9–September 7	Libra
September 8–December 31	Scorpio

1971

January 1–7	Scorpio
January 8–February 5	Sagittarius
February 6–March 4	Capricorn
March 5–29	Aquarius
March 30–April 23	Pisces
April 24–May 17	Aries
May 18–June 12	Taurus
June 13–July 6	Gemini
July 7–31	Cancer
August 1–24	Leo
August 25–September 17	Virgo
September 18–October 17	Libra
October 18–November 5	Scorpio
November 6–29	Sagittarius
November 30–December 23	Capricorn
December 24–31	Aquarius

1972

January 1–16	Aquarius
January 17–February 10	Pisces
February 11–March 7	Aries
March 8–April 3	Taurus
April 4–May 10	Gemini
May 11–June 11	Cancer
June 12–August 6	Gemini
August 7–September 7	Cancer
September 8–October 4	Leo
October 5–30	Virgo
October 31–November 24	Libra
November 25–December 18	Scorpio
December 19–31	Sagittarius

1974

January 1–29	Aquarius
January 30–February 28	Capricorn
March 1–April 6	Aquarius
April 7–May 4	Pisces
May 5–31	Aries
June 1–25	Taurus
June 26–July 21	Gemini
July 22–August 14	Cancer
August 15–September 8	Leo
September 9–October 2	Virgo
October 3–26	Libra
October 27–November 19	Scorpio
November 20–December 13	Sagittarius
December 14–31	Capricorn

1973

January 1–11	Sagittarius
January 12–February 4	Capricorn
February 5–28	Aquarius
March 1–24	Pisces
March 25–April 18	Aries
April 19–May 12	Taurus
May 13–June 5	Gemini
June 6–30	Cancer
July 1–25	Leo
July 26–August 19	Virgo
August 20–September 13	Libra
September 14–October 9	Scorpio
October 10–November 5	Sagittarius
November 6–December 7	Capricorn
December 8–31	Aquarius

1975

January 1–6	Capricorn
January 7–30	Aquarius
January 31–February 23	Pisces
February 24–March 19	Aries
March 20–April 13	Taurus
April 14–May 9	Gemini
May 10–June 6	Cancer
June 7–July 9	Leo
July 10–September 2	Virgo
September 3–October 4	Leo
October 5–November 9	Virgo
November 10–December 7	Libra
December 8–31	Scorpio

1976

January 1	Scorpio
January 2–26	Sagittarius
January 27–February 19	Capricorn
February 20–March 15	Aquarius
March 16–April 8	Pisces
April 9–May 2	Aries
May 3–27	Taurus
May 28–June 20	Gemini
June 21–July 14	Cancer
July 15–August 8	Leo
August 9–September 1	Virgo
September 2–26	Libra
September 27–October 20	Scorpio
October 21–November 14	Sagittarius
November 15–December 9	Capricorn
December 10–31	Aquarius

1977

January 1–4	Aquarius
January 5–February 2	Pisces
February 3–June 6	Aries
June 7–August 2	Gemini
August 3–28	Cancer
August 29–September 22	Leo
September 23–October 17	Virgo
October 18–November 10	Libra
November 11–December 4	Scorpio
December 5–27	Sagittarius
December 28–31	Capricorn

1978

January 1–20	Capricorn
January 21–February 13	Aquarius
February 14–March 9	Pisces
March 10–April 2	Aries
April 3–27	Taurus
April 28–May 22	Gemini
May 23–June 16	Cancer
June 17–July 12	Leo
July 13–August 8	Virgo
August 9–September 7	Libra
September 8–December 31	Scorpio

1979

January 1–7	Scoprio
January 8–February 5	Sagittarius
February 6–March 3	Capricorn
March 4–29	Aquarius
March 30–April 23	Pisces
April 24–May 18	Aries
May 19–June 11	Taurus
June 12–July 6	Gemini
July 7–30	Cancer
July 31–August 24	Leo
August 25–September 17	Virgo
September 18–October 11	Libra
October 12–November 4	Scorpio
November 5–28	Sagittarius
November 29–December 22	Capricorn
December 23–31	Aquarius

1980

January 1–16	Aquarius
January 17–February 9	Pisces
February 10–March 6	Aries
March 7–April 3	Taurus
April 4–May 12	Gemini
May 13–June 5	Cancer
June 6–August 6	Gemini
August 7–September 7	Cancer
September 8–October 4	Leo
October 5–30	Virgo
October 31–November 24	Libra
November 25–December 18	Scorpio
December 19–31	Sagittarius

1981

January 1–11	Sagittarius
January 12–February 4	Capricorn
February 5–28	Aquarius
March 1–24	Pisces
March 24–April 17	Aries
April 18–May 12	Taurus
May 13–June 5	Gemini
June 6–29	Cancer
June 30–July 24	Leo
July 25–August 18	Virgo
August 19–September 12	Libra
September 13–October 8	Scorpio
October 9–November 5	Sagittarius
November 6–December 8	Capricorn
December 9–31	Aquarius

1982

January 1–23	Aquarius
January 24–March 2	Capricorn
March 3–April 6	Aquarius
April 7–May 4	Pisces
May 5–30	Aries
May 31–June 25	Taurus
June 26–July 20	Gemini
July 21–August 14	Cancer
August 15–September 7	Leo
September 8–October 2	Virgo
October 3–26	Libra
October 27–November 18	Scorpio
November 19–December 12	Sagittarius
December 13–31	Capricorn

1983

January 1–5	Capricorn
January 6–29	Aquarius
January 30–February 22	Pisces
February 23–March 19	Aries
March 20–April 13	Taurus
April 14–May 9	Gemini
May 10–June 6	Cancer
June 7–July 10	Leo
July 11–August 27	Virgo
August 28–October 5	Leo
October 6–November 9	Virgo
November 10–December 6	Libra
December 7–31	Scorpio

1984

January 1	Scorpio
January 2–25	Sagittarius
January 26–February 19	Capricorn
February 20–March 14	Aquarius
March 15–April 7	Pisces
April 8–May 2	Aries
May 3–26	Taurus
May 27–June 20	Gemini
June 21–July 14	Cancer
July 15–August 7	Leo
August 8–September 1	Virgo
September 2–25	Libra
September 26–October 20	Scorpio
October 21–November 13	Sagittarius
November 14–December 9	Capricorn
December 10–31	Aquarius

1985

January 1–4	Aquarius
January 5–February 2	Pisces
February 3–June 6	Aries
June 7–July 6	Taurus
July 7–August 2	Gemini
August 3–28	Cancer
August 29–September 22	Leo
September 23–October 16	Virgo
October 17–November 9	Libra
November 10–December 3	Scorpio
December 4–27	Sagittarius
December 28–31	Capricorn

1986

January 1–20	Capricorn
January 21–February 13	Aquarius
February 14–March 9	Pisces
March 10–April 2	Aries
April 3–26	Taurus
April 27–May 21	Gemini
May 22–June 15	Cancer
June 16–July 11	Leo
July 12–August 7	Virgo
August 8–September 7	Libra
September 8–December 31	Scorpio

1987

January 1–7	Scorpio
January 8–February 5	Sagittarius
February 6–March 3	Capricorn
March 4–28	Aquarius
March 29–April 22	Pisces
April 23–May 17	Aries
May 18–June 11	Taurus
June 12–July 5	Gemini
July 6–30	Cancer
July 31–August 23	Leo
August 24–September 16	Virgo
September 17–October 10	Libra
October 11–November 3	Scorpio
November 4–28	Sagittarius
November 29–December 22	Capricorn
December 23–31	Aquarius

1988

January 1–15	Aquarius
January 16–February 9	Pisces
February 10–March 6	Aries
March 7–April 3	Taurus
April 4–May 17	Gemini
May 18–27	Cancer
May 28–August 6	Gemini
August 7–September 7	Cancer
September 8–October 4	Leo
October 5–29	Virgo
October 30–November 23	Libra
November 24–December 17	Scorpio
December 18–31	Sagittarius

1989

January 1–10	Sagittarius
January 11–February 3	Capricorn
February 4–27	Aquarius
February 28–March 23	Pisces
March 24–April 16	Aries
April 17–May 11	Taurus
May 12–June 4	Gemini
June 5–29	Cancer
June 30–July 24	Leo
July 25–August 18	Virgo
August 19–September 12	Libra
September 13–October 8	Scorpio
October 9–November 5	Sagittarius
November 6–December 10	Capricorn
December 11–31	Aquarius

1990

January 1–16	Aquarius
January 17–March 3	Capricorn
March 4–April 6	Aquarius
April 7–May 4	Pisces
May 5–30	Aries
May 31–June 25	Taurus
June 26–July 20	Gemini
July 21–August 13	Cancer
August 14–September 7	Leo
September 8–October 1	Virgo
October 2–25	Libra
October 26–November 18	Scorpio
November 19–December 12	Sagittarius
December 13–31	Capricorn

1991

January 1–5	Capricorn
January 6–29	Aquarius
January 30–February 22	Pisces
February 23–March 18	Aries
March 19–April 13	Taurus
April 14–May 9	Gemini
May 10–June 6	Cancer
June 7–July 11	Leo
July 12–August 21	Virgo
August 22–October 6	Leo
October 7–November 9	Virgo
November 10–December 6	Libra
December 7–31	Scorpio

1992

January 1–25	Sagittarius
January 26–February 18	Capricorn
February 19–March 13	Aquarius
March 14–April 7	Pisces
April 8–May 1	Aries
May 2–26	Taurus
May 27–June 19	Gemini
June 20–July 13	Cancer
July 14–August 7	Leo
August 8–31	Virgo
September 1–25	Libra
September 26–October 19	Scorpio
October 20–November 13	Sagittarius
November 14–December 8	Capricorn
December 9–31	Aquarius

1993

January 1–3	Aquarius
January 4–February 2	Pisces
February 3–June 6	Aries
June 7–July 6	Taurus
July 7–August 1	Gemini
August 2–27	Cancer
August 28–September 21	Leo
September 22–October 16	Virgo
October 17–November 9	Libra
November 10–December 2	Scorpio
December 3–26	Sagittarius
December 27–31	Capricorn

1994

January 1–19	Capricorn
January 20–February 12	Aquarius
February 13–March 8	Pisces
March 9–April 1	Aries
April 2–26	Taurus
April 27–May 21	Gemini
May 22–June 15	Cancer
June 16–July 11	Leo
July 12–August 7	Virgo
August 8–September 7	Libra
September 8–December 31	Scorpio

1995

January 1–7	Scorpio
January 8–February 4	Sagittarius
February 5–March 2	Capricorn
March 3–28	Aquarius
March 29–April 22	Pisces
April 23–May 16	Aries
May 17–June 10	Taurus
June 11–July 5	Gemini
July 6–29	Cancer
July 30–August 23	Leo
August 24–September 16	Virgo
September 17–October 10	Libra
October 11–November 3	Scorpio
November 4–27	Sagittarius
November 28–December 21	Capricorn
December 22–31	Aquarius

1996

January 1–15	Aquarius
January 16–February 9	Pisces
February 10–March 6	Aries
March 7–April 3	Taurus
April 4–August 7	Gemini
August 8–September 7	Cancer
September 8–October 4	Leo
October 5–29	Virgo
October 30–November 23	Libra
November 24–December 17	Scorpio
December 18–31	Sagittarius

1997

January 1–10	Sagittarius
January 11–February 3	Capricorn
February 4–27	Aquarius
February 28–March 23	Pisces
March 24–April 16	Aries
April 17–May 10	Taurus
May 11–June 4	Gemini
June 5–28	Cancer
June 29–July 23	Leo
July 24–August 17	Virgo
August 18–September 12	Libra
September 13–October 8	Scorpio
October 9–November 5	Sagittarius
November 6–December 12	Capricorn
December 13–31	Aquarius

1998

January 1–9	Aquarius
January 10–March 4	Capricorn
March 5–April 6	Aquarius
April 7–May 3	Pisces
May 4–29	Aries
May 30–June 24	Taurus
June 25–July 19	Gemini
July 20–August 13	Cancer
August 14–September 6	Leo
September 7–30	Virgo
October 1–25	Libra
October 26–November 17	Scorpio
November 18–December 11	Sagittarius
December 12–31	Capricorn

1999

January 1–4	Capricorn
January 5–28	Aquarius
January 29–February 21	Pisces
February 22–March 18	Aries
March 19–April 12	Taurus
April 13–May 8	Gemini
May 9–June 5	Cancer
June 6–July 12	Leo
July 13–August 15	Virgo
August 16–October 7	Leo
October 8–November 9	Virgo
November 10–December 5	Libra
December 6–31	Scorpio

2000

January 1–24	Sagittarius
January 25–February 18	Capricorn
February 19–March 13	Aquarius
March 14–April 6	Pisces
April 7–May 1	Aries
May 2–25	Taurus
May 26–June 18	Gemini
June 19–July 13	Cancer
July 14–August 6	Leo
August 7–31	Virgo
September 1–24	Libra
September 25–October 19	Scorpio
October 20–November 13	Sagittarius
November 14–December 8	Capricorn
December 9–31	Aquarius

★
MARS

1925

January 1–February 4	Aries
February 5–March 23	Taurus
March 24–May 9	Gemini
May 10–June 25	Cancer
June 26–August 12	Leo
August 13–September 28	Virgo
September 29–November 13	Libra
November 14–December 27	Scorpio
December 28–31	Sagittarius

1926

January 1–February 8	Sagittarius
February 9–March 22	Capricorn
March 23–May 3	Aquarius
May 4–June 14	Pisces
June 15–July 31	Aries
August 1–December 31	Taurus

1927

January 1–February 21	Taurus
February 22–April 16	Gemini
April 17–June 5	Cancer
June 6–July 24	Leo
July 25–September 10	Virgo
September 11–October 25	Libra
October 26–December 7	Scorpio
December 8–31	Sagittarius

1928

January 1–18	Sagittarius
January 19–February 27	Capricorn
February 28–April 7	Aquarius
April 8–May 16	Pisces
May 17–June 25	Aries
June 26–August 8	Taurus
August 9–October 2	Gemini
October 3–December 19	Cancer
December 20–31	Gemini

1929

January 1–March 10	Gemini
March 11–May 12	Cancer
May 13–July 3	Leo
July 4–August 21	Virgo
August 22–October 5	Libra
October 6–November 18	Scorpio
November 19–December 28	Sagittarius
December 29–31	Capricorn

1930

January 1–February 6	Capricorn
February 7–March 16	Aquarius
March 17–April 24	Pisces
April 25–June 2	Aries
June 3–July 14	Taurus
July 15–August 27	Gemini
August 28–October 20	Cancer
October 21–December 31	Leo

1931

January 1–February 15	Leo
February 16–March 29	Cancer
March 30–June 9	Leo
June 10–July 31	Virgo
August 1–September 16	Libra
September 17–October 29	Scorpio
October 30–December 9	Sagittarius
December 10–31	Capricorn

1932

January 1–17	Capricorn
January 18–February 24	Aquarius
February 25–April 2	Pisces
April 3–May 11	Aries
May 12–June 21	Taurus
June 22–August 3	Gemini
August 4–September 19	Cancer
September 20–November 12	Leo
November 13–December 31	Virgo

1933

January 1–July 5	Virgo
July 6–August 25	Libra
August 26–October 8	Scorpio
October 9–November 18	Sagittarius
November 19–December 27	Capricorn
December 28–31	Aquarius

1934

January 1–February 3	Aquarius
February 4–March 13	Pisces
March 14–April 21	Aries
April 22–June 1	Taurus
June 2–July 14	Gemini
July 15–August 29	Cancer
August 30–October 17	Leo
October 18–December 10	Virgo
December 11–31	Libra

1935

January 1–July 28	Libra
July 29–September 15	Scorpio
September 16–October 27	Sagittarius
October 28–December 6	Capricorn
December 7–31	Aquarius

1936

January 1–13	Aquarius
January 14–February 21	Pisces
February 22–March 31	Aries
April 1–May 12	Taurus
May 13–June 24	Gemini
June 25–August 9	Cancer
August 10–September 25	Leo
September 26–November 13	Virgo
November 14–December 31	Libra

1937

January 1–March 12	Scorpio
March 13–May 13	Sagittarius
May 14–August 7	Scorpio
August 8–September 29	Sagittarius
September 30–November 10	Capricorn
November 11–December 20	Aquarius
December 21–31	Pisces

1938

January 1–29	Pisces
January 30–March 11	Aries
March 12–April 22	Taurus
April 23–June 6	Gemini
June 7–July 21	Cancer
July 22–September 6	Leo
September 7–October 24	Virgo
October 25–December 10	Libra
December 11–31	Scorpio

1939

January 1–28	Scorpio
January 29–March 20	Sagittarius
March 21–May 23	Capricorn
May 24–July 20	Aquarius
July 21–September 23	Capricorn
September 24–November 18	Aquarius
November 19–December 31	Pisces

1940

January 1–2	Pisces
January 3–February 16	Aries
February 17–March 31	Taurus
April 1–May 16	Gemini
May 17–July 2	Cancer
July 3–August 18	Leo
August 19–October 4	Virgo
October 5–November 19	Libra
November 20–December 31	Scorpio

1941

January 1–3	Scorpio
January 4–February 16	Sagittarius
February 17–April 1	Capricorn
April 2–May 15	Aquarius
May 16–July 1	Pisces
July 2–December 31	Aries

1942

January 1–10	Aries
January 11–March 6	Taurus
March 7–April 25	Gemini
April 26–June 13	Cancer
June 14–July 31	Leo
August 1–September 16	Virgo
September 17–October 31	Libra
November 1–December 14	Scorpio
December 15–31	Sagittarius

1943

January 1–25	Sagittarius
January 26–March 7	Capricorn
March 8–April 16	Aquarius
April 17–May 26	Pisces
May 27–June 6	Aries
June 7–August 22	Taurus
August 23–December 31	Gemini

1944

January 1–March 27	Gemini
March 28–May 21	Cancer
May 22–July 11	Leo
July 12–August 28	Virgo
August 29–October 12	Libra
October 13–November 24	Scorpio
November 25–December 31	Sagittarius

1945

January 1–4	Sagittarius
January 5–February 13	Capricorn
February 14–March 24	Aquarius
March 25–May 1	Pisces
May 2–June 10	Aries
June 11–July 22	Taurus
July 23–September 6	Gemini
September 7–November 10	Cancer
November 11–December 25	Leo
December 26–31	Cancer

1946

January 1–April 21	Cancer
April 22–June 19	Leo
June 20–August 8	Virgo
August 9–September 23	Libra
September 24–November 5	Scorpio
November 6–December 16	Sagittarius
December 17–31	Capricorn

1947

January 1–24	Capricorn
January 25–March 3	Aquarius
March 4–April 10	Pisces
April 11–May 20	Aries
May 21–June 30	Taurus
July 1–August 12	Gemini
August 13–September 30	Cancer
October 1–November 30	Leo
December 1–31	Virgo

1948

January 1–February 11	Virgo
February 12–May 17	Leo
May 18–July 16	Virgo
July 17–September 2	Libra
September 3–October 16	Scorpio
October 17–November 25	Sagittarius
November 26–December 31	Capricorn

1949

January 1–3	Capricorn
January 4–February 10	Aquarius
February 11–March 20	Pisces
March 21–April 29	Aries
April 30–June 9	Taurus
June 10–July 22	Gemini
July 23–September 6	Cancer
September 7–October 26	Leo
October 27–December 25	Virgo
December 26–30	Libra

1950

January 1–March 27	Libra
March 28–June 10	Virgo
June 11–August 9	Libra
August 10–September 24	Scorpio
September 25–November 5	Sagittarius
November 6–December 14	Capricorn
December 15–31	Aquarius

1951

January 1–21	Aquarius
January 22–February 28	Pisces
March 1–April 9	Aries
April 10–May 20	Taurus
May 21–July 2	Gemini
July 3–August 17	Cancer
August 18–October 3	Leo
October 4–November 23	Virgo
November 24–December 31	Libra

1952

January 1–19	Libra
January 20–August 26	Scorpio
August 27–October 11	Sagittarius
October 12–November 20	Capricorn
November 21–December 29	Aquarius
December 30–31	Pisces

1953

January 1–February 7	Pisces
February 8–March 19	Aries
March 20–April 30	Taurus
May 1–June 13	Gemini
June 14–July 28	Cancer
July 29–September 13	Leo
September 14–October 31	Virgo
November 1–December 19	Libra
December 20–31	Scorpio

1954

January 1–February 8	Scorpio
February 9–April 11	Sagittarius
April 12–July 2	Capricorn
July 3–August 23	Sagittarius
August 24–October 20	Capricorn
October 21–December 3	Aquarius
December 4–31	Pisces

1955

January 1–14	Pisces
January 15–February 25	Aries
February 26–April 9	Taurus
April 10–May 25	Gemini
May 26–July 10	Cancer
July 11–August 26	Leo
August 27–October 12	Virgo
October 13–November 28	Libra
November 29–December 31	Scorpio

1956

January 1–13	Scorpio
January 14–February 27	Sagittarius
February 28–April 13	Capricorn
April 14–June 2	Aquarius
June 3–December 5	Pisces
December 6–31	Aries

1957

January 1–February 27	Aries
February 28–March 16	Taurus
March 17–May 3	Gemini
May 4–June 20	Cancer
June 21–August 7	Leo
August 8–September 23	Virgo
September 24–November 7	Libra
November 8–December 22	Scorpio
December 23–31	Sagittarius

1958

January 1–February 2	Sagittarius
February 3–March 16	Capricorn
March 17–April 26	Aquarius
April 27–June 6	Pisces
June 7–July 20	Aries
July 21–September 20	Taurus
September 21–October 28	Gemini
October 29–December 31	Taurus

1959

January 1–February 9	Taurus
February 10–April 9	Gemini
April 10–May 31	Cancer
June 1–July 19	Leo
July 20–September 4	Virgo
September 5–October 20	Libra
October 21–December 2	Scorpio
December 3–31	Sagittarius

1960

January 1–13	Sagittarius
January 14–February 22	Capricorn
February 23–April 1	Aquarius
April 2–May 10	Pisces
May 11–June 19	Aries
June 20–August 1	Taurus
August 2–September 20	Gemini
September 21–December 31	Cancer

1961

January 1–May 5	Cancer
May 6–June 27	Leo
June 28–August 16	Virgo
August 17–September 30	Libra
October 1–November 12	Scorpio
November 13–December 23	Sagittarius
December 24–31	Capricorn

1962

January 1–31	Capricorn
February 1–March 11	Aquarius
March 12–April 18	Pisces
April 19–May 27	Aries
May 28–July 8	Taurus
July 9–August 21	Gemini
August 22–October 10	Cancer
October 11–December 31	Leo

1963

January 1–June 2	Leo
June 3–July 26	Virgo
July 27–September 11	Libra
September 12–October 24	Scorpio
October 25–December 4	Sagittarius
December 5–31	Capricorn

1964

January 1–12	Capricorn
January 13–February 19	Aquarius
February 20–March 28	Pisces
March 29–May 6	Aries
May 7–June 16	Taurus
June 17–July 29	Gemini
July 30–September 14	Cancer
September 15–November 5	Leo
November 6–December 31	Virgo

1965

January 1–June 28	Virgo
June 29–August 19	Libra
August 20–October 3	Scorpio
October 4–November 13	Sagittarius
November 14–December 22	Capricorn
December 23–31	Aquarius

1966

January 1–29	Aquarius
January 30–March 8	Pisces
March 9–April 16	Aries
April 17–May 27	Taurus
May 28–July 10	Gemini
July 11–August 24	Cancer
August 25–October 11	Leo
October 12–December 3	Virgo
December 4–31	Libra

1967

January 1–February 11	Libra
February 12–March 31	Scorpio
April 1–July 18	Libra
July 19–September 9	Scorpio
September 10–October 22	Sagittarius
October 23–November 30	Capricorn
December 1–31	Aquarius

1968

January 1–8	Aquarius
January 9–February 16	Pisces
February 17–March 26	Aries
March 27–May 7	Taurus
May 8–June 20	Gemini
June 21–August 4	Cancer
August 5–September 20	Leo
September 21–October 8	Virgo
October 9–December 28	Libra
December 29–31	Scorpio

1969

January 1–February 24	Scorpio
February 25–September 20	Sagittarius
September 21–November 3	Capricorn
November 4–December 13	Aquarius
December 14–31	Pisces

1970

January 1–23	Pisces
January 24–March 6	Aries
March 7–April 17	Taurus
April 18–June 1	Gemini
June 2–July 17	Cancer
July 18–September 2	Leo
September 3–October 19	Virgo
October 20–December 5	Libra
December 6–31	Scorpio

1971

January 1–23	Scorpio
January 24–March 12	Sagittarius
March 13–May 3	Capricorn
May 4–November 6	Aquarius
November 7–December 26	Pisces
December 27–31	Aries

1972

January 1–February 10	Aries
February 11–March 27	Taurus
March 28–May 12	Gemini
May 13–June 28	Cancer
June 29–August 15	Leo
August 16–September 30	Virgo
October 1–November 15	Libra
November 16–December 30	Scorpio
December 31	Sagittarius

1973

January 1–February 12	Sagittarius
February 13–March 26	Capricorn
March 27–May 8	Aquarius
May 9–June 20	Pisces
June 21–August 12	Aries
August 13–October 29	Taurus
October 30–December 24	Aries
December 25–31	Taurus

1974

January 1–February 27	Taurus
February 28–April 20	Gemini
April 21–June 9	Cancer
June 10–July 27	Leo
July 28–September 12	Virgo
September 13–October 28	Libra
October 29–December 10	Scorpio
December 11–31	Sagittarius

1975

January 1–21	Sagittarius
January 22–March 3	Capricorn
March 4–April 11	Aquarius
April 12–May 21	Pisces
May 22–July 1	Aries
July 2–August 14	Taurus
August 15–October 17	Gemini
October 18–November 25	Cancer
November 26–December 31	Gemini

1976

January 1–March 18	Gemini
March 19–May 16	Cancer
May 17–July 6	Leo
July 7–August 24	Virgo
August 25–October 8	Libra
October 9–November 20	Scorpio
November 21–December 31	Sagittarius

1977

January 1–2	Sagittarius
January 3–February 9	Capricorn
February 10–March 20	Aquarius
March 21–April 27	Pisces
April 28–June 6	Aries
June 7–July 17	Taurus
July 18–September 1	Gemini
September 2–October 26	Cancer
October 27–December 31	Leo

1978

January 1–26	Leo
January 27–April 10	Cancer
April 11–June 14	Leo
June 15–August 4	Virgo
August 5–September 19	Libra
September 20–November 2	Scorpio
November 3–December 12	Sagittarius
December 13–31	Capricorn

1979

January 1–20	Capricorn
January 21–February 27	Aquarius
February 28–April 7	Pisces
April 8–May 16	Aries
May 17–June 26	Taurus
June 27–August 8	Gemini
August 9–September 24	Cancer
September 25–November 19	Leo
November 20–December 31	Virgo

1980

January 1–March 11	Virgo
March 12–May 4	Libra
May 5–July 10	Scorpio
July 11–August 29	Sagittarius
August 30–October 12	Capricorn
October 13–November 22	Aquarius
November 23–December 31	Pisces

1981

January 1–February 6	Aquarius
February 7–March 17	Pisces
March 18–April 25	Aries
April 26–June 5	Taurus
June 6–July 18	Gemini
July 19–September 2	Cancer
September 3–October 21	Leo
October 22–December 16	Virgo
December 17–31	Libra

1982

January 1–August 3	Libra
August 4–September 20	Scorpio
September 21–October 31	Sagittarius
November 1–December 10	Capricorn
December 11–31	Aquarius

1983

January 1–17	Aquarius
January 18–February 24	Pisces
February 25–April 5	Aries
April 6–May 16	Taurus
May 17–June 29	Gemini
June 30–August 13	Cancer
August 14–September 29	Leo
September 30–November 18	Virgo
November 19–December 31	Libra

1984

January 1–11	Libra
January 12–August 17	Scorpio
August 18–October 5	Sagittarius
October 6–November 15	Capricorn
November 16–December 25	Aquarius
December 26–31	Pisces

1985

January 1–February 2	Pisces
February 3–March 15	Aries
March 16–April 26	Taurus
April 27–June 10	Gemini
June 11–July 25	Cancer
July 26–September 10	Leo
September 11–October 27	Virgo
October 28–December 14	Libra
December 15–31	Scorpio

1986

January 1–February 2	Scorpio
February 3–March 29	Sagittarius
March 30–October 9	Capricorn
October 10–November 26	Aquarius
November 27–December 31	Pisces

1987

January 1–8	Pisces
January 9–February 20	Aries
February 21–April 5	Taurus
April 6–May 21	Gemini
May 22–July 6	Cancer
July 7–August 22	Leo
August 23–October 8	Virgo
October 9–November 24	Libra
November 25–December 31	Scorpio

1988

January 1–8	Scorpio
January 9–February 22	Sagittarius
February 23–April 6	Capricorn
April 7–May 22	Aquarius
May 23–July 13	Pisces
July 14–October 23	Aries
October 24–November 1	Pisces
November 2–December 31	Aries

1989

January 1–19	Aries
January 20–March 11	Taurus
March 12–April 29	Gemini
April 30–June 16	Cancer
June 17–August 3	Leo
August 4–September 19	Virgo
September 20–November 14	Libra
November 15–December 18	Scorpio
December 19–31	Sagittarius

1990

January 1–29	Sagittarius
January 30–March 11	Capricorn
March 12–April 20	Aquarius
April 21–May 31	Pisces
June 1–July 12	Aries
July 13–August 31	Taurus
September 1–December 14	Gemini
December 15–31	Taurus

1991

January 1–21	Taurus
January 22–April 3	Gemini
April 4–May 26	Cancer
May 27–July 15	Leo
July 16–September 1	Virgo
September 2–October 16	Libra
October 17–November 29	Scorpio
November 30–December 31	Sagittarius

1992

January 1–9	Sagittarius
January 10–February 18	Capricorn
February 19–March 28	Aquarius
March 29–May 5	Pisces
May 6–June 14	Aries
June 15–July 26	Taurus
July 27–September 12	Gemini
September 13–December 31	Cancer

1993

January 1–April 27	Cancer
April 28–June 23	Leo
June 24–August 12	Virgo
August 13–September 27	Libra
September 28–November 9	Scorpio
November 10–December 20	Sagittarius
December 21–31	Capricorn

1994

January 1–28	Capricorn
January 29–March 7	Aquarius
March 8–April 14	Pisces
April 15–May 23	Aries
May 24–July 3	Taurus
July 4–August 16	Gemini
August 17–October 4	Cancer
October 5–December 12	Leo
December 13–31	Virgo

1995

January 1–22	Virgo
January 23–May 25	Leo
May 26–July 21	Virgo
July 22–September 7	Libra
September 8–October 20	Scorpio
October 21–November 30	Sagittarius
December 1–31	Capricorn

1996

January 1–8	Capricorn
January 9–February 15	Aquarius
February 16–March 24	Pisces
March 25–May 2	Aries
May 3–June 12	Taurus
June 13–July 25	Gemini
July 26–September 9	Cancer
September 10–October 30	Leo
October 31–December 31	Virgo

1997

January 1–3	Virgo
January 4–March 8	Libra
March 9–June 19	Virgo
June 20–August 14	Libra
August 15–September 28	Scorpio
September 29–November 9	Sagittarius
November 10–December 18	Capricorn
December 19–31	Aquarius

1998

January 1–25	Aquarius
January 26–March 4	Pisces
March 5–April 13	Aries
April 14–May 24	Taurus
May 25–July 6	Gemini
July 7–August 20	Cancer
August 21–October 7	Leo
October 8–November 27	Virgo
November 28–December 31	Libra

1999

January 1–26	Libra
January 27–May 5	Scorpio
May 6–July 5	Libra
July 6–September 2	Scorpio
September 3–October 17	Sagittarius
October 18–November 26	Capricorn
November 27–December 31	Aquarius

2000

January 1–4	Aquarius
January 5–February 12	Pisces
February 13–March 23	Aries
March 24–May 3	Taurus
May 4–June 16	Gemini
June 17–August 1	Cancer
August 2–September 16	Leo
September 17–November 4	Virgo
November 5–December 23	Libra
December 24–31	Scorpio

Jupiter

January 1, 1921–September 25, 1921	Virgo
September 26, 1921–October 26, 1922	Libra
October 27, 1922–November 24, 1923	Scorpio
November 25, 1923–	
December 17, 1924	Sagittarius
December 18, 1924–January 5, 1926	Capricorn
January 6, 1926–January 17, 1927	Aquarius
January 18, 1927–June 10, 1927	Pisces
June 11, 1927–September 10, 1927	Aries
September 11, 1927–January 22, 1928	Pisces
January 23, 1928–June 3, 1928	Aries
June 4, 1928–June 11, 1929	Taurus
June 12, 1929–June 26, 1930	Gemini
June 27, 1930–July 16, 1931	Cancer
July 17, 1931–August 10, 1932	Leo
August 11, 1932–September 9, 1933	Virgo
September 10, 1933–October 10, 1934	Libra
October 11, 1934–November 8, 1935	Scorpio
November 9, 1935–	
December 2, 1936	Sagittarius
December 3, 1936–	
December 20, 1937	Capricorn
December 21, 1937–May 15, 1938	Aquarius
May 16, 1938–July 30, 1938	Pisces
July 31, 1938–December 30, 1938	Aquarius
December 31, 1938–May 13, 1939	Pisces
May 14, 1939–October 30, 1939	Aries
October 31, 1939–December 20, 1939	Pisces
December 21, 1939–May 17, 1940	Aries
May 18, 1940–May 27, 1941	Taurus
May 28, 1941–June 11, 1942	Gemini
June 12, 1942–June 30, 1943	Cancer
July 1, 1943–July 27, 1944	Leo
July 28, 1944–August 26, 1945	Virgo
August 27, 1945–September 26, 1946	Libra
September 27, 1946–October 25, 1947	Scorpio
October 26, 1947–	
November 16, 1948	Sagittarius
November 17, 1948–April 12, 1949	Capricorn
April 13, 1949–June 28, 1949	Aquarius
June 29, 1949–November 30, 1949	Capricorn
December 1, 1949–April 16, 1950	Aquarius
April 17, 1950–September 16, 1950	Pisces
September 17, 1950–	
December 3, 1950	Aquarius
December 4, 1950–April 20, 1951	Pisces
April 21, 1951–April 26, 1952	Aries
April 27, 1952–May 10, 1953	Taurus
May 11, 1953–May 21, 1954	Gemini
May 22, 1954–June 10, 1955	Cancer
June 11, 1955–November 20, 1955	Leo
November 21, 1955–January 10, 1956	Virgo
January 11, 1956–July 5, 1956	Leo
July 6, 1956–December 15, 1956	Virgo
December 16, 1956–February 15, 1957	Libra
February 16, 1957–August 5, 1957	Virgo
August 6, 1957–January 14, 1958	Libra
January 15, 1958–March 15, 1958	Scorpio
March 16, 1958–September 5, 1958	Libra
September 6, 1958–February 9, 1959	Scorpio
February 10, 1959–April 20, 1959	Sagittarius
April 21, 1959–October 5, 1959	Scorpio

October 6, 1959–	
February 29, 1960	Sagittarius
March 1, 1960–June 7, 1960	Capricorn
June 8, 1960–October 21, 1960	Sagittarius
October 22, 1960–March 16, 1961	Capricorn
March 17, 1961–August 11, 1961	Aquarius
August 12, 1961–October 31, 1961	Capricorn
November 1, 1961–March 25, 1962	Aquarius
March 26, 1962–April 4, 1963	Pisces
April 5, 1963–April 9, 1964	Aries
April 10, 1964–April 20, 1965	Taurus
April 21, 1965–September 20, 1965	Gemini
September 21, 1965–	
November 15, 1965	Cancer
November 16, 1965–May 5, 1966	Gemini
May 6, 1966–September 27, 1966	Cancer
September 28, 1966–January 16, 1967	Leo
January 17, 1967–May 23, 1967	Cancer
May 24, 1967–October 19, 1967	Leo
October 20, 1967–February 27, 1968	Virgo
February 28, 1968–June 15, 1968	Leo
June 16, 1968–November 15, 1968	Virgo
November 16, 1968–March 30, 1969	Libra
March 31, 1969–July 15, 1969	Virgo
July 16, 1969–December 16, 1969	Libra
December 17, 1969–April 30, 1970	Scorpio
May 1, 1970–August 15, 1970	Libra
August 16, 1970–January 14, 1971	Scorpio
January 15, 1971–June 5, 1971	Sagittarius
June 6, 1971–September 11, 1971	Libra
September 12, 1971–	
February 6, 1972	Sagittarius
February 7, 1972–July 24, 1972	Capricorn
July 25, 1972–September 25, 1972	Sagittarius
September 26, 1972–	
February 23, 1973	Capricorn
February 24, 1973–March 8, 1974	Aquarius
March 9, 1974–March 18, 1975	Pisces
March 19, 1975–March 26, 1976	Aries
March 27, 1976–August 23, 1976	Taurus

August 24, 1976–October 16, 1976	Gemini
October 17, 1976–April 3, 1977	Taurus
April 4, 1977–August 20, 1977	Gemini
August 21, 1977–December 31, 1977	Cancer
January 1, 1978–April 11, 1978	Gemini
April 12, 1978–September 5, 1978	Cancer
September 6, 1978–March 1, 1979	Leo
March 2, 1979–April 20, 1979	Cancer
April 21, 1979–September 29, 1979	Leo
September 30, 1979–October 27, 1980	Virgo
October 28, 1980–November 27, 1981	Libra
November 28, 1981–	
December 26, 1982	Scorpio
December 27, 1982–	
January 19, 1984	Sagittarius
January 20, 1984–February 6, 1985	Capricorn
February 7, 1985–February 20, 1986	Aquarius
February 21, 1986–March 2, 1987	Pisces
March 3, 1987–March 8, 1988	Aries
March 9, 1988–July 21, 1988	Taurus
July 22, 1988–November 30, 1988	Gemini
December 1, 1988–March 11, 1989	Taurus
March 12, 1989–July 30, 1989	Gemini
July 31, 1989–August 18, 1990	Cancer
August 19, 1990–September 12, 1991	Leo
September 13, 1991–October 10, 1992	Virgo
October 11, 1992–November 10, 1993	Libra
November 11, 1993–	
December 9, 1994	Scorpio
December 10, 1994–	
January 3, 1996	Sagittarius
January 4, 1996–January 21, 1997	Capricorn
January 22, 1997–February 4, 1998	Aquarius
February 5, 1998–February 13, 1999	Pisces
February 14, 1999–June 28, 1999	Aries
June 29, 1999–October 23, 1999	Taurus
October 24, 1999–February 15, 2000	Aries
February 16, 2000–June 26, 2000	Taurus
June 27, 2000–December 31, 2000	Gemini

Saturn

January 1, 1920–October 7, 1921	Virgo	October 21, 1953–January 10, 1956	Scorpio
October 8, 1921–December 19, 1923	Libra	January 11, 1956–May 14, 1956	Sagittarius
December 20, 1923–April 5, 1924	Scorpio	May 15, 1956–October 13, 1956	Scorpio
April 6, 1924–September 13, 1924	Libra	October 14, 1956–January 9, 1959	Sagittarius
September 14, 1924–		January 10, 1959–January 3, 1962	Capricorn
December 2, 1926	Scorpio	January 4, 1962–March 25, 1964	Aquarius
December 3, 1926–March 14, 1929	Sagittarius	March 26, 1964–September 15, 1964	Pisces
March 15, 1929–May 4, 1929	Capricorn	September 16, 1964–	
May 5, 1929–November 29, 1929	Sagittarius	December 15, 1964	Aquarius
November 30, 1929–		December 16, 1964–March 3, 1967	Pisces
February 23, 1932	Capricorn	March 4, 1967–April 29, 1969	Aries
February 24, 1932–August 13, 1932	Aquarius	April 30, 1969–June 18, 1971	Taurus
August 14, 1932–November 19, 1932	Capricorn	June 19, 1971–January 10, 1972	Aries
November 20, 1932–		January 11, 1972–February 21, 1972	Taurus
February 13, 1935	Aquarius	February 22, 1972–August 1, 1973	Gemini
February 14, 1935–April 25, 1937	Pisces	August 2, 1973–January 7, 1974	Cancer
April 26, 1937–October 18, 1937	Aries	January 8, 1974–April 18, 1974	Gemini
October 19, 1937–January 15, 1938	Pisces	April 19, 1974–September 17, 1975	Cancer
January 16, 1938–July 7, 1939	Aries	September 18, 1975–January 15, 1976	Leo
July 8, 1939–September 23, 1939	Taurus	January 16, 1976–June 5, 1976	Cancer
September 24, 1939–January 20, 1940	Aries	June 6, 1976–November 16, 1977	Leo
January 21, 1940–May 9, 1942	Taurus	November 17, 1977–January 5, 1978	Virgo
May 10, 1942–June 21, 1944	Gemini	January 6, 1978–July 26, 1978	Leo
June 22, 1944–August 3, 1946	Cancer	July 27, 1978–September 21, 1980	Virgo
August 4, 1946–September 20, 1948	Leo	September 22, 1980–	
September 21, 1948–April 4, 1949	Virgo	November 29, 1982	Libra
April 5, 1949–May 30, 1949	Leo	November 30, 1982–May 6, 1983	Scorpio
May 31, 1949–November 21, 1950	Virgo	May 7, 1983–August 25, 1983	Libra
November 22, 1950–March 7, 1951	Libra	August 26, 1983–November 17, 1985	Scorpio
March 8, 1951–August 13, 1951	Virgo	November 18, 1985–	
August 14, 1951–October 20, 1953	Libra	February 13, 1988	Sagittarius

February 14, 1988–June 10, 1988	Capricorn	January 29, 1994–April 7, 1996	Pisces
June 11, 1988–November 12, 1988	Sagittarius	April 8, 1996–June 9, 1998	Aries
November 13, 1988–		June 10, 1998–October 25, 1998	Taurus
February 6, 1991	Capricorn	October 26, 1998–February 28, 1999	Aries
February 7, 1991–May 21, 1993	Aquarius	March 1, 1999–August 10, 2000	Taurus
May 22, 1993–June 30, 1993	Pisces	August 11, 2000–October 20, 2000	Gemini
July 1, 1993–January 28, 1994	Aquarius	October 21, 2000–December 31, 2000	Taurus

Uranus

January 1, 1900–		August 24, 1955–January 27, 1956	Leo
December 19, 1904	Sagittarius	January 28, 1956–June 8, 1956	Cancer
December 20, 1904–		June 9, 1956–October 31, 1961	Leo
January 30, 1912	Capricorn	November 1, 1961–January 11, 1962	Virgo
January 31, 1912–September 4, 1912	Aquarius	January 12, 1962–August 8, 1962	Leo
September 5, 1912–		August 9, 1962–September 27, 1968	Virgo
November 11, 1912	Capricorn	September 28, 1968–May 20, 1969	Libra
November 12, 1912–March 31, 1919	Aquarius	May 21, 1969–June 23, 1969	Virgo
April 1, 1919–August 16, 1919	Pisces	June 24, 1969–November 22, 1974	Libra
August 17, 1919–January 21, 1920	Aquarius	November 23, 1974–May 2, 1975	Scorpio
January 22, 1920–March 30, 1927	Pisces	May 3, 1975–September 8, 1975	Libra
March 31, 1927–November 4, 1927	Aries	September 9, 1975–February 17, 1981	Scorpio
November 5, 1927–January 12, 1928	Pisces	February 18, 1981–March 20, 1981	Sagittarius
January 13, 1928–June 6, 1934	Aries	March 21, 1981–November 16, 1981	Scorpio
June 7, 1934–October 9, 1934	Taurus	November 17, 1981–	
October 10, 1934–March 28, 1935	Aries	February 14, 1988	Sagittarius
March 29, 1935–August 6, 1941	Taurus	February 15, 1988–May 26, 1988	Capricorn
August 7, 1941–October 4, 1941	Gemini	May 27, 1988–December 2, 1988	Sagittarius
October 5, 1941–May 13, 1942	Taurus	December 3, 1988–April 1, 1995	Capricorn
May 14, 1942–August 29, 1948	Gemini	April 2, 1995–June 9, 1995	Aquarius
August 30, 1948–November 11, 1948	Cancer	June 10, 1995–January 12, 1996	Capricorn
November 12, 1948–June 9, 1949	Gemini	January 13, 1996–December 31, 2000	Aquarius
June 10, 1949–August 23, 1955	Cancer		

★

Neptune

January 1, 1900–July 19, 1901	Gemini	October 16, 1956–January 4, 1970	Scorpio
July 20, 1901–December 25, 1901	Cancer	January 5, 1970–May 2, 1970	Sagittarius
December 26, 1901–May 20, 1902	Gemini	May 3, 1970–November 6, 1970	Scorpio
May 21, 1902–September 23, 1914	Cancer	November 7, 1970–	
September 24, 1914–December 14, 1914	Leo	January 18, 1984	Sagittarius
December 15, 1914–July 18, 1915	Cancer	January 19, 1984–June 22, 1984	Capricorn
July 19, 1915–March 19, 1916	Leo	June 23, 1984–November 21, 1984	Sagittarius
March 20, 1916–May 1, 1916	Cancer	November 22, 1984–	
May 2, 1916–September 20, 1928	Leo	January 28, 1998	Capricorn
September 21, 1928–February 19, 1929	Virgo	January 29, 1998–August 23, 1998	Aquarius
February 20, 1929–July 23, 1929	Leo	August 24, 1998–	
July 24, 1929–October 4, 1942	Virgo	November 27, 1998	Capricorn
October 5, 1942–April 19, 1943	Libra	November 28, 1998–April 30, 2011	Aquarius
April 20, 1943–August 3, 1943	Virgo	May 1, 2011–September 29, 2011	Pisces
August 4, 1943–December 31, 1955	Libra	September 30, 2011–	
January 1, 1956–April 30, 1956	Scorpio	February 29, 2012	Aquarius
May 1, 1956–October 15, 1956	Libra	March 1, 2012–December 31, 2020	Pisces

Pluto

January 1, 1900–September 24, 1912	Gemini	October 5, 1971–April 17, 1972	Libra
September 25, 1912–October 2, 1912	Taurus	April 18, 1972–July 30, 1972	Virgo
October 3, 1912–July 12, 1913	Gemini	July 31, 1972–November 20, 1983	Libra
July 13, 1913–December 24, 1913	Cancer	November 21, 1983–May 20, 1984	Scorpio
December 25, 1913–May 23, 1914	Gemini	May 21, 1984–July 29, 1984	Libra
May 24, 1914–October 8, 1937	Cancer	July 30, 1984–January 1, 1995	Scorpio
October 9, 1937–November 15, 1937	Leo	January 2, 1995–April 22, 1995	Sagittarius
November 16, 1937–August 5, 1938	Cancer	April 23, 1995–November 18, 1995	Scorpio
August 6, 1938–February 7, 1939	Leo	November 19, 1995–	
February 8, 1939–June 15, 1939	Cancer	January 29, 2008	Sagittarius
June 16, 1939–October 19, 1956	Leo	January 30, 2008–July 29, 2008	Capricorn
October 20, 1956–January 16, 1957	Virgo	July 30, 2008–December 1, 2008	Sagittarius
January 17, 1957–August 18, 1957	Leo	December 2, 2008–	
August 19, 1957–October 4, 1971	Virgo	December 31, 2020	Capricorn

WORKSHEET

Name _____

Date of Birth _____

Time of Birth _____

Place of Birth _____

	PLANETS	HOUSE
Sun	_____	_____
Moon	_____	_____
Mercury	_____	_____
Venus	_____	_____
Mars	_____	_____
Jupiter	_____	_____
Saturn	_____	_____
Uranus	_____	_____
Neptune	_____	_____
Pluto	_____	_____
Ascendant	_____	_____
Moon Node	_____	_____
	_____	_____
Decanate:	_____	_____

BIRTH CHART

Glyph Identifier

♈	Aries	☉	Sun
♉	Taurus	☽	Moon
♊	Gemini	☿	Mercury
♋	Cancer	♀	Venus
♌	Leo	♂	Mars
♍	Virgo	♃	Jupiter
♎	Libra	♄	Saturn
♏	Scorpio	♅	Uranus
♐	Sagittarius	♆	Neptune
♑	Capricorn	♇	Pluto
♒	Aquarius	☊	North Node
♓	Pisces	☋	South Node
		ASC	Ascendant
□	Square	MID	Midheaven
☍	Opposition		
☌	Conjunction		
△	Trine		
✳	Sextile		
⚻	Quincunx		

Resources

All of these resources have been compiled at press time and may be subject to changes. Since new information, software programs, and Web sites become available every week, there will probably be more to choose from than what's listed here. The following items should help you get started.

NATAL CHARTS

To obtain or create an accurate natal chart, be sure you have your exact date, time, and place of birth. A natal chart usually costs about ten to fifteen dollars when provided by an astrological computer service.

COMPUTER SOFTWARE

There are an array of software programs available, though most of them are for professional astrologers and can be quite expensive. These have been included along with more entertainment-related astrology programs, which are priced at street value.

For Windows
Expert Astrologer V1.01, Expert Software, $13.95

Astrologer, SoftKey, $9.99
Astrology for Windows, Halloran Software, $26.50
Kaleidoscope, Matrix Software, $49.95
AstrolDeluxe for Windows, Halloran Software, $149.00
Win*Star & Win*Star Plus, Matrix Software, $200.00–$295.00

For Macintosh
Astrology Source, Multicom, $29.95
IO Edition, Time Cycles Research, $195.00
Contact Astro-Report, Astrolabe, $195.00
Mercury, Matrix Software, $200.00

Software Companies
Time Cycles Research
375 Willets Avenue
Waterford, CT 06385-3804
1-800-827-2270

Matrix Software
315 Marion Avenue
Big Rapids, MI 49307
www.thenewage.com

The Learning Company
1 Athenaeum Street
Cambridge, MA 02142
1-800-323-8088

Astrolabe
P.O. Box 1750
Brewster, MA 02631
1-800-843-6682

INTERNET CHARTS/FREEWARE
Astrodienst Online (www.astro.ch/atlas)
This is a great site. Just type in your place and date/time of birth
and a quick, full-color chart (using the Astrolog program) is available
to print in minutes. Best of all, it's free.

Astrolog 5.30 (www.magitech.com/~cruiser1/astrolog/htm)

This is a freeware program that can be downloaded for DOS, Windows, or Mac. Input birth information and the program will create a detailed natal chart that even includes retrograde planets. The only drawback is having to look up latitude and longitude for your place of birth (which you can find in a good atlas or encyclopedia, or at the Astrodienst site mentioned above).

CHARTING SERVICES (VIA MAIL OR PHONE ORDER)

Many astrological charting services abound, too numerous to mention here. Check your local Yellow Pages under "Astrology," visit a New Age shop or bookstore, or simply visit a health food store (these stores, in particular, always seem to have free directories or newspapers pertaining to New Age/healthy living that can be great references for resources in your area).

Index

About the Authors

ADA AUBIN, a Taurus, has been a professional astrologer for over thirty years. Her introduction to the field came unexpectedly. The daughter of a Presbyterian minister and Sunday School teacher, Ada was coaxed by a neighbor into attending a lecture led by astrologer Lionel Day. She entered the lecture as a skeptic and left inspired. Ada wholeheartedly began studying astrology in the 1960s under the guidance of Mr. Day and other noted astrologers of the era, including Isabel Hickey, Zipporah Dobyns, and Barbara Watters. She studied at Suffolk Community College and Dowling State in New York, and she attended astrology symposiums conducted through New York University.

In April 1973, Ada received certification by the Astrologer's Guild of America. Since that time, she has lectured at Suffolk Community College, participated in a variety of seminars, and led many classes in astrology. The majority of Ada's work is done in private sessions. Over the last three decades, she has developed a vast clientele who contact her on a regular basis for guidance and enlightenment.

Ada is the mother of four, has several grandchildren, and currently resides in Aurora, Colorado.

JUNE RIFKIN, a Pisces, has had a dual career. Since graduating from Queens College in New York, she has spent twenty years in the cable television industry, working in marketing, advertising, and promotion for several major operators and program services. She is the recipient of industry merits, including an ACE Award.

In 1990 June switched gears to pursue writing through studies at Emerson College in Boston, where she received her M.A. in Writing and Publishing with a concentration in playwriting. In 1992 her comedy *Separation Anxiety* was produced at the Brimmer Street Theater in Boston.

June currently divides her time between working as a promotion copywriter and writing on her own. She is the author of three plays and a screenplay and is working on a novel and a nonfiction book.

June lives in New York City with her husband, Dick, and son, Colin.